THE NEW LAW AND ECONOMIC DEVELOPMENT

In this book authors from the United States, Canada, Mexico, and the United Kingdom identify and analyze a new phase in thinking about the role of law in economic development and the practices of the development agencies that support law reform. The essays describe an emerging paradigm that is changing ideas and shaping practice. The book is the first to draw attention to this new consensus and analyze the tensions and contradictions it reflects. Tracing how ideas about the role of law in economic development have changed over time, the authors situate the new paradigm in the history of changing development models and related legal reform strategies since World War II.

David M. Trubek is Voss-Bascom Professor of Law and Senior Fellow of the Center for World Affairs and the Global Economy (WAGE) at the University of Wisconsin-Madison. He served with the United States Agency for International Development and worked on legal development projects in Latin America, Africa, and Russia. He has taught at Wisconsin, Yale, Harvard, and the Catholic University Law School in Rio de Janeiro and has published books and articles on the role of law in economic development, the social and economic role of the legal profession, the impact of globalization on legal systems, the sociology of law, the role of courts in society, labor rights and the governance of work, new forms of governance in a globalized world, and critical legal studies. From 1989 to 2001 he was the UW-Madison's Dean of International Studies and Director of the International Institute. He was appointed *Chevalier dans l'Ordre des Palmes Academiques* by the French government for his work on globalization.

Alvaro Santos is Emerging Scholars Program Assistant Professor at the University of Texas at Austin School of Law. He teaches law and economic development and international trade law, and his scholarly interests also include international law, transnational labor law, and legal theory. Santos is an S.J.D. candidate and Byse Fellow at Harvard Law School. His research focuses on the impact of the global economic integration on domestic labor regimes, particularly on the North American economic integration and its effects on Mexican labor relations. He received an LL.M. from Harvard (2000), where he held a Ford Foundation scholarship, and obtained a J.D. with high honors from Universidad Nacional Autónoma de México (1999). He has taught international law at Tufts University and law and development in the Master's Degree on Management of Development offered by the University of Turin and the International Labour Organization.

The New Law and Economic Development

A CRITICAL APPRAISAL

Edited by

David M. Trubek
University of Wisconsin Law School

Alvaro Santos
The University of Texas at Austin School of Law

CAMBRIDGE
UNIVERSITY PRESS

CAMBRIDGE UNIVERSITY PRESS
Cambridge, New York, Melbourne, Madrid, Cape Town,
Singapore, São Paulo, Delhi, Tokyo, Mexico City

Cambridge University Press
32 Avenue of the Americas, New York, NY 10013-2473, USA

www.cambridge.org
Information on this title: www.cambridge.org/9780521677578

First published 2006
Reprinted 2008, 2009, 2011

A catalog record for this publication is available from the British Library.

Library of Congress Cataloging in Publication Data

Trubek, David M., 1935–
The new law and economic development : a critical appraisal / David M.
Trubek, Alvaro Santos.
p. cm.
ISBN 0-521-86021-0 (hardback : alk. paper) – ISBN 0-521-67757-2 (pbk. : alk. paper)
1. Law and economic development. 2. Rule of law. 3. Economic assistance.
4. International economic relations. I. Santos, Alvaro, 1975– II. Title.
K3820.T78 2006
340´.11 – dc22 2006005046

ISBN 978-0-521-86021-5 Hardback
ISBN 978-0-521-67757-8 Paperback

CONTENTS

CONTRIBUTORS

David Kennedy is Manley O. Hudson Professor of Law at Harvard Law School.

Duncan Kennedy is Carter Professor of General Jurisprudence at Harvard Law School.

Scott Newton is Lecturer in Law and Chair of the Centre of Contemporary Central Asia and the Caucasus in the School of Oriental and African Studies, University of London.

Kerry Rittich is Associate Professor, Faculty of Law and Women's and Gender Studies Institute at the University of Toronto.

Alvaro Santos is Emerging Scholars Program Assistant Professor at the University of Texas School of Law.

David M. Trubek is Voss-Bascom Professor of Law and Senior Fellow of the Center for World Affairs and the Global Economy (WAGE) at the University of Wisconsin-Madison.

1 INTRODUCTION: THE THIRD MOMENT IN LAW AND DEVELOPMENT THEORY AND THE EMERGENCE OF A NEW CRITICAL PRACTICE

David M. Trubek and Alvaro Santos

The study of the relationship between law and economic development goes back at least to the nineteenth century. It is a question that attracted the attention of classical thinkers like Marx and Weber. And there were some early efforts to craft policy in this area; for example, under the Raj, some English Utilitarians tried to put Jeremy Bentham's ideas about law and economic progress into practice in India. But it was only after World War II that systematic and organized efforts to reform legal systems became part of the practice of international development agencies.

Initially, development agencies turned to law as an instrument for state policy aimed at generating economic growth. Starting in the 1980s, interest in the role of law in economic development grew, but it was an interest in law more as a framework for market activity than as an instrument of state power. This book argues that, starting in the mid-1990s, development practitioners approached law in a fundamentally new way – as a correction for market failures and as a constitutive part of "development" itself. As a result, "the rule of law" has become significant not only as a tool of development policy, but as an objective for development policy in its own right.

This book charts the history of this growing interest in the legal field, explores the shifting rationales behind development policy initiatives, and explores in detail the newest – and most surprising – of these rationales. To do that, we trace the history of a body of ideas about law and economic development that have been employed not just by academics but also by development practitioners responsible for allocating funds and designing projects. In this introduction, we refer to that body of ideas as *law and development doctrine.* Although this doctrine has academic roots in economic and legal theory, it is a practical working tool of development agencies.

This is not a static body of thought. Views on the relationship between law and development, and thus on the nature of legal assistance efforts, change over time. As ideas change and practices evolve, older ideas are challenged and a new vision crystallizes. As a result, there have been several different versions of law and development doctrine since the 1950s. In this introduction, we use the term "Moment" to refer to a period in which law and development doctrine has crystallized into an orthodoxy that is relatively comprehensive and widely accepted. While the authors in this collection employ different terms to refer to such "Moments" of crystallization, all agree that there have been three primary forms of orthodox law and development doctrine since World War II.

The first such Moment emerged during the 1950s and 1960s. Development policy focused on the role of the state in managing the economy and transforming traditional societies. Development practitioners assumed that law could be used as a tool for economic management and a lever for social change. Initially, these assumptions were largely tacit but eventually a body of theory and doctrine emerged. First Moment doctrine stressed the importance of law as an instrument for effective state intervention in the economy. It helped guide a small number of law reform projects in a few parts of the world.

In the 1980s, however, law moved to the center of development policy making and the scope of the reform effort expanded exponentially. This renewed interest in law was heavily influenced by the emergence of neoliberal ideas about development. Neoliberal thinkers stressed the primary role of markets in economic growth. As development policymakers sought to transform command and *dirigiste* economies into market systems, and integrate developing nations into the world economy, they began to see law as an important arena for policy.

Like the previous period, this was not a turn to law in general, but to a particular vision of law and its role in the economy. The particular vision of this period, however, could hardly have been more distinct from that which came before. Rather than an instrument for state policy, law was understood as the foundation for market relations and as a *limit* on the state. Of course, new laws would be needed to dismantle state controls. But, consistent with the dominant economic theory that working markets were both necessary and sufficient for growth, the primary role assigned to legal institutions was one of a foundation for market relations.

Attention shifted from the establishment of an administrative state to the core institutions of private law, the role of the judiciary in protecting business against the intrusions of government, and the need to change local laws to facilitate integration into the world economy. Not much attention was paid to regulatory law. When it was, regulation was often presented as an unnecessary intrusion on the market. Neoliberal law and development thought focused primarily on the law of the market: relatively little concern was shown for law as a guarantor of political and civil rights or as protector of the weak and disadvantaged.

This neoliberal turn led to the Second Moment in law and development doctrine and to a remarkable expansion of the assistance effort. The first law and development efforts were small in scale, involving a few projects mostly in Africa and Latin America. The neoliberal era ushered in a massive increase in the level of investment and the scale of projects. Investments by bilateral and multilateral agencies as well as by private foundations reached into the billions. "Law and development" became big business.

The results of the neoliberal Second Moment have been analyzed and critiqued from many points of view. In this book we recapitulate and expand on some of these analyses. But the real focus of the volume is on the description, analysis, and critique of the Third and current Moment. We argue that a major shift in law and development doctrine is going on today. In the 1990s and the early years of this century, changes have occurred in development economics, assistance policy and practice, and legal thought. Neoliberal ideas have been revised and additional elements added to the definition of development. In this context, mainstream law and development doctrine has changed. This change has influenced and been influenced by shifts in development policy more generally.

This book had its origins in a consensus among the authors that emerged during a conference on "Law and Economic Development: Critiques and Beyond" held at Harvard Law School in 2003.[1] All of us have been studying the relationship between law and economic development, some for many years. As we prepared for the 2003 event, we all realized that a significant shift had occurred in this field during the 1990s. We gave the shift different names, we offered somewhat different explanations for the changes, and we held differing views about the possible relationship between changes in theory and changes in practice. But we all saw that something important was taking place.

We thought this shift might presage the emergence of a new paradigm and the inauguration of the Third Moment in Law and Development. Some thought that a basic change had occurred; others were not sure that the neoliberal era had really ended. Was there a new paradigm, or simply a chastened form of neoliberalism? We decided to pool our efforts to better understand this shift. The group met several times over the following year.[2] This volume is the result.

"LAW AND DEVELOPMENT" DOCTRINE AS THE NODE OF THREE DISCIPLINARY FIELDS

"Law and development doctrine" orients and explains the current practices of those who seek to change legal systems in the name of development,

1 The conference was sponsored by the Harvard Law School European Law Research Center.

2 The group met at the University of Wisconsin in October, 2003, and at Cornell University and the University of Toronto in April, 2004.

however defined. This doctrine is more than a detailed blueprint and less than a robust theory. Our thesis is that at any point in time, the doctrine can best be understood if it is seen as the intersection of current ideas in the spheres of economic theory, legal ideas, and the policies and practices of development institutions.

These spheres are analytically separable but practically intertwined. They influence each other in complex and reciprocal ways. Both the theory and the practice of law and development are shaped by, and at the same time shape, the spheres of economic theory, legal theory, and institutional practice. The book does not suggest a relation of causality between these various spheres. Our goal is to disentangle the separate spheres, understand how each has changed in recent years, study how they have interacted, and chart the multiple dynamics of influence.

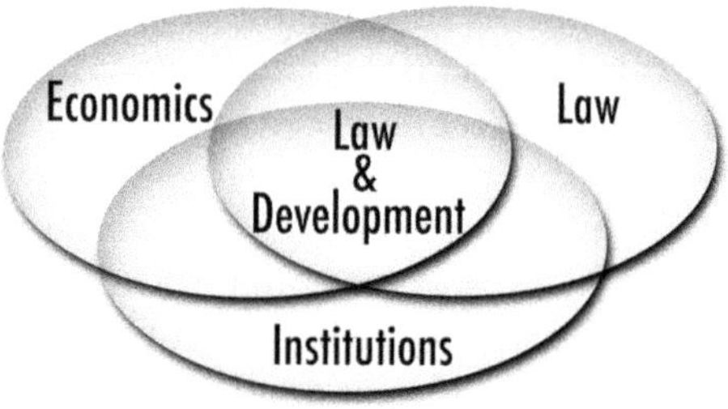

As the chart shows, law and development doctrine emerges from the intersection of economics, law, and institutional practice. Economics influences the practices and policies of the development agencies but these policies and practices may also be taken into account in shaping economic theory. So there is an area of overlap between institutional practice and economic theory. But the shape of this space is also constituted by the world of legal ideas: when economic theory and institutional practice turn to law, they must take their ideas about law from the realm of legal thought. Law and development doctrine, then, crystallizes when all three of these sources come together.

The analysis of the spheres and their interaction in the following chapters helps us chart recent changes and understand the emergence of a new vocabulary and an increasingly dominant way of thinking about development. The resulting maps are an effective guide for understanding and contesting current mainstream thought and practice.

Our authors suggest many reasons why a new law and development mainstream vision is emerging. These include changes within the field of development economics, reactions to failures of the neoliberal Moment, changing policies and practices of the World Bank and other development agencies, developments within legal theory in the center, and the spread of a new legal consciousness to the periphery.

One of the recurring themes in this volume is the complex relationship between changes in development economics and practices and changes at any point in time in ideas about law's role in development. All the authors recognize the relationship between these bodies of ideas. They may not agree on the exact nature of this relationship but all acknowledge that at given points in time ideas from the several spheres seem to fit together and a new Moment begins.

THE FIRST TWO MOMENTS IN LAW AND DEVELOPMENT

We can think of the First Moment as "Law and the Developmental State." The developmental state was based on a series of assumptions that included the idea that import substitution in the internal market is the engine of growth; scarce savings must be directed to key investment areas; the private sector is too weak to provide "take-off" to self-sustaining growth; and "traditional sectors" will resist change. Foreign capital may help but it is scarce and possibly exploitative. As a result, in order to secure self-sustaining growth, the national state should create plans, reallocate surplus, combat resistance, invest and manage key sectors, and control foreign capital.

The primary use of law in the developmental state is as a tool to remove "traditional" barriers and change economic behavior. Laws are needed to create the formal structure for macroeconomic control. Legislation can translate policy goals into action by channeling economic behavior in accordance with national plans. The law is needed to create the framework for operation of an efficient governmental bureaucracy and the governance of public sector corporations. Legal rules are needed to manage complex exchange controls and import regulations.

Law and development doctrine and practice in the First Moment followed from this vision. The focus was on modernizing regulation and the legal profession. Emphasis was placed on public law and transplanting regulatory laws from advanced states. It was important to strengthen the legal capacity of state agencies and state corporations and modernize the legal profession by encouraging pragmatic, policy-oriented lawyering. Because modernization was thought to come about primarily through university training, a great deal of emphasis was placed on the reform of legal education.

The Second Moment might be called "Law and the Neoliberal Market." The development policy of the neoliberal market was based on the view that the best way to achieve growth was by getting prices right, promoting fiscal discipline, removing distortions created by state intervention, promoting free trade, and encouraging foreign investment.

The vision of law in the Second Moment was as an instrument to foster private transactions. In the Second Moment, law and development doctrine placed its emphasis on private law in order to protect property and facilitate contractual exchange. It sought to use the law to place strict limits on state intervention and ensure equal treatment for foreign capital.

Second Moment legal reforms were designed to strengthen the rights of property and ensure that contracts would be enforceable. Emphasis was placed on the role of the judiciary both as a way to restrain the state and to facilitate markets. It was thought that an independent judiciary using formalistic methods would provide fidelity to the law and predictability. The model was thought to be universal: markets were markets, and the same legal foundations would be needed and could operate anywhere.

THE TRANSITION TO THE PRESENT: THE CRITIQUE OF NEOLIBERALISM AND THE EMERGENCE OF NEW PRINCIPLES FOR DEVELOPMENT POLICY

As the last century came to an end, reactions to the neoliberal program in development economics grew stronger. Many developing and transition countries that had adopted these policies experienced severe economic crises. When it became clear that neoliberal policies were not delivering the growth that had been promised, the voices of skeptical economists became louder, and confidence in the so-called Washington Consensus that codified neoliberal policies began to erode.

The devastating experience with market-shock therapy in Russia, the severe economic emergency experienced by a number of Latin American countries, and the Asian financial crisis made clear that markets do not create the conditions for their own success. People recognized that unrestricted markets were often inefficient and that state intervention was necessary to correct such market failures as transaction costs or information asymmetries. Critics charged neoliberal policymakers for not having paid attention to existing local institutions and to timing of reforms. They noted that transplanted laws, thought to reflect best practices, often did not take hold, or produced results diametrically opposite from what was intended. They emphasized that success of economic policies could not be disentangled from local context and from concern with sequencing and pacing of reforms.

Another set of critiques questioned the exclusive focus on economic growth that had dominated development thinking. One set of critics noted that growth did not necessarily lead to poverty reduction. Others questioned the very idea that "development" should be seen exclusively as a matter of economic growth and poverty alleviation.

These critiques have led to two distinct lines of new ideas about development: the recognition of the limits of markets and the expansion of the definition of development. Mainstream development thinkers continue to stress the importance of markets as the main mechanism for production and distribution of resources in societies and as the main leverage for economic growth. But they now also recognize that there may be significant market failures, which could justify state intervention. Development economists no longer insist on "deregulation" of internal markets, but rather focus on introducing "appropriate regulation." Similarly, they have come to qualify their faith in open international borders and unrestricted flows of capital and goods. While the faith in free trade is still robust, it has been qualified by recognition that countries need to pace the liberalization of their borders.

Second, there is an appeal for a reconceptualization of development that would decenter the focus on economic growth. Advocates of this view argue that development policies should broaden their scope in the pursuit of human development, of which income is only an aspect, and equal consideration should be paid to political, social, and legal development. Taken together, these multiple aspects of development aim at promoting development as *freedom*: the goal is to enhance people's capabilities and to enable individuals to lead the life they choose to live. These objectives have been captured in the promotion of a "Comprehensive Development Framework" and in the incorporation of a social agenda in policy recommendations.

In addition to these two major efforts to rethink development, other changes occurred as academics and practitioners reflected on the limits of the neoliberal model. Thus, more stress is being put on the need to consider local institutions and to avoid one size fits all approaches. Also, there is more attention to local participation in the design and implementation of economic reforms so that local groups take "ownership" of reforms and projects. Finally, there has been a renewed interest in establishing social safety nets and focusing policy more explicitly on poverty reduction.

The new attention to the limits of markets, the effort to define development as freedom not just growth, the stress on the local, the interest in participation, and the focus on poverty reduction have helped set in motion new thinking about law and have ushered in a new Moment in law and development doctrine.

THE THIRD MOMENT IN LAW AND DEVELOPMENT THEORY: AN EMERGING PARADIGM?

As the critique of neoliberal policies took shape and new visions of development policy emerged, people interested in the role of law started to rethink Law and Development doctrine. As a result, a new set of ideas about law have appeared and gained support, allowing us to speak of a Third Moment in Law and Development. Unlike the first two, however, this Moment is still in a formative phase. While the basic outlines of a new vision have become clear, some aspects are still contested.

This new "paradigm" contains a mix of different ideas for development policy. These include the idea that markets can fail and compensatory intervention is necessary, as well as the idea that "development" means more than economic growth and must be redefined to include "human freedom." While Third Moment doctrine embraces these broad notions, each encompasses a great range of options with very different implications for policy. Take "market failure" as a rationale for intervention. This can be construed very broadly, allowing wide scope for government intervention, or very narrowly. Similarly, while everyone is committed to including human rights in development, there is room for very different interpretations of what that might mean. For some, human rights might mean limiting state action while others might deploy a more expansive notion. The same terminology of human rights can be used to promote the interests of oppressed minorities and holders of property.

These two key ideas are not only subject to very different interpretations; they may also be deployed in ways that make them incompatible. A vision of development that embraces human flourishing as its benchmark certainly goes beyond a purely economic conception of development. Those pursuing a holistic vision of development may choose policies that sacrifice long-term growth results to avoid a decrease in or promote an increase of people's capabilities and freedom. In contrast, those supporting a wealth maximization yardstick for development may opt for policies having a prospect for long-term growth results at the expense of investing in people's capabilities.

Another feature that marks the Third Moment as more unsettled than the prior two periods of orthodoxy is the simultaneous presence of critique. At the same time that these new conceptions of development are taking root, a new set of critiques is also being developed. The critiques, including those presented in this book, include some of the concerns raised during the Second Moment. But the new critique adds elements unique to the present because it looks closely at the new elements of doctrine that have appeared in this Third Moment.

In addition to delineating the Third Moment vision, the authors in this book articulate a critique of this emerging orthodoxy. They use different terminologies but all agree that a new form of development doctrine is emerging.[3] They see that the new doctrine accepts the use of law not only to create and protect markets, but also to curb market excess, support the social, and provide direct relief to the poor. They believe that while Third Moment doctrine continues the neoliberal project of private law development, the new vision also seeks to construct an appropriate framework for regulation of economic behavior.

[3] All but one of the chapters focus on the description and analysis of the Third Moment although many do this in the light of a history of earlier periods. They give different names to, and different accounts of, the new orthodoxy and take different approaches to the emerging critique. For example, in describing mainstream theory David Kennedy refers to "chastened neoliberalism" while Trubek calls it "Rule of Law II," Rittich talks about the "incorporation of the social," Newton speaks of the "post Moment," and Santos identifies it with the World Bank's Comprehensive Development Framework.

The authors note that the judiciary remains a central actor and judicial reform still is a major focus of development assistance. But they see that there are subtle differences in the role ascribed to judges in Third Moment doctrine. Now judges not only have to protect property rights and be sure contracts are enforced; they also have to be sure they interpret regulatory law correctly, protect a wider range of human rights, and contribute to poverty reduction. As a result, they cannot rely exclusively on formalist reasoning but must also deploy consequentialist thought. And since the judiciary is now linked to poverty reduction and the social, it is important to provide access to justice for those most in need.

Finally, there is some recognition that one size does not fit all. As the agencies gain more experience and the tasks ascribed to law become more complex, they at least say they are willing to accommodate local conditions and national diversities.

Legal ideas: The Third Moment and the history of legal thought

The progress from the First to the Third Moment in law and development not only moves law to the center of development policy making; it also changes the rationale for legal development assistance. Up to now, the rationale for such assistance has been instrumental. Proponents argued that in one way or another law was a tool to bring about development, and development meant economic growth. But in the current era, the concept of development has been expanded to include law reform as an *end in itself*. Third Moment development thinkers have not rejected instrumental arguments; they still think that law is important to constitute markets and implement a host of policies. But they also see legal institutions as part of what is meant by development, so that legal reform is now justified whether or not it can be tied directly to growth.

To understand the current Moment in thinking about "law and development," we must first look at developments within the sphere of legal theory. And to do that, we must first go back a long way in time. That is the role of Duncan Kennedy's chapter on the globalization of legal consciousness.

Kennedy's chapter provides a sweeping history of law and legal thought from the mid-nineteenth century to the present. He shows how several times in that period a dominant set of ideas about law and its relation to economy and society emerged and was gradually diffused around the world. He identifies three such sets of ideas or "globalizations": the first one going approximately from 1850 to 1914, the second from 1900 to 1968, and the third from 1945 to 2000.

The first of these modes or globalizations is classical legal thought, which consolidates nineteenth-century liberal ideas about law in a market society. It stresses the importance of individual autonomy and sees the primary role of law being protection of property and free transactions. Classical legal thought embraces legal formalism – the deduction of legal results within a coherent and autonomous legal order.

The second globalization was based on the idea of law as means to an end, an instrument to pursue social goals. In this mode, social law emerges to supplement market relations. Laws are consciously designed to achieve social ends. To pursue social welfare, law's domain expands into areas previously left to the market or the will of the parties. Because law is a means to achieve such ends, legal thought must embrace consequentialist analysis.

Duncan Kennedy's analysis helps us understand the past of law and development doctrine. The First Moment in Law and Development embraced the core ideas of social law and consequentialism while the Second or neoliberal Moment was an effort to revive the free market ideas of classical legal thought. But it also helps illuminate the present. For in his chapter Duncan Kennedy sketches a third mode of legal reasoning. He describes this third mode as an amalgam of the prior modes of legal consciousness, which incorporates two separate elements: *policy analysis* and *public law neoformalism.*

Policy analysis involves balancing the competing considerations and conflicting interests present in complex legal problems and finding a supposedly rational solution. In this mode, judges are expected to make decisions by assessing consequential outcomes out of conflicting considerations. Neoformalism, on the other hand, involves purportedly deductive reasoning by reference to rights and principles in foundational texts like treaties and constitutions. Policy analysis draws from ideas of the second globalization of legal thought while new formalism relies on ideas developed in the initial one.

This mode of legal thought emerged after World War II and has gradually diffused around the world. Many factors may account for this diffusion: Duncan Kennedy lists a number of them, including the spread of constitutional courts, the role of transnational law firms and transnational legal NGOs, the incorporation of this mode of thought in the work of international organizations, the global reach of U.S. courts, and the emergence of a transnational legal elite.

The rise of this mode of thought is a key element in the emergence of the Third Moment. Because this mode of consciousness includes attention to the social and to consequentialism, it served as one foundation for the critique of the neoliberal revival of classical legal thought and as a building block for a new form of doctrine. As it was widely diffused already, it provided cultural support for legal projects built around Third Moment premises.

Economic ideas

The current Moment is to a great extent the result of the acknowledged failures of neoliberalism. Of course, voices on the left have pointed to the limits of neoliberalism from the very beginning. But voices from within the original mainstream have been far more influential in defining the current Moment.

As the neoliberal Moment played itself out, even those who believe that the market is the only way to allocate resources for growth came to recognize that markets do not create themselves, may sometimes fail, and cannot deal with all issues of concern to developing countries.

When institutional economists began to posit the need for state intervention to create institutional infrastructure, and people like Joseph Stiglitz reminded everyone that markets have inherent imperfections, there emerged within development economics itself the recognition that law might be needed to create the necessary infrastructure for markets, regulate activity when markets fail, and provide for social needs that markets could not meet. An even broader role for law emerged from the views of economists like Amartya Sen who argued that law, democracy, and freedom should be included in the very *definition* of development.

For David Kennedy, thanks to changes in development theory and legal theory, a new law and development mainstream has emerged. This new mainstream includes the basic neoliberal ideas concerning the importance of law for the operation of private markets. But it also has room for a limited form of state intervention in markets as well as for protection of human rights. The new mainstream rejects the strong neoliberal presumption against regulatory law and accepts the need for legal intervention to reduce transaction costs and compensate for market failures.

David Kennedy observes that whereas neoliberals thought that the market required a highly formalist approach to the judicial role, the new mainstream accepts the importance of consequentialist thought in the law of the market. But while instrumental or consequentialist policy analysis is central to mainstream law and development theory in the Third Moment, it is only one part of a complex amalgam. It may seem strange that the new mainstream can embrace instrumental legal thought for the law of the market but rely on formalism for the interpretation of treaties, constitutions, and similar fundamental texts. This amalgam can be seen as related both to the disillusion with extensive state intervention in the economy and the spread of constitutionalism and judicial review around the world. Kennedy's chapter argues that it is just this form of legal consciousness that has been embraced by the development policy mainstream.

A distinctive aspect of the new development theory mainstream could be called, following Rittich, the "incorporation of the social." With the introduction of the World Bank's Comprehensive Development Framework (CDF), the leading development assistance institution has proclaimed the need to pay greater attention to social, structural, and human dimensions of development. This has meant more concern for human rights, gender equity, direct poverty alleviation, democracy, and access to justice.

The move to the social reinforces the importance of the judge in the current Moment and helps explain the importance given to the judiciary in today's development assistance practices. We can call it social, because it deemphasizes the economic side of the development equation – and emphasizes the social and human side of the process. It appeals to a "holistic" or integral definition of development in which each of the constitutive dimensions of development (economic, social, political, and legal) is in a relation of *interdependence*. On the *instrumental* or policy-analysis side, policies have to be attuned to the local conditions of the market and its existing institutional forms. Judges are expected to make decisions by assessing consequential outcomes and balancing competing considerations in light of the local context. There is an emphasis on *consensus* building, on increasing participation of all stakeholders to reach agreement and thus *ownership* of the projects. On the other hand, there is a clear *rights* analysis, "neoformalist" component associated with CDF that has made "freedom" the paramount consideration of development. In other words, the CDF has enhanced both the instrumental and the rights-analysis aspects of the third globalization.

Institutional practices

The changes in economic and legal ideas affected, and were affected by, changes in the rhetoric and sometimes in the practices of the development agencies. Accused by critics of not doing enough to create the conditions for markets, placing too much faith in markets as development mechanisms, ignoring issues of equality, being insensitive to the needs of women, and not doing enough to promote democracy, development agencies began to redefine what they meant by development and increase their investment in law reform projects.

Take the issue of judicial reform, for example. Judicial reform has been a central feature of legal development assistance for a long time. As Santos explains, however, the World Bank's rationale for its judicial projects has shifted over time. Initially, interest in judicial reform was justified almost exclusively by the need to create basic institutions for securing private entitlements, facilitating transactions, and limiting state intervention in markets. This helps explain why neoliberal theory and legal development practice stressed the importance of formalism in the private law of the market. Formalism seemed like a method to both increase the predictability of judicial action and to constrain any judicial temptation to interfere in market relations.

This has changed with the recognition that limited interventionism may be needed to avoid market failures. Once it became clear that some degree of regulation would be needed, it became obvious that judges would have to employ consequentialist thought to ensure fulfillment of regulatory objectives. That helps explain the reemergence of policy analysis in law and development thinking. A similar change in policy and perhaps in the practice of judicial reform is related to the introduction of the social. The World Bank has continued to support judicial efficiency among the objectives of judicial reform projects. But as Rittich and Santos show, with the appearance of the CDF, it has also begun to focus on "access to justice" and has supported direct efforts to empower advocates for the poor and other "unrepresented interests."

The integration of the spheres

Taken together, developments in these distinctive spheres help explain why the legal consciousness of the Third Moment embraces both the market *and* the social and deploys formalism *and* consequentialism. The Third Moment in law and development doctrine began to take shape when the limits of the revival of classical thought and formalism that marked the Second Moment became apparent. Once mainstream thinkers saw that state intervention was needed to maintain and supplement markets and started paying more attention to social concerns it became clear that the pure neoliberal model of law was inadequate. But at the same time it seemed important to preserve some of the elements of classical formalism as a protection against abuse of state and judicial powers. What was needed was a way of thinking that would allow intervention, albeit a limited one, and would permit the use of law as an instrument of economic transformation without trampling on fundamental rights. Law and development thinkers had this mode of legal thought handy in the amalgam Duncan Kennedy describes as the Third Globalization that had already diffused in many parts of the world. By incorporating policy analysis and public law formalism into law and development doctrine, policy makers were able to link development assistance projects and lend their institutional support to these increasingly influential ideas.

THE NEW CRITICAL PRACTICE

A distinctive feature of the Third Moment in law and development thought is the emergence of a new critical practice. The critique of law and development orthodoxy has a long history, dating back to Trubek and Galanter's "Scholars in Self-Estrangement,"[4] which challenged much of the theory and practice of the First Moment. Today's critical practice started as a reaction against the neoliberal Moment. It included a critique of such elements as neoformalism in the law of markets, the strong antiregulatory presumption, simple-minded legal transplantation, subordination of issues of equity and social development to the overarching goal of rapid economic growth, and

[4] David M. Trubek and Marc Galanter, *Scholars in Self-Estrangement: Reflections on the Crisis in Law and Development Studies in the United States*, 1974 Wis. L. Rev. 1062 (1974).

the costs involved in rapid integration of developing nations into an open global economy.

But the emergence of the new mainstream in the Third Moment, with its subtle softening of neoliberal orthodoxy, introduction of constitutionalism and human rights, and apparent reintroduction of the social, presents a more complex challenge. To deal with the emerging new mainstream we must not only account for the most recent changes, but also develop a critical analysis of a more complex situation. This volume seeks to meet those challenges.

In addition to describing the emergence of a new form of mainstream theory about the role of law in development, our authors seek to launch a new critical practice. This practice builds on and incorporates earlier critical approaches but goes beyond them to confront the rhetoric and practices of the Third Moment.

Antecedents and foundations

Not all of the "new" critical practice is new. Indeed, many of its guiding ideas have their origins in critiques developed in the previous law and development Moments. This should be no surprise as many of the issues that earlier critics raised are still with us. Mainstream thought may have changed, but many of its assumptions haven't changed completely. And even where there seem to be new theories animating development policy, it is far from clear that development practice follows the new rhetoric.

The politics of private law

Drawing on the tradition of American legal realism, our authors challenge commonly held assumptions about private law. They question the economic neutrality of the private law regime of property and contract, the distinction between public and private law, and the related idea that judges do not make law.

Much current development thought continues to present private law as a neutral framework in which economic actors establish relations in a realm of freedom. This is contrasted with the sphere of public or "regulatory" law, which is presented as coercive, and an "intervention" in an otherwise level playing field. Moreover, in this vision, the judges who decide cases involving private law issues are represented not as making regulatory or distributional decisions; they are simply deriving results from abstract principles.

Our authors challenge this body of thought, which has played a major role in the Second Moment and has a continued presence in some circles today. They reject the public/private distinction on which it is based, making clear that the background rules of property and contract, constructed by judicial decisions, are just as coercive and interventionist as public regulatory law. They show that these background norms structure behavioral incentives and play a key role in the distribution of economic resources and power in society.

They also show that the idea that judges do not make law, but just use deductive techniques to discover preordained conclusions, is pure myth. They emphasize that law is not a closed, coherent, and consistent conceptual system with potential answers to all legal questions and factual situations, but rather is ridden with gaps, conflicts, and ambiguities that need to be resolved by judges or other decisionmakers when interpreting and applying the law. They remind us of the enormous discretion of judges and of their role as lawmakers, establishing policies with distributional stakes.

Unreconstructed market fundamentalism

All of our authors suggest that despite rhetorical change, the development assistance world still places primary faith in markets. Despite the rhetoric of the social, World Bank legal projects still focus primarily on creating the conditions for market activity. And while there is now a recognition that market failure may justify limited state intervention, it seems that the assistance agencies have a very narrow definition of market failure and thus relatively little tolerance for a more active participation of the state in the economy. Further, as Santos has documented, development agencies like the World Bank are not monoliths, and even if some units are committed to change, others, possibly more powerful, may stick to the core ideas of the neoliberal Moment.

The gap between rhetoric and reality

A recurring theme in the analysis of the Third Moment is the extent to which development practice follows changes in law and development theory. Several of our authors question whether the changes that we have observed reflect deep changes in policy and practice, or whether they really are little more than a smokescreen to deflect critics.

Containment

Several of the chapters suggest that even when doctrine has actually changed, the new policies may severely restrict the scope of any change. Take, for example, the recognition that law may be needed to correct market failure. This may seem like a significant expansion of the neoliberal model, but if market failure is defined very narrowly this doctrinal shift may leave much of the original model unchanged. Similarly, as Rittich argues, the "incorporation of the social" may add something but it also allows development agencies to control what is meant by the social and define it in ways fully compatible with the core strategy. Thus, the critics suggest that the Third Moment may involve some real change, but only enough to contain critics of the neoliberal mainstream.

The continuing vitality of the critique of formalism

A major feature of prior critical practices was the critique of formalism. This critique has a long and distinguished pedigree in legal thought. For much of the twentieth century, legal scholars have pointed out that formalist objectives were unrealizable and formalist ideology masked judicial discretion. This critique was applied to critique of the reliance of formalism in the neoliberal law of the market. To the extent that continued market fundamentalism keeps those ideas alive, the critique remains valid. Further, although Third Moment legal thinkers have introduced an element of consequentialism into their revised law of the market, they have added public law neoformalism to the law and development amalgam thus creating a new target for this type of critique.

The critique of efficiency

During the neoliberal Moment, legal reforms in a wide array of areas were justified on grounds of economic efficiency. The new critical practice incorporates both an internal and external critique of efficiency claims. First, the internal critique emphasizes that efficiency analysis does not deliver determinate solutions for the choice of particular rules. Rather, there are a number of possible efficient solutions with different distributional consequences. So, efficiency analysis does not offer an escape from the need of making choices when making law. Nor does it justify any a priori preference for private legal ordering over regulatory intervention. Second, the external critique challenges the self-proclaimed scientificity of efficiency analysis and its appeal to neutrality, showing that this type of reasoning is logically fallible and politically contestable. In the end, there is no reason for thinking that a one-time efficiency gain will be translated into "development" rather than another stable, low level, equilibrium.

The forgotten issue of distribution

A very central objective of our effort has been to reinstate distributional issues on the development agenda. Critics in this volume have challenged two features of Third Moment thought. The first, inherited from the neoliberal Moment, is the idea that a mature system of private law creates a level playing field. The myth of the distributional neutrality of the private law order was exposed by the Legal Realists decades ago and continues to be a major point of critique in the present Moment.

This effort to demonstrate that private law as well as regulatory interventions has distributional consequences merges with the critique of neoliberal tendencies to efface distributional questions in development doctrine more generally. As both Newton and David Kennedy point out, where all earlier theories of economic development assumed that distributional issues were fundamental to an effective growth strategy, market fundamentalists focus exclusively on the role of allocative efficiency through markets to promote growth.

Finally, the critics note that the redefinition of law reform as an end of development in its own right further obscures the issue of distribution. Even if instrumental rationales for legal reform downplay distributional consequences, at least they make claims about the relationship between these changes and growth that can be met by distributional analysis. But, if law reform is an end in itself, the whole issue seems to go away.

False universalism

Another feature of the new critical practice is the challenge it poses to the idea that there is one model of development and thus one model for law in development. At the height of the neoliberal Moment, Margaret Thatcher issued her famous dictum that "there is no alternative" and the development agencies of that time adopted the so-called "Washington Consensus," which preached market fundamentalism and economic integration as the solution for all countries. In the legal sphere, this view led to what Newton calls "prescriptive transplantism" in which Western legal models are imposed on transitional and developing countries.

Although Third Moment development thinking has expanded to include issues of democracy and the social, and to recognize the need for limited interventionism, the development agencies still are largely committed to the idea that there is one basic model that should be followed by all developing and transition countries. While revisionist mainstream thinkers accept the need for limited differences and sequencing of reforms, the critics seek to challenge the continued adherence to a basic universalism and suggest the possibility of alternative development paths and legal models.

The hegemony of the world economic order

The new critical practice questions the relationship between the legal systems of developing and transition countries and the hegemony of the world economic order. Although the focus of critical practice is on the policies of the development agencies, critics recognize that their actions are only one of many international forces that affect the legal orders of developing and transition economies. These legal orders are affected by trade regimes like the World Trade Organization (WTO) and North American Free Trade Agreement (NAFTA), by the role played by transnational legal actors, by cultural flows, and other factors. To the extent that these forces constrain alternatives to a one-size-fits-all model of capitalism, critics seek to expose their impact and question their necessity.

The possibility of contestation

Fundamental to the critical practice is the desire to open things up for challenge and contestation. Contributors to this volume believe that more equitable and fairer approaches to development are possible. They think that legal rules, practice, culture, and consciousness are arenas in which false universalism and appeal to professional expertise can be contested and alternatives proposed. They all hope that this volume will encourage such contestation.

CONCLUSION

The current literature reveals several very different approaches to law and development that contrast with the argument of this volume. The first are the "chastened neoliberals" who think that minor adjustments in the neoliberal model, plus better implementation of reforms, are all that is needed. Included in that group are those who see the problems as largely technical, simply requiring better indicators and more empirical studies to perfect the model. The second are those who think that all that we need is a turn to a holistic view of development to fully implement the move to the social and the embrace of policy analysis and public law formalism. In contrast, these essays suggest that the practice of law and development must pay close attention to issues of distribution, question the alleged neutrality of both policy analysis and public law formalism, and explore alternative models of development and the role law might play in advancing them.

2 THREE GLOBALIZATIONS OF LAW AND LEGAL THOUGHT: 1850–2000

Duncan Kennedy

The study of law and development began with a particular positioning of its two terms, "law" in relation to "development." The question was how legal reform might contribute to the takeoff into self-sustaining growth in the Cold War, postcolonial Third World of the 1960s. Trubek and Galanter's famous article, "Scholars in Self Estrangement,"[1] published in 1974, stands, among other things, for the repositioning of the two terms, problematizing the relatively simple instrumental idea of law with which the field had begun, and politicizing our understanding of development. I hope this essay will contribute to the renewal of the project that this book represents.

The three globalizations of my title refer to two overlapping periods of legal institutional and conceptual change in the West: to the rise of Classical Legal Thought between 1850 and 1914, and of socially oriented legal thought between 1900 and 1968; and to the transformation of the characteristic traits of the two periods in two distinct processes of diffusion across the world of colonies and recently independent nation states. The briefer third part sketches a similar institutional and legal theoretical development – a third globalization – for the period 1945–2000 (for a summary overview, see Table 1).

These institutional and conceptual transformations might be described as one of the frameworks or contexts for what development did or did not occur in the world beyond the industrial West over these 150 years. But framework and context are misleading terms for describing the relationship between legal and economic activities. This is because economic activity can't be understood as something autonomous in relation to a set of passive institutional and legal conceptual constraints, as the terms framework and context suggest. Legal institutions and ideas have a dynamic, or dialectical, or constitutive relationship to economic activity.

[1] David M. Trubek and Marc Galanter, *Scholars in Self-Estrangement: Some Reflections on the Crisis in Law and Development Studies in the United States*, 1974 Wisc. L. Rev. 1062–1101 (1974).

The changing "framework" described below was also a "plan," or project of those with access to the legal, administrative, and judicial processes in colonies and states, a project for influencing economic activity. Since the middle of the eighteenth century (the French Physiocrats), one of the objects of legislation, administration, and adjudication has, at least some of the time, been economic development (as it happened to be understood at the time). The first globalization can be seen as the culmination of the liberal attack on mercantilist or "early modern" economic and social policy making, and the second as the policy program of the first generation of critics of the fruits of laissez-faire.

But the framework is not just a plan of "policymakers." In the capitalist West and its periphery strong economic actors influence law making just as much as they are constrained by it. They too have projects, both with respect to specific legal rules that they want or don't want to constrain their pursuit of power and profit and with respect to contours of the legal regime taken as a whole. The transition from mercantilism to liberalism was as much or more their doing as that of statesmen and thinkers. And the rise of what I will be calling "the social" was a function of the rise of political parties that aggregated the interests of weak economic actors, particularly farmers and workers, in response to the influence of capital.

In struggles over the regime, the institutional and conceptual possibilities of law are at stake, the repertoire of possible policies, as well as large numbers of particular rules that make up contested wholes like laissez-faire or socially oriented law. In these struggles, actors with privileged access to the legal apparatus – lawyers for economic actors, lawyers working as legislators, judges and legal academics – have a professionally legitimated role to play, a role that parallels and overlaps that of the economic power holders. They change what the public understands about law and its appropriate role as they argue about how to channel or direct economic and social change, and they participate in the continuous transformation of how the society understands economic development.

This chapter provides an introduction to these processes, but it seems only fair to warn the reader that it is very much a version of a work in progress. It covers a very large amount of material, both in time and in space, and I am sure I've made significant errors both of detail and of substance. The sweeping assertions in the text are supported by a minimal footnote apparatus that reflects the vagaries of my interests and reading over the years rather than sustained research on each topic covered. I hope readers will challenge rather than dismiss me for this weakness, so that I can improve the next version.

Between 1850 and 1914 what globalized was Classical Legal Thought (CLT). It had no essence. But among its important traits were that it was a way of thinking about law as a system of spheres of autonomy for private and public actors, with the boundaries of spheres defined by legal reasoning understood

TABLE 1. The Three Globalizations of Legal Thought

	1st: 1850–1914, Classical legal thought	2nd: 1900–1968, The social	3rd: 1945–2000, Policy analysis, neoformalism, and adjudication
Rights	Individual rights, property rights	Group rights, social rights	Human rights
Equality	Formal equality	Social justice	Nondiscrimination
Legal ideal	Freedom, system, and legal science	Solidarity, evolution, and social science	Democracy, rights, rule of law, and pragmatism
Legal core	Private law	Social law	Constitutional law
Legal philosophy	Legal positivism	Legal pluralism	Multiple normative reconstruction projects
Normative ideas	Right, will, fault	Social welfare	Human rights and social policies
Governance idea	Unitary state	Corporatism	Federalism
Societal unit	People	Social classes, national minorities	Plural identities
Sociolegal unit	Nation state	The institution	Civil society
Boundary	Law/morality	Law/society	Law/politics
Legal instrument	Code	Special legislation	Constitution, treaty, charter
Legal technique	Deduction within coherent and autonomous legal order	Rational development of law as means to social ends	Public law neoformalism and balancing of conflicting considerations
Legal agency	Law professor (drafts code and expounds it)	Legal sociologist and legislator and administrator	The judge (and the litigants)
Economic image	The free market	Alternatives to the market	The pragmatically regulated market
Family image	*Patria potestas* with unenforceable high moral duties	The family regulated in the interest of the state/society	The liberal family
Public international law	Nation states + colonies + treaties	International institutions	International civil society, human rights, and adjudication
International economic law	Gold standard, free trade, private international law	Autarchy, bilateralism, blocs, IMF, World Bank, GATT	EC, NAFTA, WTO, structural adjustment
Privileged legal fields	Contract law, commercial law	Labor law, administrative law, family law, international law	Constitutional law, business law, international law

as a scientific practice. The mechanisms of globalization were direct Western imposition in the colonized world, forced "opening" of non-Western regimes that remained independent, and the prestige of German legal science in the European and Western Hemisphere world of nation states.

Between 1900 and 1968, what globalized was The Social, again a way of thinking without an essence, but with, as an important trait, preoccupation with rethinking law as a purposive activity, as a regulatory mechanism that could and should facilitate the evolution of social life in accordance with ever greater perceived social interdependence at every level, from the family to the world of nations. The agents of globalization were reform movements, of every political stripe, in the developed West, nationalist movements in the periphery, and the elites of newly independent nation states after 1945.

Between 1945 and 2000, one trend was to think about legal technique, in the aftermath of the critiques of CLT and the social, as the pragmatic balancing of conflicting considerations in administering the system created by the social jurists. At the same time, there was a seemingly contrary trend to envisage law as the guarantor of human and property rights and of intergovernmental order through the gradual extension of the rule of law, understood as judicial supremacy. The mechanisms of globalization were American victory in World War II and the Cold War, the "opening" of nation states to the new legal consciousness through participation in the world market on the conditions set by multinational corporations and international regulatory institutions, and the prestige of American culture.

The "thing" that globalized was not, in any of the three periods, the view of law of a particular political ideology. Classical Legal Thought was liberal in either a conservative or a progressive way, according to how it balanced public and private in market and household. The Social could be socialist or social democratic or Catholic or Social Christian or fascist (but not communist or classical liberal). Modern legal consciousness is the common property of right wing and left wing rights theorists, and right wing and left wing policy analysts.

Nor was it a philosophy of law in the usual sense: in each period there was positivism and natural law within the mode of thought, various theories of rights, and, as time went on, varieties of pragmatism, all comfortably within the Big Tent. And what was globalized was most definitely not a particular body of legal rules: each mode provided materials from which jurists and legislators could produce an infinite variety of particular positive laws to govern particular situations, and they did in fact produce an infinite variety, even when they claimed to be merely transplanting rules from milieu to milieu.

The mode of thought provided a conceptual vocabulary, organizational schemes, modes of reasoning, and characteristic arguments. These were used in everything from jurists' writings for lay audiences to legal briefs, judicial opinions, treatises and doctrinal writing and legal philosophy. Using the mode of thought, jurists in each period critiqued the previous mode, and reconceptualized, and to one degree or another substantively reformed, every area of law. We can find The Social, for example, at work everywhere from family law to civil procedure, to criminal law, to contracts, to administrative, international, and constitutional law.

I will refer repeatedly to the consciousness, understood as a vocabulary, of concepts and typical arguments, as a *langue*, or language, and to the specific, positively enacted rules of the various countries to which the *langue* globalized as *parole*, or speech. Just as a specific sentence, for example, "shut the door," is uttered in a specific language, in this case, English, a legal norm is binding utterance in a specific legal discourse, say, that of Classical Legal Thought or The Social. Just as there are an infinity of grammatically correct sentences that can be uttered in English, there are an infinity of regulatory statutes that can be formulated in the conceptual vocabulary of the social and defended through an infinite variety of specific justificatory arguments formulated by combining and recombining the policy "sound bites" of the social.[2]

The elements of the mode of thought were produced piecemeal in different civil and common law countries. We can distinguish two processes. There is that by which a transnational mode of thought comes into existence as jurists combine ideas with distinct origins, displacing a *previous transnational mode*. And the process of *geographic diffusion* of a transnational mode, either by direct and complete replacement of an earlier legal regime by a new one, as in colonial expansion, or through the "reception" of an emergent transnational mode, combining it with "indigenous" elements, and the residuum of the previous mode, into a new national synthesis.

As Diego Lopez Medina argues,[3] we can identify locales of "production" of a new transnational mode, contrasting locales where what happens is reception with only minimal dialectical counterinfluence on the transnational mode, and cases in between. German legal thought was in this sense hegemonic between 1850 and 1900, French legal thought between 1900 and some time in the 1930s, and Unitedstatesean legal thought after 1950.

I do not propose, in this chapter, an overarching theory of what caused these modes of thought to emerge when they did, of what determined their

[2] On 'langue' and 'parole,' see Duncan Kennedy, *A Semiotics of Critique*, 22 Cardozo L. Rev. 1147, 1175 (2001); Duncan Kennedy, A Critique of Adjudication [fin de siecle] 133–135 (1997). On argument-bites, see Duncan Kennedy, *A Semiotics of Legal Argument*, 42 Syracuse L. Rev. 75 (1991), reprinted with a European Introduction in 3 Courses of the Academy of European Law, Book 2 at 309 (1994).

[3] Diego Lopez Medina, *Teoria Impura de Derecho* (2004), and see Diego Lopez Medina, *Comparative Jurisprudence: Reception and Misreading of Transnational Legal Theory in Latin America* (2001) (unpublished doctoral dissertation, Harvard Law School) (on file with the Harvard Law School Library).

internal structural properties, of the particulars of their geographic reception, or of their effects or functions in social life. The scheme of periods, modes, and production/reception across the world is a set of boxes for the organization of facts and factoids, a structure within which to propose low-level hypotheses, and the locale of a narrative.

One can have three modest, though not negligible, ambitions for this kind of exercise. First, one hopes that the narrative will bring together and relate to one another a large number of previously disparate events in the intellectual history of Western law in the world, thereby increasing the ex post intelligibility of that history.

Second, one small notch higher on the scale of ambition, one can hope that other researchers (or oneself at a later date) will "confirm" the hypotheses by finding things that uncannily correspond to what one would have predicted given the narrative. Thus, for example, it gave me, recently, great pleasure, for reasons that will become clear, when it was brought to my attention that a survey of Scandinavian law published in 1963 claims first, that Danish-Norwegian law is part neither of the civil nor of the common law system, and, second that this body of law is "further influenced by social welfare trends than the law of most other societies."[4]

One can also hope that the narrative will operate in support of political interventions, in this case, I hope, of left or radical left interventions. It might do so because, in any given period, the plausibility even to ourselves of our political convictions is, to a limited but important degree, a function of how we understand our history. In this case, my hope is that the "three globalizations" narrative will support the conviction that progressive elites of the periphery can and should devise national progressive strategies, rather than accept the prescription of the center, that they simply "open" their economies and "reform" their legal systems, and accept the consequences for good or ill. But to avoid false advertising, let me emphasize that the connection between narrative and political intuition is tenuous.[5]

Speaking for a moment of the history of Unitedstatesean law, the account that follows is heterodox in four main ways. First, it portrays the United States up to the 1930s as a context of legal reception, that is, as part of the periphery or semi-periphery. Legal development was heavily determined by what was happening in Germany and later France, but the original Unitedstatesean synthesis had no influence on those countries. I mean here to challenge the main tradition in Unitedstatesean legal history, which represents

[4] Danish and Norwegian Law: A General Survey 70 (The Danish Committee on Comparative Law, 1963).

[5] For an analogous decentering effort in the context of the process of global change, and with similar methodological premises, see P.G. Monateri, *Black Gaius: A Quest for the Multicultural Origins of the 'Western Legal Tradition,'* 51 Hastings L. J. 479, 481 (2000).

the transformations of Unitedstatesean legal thought as determined by internal social and economic developments.[6]

Second, this account emphasizes the extent to which developments in different fields of law over the last century followed a single pattern. Histories of fields constantly attribute to internal dynamics changes that were happening in strictly analogous ways in other fields, and therefore are unconvincing in the same way as national histories that disregard the transnational movement of legal thought. Third, I depart from current fashion by treating legal realism as the critical devastation of sociological jurisprudence ("the social," in the lingo of this article), rather than as "essentially" an extension of the sociological jurisprudes critique of CLT. Fourth, in this account post-WWII developments are characterized just as much by the neoformalist rights consciousness of the Warren Court and the neoliberals as by the conflicting considerations consciousness of the Legal Process School, and both were responses to the demise of the social, rather than of CLT.[7]

In terms of classic comparative law categories, the narrative treats the contrast between civil and common law as useful in providing explanations of how the emergent transnational mode of thought penetrated and transformed different national contexts. But it rejects the notion that the Western rivals evolved through time according to distinct, internally determined system logics. This is analogous to denying that we can explain any important aspect of Unitedstatesean legal thought by reference to uniquely Unitedstatesean conditions.

THE FIRST GLOBALIZATION

The first globalization occurred during the second half of the nineteenth century and was over by WWI. What was globalized was a mode of legal consciousness. According to its social critics[8] and according to most (not all) of today's historians,[9] the late nineteenth-century mainstream saw law as "a system," having a strong internal structural coherence based on the three traits of exhaustive elaboration of the distinction between private and public law, "individualism," and commitment to legal interpretive formalism. These

[6] *E.g.*, Morton Horwitz, The Transformation of American Law: 1780–1860 (1977); Thomas Grey, *Langdell's Orthodoxy*, 45 U.Pitt L .Rev. 1 (1983) (paying more attention to European analogies, but ironically, missing both the will theory and what was uniquely Unitedstatesean about the story, namely the extension of CLT to public law).

[7] *Contrast* Morton Horwitz, The Transformation of American Law 1870–1960: The Crisis of Legal Orthodoxy (1992).

[8] *E.g.*, Roscoe Pound, *The End of Law as Developed in Juristic Thought* II, 30 Harv. L. Rev. 201, 202, 223–225 (1917); *see infra* notes 42–119 and accompanying text.

[9] *See* Horwtiz, *supra* note 7; Grey, *supra* note 6; Duncan Kennedy, *Towards an Historical Understanding of Legal Consciousness: The Case of Classical Legal Thought*, 3 Res. in Law and Soc., 3–24 (1980).

traits combined in "the will theory."[10] The will theory was that the private law rules of the "advanced" Western nation states were well understood as a set of rational derivations from the notion that government should protect the rights of legal persons, which meant helping them realize their wills, restrained only as necessary to permit others to do the same.

The will theory was an attempt to identify the rules that should follow from consensus in favor of the goal of individual self-realization. It was not a political or moral philosophy justifying this goal; nor was it a positive historical or sociological theory about how this had come to be the goal. Rather, the theory offered a specific, will-based and deductive interpretation of the interrelationship of the dozens or hundreds of relatively concrete norms of the extant national legal orders, and of the legislative and adjudicative institutions that generated and applied the norms.

"Outside" or "above" legal theory, there were a variety of rationales for the legal commitment to individualism thus understood. Of these, only natural rights theory was also highly relevant on the "inside," that is, in the development of the technique of legal analysis based on deduction. Natural rights theorists had elaborated the will theory, beginning in the seventeenth century, as a set of implications from their normative premises, and their specific legal technique was the direct ancestor of the legal formalism that the socially oriented reformers were to attack in its positivized form.[11]

In the nineteenth century, the German historical school developed a positivist version of normative formalism. A national system of law reflects as a matter of fact the normative order of the underlying society; such a normative order is coherent or tends toward coherence on the basis of the spirit and history of the people in question; "legal scientists" can and should elaborate the positive legal rules composing "the system" on the premise of its internal coherence.[12] In the late nineteenth century, the German pandectists (e.g., Windschied) worked at the analysis of the basic conceptions of the German common law version of Roman law (right, will, fault, person) with the aim of establishing that this particular system could be made internally coherent, and also be made to approach gaplessness. Many Continental legal scholars understood the German Civil Code of 1900 as the legislative adoption of this system.[13]

[10] *See* Duncan Kennedy, *From the Will Theory to the Principle of Private Autonomy: Lon Fuller's 'Consideration and Form,'* 100 Colum. L. Rev. 94, 106–108, 115–116 (2000).

[11] On the history of the will theory, see Franz Wieacker, History of Private Law in Europe with Special Reference to Germany (1995, 1967); James Gordley, The Philosophical Origins of Modern Contract Doctrine (1991).

[12] *See* Friedrich Carl von Savigny, On the Vocation of our Age for Legislation and Jurisprudence (London, Littlewood and Co., 1831); Friedrich Carl von Savigny, The System of Modern Roman Law, I (William Holloway, trans., Hyperion Press, 1979) (1839).

[13] *See* Franz Neumann, *The Change in the Function of Law in Modern Society, in* The Democratic and The Authoritarian State 22 (Herbert Marcuse ed., 1957).

The hero figure of the first globalization was the law professor (author of codes and statutory modifications of codes, as well as of treatises), and the great and inspiring precursor initiator was the founder of the historical school, Friedrich Carl von Savigny (1779–1861). The paradox of Savigny, and the probable source of his seminal importance, was the combination, in the single idea of legal science as the elaboration of "the system," of a universalizing legal formalist will theory with the idea that particular regimes of state law reflect diverse underlying nonlegal societal normative orders. His approach sharply attacked the notion that all national legal regimes are simply better or worse approaches to a religiously or rationally based transnational natural law. Outside Germany, the historical school was a minor tendency, but the same conception of a will theory combining individualism and deductive form gradually supplanted earlier ways of understanding private law. Austin was a follower of the Germans, and his *Lectures on Jurisprudence,* written in 1831–2 but not published until 1863, was the manifesto of CLT for the common law world.[14] The normative or "outside" force for the theory might come from utilitarianism, or from Lockean or Kantian or French revolutionary natural rights, or from a variant of evolutionism (the movement of the progressive societies has been from contract to status; social Darwinism). But however derived, normative individualism was closely connected with logical method in the constitution of some version of the will theory.[15]

The will theory in turn served a variety of purposes within legal discourse. It guided the scholarly reconceptualization, reorganization, and reform of private law rules, in what the participants understood as an apolitical rationalization project. But it also provided the discursive framework for the decision of hundreds or perhaps thousands of cases, throughout the industrializing West, in which labor confronted capital and small business confronted big business. And it provided an abstract, overarching ideological formulation of the meaning of the rule of law as an essential element in a Liberal legal order.

Left and right political projects could coexist within Classical Legal Thought in its heyday because the "will theory," for all its pretensions to scientificity, was highly manipulable when it came to defining just what fell into the categories of right and will (not to speak of the ambiguities of the notion of legal personality, as applied to private corporations and labor unions). CLT firmly excluded only hierarchical organicism in the mode of monarchism or neofeudalism (DeMaistre), and left wing collectivism in the mode of communism or utopian socialism (Fourier).

A minority current in CLT, but a major current in lay left thinking in the late-nineteenth and early-twentieth centuries developed the two ideas that the legal order gave inadequate protection to "workers rights," and that bargains

[14] John Austin, Lectures on Jurisprudence (1863).

[15] Pound, *supra* note 8.

under capitalism did not represent "free will."[16] For all Karl Marx's railing against it,[17] the populist idea that the problem was that the rules were skewed against the masses, and in favor of "the interests," never lost its hold, and was available for appropriation by pre-1914 feminists and anticolonialists. While progressives generally abandoned rights rhetoric during the period of the social, they revived it after WWII, as we will see, in the two forms of civil libertarianism and international human rights ideology.

Nonetheless, it is fair to say that a large majority of the juristic elite that developed and propagated CLT was conservative, and that, over the course of the twentieth century, the mainstream ideas of the first globalization turned from a "consciousness," within which a multitude of political projects were at least possible, into an "ideology," classical liberalism and then neoliberalism, one of the central political theoretical projects of the modern right wing (the other one being "tradition").

The mechanism of the first globalization was a combination of influence within the system of autonomous Western nation states, and imperialism broadly conceived. The German model spread not just to France[18] but across Europe (both Western and Eastern) and across the Channel and to the United States and Latin America. The United States and British colonies, like Britain itself, adopted German legal science and vast numbers of statutes, while resisting codification. The former Spanish colonies were more influenced by France, and codified.

The English, French, and Dutch, and later the Germans, Americans, and Belgians, spread their national versions of CLT directly to their colonies, with or without codification. (The Portuguese and Spanish did the same in the remains of their empires in decline.) The Great Powers forced "opening" to Western law, as a mandatory aspect of opening to Western trade, on states not directly colonized, such as the Ottoman Empire, Japan, China, Thailand, Egypt, and Iran. These sometimes adopted codes on the European model and sometimes submitted to the creation of special courts to apply European law in transactions with Europeans.

A more subtle mode of globalization of CLT was implicit in the eventual universalization (that is, literally, globalization) of a single Classical system of public international law, devised by the Western Great Powers, based on the conceptual innovations of the seventeenth century natural law theorists of sovereignty as a territorial (not personal) power absolute within its

[16] William Forbath, Law and the Shaping of the American Labor Movement (1991).

[17] Karl Marx, Critique of the Gotha Programme (Scientific Socialism Series, Progress Publishers, 1971) (1875).

[18] Mikhail Xifaras, *L'ecole de l'exegese etait-elle historique?*, *in* Influences et receptions mutuelles du droit et de la philosophie en France et en Allemagne (Kervegan & Mohnhaupt eds., 2001).

sphere.[19] In CLT, the "nation state and colonies" model was universal except for anachronisms, and the heterogeneous mish mash of governance structures of the world in 1800 was no more than a memory.

Finally, there was the creation of a first global system of international economic law, based on free trade, the gold standard, and private international law (often applied by arbitrators) to settle disputes. Money was depoliticized,[20] and an international capital market, with accompanying gunboat diplomacy, came into existence. Within this complex (and fragile, and violent) structure, the combination of the growth of world trade and the infrastructural and primary product investments of the center in the periphery unleashed a process of social transformation, irreversible as it has turned out, out of which emerged (only in the second half of the nineteenth century) the "tradition/modernity" dichotomy that still rules our lives.[21]

The historicist idea (Savigny), as I remarked above, was double, if not contradictory. The law of a nation was a reflection of the spirit or culture of its people, and in this sense inherently political, but could be developed in a scientific manner by jurists who presupposed its internal coherence. In Germany, according to Savigny, the people had received Roman law, and Christianized and modernized it through evolutionary popular action. This particular law revealed itself, when worked over by the science of the jurists, to be based on the highly abstract ideas of right and will. Moreover, it corresponded in its fundamentals to the *ius gentium*, or law of peoples, the minimal substratum of legal rules that were shared, as a matter of fact, or at least should be shared, by all peoples. This formulation "fit" globalization in the mode described in the last four paragraphs.[22]

Of course, when what happened was direct colonization, there was, initially, little effective resistance to whatever legal ideas the colonizer chose to impose. But in Western and Eastern Europe, and North and South America, CLT had to win over the elites of independent nation states. In the territories of the Ottoman Empire and in Southeast and East Asia, what was happening was "opening," not direct conquest. In the Ottoman lands and across Asia, there were highly developed preexisting modes of legal consciousness

[19] *See* Anthony Carty, The Decay of International Law? (1986); David Kennedy, *Primitive Legal Scholarship*, 27 Harv. Int'l L.J. 1 (1986); David Kennedy, *International Law and the Nineteenth Century: History of an Illusion*, 65 Nordic J. Int'l L. 385 (1996); Richard Ford, *Law's Territory (A History of Jurisdiction)*, 97 Mich. L. Rev. 843, 922–927 (1999); Antony Anghie, *Francisco de Vitoria and the Colonial Origins of International Law*, 5 Soc. & Legal Stud. 321 (1996); Antony Anghie, *Finding the Peripheries: Sovereignty and Colonialism in Nineteenth-Century International Law*, 40 Harv. Int'l L.J. 1, 54–57 (1999).

[20] Barry Eichengreen, Globalizing Capital: A History of the International Monetary System (1998); Christine Desan, *The Market as a Matter of Money: Denaturalizing Economic Currency in American Constitutional History*, 30 Law & Soc. Inquiry 1 (2005).

[21] *See* Karl Polanyi, The Great Transformation (1957).

[22] Savigny, The System of Modern Roman Law, *supra* note 12.

(Islamic, Hindu, Confucian, Shinto) that had at least a chance of resisting or transforming themselves into local competitors. For example, the *Majalla*, the Ottoman codification of the Islamic Hanafi law of obligations, 1869–76, was a serious peripheral attempt to adapt the European legal form of codification (not without earlier Ottoman analogues) to Islamic substance.[23] Something at least resembling "selection,"[24] along with "imposition," was probably a factor, in these complex contexts, in the success of CLT. In other words, CLT probably had some intrinsic appeal to the elites that chose it.

CLT replaced an earlier Western transnational mode of thought that had asserted the existence of a universal law of reason, either Catholic or based on natural rights theory, and a sharp legal distinction between civilized (participant in the *ius gentium*) and barbarous nations. CLT offered the legal elites of the peripheral, newly formed nation states of Europe, North and South America, and Asia something at least superficially more attractive. The national elites could identify themselves with their respective "peoples," and sharply dissociate, if they were English or Russian, or for that matter Argentinean, or Egyptian, or Japanese, from the Germans and French.

They could deploy European historicist legal theory to defend themselves against European legal hegemony – only Latin American jurists could "own" a Latin American law reflecting *criollo* consciousness,[25] Japanese law should reflect the "spirit" of the Japanese people. The mission was the development of that law in particular, not universal or natural law, and its development in a world of formally equal nation states, rather than in the outer darkness of "barbarism."[26]

On the other side of the contradictory structure, CLT affirmed that every country with a Western legal heritage shared the Roman legacy along with Savigny's Germans, including, for example, the newly independent Bulgarians (1878/1908) and the Bolivians (1825), and that every nation that participated in the global order of commerce and finance participated in the *ius gentium*. Along with the particularist notion that every people had its own unique normative order, the jurists scattered across the periphery of independent nations and modernizing empires could affirm their participation in the developing sciences of legal obligation and international law, based as they were on an analytics of will, right, and sovereignty that had no obvious national particularity at all. They could develop their own slightly modified

[23] Niyazi Berkes, The Development of Secularism in Turkey 160–169 (1988); Hava Guney, The Ottoman Codification Movement Compared with the American (2002) (unpublished manuscript on file with the Suffolk University Law Review).

[24] *See* Jared Diamond, Guns, Germs and Steel (1997).

[25] Liliana Obregón, Completing Civilization: Nineteenth Century Criollo Interventions in International Law (2002) (unpublished doctoral dissertation, Harvard Law School) (on file with the Harvard Law School Library).

[26] *See* Joseph Levinson, Confucian China and its Modern Fate: A Trilogy (1972); Masao Maruyami, Studies in the Intellectual History of Tokugawa Japan (1974).

national versions of the Civil and Commercial Codes of the commercially, financially, and militarily dominant European powers, facilitating integration into the world market, without seeing themselves as traitors to their national constituencies. And they could work, as jurists, for their nations' interests within the structure of international law, deploying the norms of sovereign equality and autonomy against the Great Powers. At home, the universal, transnational element in CLT was the basis of a claim to power as mediators of the participation of the periphery in the normative order, as well as the culture, of the metropoles.[27]

There are no fewer than three other structural characteristics of CLT that may have facilitated its reception, first across Europe and then across the non-European periphery. These are: the distinction between the "subjects" of municipal law and international law; the distinction between public and private law; and the distinction between the law of the market and the law of the household.

The "subjects" of municipal law include "persons," but the "subjects" of international law were, in CLT, only "sovereigns." Citizens as citizens had no rights at all under international law. If they had no rights under international law, then sovereigns, and in particular powerful sovereigns, had no legal basis for interfering with the way independent states treated their citizens. This was the globalization of a legal consciousness within which a basic structural trait was that *jurisdiction* must *not* be global. The people doing the receiving were legal elites scattered around the world. They were closely integrated with, but not everywhere identical with, the political and economic elites of their respective countries. Receiving CLT permitted a gesture of striking cosmopolitanism, without any sacrifice of local autonomy (in the sense of legal autonomy vis à vis other countries).

In CLT, everyone understood (and jurists often explicitly affirmed) that private law was the core of law.[28] That distinguished not only international law, but public law as well, as not part of the core. Public law was the law of the state: criminal law, administrative law (law of the bureaucracy – every state has one), and constitutional law. Public law differed from private law because it was less scientific and more political than private law. It was more political because criminal law directly reflected the normative order of the common people; administrative law was the law of the sovereign, whose legal autonomy was, arguably, inherently unlimited; and constitutional law was created by the people, or by the constituent orders of civil society, in their capacity as ultimate legal authors.

International law had only sovereigns as subjects, so the jurist could not be called on to denounce, in the name of international law, the conduct of his sovereign toward his fellow citizens – indeed must resist the illegal efforts of

[27] *See* Jorge Esquirol, *The Fictions of Latin American Law (Part I)*, 1997 Utah L. Rev. 425 (1997).

[28] *E.g.*, Savigny, The System of Modern Roman Law, *supra* note 11.

other sovereigns to interfere. Public law was political rather than scientific, with the same result: science did not oblige the jurist one way or another on the issue of local dictatorship or oligarchic rule by large landowners. At the same time, public law was still, in spite of all, "Law," so the jurist could, if he wanted to risk it, try to parlay Law's prestige in favor of one outcome or another at the moment of coup d'etat, and the jurist should certainly be in charge of drafting when the new regime required a new constitution.

CLT dealt with the issue of patriarchy, meaning not just "gender" but the whole "household," through the distinction, within private law, between the law of obligations and family law. The first globalization globalized a compromise in which the will theory came to an end at the family. There was a big difference between liberalism in the economy and liberalism with respect to the relations of seducers and virgins; husbands and wives; fathers and abused or rebellious daughters; husbands and mistresses; ex-husbands, ex-wives; and their children; rich patriarchs and their proletarian boy lovers; and so on.

The starting point was the "early modern" system of family law described, for example, by Blackstone,[29] in which the patriarch was legally obliged to support his wife and minor children, entitled to their obedience, which he could enforce through moderate physical punishment, had arbitrary power with respect to many aspects of their welfare and property, and was protected against sexual and economic interference by third parties.

This was a limited, Christianized, supervised form of patriarchy, nothing like the Roman *patria potestas*. The father was understood to be subject to "natural" obligations to family members, obligations of care and protection that went well beyond those owed one another by market actors. These were legally enforceable against the patriarch in court, when he went beyond the bounds of culturally sanctioned physical abuse or denial of necessaries, but only at the outer limits of outrage. Fathers legally owed less to family than to strangers except that in exceptional cases they owed more. Within the wide range of discretion thus granted him by positive law, jurists presented his high altruistic obligations as moral or ethical rather than properly legal (therefore described as of "imperfect obligation," by contrast with obligations "perfected" by the addition of state enforcement mechanisms).

The regimes in place in the North Atlantic when CLT began to take off around 1850 also included some or all of the following: divorce only for fault or not all, inheritance rules designed to preserve legitimate family assets, criminal prohibition of "unnatural" and "dishonorable" sexuality, including same-sex sex and female adultery (male adultery was usually punished only if there was also cohabitation or concubinage), snuffing of legal claims arising out of "immoral" relationships (particularly the claims of mistresses and

[29] William Blackstone, Commentaries, *421–447 (1765–9).

illegitimate children), and child custody in the father. Within these broad initial contours, family law moved toward liberalization at different speeds in different countries, with different political and religious balances of power producing diverse and unstable bodies of positive law.

The Code Napoleon (1804), for example, was liberal in that it permitted divorce by mutual consent. That provision was abrogated in 1815 (at the Restoration), and not restored until 1975. The Chilean Bello Code of 1857 adapted much of the liberal law of obligations of the French Code, but remitted the whole of the law of marriage and divorce to the Catholic Church for administration under canon law. The Bello Code in some cases adopted and in others rejected liberal rules designed to impede the formation of stable dynastic families (e.g., forbidding entails, increasing the rights of illegitimate children, reducing forced shares in inheritance), according to the balance of local forces.[30]

In 1850, the family law of the North Atlantic countries still looked, at the formal level, quite similar to the then existing regimes of Muslim or Hindu or Confucian family law. In some cases, for example the Muslim law of marriage, which recognized the wife's separate property and treated domestic violence and the husband's duty of support as fully justiciable, the West was well "behind" the East.[31] North Atlantic family law was only somewhat more liberal than the traditionalist Catholic regime that Spain had imposed on its American colonies.[32] In North and South America, Eastern Europe and the Ottoman lands, exactly as in Western Europe, local elites did battle as to how far the reforms of the middle of the nineteenth century should go in a liberalizing direction.

The substance of the North Atlantic regime changed rapidly, by historical standards, at the same time that it was reconceptualized by the Classical jurists. Legally legitimized hierarchy gave way, step by step, sometimes with steps backward, in the direction of a regime of formal equality with reciprocal duties. For family relations, it was formal equality within what the Classics defined as a "status" rather than a contract, so that it was the "will of the state" rather than that of the parties that fixed the relations of the parties. In this way, CLT sharply split family law from the law of obligations (contract, property, and tort), placing it on the side of morals and politics, rather than science and will.[33]

30 M. C. Mirow, *Borrowing Private Law in Latin America: Andres Bello's Use of the 'Code Napoleon' in Drafting the Chilean Civil Code*, 61 La. L. Rev. 291 (2001).

31 Lama Abu-Odeh, *Modernizing Muslim Family Law: The Case of Egypt* 37 Vand. J. Transnat'l L. 1043 (2004).

32 *See* Isabel Cristina Jaramillo, A History of Family Law in Colombia, 1800–2000 (2003) (unpublished manuscript on file with the Suffolk University Law Review).

33 Michael Grossberg, Governing the Hearth (1985).

It was no less and perhaps more important that CLT combined movement toward formal equality with a powerful doctrine of legal nonintervention in the family that rendered many of the formally equal rights of wives unenforceable (e.g., domestic violence, marital rape).[34] Nonintervention was rationalized on the CLT ground that the "sphere" of the family, based on the principle of egalitarian altruism, would be corrupted or destroyed by judicial intervention that would have to use legal tools closely associated with the conflictual individualist ethos of market law.[35]

The colonial powers everywhere declined to replace "native" family law with their own systems. Even the French, famous for "direct rule" and "assimilation," did no more than promote the codification of Muslim family law in the Maghreb. The British did the same in India, with separate Hindu, Muslim, and Christian rules. In the Netherlands Indies, the Dutch preserved *adat* law for the family. But everywhere the process of formalization within the colonial legal and political system included some deliberate change (for example, with respect to practices like widow burning in India),[36] and initiated many indirect, intended and unintended changes.[37] These might reinforce rather than weaken the powers of heads of households by reducing responsibilities of titular landholders to extended family members.[38]

There seem to have been a very large number of solutions, along a highly predictable continuum of options, with the outcome in many countries determined in sharp conflicts between the Catholic Church, socially conservative Protestant sects, or Muslim clerics, on one side, and "modernizing" secular forces on the other. Though the continuum of solutions and the arguments back and forth seems to have been the same everywhere, the solutions adopted in North America were much more "liberal" than those in South America and the ex-Ottoman Empire. As in Europe, there were as many compromises as there were countries, and they were everywhere unstable, with change generally in the liberalizing direction interrupted by periods of reaction.[39]

It seems plausible that the distinction between market law and family law functioned in the same way that the municipal/international and public/private distinctions did in the context of historicism. CLT did *not*

[34] *See* Frances Olsen, *The Myth of State Intervention in the Family*, 18 Mich. J. Law Reform 835 (1985); Reva Siegal, *"The Rule of Love": Wife Beating as Prerogative and Privacy*, 105 Yale L. J. 2117, 2196–2206 (1996).

[35] *See* Frances Olsen, *The Family and the Market*, 96 Harv. L. Rev. 1497 (1983).

[36] *See* Ratna Kapur and Brenda Cossman, Subversive Sites: Feminist Engagements With the Law in India (1996).

[37] *See id.*

[38] J. S. Furnivall, Colonial Policy and Practice 296 (1948); Celestine Nyamu, Gender, Culture and Property Relations in a Pluralistic Social Setting (2000) (unpublished doctoral dissertation, Harvard Law School) (on file with the Harvard Law School Library).

[39] *See, e.g.*, Jaramillo, *supra* note 32.

claim substantive universality – quite the contrary. Beginning with Savigny, it offered peripheral elites the categorization of their family law as popular, political, religious, cultural, and particular, and therefore as eminently *national*. In exchange they accepted (usually with alacrity) that the law of the market would be, not positively and in every detail, but generally and "essentially," the property and contract-based law of a national "free" market, linked to other free markets by free trade, the gold standard, and a private international law that was conceptually identical to municipal civil law.

In the first half of the nineteenth century, the major boundary issue that had to be resolved before the consciousness of the first globalization could gel had nothing to do with the blood family. For the blood family, the solution according to which full liberalization didn't apply, and every country could have its own compromise between equality and tradition, produced a stable overarching context for local battles. The more difficult question was the status of what the eighteenth century had conceived as domestic labor, the labor of slaves, apprentices, indentured servants, and dependent agricultural laborers.

In the North Atlantic, the ultimate resolution came about through the emergence of the factory, the small farm, and the bourgeois (as opposed to aristocratic) institution of domestic service as the dominant labor forms. All of these classes of labor were categorized, within the liberal CLT regime of will theory and free contract, through the notion of "self-ownership," rather than within the eighteenth-century model of the servant as part of the household. Duties of obedience were eliminated along with rights to support; the arbitrary authority of the employer replaced the arbitrary authority of the patriarch.

The intermediate forms of semifree labor (serfdom, apprenticeship, the indenture) disappeared – through the French Revolution and Napoleon's conquests in Western Europe, at the moment of independence from Spain in Latin America, after the middle of the century in Russia. Slavery flourished in many countries of the Americas over the nineteenth century, and wasn't abolished in the United States until 1863, Brazil in 1871, and, finally, Cuba in 1886. At this point, all that was left of the legal household was the family.[40]

In the world's South, or the capitalist periphery broadly conceived, what emerged was not the small farm so central to North Atlantic republican ideology. European diseases and slaughtering eliminated most of the remaining hunter gatherers and nomadic pastoralists, and amalgamated tribal societies and small states into colonies. At the same time, the precapitalist empires

40 *See generally* Robert Steinfeld, The Invention of Free Labor: The Employment Relationship in English and American Law and Culture: 1350–1870 (1991).

disintegrated into nation states and/or colonies. Within this structure, a very large part of the world's population came to be organized either in *latifundia*, large estates or plantations, owned first by planters and then by multinationals, worked by nominally free but factually dependent laborers, or in *minifundia*, small plots worked by peasant villagers with various forms of customary or sharecropping tenure. Both types produced old or new cash crops for a new world market, but the smallholders did so in unstable combination with subsistence crops. The latifundia/minifundia contrast has something to say about Latin America, Africa, India, Eastern Europe, the Ottoman Empire successor states, Indonesia, China, and the post-Reconstruction Unitedstatesean South.[41]

Incorporation of these labor forms through CLT's categories – the sale of labor power for the agricultural laborer, private property in land for the peasant – meant sometimes that the colonial powers and the independent states of the periphery simply ratified, by adopting a formal, abstract idea of free will rather than a more substantive one, whatever schemes of economic and social hierarchy emerged out of the play of violence and culture on the ground. And sometimes they transformed, in their own interests, but without understanding exactly what they were doing, the preexisting social arrangements by forcing them into the mold of the "Western idea of property."[42] Through the long transition, a whole series of legal dodges were available so that something like serfdom could be maintained within liberal forms, and something like capitalism maintained within feudal forms. (The great exception is British India, where land reform was a major strategy of control and colonial reconstitution from the middle of the nineteenth century.[43])

Once again, it seems plausible that CLT could globalize precisely because it had so little to say one way or the other about the legal treatment of the legally free but obviously subordinated peasants and agricultural laborers of the South.

As we will see, it is no more possible to understand the second and third globalizations than the first without an analysis of how the liberal idea (of a regime based on state action to guarantee the exercise of free will and also the limits on free will necessary for everyone to enjoy it) worked in symbiosis

[41] Eric R. Wolf, Europe and the People without History (1983).

[42] J. S. Furnivall, An Introduction to the Political Economy of Burma (3d ed., 1957); Sylvia Kang'ara, Analytical, Prescriptive and Resistant Characterizations of "African" Conceptions of Property: A Critique of Mainstream Assumptions about African-Western Incompatibility (2003) (unpublished doctoral dissertation available from the author); Joel Ngugi, Searching for the Market Criteria: Market Oriented Reforms in Legal and Economic Development Discourses (2002) (unpublished doctoral dissertation, available in the Harvard Law School Library).

[43] Eric Stokes, The English Utilitarians and India (1959); Robert Eric Frykenberg, Land Control and Social Structure in Indian History (2d ed. 1979).

with or in contradiction of the counterideal, counterethic, counterreality represented by the household.

THE SECOND GLOBALIZATION

society
sociology
social anthropology
social science
social function
social justice
social revolution
socialism
national socialism
social democracy
social Catholicism
social Christianity
social welfare
social purpose
social need
social question
social problem
social policy
social law
social rights
social legislation
social insurance
social work

The second globalization began around 1900 and had spent its force by the end of WWII, but strongly influenced thinking both about the international and about third world economic development strategies through the 1960s. What was globalized this time was a critique of the first globalization and a reconstruction project. The critique was that the late nineteenth-century European mainstream abused deduction in legal method and was "individualist" in legal substance. The slogan of the second globalization was "the social," an abstraction that played much the same role during this period that will, right, and fault played in CLT.

The social as a transnational legal consciousness

The initial innovators of the social were German-speaking, including Jhering,[44] Gierke,[45] and Ehrlich,[46] but the main globalizers were French-speaking,[47] Saleilles,[48] Geny,[49] Duguit,[50] Lambert,[51] Josserand,[52] Gounod,[53]

[44] Rudolf von Jhering, Law as a Means to an End (Isaac Husik trans., Macmillan 1924) (1914).

[45] Otto von Gierke, Political Theories of the Middle Age (Frederic William Maitland trans., 1913).

[46] Eugen Ehrlich, Fundamental Principles of the Sociology of Law (Walter L. Moll trans., 1936, 1913).

[47] Marie-Claire Belleau, *The 'Juristes Inquiets': Legal Classicism and Criticism in Early Twentieth Century France*, 1997 Utah L. Rev. 379.

[48] Raymond Saleilles, De la declaration de la volonte (1901).

[49] Francois Geny, Method of Interpretation and Sources of Private Positive Law (Louisiana State Law Institute trans., 2d ed. 1963) (1899).

[50] Leon Duguit, *Theory of Objective Law Anterior to the State, in* Modern French Philosophy, VII The Modern Legal Philosophy Series (1916).

[51] Edouard Lambert, La Fonction du Droit Civile Compare (1903).

[52] Josserand, De l'esprit des droits et de leur relativite: Theorie dite de L'abus des droits (1927, 1939).

[53] Emmanuel Gounod, Le principe de l'autonomie de la volonte (1912).

and Gurvitch.[54] They had in common with the Marxists (the other significant early twentieth-century school critical of CLT) that they interpreted the actual regime of the will theory as an epiphenomenon in relation to a "base," in the case of the Marxists, the capitalist economy and in the case of the social, "society" conceived as an organism. The idea of both was that the will theory in some sense "suited" the socioeconomic conditions of the first half of the nineteenth century. But the social people were anti-Marxist, just as much as they were antilaissez-faire. Their goal was to save liberalism from itself.[55]

Their basic idea was that the conditions of late nineteenth-century life represented a social transformation, consisting of urbanization, industrialization, organizational society, globalization of markets, all summarized in the idea of interdependence."[56] Because the will theory was individualist, it ignored interdependence, and endorsed particular legal rules that permitted antisocial behavior of many kinds. The crises of the modern factory (industrial accidents, pauperization) and the urban slum, and later the crisis of the financial markets and the Great Depression, all derived from the failure of coherently individualist law to respond to the coherently social needs of modern conditions of interdependence. After 1919, they extended this analysis to the problem of war, understood as the product of failures of an international order based on the logic of sovereignty, highly analogous to the problems of markets based on the logic of property.[57]

From this "is" analysis, they derived the "ought" of a reform program, one that was astonishingly successful. There was labor legislation, the regulation of urban areas through landlord/tenant, sanitary and zoning regimes, the regulation of financial markets, and the development of new institutions of

[54] Georges Gurvitch, L'idee du droit social (1932).

[55] See generally on the social as legal consciousness, Wieacker, *supra* note 7; G. Edward White, *From Sociological Jurisprudence to Realism: Jurisprudence and Social Change in Early Twentieth-Century America*, 58 VA. L. REV. 999 (1972); Andre-Jean Arnaud, Les juristes face a la societe du XIXieme siecle a nos jours (1975); Horwitz, The Transformation of American Law 1870–1960: The Crisis of Legal Orthodoxy, *supra* note 6; Nestor DeBuen, La Decadencia del Contrato (1965); Duncan Kennedy and Marie Claire Belleau, *Francois Geny aux Etats* in Francois Geny: Mythes et realities (2000); Duncan Kennedy, *From the Will Theory to the Principle of Private Autonomy: Lon Fuller's "Consideration and Form,"* 100 Col. L. Rev. 94 (2000); Christophe Jamin, *Une breve histoire politique des interpretations de l'article 1134 du code civil*, Le Dalloz, March 14, 2002, p. 901.

[56] On the social as characteristic of early nineteenth-century thought in general, see Morton White, Social Thought in America: The Revolt against Formalism (1949); Ben Seligman, 1 Main Currents of Economic Thought: The Revolt against Formalism (1962); Edward Purcell, The Crisis of Democratic Theory (1973); Yves Donzelot, L'invention du social (1984); Michel Borgetto and Robert Lafore, La republique sociale: contribution a l'etude de la question democratique en france (2000); Francois Ewald, Histoire de l'etat providence (1986).

[57] Alejandro Alvarez, The New International Law (1924).

international law. The is-to-ought move appealed to a very wide range of legitimating rhetorics. These traversed the left/right spectrum, leaving out only Marxist collectivism at one extreme and pure Manchesterism at the other.

So the social could be based on socialist or social democratic ideology (perhaps Durkheimian), on the social Christianity of Protestant sects, on neo-Kantian "situational natural law," on Comtean positivism, on Catholic natural law, on Bismark/Disraeli social conservatism, or on fascist ideology.[58] In other words, the social, like CLT, was initially a consciousness (though always in an embattled relationship with CLT, rather than straightforwardly hegemonic in the way CLT had been in the brief period between about 1850 and 1890) within which it was possible to develop different and conflicting ideological projects. Regardless of which it was, the slogans included organicism, purpose, function, reproduction, welfare, instrumentalism (law is a means to an end) – and so antideduction, because a legal rule is just a means to accomplishment of social purposes.

A crucial part of the social critique of classical legal thought was the claim that it maintained an appearance of objectivity in legal interpretation only through the abuse of deduction. According to the social people, CLT people understood themselves to operate as interpreters (judges, administrators, law professors) according to a system of induction and deduction premised on the coherence, or internal logical consistency, of the system of enacted legal norms. One mode was to locate the applicable enacted rule; a second was to develop a rule to fill a gap by a chain of deductions from a more abstract enacted rule or principle; a third, the method of "constructions," was to determine what unenacted principle must be part of "the system," given the various enacted elements in it, if we were to regard it as internally coherent, and then derive a gap-filling rule from the construction.

In the social analysis, because interpreters within CLT had always to understand themselves as logically compelled in one of these ways, they could never legitimately work consciously to adapt the law to the new conditions of the late nineteenth century. Nonetheless, those conditions constantly presented them, as interpreters, with gaps. What the CLT people had to do, to stay loyal to their role as they conceived it, was to "abuse deduction."[59] They had to make decisions reached on other grounds look like the operation of deductive work premised on the coherence of the system. And the abuse of deduction permitted the smuggling in not of the general desiderata of social evolution, but of

[58] *See* DEBUEN, *supra* note 55.

[59] On the role of "abuse of deduction," see DUNCAN KENNEDY, A CRITIQUE OF ADJUDICATION [*FIN DE SIECLE*] 82–92 (1997), Kennedy, *From the Will Theory*, *supra* note 9; Duncan Kennedy, *Legal Formalism*, *in* 13 ENCYCLOPEDIA OF THE SOCIAL AND BEHAVIORAL SCIENCES 8634 (2001); KENNEDY & BELLEAU, *supra* note 55. *See also*, ESQUIROL, *supra* note 27.

the partisan ideologies of the parties to the conflicts between labor and capital, large and small business, of the century's end. (Important antiformalists, aside from the social people, were Demogue,[60] Heck,[61] Holmes,[62] Hohfeld,[63] and Llewellyn.[64])

The social people had four positive proposals: (1) from the social "is" to the adaptive ought for law, (2) from the deductive to the instrumental approach to the formulation of norms, (3) not only by the legislature but also by legal scientists and judges and administrative agencies openly acknowledging gaps in the formally valid order, and (4) anchored in the normative practices ("living law") that groups intermediate between the state and the individual were continuously developing in response to the needs of the new interdependent social formation.

Pluralism. Many advocates of the social argued that various groups within the emerging interdependent society, including, for example, merchant communities and labor unions, were developing new norms to fit the new "social needs." These norms, regarded as "valid" "living law," rather than deduction from individualist postulates, should, and also would, in this "legal pluralist" view, be the basis for legislative, administrative and judicial elaboration of new rules of state law. The pluralist position, like so much in the social, was a complex is/ought mixture. Pluralists identified the multiple substate and suprastate normative orders in actual operation in the modern world, and the various kinds of institutionalized or informal sanctioning systems that contributed to their effectiveness in influencing behavior. In this mode, the Mafia code of *omerta* and canon law were as important and interesting as any other nonstate order. But in their normative role, the pluralists were much more interested in medieval corporations, the law of merchants, the law of the industrial shop, and customary international law. My hypothesis is that this was because in each of these, it was possible to argue that nonstate law was more "social" than state law, and provided a basis for reform of the latter in the particular direction they favored.[65]

60 Rene Demogue, *Fundamental Notions of Private Law, in* MODERN FRENCH PHILOSOPHY, VII THE MODERN LEGAL PHILOSOPHY SERIES (1916).

61 Phillip Heck, *The Jurisprudence of Interests: An Outline, in* THE JURISPRUDENCE OF INTERESTS (Magdalena Schoch, trans. & ed., 1948).

62 OLIVER WENDELL HOLMES, *Privilege, Malice and Intent, in* COLLECTED LEGAL PAPERS OF OLIVER WENDALL HOLMES (1920); HOLMES, *The Path of the Law, in* COLLECTED PAPERS, *supra*; HOLMES, *Natural Law, in* COLLECTED PAPERS, *supra*.

63 Wesley Hohfeld, *Fundamental Conceptions in Legal Reasoning*, 26 YALE L. J. 710 (1917).

64 *E.g.*, Karl Llewellyn, *On Reading and Using the Newer Jurisprudence*, 40 COLUM. L. REV. 581 (1940).

65 *See* EHRLICH, *supra* note 63; SANTI ROMANO, L'ORDINAMENTO GIURIDICO (1918); GURVITCH, *supra* note 62, for a listing of the most important pluralists up to the 1930s. *See* John Griffiths, *What Is Legal Pluralism?*, 24 J. LEGAL PLURALISM 1 (1986); B. DE SOUSA SANTOS, TOWARD A NEW COMMON

Institutionalism. This was the view that in order to understand nonstate orders, within the pluralist enterprise broadly conceived, it was necessary to do two things: identify the social practices distinguishing nonstate law from mere customs or mores, and explain how to conceptualize the coherence of nonstate law, that is, how we know that a given specific norm is part of a system of nonstate law. The notion of the institution served both of these purposes: the reference was to an organization, a set of roles, persistent in time but with shifting personnel, oriented in a founding moment to some set of (changeable) purposes going beyond the individual interests of the role incumbents. A purely for-profit private corporation is an institution if it has, as all do, an explicit or implicit business plan. (The State becomes an institution among many, in this mode of analysis.)

We observe that as a matter of fact institutions develop complex normative orders, enforced by a wide variety of sanctions, from formal "staff" (Weber) to popular assemblies to mere social pressure. The institutionalist idea was that the norms derived both their rational coherence and their "validity" from the combination of the devotion of the institution to a purpose or purposes and its history of development in response to changing circumstances. The is/ought move was to say that institutions should define and develop norms in ways that furthered their purposes. And the state, as an institution with the purpose of coordinating normative orders, should recognize and facilitate, rather than ignore or oppose, this process of internal institutional development.[66]

Corporatism. This was the view that the plural institutions all had purposes that contributed to the self-preservation or reproduction and evolution of society as a whole, and that taken together they were a better "representative" of society than, say, an electoral process based on voting by individuals. Moreover, a legislative process that emerged from individual voting was unlikely to perform in a rational way the function of overseeing the self-regulating activities of institutions.

In the corporatist view, it would be better to give the institutions one mode or another of direct access to state power, rather than constituting the state either in opposition to or without relation to them. The fascist regimes of the 1930s embraced corporatism along with presidentialism as an alternative to parliamentary democracy. They so thoroughly discredited it in the process that it is hard to remember that, in the form of industry labor/management

SENSE: LAW, SCIENCE AND POLITICS IN THE PARADIGMATIC TRANSITION (1995) and the excellent review article, Brian Tamanaha, *A Non-essentialist Version of Legal Pluralism.*, 27 J. Law & Soc. 296 (2000), for a sampling of modern pluralism.

66 *See* THE FRENCH INSTITUTIONALISTS: MAURICE HAURIOU, GEORGES RENARD, JOSEPH T. DELOS (Albert Broderick ed., 1970); and SANTI ROMANO, *supra* note 73.

councils with power to make legally binding regulations, it was the central element of Roosevelt's First New Deal.[67]

Social legislation. One way to understand the social is as a transformation of the CLT model in which individuals constitute a people, with rights secured by a state, that is sovereign, in decentralized association with other sovereign states, representing and securing the rights of other peoples. In the social, there was an intense focus not just on the plurality of institutions below and above the level of the state, but also on groups between the level of the individual and the people. The most important of these were social classes, and particularly labor and capital, and national minorities. Whereas Marxism was a "conflict ideology," prophesying the triumph of the working class in death struggle with the capitalist class, the social was a "harmony ideology," preaching a function for each organized interest, and the existence of a "public interest" in the coordination of their interdependent activities in order to maximize social welfare.[68] So the social people were against the tendency in CLT to deny the juristic reality of anything other than an individual or a state.

In labor law, the goal was to devise new legal forms, such as social insurance against industrial accidents as a compulsory element of the wage bargain, the labor union as an involuntary association, and compulsory collective bargaining, all in the context of pervasive regulation from above. The notion was that given the interdependence of labor and capital, and the interdependence of all the different sectors of a modern economy, "industrial warfare" (or "strife" or "class war") threatened the whole society with breakdowns of production that might be truly catastrophic. In this situation, the "public interest" was in "industrial peace," and the public interest justified jettisoning individualist and formalist notions, such that it would violate basic premises if a union's collectively bargained agreement could determine the terms of employment of a worker who was not a member.[69]

In CLT, as we saw, plurality was an essential part of the picture, but it was, first of all, the plurality of right bearing individuals. Second, there was the plurality of volksgeists, the plurality of family law regimes corresponding to different national cultures, the plurality of public law arrangements corresponding to the different modes of political life of different peoples. These pluralities were peripheral in relation to the legal core, which consisted of the private law of obligations, with contract law, the law of free will from the starting point of property rights, as the core of the core.

[67] *See* Donald Brand, Corporatism and the Rule of Law (1988). On the influence of corporatism on U.S. legal realism, see also Allen Kamp, *Downtown Code: A History of the Uniform Commercial Code 1949–1954*, 49 Buffalo L. Rev. 359 (2001).

[68] *See* Rexford Tugwell, The Economic Basis of Public Interest (1922).

[69] *See* Karl Klare, *The Deradicalization of the Wagner Act and the Origins of Modern Legal Consciousness*, 62 Minn. L. Rev. 265 (1978).

Social legislation meant expanding the regulatory functions of the state, carving out and redefining as public law vast areas that had fallen safely within the domain of right, will, and fault. Social law coordinated the various individual willing subjects of CLT in the public interest, through public agencies that were to make rules to instantiate relatively abstract and vague legislative pronouncements (for example, in the U.S. context, a federal statute banning "contracts in restraint of tradec" or "unfair competition," "unfair labor practices," or "deceptive practices" in securities law).

Expertise and studies. The agencies were supposed to bring "expertise" to bear, meaning both social science and concrete pragmatic knowledge. They were to act through inspectorates applying low-level criminal sanctions or injunctions, in proceedings much less formal than those emblematic of CLT. In place of the law of obligations, the salient fields were administrative law, applicable to all social legislation, and then labor law, family law, and international law.[70] By the 1930s, the social people had flipped the structure of CLT and the periphery had become the core.

After a brief flirtation with the judge (both in France and in Germany at the beginning of the twentieth century), the hero figures of the social current became, in principal, the legislators who drafted the multiplicity of special laws that constituted the new order, along with the administrator who produced and enforced the detailed regulations that put legislative regimes into effect. The literature of the social, however, was the product of a new breed of law professors. These were not the magisterial authors of codes and expounders of their inner logic. They were law reformers, writing theory, doing studies, drafting legislation, overseeing, in doctrinal literature, its implementation and eventual amendment in the light of practical experience.

Because of the diverse political currents that supported reform, the professors of the social weren't pigeonholed politically. Nor were they open to the charge that they rejected scientific objectivity. The social was social scientific. The legal science of CLT was the science of legal categories. It was the science of the technique of law. The social, by contrast, was associated with sociology, economics, and psychology.

A key element of is-to-ought was the "study," beginning with industrial accidents at the beginning of the century. The premise of the "study" was that there was a politically powerful, centrist, middle-class audience, that tended to assume that things in general were going fine. When alerted by a study either to dangers to themselves (e.g., unsanitary food processing) or to sufficiently flagrant abuse of others (conditions in the mines), this group would support a regulatory regime on "public interest" rather than partisan political grounds.

70 *See* James Landis, The Administrative Process (1938).

The social and its studies were scientific in the way characteristic of the social science of that period, which was a mish mash of evolutionism, pragmatism in the Dewey tradition, and diverse forms of positivism, such as statistics-based empirical surveying. When the social jurist squared off against his Classical legal positivist colleague, treating him as a formalist dinosaur, hopelessly rigid and out of contact with reality, he did not do it in the name of subjectivism or whatever his political preferences might be. He did it in the name of his own discipline, because the social was a discipline, not just a political position.

The combination of pluralism, institutionalism, and commitment to empirical investigation, in the is-to-ought context, meant that the "other" of law was no longer morality, as it had been in CLT, but "society." Law did or did not adapt to it, did or did not constitute while pretending to merely mirror it; society did or did not have powerful long-run immanent tendencies, and so on.

Innovation across the whole juristic field. One juristic response to social legislation was to assimilate it to the Classical positivist model by adding new legal topics corresponding to new statutes, without modifying the premises or the methods of doctrinal analysis in any way. The advent of the social added norms and provided new fields for legal science. In every country that has a Western system of legal education, it seems that something between a part and a very large part of instruction proceeds in this way, with classical fields coherent in a classical way, and social fields coherent in a social way.

The social jurists themselves were more ambitious. Their notion was that the reform effort to make law adapt to society required a thorough revamping of the juristic universe. In civil procedure, for example, the adversary system was obviously maladapted to a modern, interdependent, flexible complex industrial system. We needed many new types of procedures that would get us out of the typical individualist battle model.[71] In criminal law, we needed to individualize punishment but also to make it socially effective by identifying the types of criminals and the social causes of crime.[72] Even contract law, the core of the core, needed revision, in the direction, for example, of pre-contractual duties, liberalization of excuses, functional rather than formalist interpretation of formalities.[73]

We needed new types of courts – labor courts, merchant courts, juvenile courts, and family courts – as well as new types of procedure. Commercial law needed to be reformed to meet the requirements of the new style of

[71] *See* Charles C. Clark, *The Federal Rules of Civil Procedure, 1938–58, Two Decades of the Federal Civil Rules*, 58 Colum. L. Rev. 435 (1958).

[72] *See* Richard Wasserstrom, *Some Problems in the Definition and Justification and Punishment, in* Values & Morals, 299–315 (Alvin Goodman and Jaegwon Kim eds., 1978).

[73] *See* Kennedy, *From the Will Theory, supra* note 10.

enterprise, particularly the fact that most transactions were between very large companies, or between large enterprises and individual actors with no bargaining power at all. Corporate law needed to be revamped on the basis of the notion of the radical separation of ownership and control.[74]

It was not just a matter of reconceptualizing, reformulating, and then reforming the maladaptive, ideologically individualist doctrinal substance that had emerged in the late-nineteenth century. The antiformalist strand in the social current emphasized gaps, conflicts, and ambiguities in the corpus of positive law, and consequently the role of the judge, either as an abuser of deduction or as a rational lawmaker. In the United States, stare decisis was discredited as abuse of deduction par excellence, and layers of socially oriented early case law were discovered in order to multiply conflicts and open the space for reform.

The civilian dispute about what counted as a "source of law" was resolved in favor of the legitimacy of *jurisprudence* (judge-made law), whatever the "official portrait" might continue to be.[75] Moreover, all law interpreters, in the social vision, including professors and administrators, and lawyers when they draft contracts, lawyers when they choose litigation and settlement strategies, and lawyers when they give advice on liability, are engaged in law making. What the enterprise does will be effected at every stage by interpretations made by the lawyers that will be contestable.

They will be contestable because, given gaps, there will often be a plausible social interpretation and an individualist or formalist or positivist interpretation of the relevant valid norms. The social could be snuffed out by judicial hostility – labor courts or family courts required judges who didn't hate the whole idea of new juridical institutions. If they did, they would find means of sabotage or just bungle things. Only if judges, administrators, and lawyers understood not just the rationale but also the technique of reform would reform work.

That produced new ideas about the law school curriculum. The person teaching a new course on the new labor law statute should know some sociology, economics, and psychology, and it would be a good idea to have a small number of docile economists, sociologists, and psychologists on the faculty. Ones who would never claim to know anything about law, but would be a useful resource for us in developing our interdisciplinary projects. Interdisciplinarity for the social meant the law professor as a generalist whose skills allowed acquisition of all other disciplines without formal training.[76]

74 *See* Adolph Berle and Gardiner Means, The Modern Corporation and Private Property (1932).

75 Mitchel de S.-O.-l'E. Lasser, *Judicial (Self-)Portraits: Judicial Discourse in the French Legal System*, 104 Yale L. J. 1325 (1995).

76 *See* Harold D. Lasswell and Myres S. McDougall, *Legal Education and Public Policy: Professional Training in the Public Interest*, 52 Yale L. J. 203 (1943).

As I've said already, this was not about politics. It might be true that their version of social justice could be characterized politically as more corporatist, communitarian, antiformalist, and pluralist than the thought of their enemies in the liberal traditions of the center and right. But they didn't think that the mere commitment to social justice in the is-to-ought mode of the social put them in the danger of eroding the distinction between law and politics.

The social jurists generally conceded the internal coherence of individualist deductive law (emphasizing gaps, not inescapable contradictions); they claimed the same kind of coherence for social law. The latter claim was strongly contested. Those we might broadly denominate liberals stuck to the apparatus and aspirations of CLT, while being willing to modernize, say by reading the concepts of *ordre publique* and "good faith" very broadly. But they understood the social to be chaotic, without a single counterprinciple to oppose to right and will. Moreover, while they recognized that the social had many different forms of politics, from left to right, they saw this as a symptom of the tragic politicization of law that followed the premature renunciation of legal science for social science, rather than as evidence of the suprapolitical truth of the social.[77]

The global reception of the social

The second globalization followed the channels established by the first. Students from all over Europe went to France and Germany to study law.[78] From the middle of the nineteenth century up to the 1930s, students from the part of the rest of the world under Western influence flocked to Europe. From the colonies, they went to their respective "metropoles," the Senegalese to Paris, the Indonesians to Amsterdam, and so forth. If they had a choice, they went to the European capital with most prestige in their part of the periphery (Latin Americans to Paris, Unitedstateseans to Germany).

First Germany and later France were the fountains of the social, but it developed simultaneously in many places, even though most of those places imported elements from Germany and France and had relatively little or no influence back.[79] In Italy it was first moderately left, and then fascist.[80] In Spain (Franco), Portugal (Salazar), and Greece (Metaxas), it was fascist; in the

[77] *See* WIEACKER, *supra* note 11; KENNEDY, *From the Will Theory, supra* note 10.

[78] *See* Lopez Medina, *supra* note 3.

[79] *See* GENY, *Appendix* to METHOD OF INTERPRETATION, *supra* note 49 (providing an egocentric summary of developments up to 1919).

[80] *See* PAOLO GROSSI, SCIENZA GIURIDICA ITALIANA: UN PROFILO STORICO, 1860–1950 (2000); Alessandro Somma, *Il diritto fascista dei contratti: raffronti con il modello nazionalsocialista*, 18 RIVISTA CRITICA DEL DIRITTO PRIVATO 639 (2000); Alessandro Somma, *Fascismo e diritto: una ricerca sul nulla?*, 55 RIVISTA TRIMESTRIALE DI DIRITTO E PROCEDURA CIVILE 597 (2001).

Netherlands[81] and (Fabian) Britain,[82] moderately left. The Unitedstatesean sociological jurisprudes (Pound,[83] Cardozo,[84] and Brandeis[85] were the most important) developed a version that was first moderately left and then moderately right. They drew extensively on the French and Germans, but were also strongly influenced by Holmes, who developed, before Geny, a peculiarly American variant of the "abuse of deduction" thesis.[86]

Nationalism. *As* the social established itself in the West, students from Eastern Europe, Latin America, South, East, and Southeast Asia, the Arab world, and Africa appropriated it and took it home. A crucial dimension of the spread of the social was nationalism, but in at least three modes, rather than as a unitary phenomenon. First, nationalism, as irredentism and as the drive for ethnic purity, was understood by the progressive European social people to be, along with class conflict, the scourge that might well destroy European civilization. Theorists of the social undertook a deep rethinking of public international law in an effort to contain and shape nationalism understood as a life-creating and also life-destroying irrational force. In public international law, the mandate system, the move to institutions (the League of Nations), the creation of bricolage type governing institutions such as the free city of Danzig, and the interwar regimes of minority protection all involved innovative forms, and the self-conscious rejection of the "logic of sovereignty."[87] They were inspired by and in turn inspired the innovations in labor law described above ("industrial warfare" contained in ways analogous to "real" warfare; flaws of the logic of property parallel the flaws of the logic of sovereignty).[88]

At the very same time, the social was one of the key slogans of nationalism itself, in its fascist form, and also in authoritarian right wing variants in many parts of the world, including the new states carved out of the Ottoman and

[81] Paul Scholten, Allgemeen Deel (1974) is the locus classicus, not translated into English.

[82] Harold Laski, The State in the New Social Order (1921).

[83] Compare Pound, *supra* note 8, with the more conservative version in *The New Feudal System*, 35 Com. L.J. 397 (1930).

[84] Benjamin Cardozo, The Nature of the Judicial Process (1921).

[85] *See* Samuel D. Warren and Louis D. Brandeis, *The Right to Privacy*, 4 Harv. L. Rev. 193 (1890) for a typical early example of the social; see also Brandeis' famous brief in *Muller v. Oregon*, in which the U.S. Supreme Court upheld protective labor legislation for women on conservative social grounds.

[86] Holmes, *supra* note 62; Kennedy and Belleau, *supra* note 55.

[87] David Kennedy, *The Move to Institutions*, 8 Cardozo L. Rev. 841 (1987); David Kennedy, *The International Style in Post-War Law and Policy*, 1994 Utah L. Rev. 7; Nathaniel Berman, *But the Alternative is Despair: Nationalism and Modernist Renewal of International Law*, 106 Harv. L. Rev. 1792 (1993); Nathaniel Berman, *Modernism, Nationalism and the Rhetoric of Reconstruction*, 4 Yale J. Law & Hum. 351 (1992).

[88] Hani Sayed, A Genealogy of Third World Approaches to International Law: The Social in Public International Law (2004) (unpublished doctoral dissertation on file with the Suffolk University Law Review).

Austro-Hungarian Empires, and Latin American countries such as Argentina (Peron)[89] and Brazil (Vargas). This meant that, during the interwar period, progressive or revolutionary left wing reformers in countries like Colombia and Mexico, and their right wing enemies, employed virtually identical social, corporatist, anticapitalist, antiliberal rhetorics. The Mexican federal labor laws of the 1930s, a famous accomplishment of the revival of the Mexican left under Cardenas, closely resembled, if they were not actually modeled on, Mussolini's *Carta di Lavoro*.[90]

Finally, in the colonies, nationalism meant national independence, and was the call of the people as a whole to arms against the colonial master. The colonial powers recruited natives to staff the lower levels of their administrations, and elements from precolonial elites survived and pursued success in the new order through European education. Some of them found French, British, Dutch, and Unitedstatesean academic mentors-turned-allies to help them transform the progressive metropolitan social ideology into an argument for everything from "native welfare" to national independence (Furnivall,[91] some Dutch *adat* law sociologists,[92] Lambert,[93] Tugwell[94]).

There was a pattern, identified for the Egyptian case by Amr Shalakany,[95] to the process by which a part of the legal elite of one country after another made the social its own. In case after case, the importing elite found something in the national culture that would make the social, as opposed to the formalist individualism imputed to CLT, *uniquely appropriate to the nation in question.*

In Europe, the Catholic South (Portugal, Spain, Italy, along with Hungary) could emphasize that the social was the philosophy of the Church enunciated in *Rerum Novarum* (1897), which means "Of new things," and the "new things" were industrialization, urbanization, interdependence, and the rest of the social. In the thirties the Vatican struck its infamous deal with fascism, memorialized in the social rhetoric of *Quadrigessimo Anno* (the encyclical of 1937 marking the fortieth anniversary of *Rerum Novarum*). In the Protestant North, the Dutch were able to interpret the social as particularly appropriate

[89] *See* David Rock, Authoritarian Argentina: The Nationalist Movement, Its History and its Impact (1993).

[90] *Compare* Lopez Medina, *supra* note 3, *with* Alvaro Santos, *The Reception of Social Law in Mexico and the Supposed Originality and Progressiveness of Mexican Labor Law* (2004) (unpublished paper on file with the Suffolk University Law Review).

[91] *See* J. S. Furnivall, An Introduction to the Political Economy of Burma, *supra* note 42.

[92] J. Griffiths, *Current Legal Anthropology in the Netherlands: A Trend Report,* in Sociology of law and legal anthropology in the Dutch speaking countries (J. van Houtte, ed. 1985).

[93] Amr Shalakany, *Sanhuri and the Historical Origins of Comparative Law in the Arab World,* in Rethinking the Masters of Comparative Law 152 (Annelise Riles, ed. 2001).

[94] Rexford Guy Tugwell, The Stricken Land: The Story of Puerto Rico (1946).

[95] Amr Shalakany, *Between Identity and the Redistribution: Sanhuri, Genealogy and the Will to Islamise,* 8 Islamic Law & Society 201 (2001).

to the interdependent culture of dike-based land reclamation. In Russia, there was the famous peasant village community, or *mir*.[96]

In a striking essay published in the *Harvard Law Review* in January 1917,[97] Roscoe Pound laid the ills of modern Unitedstatesean society at the door of the "Romanization" of Unitedstatesean law during the second half of the nineteenth century. He presented CLT as an "alien" mode of legal thought, whose formalist individualism had displaced the "organic" common law mode based on the notion of "relation" (husband and wife, master and servant, landlord and tenant). The rediscovery of common law medieval tradition was to be the basis for bringing Unitedstatesean law into harmony with twentieth-century conditions of social interdependence. Citations to the German and French civilian originators of the program he proposed were few and far between (though plentiful in his later works[98] representing the social as the consensus of advanced European legal thought).

In Latin America, the right wing authoritarians appealed to *Hispanidad,* whose social essence was Catholic but also uniquely American.[99] In Mexico, land reform and the *ejido* system of state regulated and subsidized cooperative peasant agriculture was supposedly a return to pre-Colombian modes of social organization.[100] In Egypt, Sanhouri's eclectic, socially oriented civil code, later adopted or adapted in many other Arab countries, was indigenous and eminently traditional, as well as ultramodern, because Islamic law was and had always been social.[101]

In Africa, there was Senghor's *negritude,* Kenyatta's "African idea of property," and Nyerere's African socialism or *Ujaama.*[102] Sun Yat Sen and then Chiang Kai-shek in China developed the nationalist ideology of the Kuomintang, the main opponent of Chinese communism, as a complex and subtle blend of Confucian "social" and liberal elements.[103] After World War II, Chiang hired Roscoe Pound as a legal consultant on the construction of the legal regime of the Republic of China on Taiwan.[104]

The social could be the public law ideology of a disempowered subgroup in a British colonial structure, for example, of the Quebecois in Canada,[105] or the

[96] *See* Peasant Economy, Culture, and Politics of European Russia, 1800–1921 (Esther Kingston–Mann & Timothy Mixter, eds. 1991).

[97] Pound, *supra* note 7.

[98] *E.g.*, Roscoe Pound, An Introduction to the Philosophy of Law (1922).

[99] Rock, *supra* note 89.

[100] Eyler N. Simpson, The Ejido: Mexico's Way Out (1937).

[101] Shalakany, *supra* note 91.

[102] Kang'ara, *supra* note 42.

[103] Levinson, *supra* note 25.

[104] Roscoe Pound, *Progress of the Law in China,* 23 Wash. L. Rev. 345, 353 (1948); Pound, *The Chinese Civil Code in Action,* 29 Tul. L. Rev. 279 (1955).

[105] Marie-Claire Belleau, *La dichotomie droit prive(droit public dans le contexte quebecois et canadien et l'intersectionnalite identitaire),* 39 C. de D. 177 (March, 1998).

Afrikaaners in South Africa,[106] with civilian private law retaining the formalism of the minority's metropole as a symbol of resistance to the common law of the colonial power. In Palestine, jurists influenced by Savigny and Ehrlich developed a secular "Hebrew law" that was first supposed to be individualist and then social, and then went out of fashion, at the moment when the State of Israel began to develop a highly social regime of public law.[107]

Savigny's formalist derivation of all private law from right and will gave way to Savigny's insistence that national legal orders did and should represent the particular normative order of the people involved. But we are left with the question of why, at the moment of discovering national particularity, *each nation discovered the same thing?*

A facile, but initially plausible interpretation would be that the social was a tool of elites facing precisely the absence of the social. That is, of elites put in charge of governing territories torn apart by class conflict, or containing wildly heterogeneous tribal, cultural, racial, and religious groups, first assembled as colonies according to the interests of the Empires and Great Powers, and then reparceled at the moment of national independence according to the interests of the Great Powers and of the local elites who were to take their place. The ideology of the social was (perhaps) not a reflection of national particularity, but an instrument in the "imagining" of presently nonexistent national communities.[108] This hypothesis gets some support from the story of gender in the social.

Sex and family. In the second globalization, the idea of the "social" was dramatically ambiguous when applied to familial and sexual relations. The social involved the demand that employers treat workers and that merchants treat consumers according to a social ethic, and the rhetoric was one of solidarity and community. The construction of relations of family members as intrinsically altruistic and protective was an obvious reference and support for the demands of workers and consumers. In a sense, the demand was to roll back the nineteenth-century disintegration of the household, and reimpose on the capitalist the duties of the patriarch, this time with state enforcement of solidarity, rather than the toleration of arbitrariness. Enemies of the social never tired of pointing out that it was a "regression" from contract to status, and that it was "demeaning" to the beneficiaries to be treated as though, like the member of the Roman or feudal household, they lacked legal capacity.[109]

[106] Andre Van de Waalt, *Tradition on Trial: A Critical Analysis of the Civil-Law Tradition in South African Property Law*, 11 S. Afr. J. on Hum. Rts. 169 (1995).

[107] Assaf Likhovski, *The Invention of "Hebrew Law" in Mandatory Palestine*, 46 Am. J. Comp. L. 339 (1998).

[108] Eric Hobsbawm, Nations and Nationalism Since 1780 (1990); Benedict Anderson, Imagined Communities: Reflections on the Origins and Spread of Nationalism (revised ed. 1991).

[109] Olsen, *supra* note 33; Olsen *supra* note 34.

At the same time, the social stood for modernity, for adapting law to conditions of urbanization, global market economy, technological change, and general interdependence. The progressive social approach to sex and family in the North Atlantic was notably secular, influenced by the first wave of Western feminism, and it in turn, influenced the most secular and Westernized segments of the elites of the periphery. Its program was to ease many prohibitions of the nineteenth-century gender regime, while at the same time increasing the intrusive enforcement of the duties of the patriarch that CLT had treated as merely moral, as opposed to legal.

The social ideology treated the family as an institution with functions and purposes crucial to the social whole. The family was far from a matter of merely private concern, or something to be left to the particularities of local culture, or an area quarantined as moral rather than legal. Every aspect of family life had, given social interdependence, far-reaching consequences for all other social functions, and the "public interest" therefore justified pervasive intervention against socially pathological behavior. The "study" was a crucial instrument here, as it was in the area of industrial accidents, and the strategy was identical. Revelation of bad conditions of poor families would mobilize the sympathy of the middle class in favor of regulation.

Studies could also support decriminalization and destigmatization by showing that outdated, moralistic controls on sexuality and insistence on the formalities of marriage were socially counterproductive. The public health arguments covered the whole range from child nutrition to venereal disease spread by prostitutes forced into vice by the combination of poverty and repressive social norms ("ruined" women couldn't marry). The new science of sexology suggested reform in the interest of adult sexual pleasure, but also to stabilize traditional gender arrangements in the interest of society as a whole.[110]

In the progressive version of the social, the prohibitions to be relaxed were those on nonmarital sex, as for example by decriminalizing female adultery and sex between unmarried persons, permitting divorce by mutual consent, legalizing the sale of contraceptives, destigmatizing illegitimacy, legalizing abortion (so that it would be performed in medically controlled circumstances). The decriminalization of prostitution went along with its regulation in brothels through the typical social mode of an inspectorate armed with criminal penalties and injunctive powers. The social ideology tended to pathologize and medicalize homosexuality.

The duties to be increased included controlling domestic battery both of wives and children, again by establishing administrative agencies armed with low-level criminal sanctions and power to initiate the transfer of custody

[110] Atina Grossmann, *The New Woman and the Rationalization of Sexuality in Weimar Germany*, *in* POWERS OF DESIRE (Ann Snitow, Christine Stansell, and Sharon Thompson eds., 1983).

of children. Family and juvenile courts and the newly created profession of "social work" aimed for a deformalized legal regime oriented to welfare rather than rights (best interest of the child, rehabilitation rather than punishment, Persons In Need of Supervision, Child In Need of Supervision, and so on).[111]

The progressives' main opponents in the North Atlantic were the Catholic Church and socially conservative Protestant sects (e.g., the Bible Belt in the United States, Anglicanism in the United Kingdom). As in the nineteenth century, although the agenda was transnational and the arguments and elements of reform everywhere similar, there was nothing like the globalization of a particular social-legal regime. The outcomes varied from country to country and from decade to decade, according to the local balance of forces and the strategies of the contenders. The social provided, as had CLT, a scheme of categories, arguments, and elements for legislation, out of which *langue* national speakers produced the *parole* of positive law.

The authoritarian nationalist approach was very different, though no less "social." In Nazi Germany, but I think only there, it was relentlessly "modern," eugenecist about reproduction as well as about racial extinction.[112] Authoritarians elsewhere were frankly allied with the Catholic or Greek Orthodox Church, both in peripheral Europe and in Latin America, or with Confucian or Shinto "family values" in East Asia. The family played the role of the "heart" or "soul" of the nation exactly because it was traditional rather than modern. The whole nation was a family, for example, and the authoritarian leader was a "father."

The interests of the nation required the reform of the family in the interests of society, as in the progressive agenda, but the rhetoric was of protection, rather than of freedom and equality. The family agenda was to subsidize the traditional nuclear family and the enterprise of child rearing in order to strengthen the nation against its enemies. This involved reenforcing the power of fathers while increasing services to mothers restricted to the home, pronatalism, and maintaining the system of prohibitions on extramarital sexuality of women. The main threats for the authoritarian social were "Godless communism" and the "decadent" liberalizing trend in bourgeois humanism and socialism. Homophobia and antisemitism went hand in hand.[113]

The national liberation parties in the colonized world faced yet a third configuration. Nationalists were everywhere disputed in their claim to lead the opposition to the colonial power. Of course, in many places there were communist parties. But often more important were political formations representing the fragments the nationalists hoped to bring together in coalition.

[111] Christopher Lasch, Haven in a Heartless World (1977).

[112] When Biology Became Destiny: Women in Weimar and Nazi Germany (Renate Bridenthal, Atina Grossman, Marion Kaplan eds., 1984).

[113] *See, e.g.*, Robert Aron, Histoire de Vichy 237–241 (1962).

In the Middle East, South Asia, Southeast Asia, and Africa, there were, first of all, Islamic reform parties (and Hindu parties in India). Then there were tribal political organizations (in all the above regions, not just in Africa). And there were racially organized groups, often in reaction against local minorities (for example, against the Chinese or Indians in Southeast Asia and the Pacific, against the Arabs in sub-Saharan Africa) that had arrived and prospered under colonial auspices.

The nationalist project was to develop the notion of national particularity as a secular force, against *both* the colonial power and the fragmenting elements in the local situation. The family played a big role here: the nation could be unified around its unique family values, social values, that provided a clear point of contrast with the imagined sexual and familial degeneracy of the metropole and "the West" in general.[114] This made possible a complex set of compromises. First, in the name of modernity, nationalists could endorse education and employment for women, under the regulated conditions that the social program attempted to establish for all workers. Second, women should (ideally through state-supported organizations) participate in national struggles as one of the social groups (along with labor, farmers, youth, intellectuals, etc.) making up the corporatist side of the national liberation coalition.

At the same time, the nationalists could compromise, in the regulation of gender roles in marriage and extramarital sexuality, with the local forces that identified with tradition. Social rights for labor, land reform, and public/private collaboration in infrastructure development and import substitution industrialization, could not just coexist with, they could harmonize with immobility on formal inequality under Islamic law, toleration of domestic violence and crimes of honor, and the celebration of female virginity before marriage.[115] Activists for women's rights found themselves up against the problem that modernizing secular male elites had chosen to split the difference, on issues of sex and the family, with the conservative *ulema* in the Muslim world or the priests in the Catholic world.[116]

Thus, the Savignian compromise took a new turn. Progressive views about labor law, consumer law, housing law, and so forth, sometimes combined with fascist or traditionalist views about family law and in general about the status of women. (In the nineteenth-century codes, it had been economic liberalism that combined with family law conservatism.) The social, which could be thoroughly progressive or thoroughly fascist in the political and

[114] *See* Partha Chatterjee, The Nation and its Fragments: Colonial and Postcolonial Histories (1993).

[115] Lama Abu-Odeh, *Crimes of Honor and the Construction of Gender in Arab Societies*, in Feminism and Islam: Legal and Literary Perspectives (Mai Yamani, ed., 1996).

[116] Lama Abu-Odeh, *Egyptian Feminism: Trapped in the Identity Debate*, in Yale J. Law & Feminism (2004).

market domains, could also be progressive or traditionalist on sex and family, and there were always compromises in both domains, and the compromises could go in all directions.

The welfare state.[117] The welfare state figures heavily in the social and political history of the period of the social, but as I hope is already clear, it would be wrong to treat it as the "essence" or, from the point of view of law, as the central development. The legal concepts that seem most important are those of social insurance (unemployment, accidents, health and old age pensions) and entitlements based on need, conceptualized as rehabilitative, with an administration that does the need assessment and delivers services (social work) that are supposed to reintegrate the recipient into the presumably normal universe of the labor market.

These are typical manifestations of the social, with Bismarkian German origins, adopted throughout the capitalist West. There is an easy transition to the notion of social rights, understood as "third generation" (after private law and political rights), occupying a position of juristic ambiguity typical of the innovations of the period. Social rights were both legal, and even constitutional (first in Mexico, 1917), but nonjusticiable as to the level of benefits provided, although justiciable as entitlements once legislatively established within the administrative law regime of the country in question.

Of course, the welfare state could globalize only to a limited extent, because it presupposed a particular kind of economic, social, and administrative development, a measure of political autonomy (i.e., something other than colonial status), and a political configuration. I would characterize the political configuration as one in which a significant measure of redistribution from the middle- to the lower-middle and working-class strata, and a significant measure of paternalist control of the spending decisions of those strata (that is, compelling them to insure), could be made plausible to an electoral majority (e.g., the New Deal in the United States, the Front Populaire in France, the corporatist social democracy of Austria) or an authoritarian elite (e.g., Germany, Argentina), as protection of the social whole. Note that as was the case for the liberalization of the law of the household, there developed a single transnational programmatic repertoire and policy vocabulary for social programs (*langue*), but an infinite diversity of specific national regimes (*parole*).

Land regimes. The social jurists took a deep interest in the agricultural workers of the South, the very ones that CLT had lumped into the *locatio operaia*, or freedom of contract regime, blithely ignoring their obvious lack of "free will."

[117] *See generally* THEDA SKOCPOL, SOCIAL REVOLUTIONS IN THE MODERN WORLD (1994); EWALD, *supra* note 56.

This was the period of the beginning of the population explosion in the South, as death rates in many areas began to fall while birth rates remained constant. The latifundia/minifundia structure began to come apart as the minifundia lost their capacity to absorb population increases, while latifundia, as they became more efficient through mechanization, needed less raw labor power. Up to 1930, capital continued to pour into the developing world, building infrastructure and creating primary product (mineral and agricultural) enterprises and stimulating smallholder cash cropping. After 1930, all of this stopped abruptly. The Southern style of urbanization, based not on the lure of expanding industrial employment, but on the collapse of rural life, got underway.[118]

This was also the period of Communist revolution in land ownership in Russia, in which both latifundia and minifundia, along with large and small landlord classes, were abolished, and agriculture collectivized. This was an epochal event, transforming the hierarchical structure of the social lives of millions of people, at a very large cost in death and suffering, and relatively little increase in calorie intake per day. Nonetheless, along with failed communist uprisings in places like Germany and Hungary (1919) and China and Indonesia (1927), it caught the attention of elites everywhere.

The challenge for the social current, after the failure of the Western powers to crush the Russian revolution militarily, was, again, to save liberalism from itself. In this domain, as in that of labor/capital and international conflict, there had to be an alternative to revolution and collectivization. The right-wing social solutions (whether in independent authoritarian regimes or in "welfare" oriented colonial ones) were right wing because they neither challenged the owners of latifundia nor tried to force foreign capitalist enterprises to subsidize the poor agricultural sector. Instead, they offered policies like road building, irrigation, and extension of power to the countryside. Another right-wing trope was resettlement. It might be internal, as in the policy of moving Javanese peasant farmers to the outer islands under the Dutch "Ethical Policy,"[119] or into newly acquired territory (e.g., Mussolini's North and East African imperial scheme).

The progressive version of the social adopted the same strategies, but with less tendency to privatize the agents of transformation as soon as possible. Roosevelt's Tennessee Valley Authority is a prime example. But their preoccupation was land reform, in the broadest sense, including the transformation of large into viable small properties, the agglomeration of minifundia into cooperatives, the abolition of tenure forms like sharecropping, and the substitution of various forms of cooperative or state credit for rural moneylenders. Cooperative marketing boards, with delegated state powers as

[118] Wolf, *supra* note 41.
[119] M. C. Ricklefs, A History of Modern Indonesia 193–205 (2001).

regulated monopsonists, were to cut out the Western commercial intermediaries between cash croppers and international commodity markets. The reformers were far less successful here than elsewhere, and, with exceptions like Mexico, the Depression scuttled most of the schemes that got to the stage of implementation.

International economic law.[120] The same kind of thinking that led to the rejection of classical liberal law as formalist and individualist led to the rejection of the nineteenth-century "gold standard/free trade/private international law" regime. Starting in the 1920s, but exploding after 1929, this is the period of "autarchy," which might better be described as "national strategy" based on bilateral agreements and then on the formation of blocs, first those of the empires and then those based on ideology in the confrontation of liberalism with fascism and communism.

Import substitution industrialization.[121] The last of the pre-War innovations I'll mention began in Latin America. The colonized peripheral countries could not react in their own interests to the Depression; they suffered passively the drying up of investment from their metropoles and the collapse of the prices of their primary product exports. The last thing their colonial rulers thought of was to open them to the price-cutting trade of the Japanese or to encourage them to reduce their imports of metropolitan textiles. But this was not the case for the independent peripheral states.

One of the nineteenth-century intellectual origins of the social had been the defense of an import substitution industrialization policy (ISI) by the German school of *nationaloeconomie*. Latin American economists who had been passionate fans of the free trade/gold standard approach when it favored rapid development rethought their position and thoroughly modernized *nationaloeconomie* as "import substitution industrialization." It became the development strategy of right wing nationalist regimes in Argentina and Brazil. One part was tariffs, manipulated exchange rates, currency controls, import licensing, and subsidized credit, all designed to favor local firms in competition with imports. Another was the development, through classic social law administrative techniques, of a state-owned or heavily state-regulated sector.

The social after WWII

If the Depression and WWII simultaneously stimulated and snuffed out institutional innovations, they made possible, through the sheer intensity of disaster, combined with the defeat of fascism and the containment of communism,

[120] *See generally* Eichengreen, *supra* note 20.

[121] Victor Bulmer-Thomas, The Economic History of Latin America since Independence (1994).

a whole collection of institutional triumphs of the progressive version of the social. The first of these was the creation, for the capitalist core countries, of the nationally and internationally regulated market economy. The second was the globalization of the Bretton Woods system. The third was the globalization, first from victors to vanquished and then from the first to the third world, of the progressive social reform program of restructuring entitlements as the basis for a highly regulated mixed capitalist economy pursuing a strategy of social peace through economic development.

Keynes. If Jhering is the undisputed grandfather of the social, John Maynard Keynes was perhaps its genius, even though he thought the save-it-from-itself strategy should operate at the state and international levels, leaving the CLT structure of private property and free contract intact. The Bretton Woods system that the Western industrial powers established for their intrabloc relations during the Cold War became eventually the world financial regulatory system. As initially conceived, it was a typical example of the social at work.

First of all, the IMF was premised on the idea of the interdependence of financial and currency markets, with the danger being runs on national currencies producing chain reaction downward spirals. The way to stop runs was to "nip them in the bud" from a position outside and above any single national strategic actor. There was a shared "public interest" in this kind of intervention, so long as it was carefully limited so as not to interfere with national sovereignty in monetary and fiscal policy.

Of course, macroeconomic monetary and fiscal policy were exactly what the CLT model of free trade, gold standard, and private international law were designed to eliminate. Keynes's contribution in this area was to show that fiscal and monetary policy could function rationally as "countercyclical," counteracting through strategic action from the center the individualist capitalist logic of boom followed by bust, and so benefitting everyone in the society. But fiscal and monetary policy also meant deficit spending in periods of economic contraction, and therefore opened the possibility of financing the whole program of the social reformers in the very periods when historically they had been forced to close up shop.

Globalization of the Bretton Woods system. The Bretton Woods institutions gradually expanded to include the whole noncommunist world. Between 1945 and the mid-1960s, decolonization brought into existence a world order of independent "nation" states. The old and new national elites of the periphery were free of direct, that is, jurisdictional control. Almost as important, without the gold standard, they were free to manipulate their currencies and national budgets for whatever sovereign purposes. They soon discovered, however, that they needed, for whatever purposes, access to world capital markets. This meant that they had to join the Bretton Woods system – either join this game strictly on the terms proposed, that is, within the structure of legal rules already in place, or starve in the dark.

Within the social, these trends produced, after WWII, a "third worldist" or Bandung reaction (Nehru, Nasser, Sukarno) and a school of progressive public international law.[122] It deployed the social critique of the individualism of classical private law against the post-WWII supposedly reformed and postcolonial international law regime. The formal liberation and enfranchisement of unfree labor in Europe simply shifted the mechanism of exploitation from the transparency of feudalism to the mystification of capitalism. The formal grant of national independence to colonized peoples likewise shifted the transparency of imperial rule to the mystification of neocolonialism. In place of the exploitative wage bargain, the modern international order worked through the unequal exchange of primary products from the Third World for industrial products from the First.[123] This seems to me to have been the last strictly analytic accomplishment of the social consciousness.

The globalization of regulated mixed economy. It seems useful to distinguish two phases here. The first occurred immediately after the War when the Allies forcefully and systematically transformed the Japanese, German, and Italian systems from a fascist to a progressive version of the social, and imposed a similar transformation on the South Korean and Taiwanese social and economic systems as the price of protection from the Chinese communists. In Japan, South Korea, and Taiwan, land reform was an important part of the transformation, along with at least paper rights for labor unions, and at least paper regulation of the financial system. Germany and Italy were incorporated into the Social Democratic/Christian Democratic model propounded by the progressive social people in the United States, Britain, and France (and by German and Italian social democrats before the War).

The second phase was the extension of the import substitution industrialization strategy across Latin America and to the newly independent Third World, first to very large economies such as those of India, Egypt, Turkey, Iran, and Indonesia, and, after 1960, to the very small economies of newly independent African states. The ISI strategy, which relied heavily on public law and government intervention, was strongly supported by the various United Nations bodies, by the World Bank, and by USAID, and it was the initial economic strategy of Taiwan and South Korea (as well as Singapore) before they gradually shifted to export-led growth.[124] It was a product of Keynesian

[122] Hani Sayed, *supra* note 88.

[123] *See* ROBERT PACKENHAM, THE DEPENDENCY MOVEMENT: SCHOLARSHIP AND POLITICS IN DEVELOPMENT STUDIES (1992).

[124] JAMES CYPHER AND JAMES DIETZ, THE PROCESS OF ECONOMIC DEVELOPMENT 265–329 (1997); ALICE AMSDEN, THE RISE OF THE REST (2001).

liberalism as much as of democratic socialism, just as strongly anticommunist as it was against laissez-faire.

ISI typically involved the exploitation of the countryside, supposedly for the sake of industrial capital formation in the cities, through tariffs and through the marketing boards that the social people had pioneered in the 1930s.[125] Aside from South Korea and Taiwan at the moment of maximum communist threat and maximum liberal influence in Washington, only a very few progressive regimes (e.g., Egypt, Bolivia) actually broke up large estates. The refusal to join the Soviet bloc was more than a matter of diplomacy. Reforming third world elites adopted the economic institutions of the social current rather than those of communism. And avoided social and economic revolution without having to give up their emoluments.

The critique of the social

It seems to me hard to overestimate the global transformation of positive law worked by the reformers in the social current. Again, what was globalized was not any particular social regime, and the rate of socialization varied from country to country and within each country from decade to decade. There was no single endpoint toward which national regimes of positive law converged, and if, as I will suggest in a moment, we take the year 1968 as a rough marker for the demise of the social as dominant legal consciousness, we would have to say that it had triumphed institutionally, but in as many forms as there were sovereigns. In other words, as *parole* rather than as structure.

The critique of the social was a cumulative phenomenon, beginning in the 1930s with the second wave of legislative reforms (the first occurred during the decade before World War I), and developing continuously along with the gradual adoption of social law over time and around the world. There was only a brief period, broadly denominated "the fifties," during which the social had no strong opponent (CLT was discredited and Marxism, in the West, disintegrating).

The critiques that reached critical mass by 1968 were, theoretically, politically and programmatically contradictory. The social at which they were directed was institutionalized, a thoroughly entrenched status quo implemented at the level of legal doctrine by a cadre of jurists who had never known anything but the social superimposed on CLT. They were administrators rather than reformers or intellectuals, and most of them ignored the critiques they happened to notice. The situation is not that different to this very day, except that the people of the social now lament the puzzling "resurgence" of CLT after 1980. By contrast, the brilliant early social people directed

[125] *See* Robert Bates, Markets and States in Tropical Africa: The Political Basis of Agricultural Policies (1981); Robert Bates, Essays in the Political Economy of Rural Africa (1983).

a relatively unitary "individualism plus abuse of deduction" critique at CLT at the moment when a relatively unitary social program of law reform was emerging transnationally as a potent threat to the established order.

The first two critiques originated in the 1930s. One was the critique of the is-to-ought move deriving reform legislation from the science of society. The two main sources of the critique of is-to-ought were Max Weber[126] and the logical positivists.[127] Weber influenced European jurists like Hans Kelsen (according to whom sociological jurisprudence was nothing but a disguised vehicle for "natural law tendencies"),[128] and Unitedstateseans like Karl Llewellyn.[129] After the War, Unitedstatesean pragmatism, in its philosophical version, turned decisively against the "is-to-ought" version of its founders, leaving behind the more Deweyan jurists of, for example, the Legal Process school.[130]

The critique of is-to-ought included a move similar to the abuse-of-deduction critique of CLT. This was that the social people were able to maintain their illusion that they were deriving legal rules from social needs or functions or purposes only by ignoring the pervasive phenomenon of conflict between desiderata – thereby producing something aptly named "social conceptualism."[131] This first critique is the intellectual ancestor of modern policy analysis.

A second, liberal and neoliberal, critique was of the association of the social with fascism and communism.[132] There are many paradoxes here. First, there was a strong Marxist critique of the social as mere bandaid,[133] and at the same time some quite striking incorporations of it into the parts of Soviet legal ideology that seem today the least "communist."[134] The social people included the dominant anticommunist and antifascist intellectual currents of the inter-War period, with the agenda, as I mentioned above, of saving

[126] Max Weber, The Methodology of the Social Sciences (Shils & Finch, eds., 1949).

[127] *E.g.*, A. J. Ayer, Language, Truth and Logic (1936). As applied in law, the logical positivist critique went far beyond Weber, advocating a purely descriptive legal science that would formulate its hypotheses without using suspect mentalist categories like "legal validity." There was a self-conscious parallel with behaviorism in psychology (getting rid of everything mental, leaving only stimulus and response) and the move to "revealed preference" (getting rid of "utility" and "choice") in economics. *See generally* Jack Schlegel, American Legal Realism and Empirical Social Science (1995).

[128] Hans Kelsen, Introduction to the Problems of Legal Theory 41 (1934, trans. 1992).

[129] Karl Llewellyn, *A Realistic Jurisprudence: The Next Step*, 30 Colum L. Rev. 431 (1930).

[130] *See generally*, Mikhal Alberstein, Pragmatism and Law: from Philosophy to Dispute Resolution (2002).

[131] Llewellyn, *supra* note 129. Karl Klare, *Radicalization, supra* note 69.

[132] Friedrich Hayek, The Road to Serfdom (1944).

[133] Gerard Farjat, Le droit economique (1971).

[134] Gianmaria Ajani, *Formalism and Anti-formalism under Socialist Law: The Case of General Clauses within the Codification of Civil Law*, Global Jurist Advances, Vol. 2, No. 2. (2002).

liberalism from itself. And in the post-WWII period in which the social jurists gradually faded from view, the liberals who treated them as tainted rested their case against communism on the post-WWII success of the 1930s reform institutions, pushed through by the social people after the War over Liberal objections.

The remaining critiques developed during the 1960s and 1970s. They have a complex internal relationship to one another that I would describe as follows. The dominant rhetoric of critique was civil libertarian, and permitted a de facto alliance of left and right, quite similar to that which had linked the social democratic and fascist versions of the social now under attack. The critique targeted the procedural dimension of the social reform program, that is, its antiformalism. In family law, criminal law, labor law, public housing, the law of civil commitment, and in the law of prisons, mental hospitals, and juvenile homes, the social program involved the creation of new institutions. These were deliberately constructed to empower administrators operating on the basis of expertise, in the public interest, and in the interest of clients lacking full capacity.

The civil libertarians attacked the institutions as denying individual rights and their administrators as arbitrary and implicitly authoritarian manipulators of vacuous general standards and empty expertise. At one level, the demand was for procedural rights, for example, to hearings applying rationally intelligible decision criteria with judicial review, before the administrators did things to their charges. But behind this demand there was a seismic cultural and political shift, occurring more or less simultaneously all over the developed West.

At the political level, the context for the jurists' critique of the social included the discrediting of the socially oriented leadership of the U.S. Vietnam War ("the best and the brightest"), with perhaps 2,000,000 deaths, the discrediting of the Soviet alternative in Prague Spring and Afghanistan, the gradual discrediting of third world revolutionary national liberation ideology in China (the Great Leap Forward, the Red Guards), Ghana, and Algeria. Don't forget the discrediting of radicalism in the West by the Weather Underground, the Black Panthers, the Red Brigades, and the Baader/Meinhoff Gang, of Pan-Arabism in the first Arab-Israeli war of 1967, not to speak of the assassination of Israeli Olympic athletes at the Munich games.

The slaughter of 500,000 communists and sympathizers by the army and Islamists in Indonesia as U.S.-backed Suharto replaced Sukarno in the economic chaos of a failed import substitution industrialization strategy, and of 1,000,000 ordinary people by the communist Pol Pot regime in Cambodia after the United States "destabilized" the country, the descent of one African state after another from import substitution into kleptocracy – none of it was "the fault" of the social, not at all. The "good" social people hated all of this.

And yet... a whole "regime" was discredited, expertise was discredited, and so on indefinitely.

The noncommunist left rebellion against the social was cultural and intellectual as much as political. Behind the civil libertarians were writers like Ken Kesey,[135] and Jean Genet,[136] and Betty Friedan,[137] who recast the supposedly benign social institutions as forms of hell analogous to the hells of the period's public sphere, and poststructuralist theorists of the social as "discipline," in the wake of Michel Foucault.[138] As Donzelot[139] argued, the New Left around the world, when it was not Marxist Leninist, was a utopian rebellion against the social, and failed because the masses on whom it called had been transformed by the social into the strongest supporters of the status quo. The striking thing about the end of the social on the left is that what replaced it had no relation to this rebellious or utopian/anarchic strand. It was rather a revival of faith in rights, this time human rather than individual or social, in legal formality in place of the standards of the social, and in the judiciary as a nonpolitical, nonmurderous defense against the military-industrial-welfare-administrative state that the social seemed to have become.

On the right, there was a two-strand attack. Social conservatives like Christopher Lasch attacked the social institutions for undermining, through social engineering and bureaucratic service provision, the very social bonds they had claimed to be preserving.[140] And emerging slowly from 1968 on, there was the neoliberal charge that the social program had perverse economic consequences as well as perverse social ones, including, particularly, that it was bad for economic growth, that it required the middle classes to subsidize the lower classes, and that it hurt the people it was trying to help by forcing them to buy social protections of various kinds that were worth less to them than they cost in increased pricing, as summarized in the slogan "nondisclaimable tenants' protections force landlords to raise the rent and evict the grandmother."[141]

The period around 1968 involved something less distinct and final than the discrediting of CLT by the events of the period from the beginning of World War I to the Depression and the rise of fascism and communism. But I don't think it mere generational prejudice (b. 1942) to see it, in neo-Hegelian organicist terms, as the moment when the chrysallis disintegrated around the legal consciousness we call contemporary.

[135] Ken Kesey, One Flew over the Cuckoo's Nest (1962).

[136] Jean Genet, Our Lady of the Flowers (1963).

[137] Betty Friedan, The Feminine Mystique (1964).

[138] Michel Foucault, Discipline and Punish (19), Karl Klare, *Critical Theory and Labor Relations Law*, in David Kairys, ed., The Politics of Law (3rd ed., 1998).

[139] Donzelot, *supra* note 56.

[140] Lasch, *supra* note 111.

[141] Richard Posner, The Economic Analysis of Law 41–65 (1st ed., 1972).

THE THIRD GLOBALIZATION

In this section, I summarize my as yet quite tentative thoughts about how the analysis above might be extended to include a third globalization. Although it is easy to see the first and second globalizations as thesis and antithesis, the third globalization cannot be seen as, does not see itself as, a synthesis. The third globalization resembles the first two in that it is founded on a brutal critique of its predecessor, in this case, the social. But it differs from both CLT and the social in the respect that there is no discernible large integrating concept, parallel to the will theory or the notion of adaptation to interdependence, mediating between normative projects and subsystems of positive law. Rather I would describe the structure of the consciousness globalized after 1945 as the unsynthesized coexistence of transformed elements of CLT with transformed elements of the social. Of course, this failure on my part to "totalize" may mean only that, because dusk has not yet fallen on "modernity," my pet owl Minerva has not been able to take flight.

The key transformed element of CLT is thinking in the mode of deduction within a system of positive law presupposed to be coherent, or "neoformalism." Neoformalism runs wild in, but also is mainly confined to, public law, including international, constitutional, and criminal law (not administrative law), and family law. It can be right or left. By contrast, CLT legal science was that of the law of obligations. The key transformed element of the social is policy analysis, but based on "conflicting considerations" (also called balancing or proportionality). It produces rules that are ad hoc compromises, rather than the social rules dictated by single social purposes in coherently adaptive new legal regimes. This mode can also be right or left, and is present everywhere, sometimes therefore, surprisingly, coexisting with neoformalism.

Between 1850 and 1950 (more or less), the plurality of schools of legal philosophy did not produce a diversity of modes of legal imagination, argument, and law making. Until around 1900, everyone ended up with a version of the will theory, and after 1900 everyone ended up either with a version of the will theory or with a version of the social. Today, all over the world, positive legal regimes in every area of law are those that emerged from the confrontation at the level of legislation or case law between CLT and the social, understood as law reform projects rather than as legal consciousnesses. There is a substratum of positively enacted classical contract law everywhere, and a superstructure of positively enacted social labor law. There are multiple administrative agencies dealing with a host of socially problematic areas, everywhere; and everywhere there is the law of the free market (itself more or less internally "socialized") governing beneath and between and among the regulatory regimes.

What there is not is a new way of conceiving the legal organization of society, a new conception at the same level of abstraction as CLT or the social.

Institutional innovation goes on constantly (e.g., structural adjustment, the European Commission, securitization). But each new piece of positive law presents itself as *parole*, dissolvable into the expanded legal *langue* that now includes as interchangeable elements all the innovative concepts of the social along with, rather than in place of, those of CLT.

On the field of positive law, structured and unstructured in a way that represents not any single logic, but rather the contingent outcomes of hundreds of confrontations of the social with CLT, it is still possible to argue as a classical person. One simply starts from and pursues the premise that the law is or should be the coherent working out of the coherent idea of individual freedom so far as compatible with the like freedom of others. In the law of market (see below for sex and the family), this mode of argument now identifies one as a neoliberal or libertarian or free market conservative. CLT in its pure or reactionary form is now a right-wing project rather than a legal consciousness.

It is also still possible to argue as though there was an obvious logic of social development, denied by CLT, that does or should animate all of positive law. Whereas up to WWII this might identify one as a fascist as probably as a progressive, the left-over social is now, in the law of the market, almost always a progressive stance. Like CLT, the social in market law has lost its political indeterminacy, but ended up on the left rather than on the right. CLT and the social, in these leftover, politicized forms, are not so much discredited as dated, or "old hat," or tired ways of proceeding, sporadically forceful, more often merely ritual.

These valences are reversed in the law of sex and the family. There, CLT is left or liberal feminist or libertarian, with equal rights still a program for transformation of the relations between men and women and for the liberation of "sexual minorities." The social, in sharp contrast, is conservative, traditionalist, or authoritarian in sex and family law, just the opposite of its valence in market law. The pre-War traditionalist or authoritarian element in the social survives here as Asian or Islamic or official Catholic or fundamentalist Christian values, opposed to the "decadence" of Western sexual and familial rule and mores.

Policy analysis, the first of the great innovations of post-War legal thought, deals with the ongoing management of preexisting legal regimes conceived as compromises between "individualist" (CLT) and social desiderata. Public law neoformalism, the second great innovation, is a disruptive, rather than managerial mode, brought to bear sometimes on the institutions that embodied the social, and sometimes on the institutions that embodied CLT. It appeals, beyond the settlement between CLT and the social represented by the institution in question, to supposedly transcendent, but also positively enacted values in constitutions or treaties, against the status quo.

In place of the unselfconscious confidence in reason and science of CLT, and of the combative self-assertion of the social, policy analysis has been, for fifty years, the vehicle of modest, workmanlike devotion to doing legal work with whatever materials are left over from the grandiose projects of the past. Its practitioners are most proud when their conclusions are warranted nonpolitical because they please and displease left and right without apparent pattern.

Public law neoformalism rebels in the name of "absolutes" outraged in a particular context. Neoformalism is unreflective in a way diametrically opposite to policy analysis. The argument that the closed shop violates the Mexican Constitution's guarantee of freedom of association, or that the failure to criminalize clitoridectomy violates the Convention on the Elimination of All Forms of Discrimination Against Women (CEDAW), or that affirmative action in U.S. university admissions violates equal protection, or that any judge in any country might authorize the detention of Pinochet for human rights abuses in violation of international law, all presuppose either a mystical union of natural and positive law or the mode of deduction from abstractions effectively trashed by the early social theorists.

In place of the professor of CLT and the legislator/administrator of the social, the hero figure of the third globalization is unmistakably the judge, who brings either policy analysis or neoformalism to bear, as best s/he can, on disputes formulated by governmental and nongovernmental organizations claiming to represent civil society.

Human rights play the same role in contemporary legal consciousness that "private rights" played in CLT and "social rights" played in the Social. Identity plays the role that the individual played in CLT, and that classes and national minorities played in the Social. The contemporary ideal is a legal regime that is pluralist, not in the sense of CLT, which coordinated atomized individuals through universally valid abstract rules, nor in that of the Social, preoccupied with finding and supporting the "valid" "living" law of subcommunities as a path toward an idea of distributive justice. But in the sense of appropriately recognizing and managing "difference."

The individual (and corporate) property and contract rights beloved of CLT were a limited class, cabined by the worship of sovereign power on the one hand and by the sharp distinction between legal and moral obligation on the other. They are an ancestor, but not the model for contemporary human rights, nor, for that matter, are they central to the human rights pantheon. The collective social rights (food, housing, work, health) beloved of The Social, are more or less vindicated in positive law, but they, like CLT property rights, are conceptually at the margin of contemporary legal consciousness in its transnational form.

Contemporary legal consciousness is the endpoint of a long process in which the general concept of a right has risen from its historical low point in the 1930s (heyday of right and left versions of the social) to become the universal legal linguistic unit. Human rights are the "hypostatization" of this trend, operating as universals, at once natural and positive, in a way oddly analogous to the operation of right, will and fault in CLT private law. Human rights also function sometimes as rules (even absolute rules) and sometimes as mere policies, potentially relevant in virtually every legal dispute even if there is no claim of violation of an enacted constitution or charter or treaty.

Contemporary legal consciousness organizes rights claimants according to their plural, cross-cutting "identities." Identity represents at once an extension of and a total transformation of the categories – social class and national minority – through which the social jurists disintegrated the Savignian "people." Contemporary identities cross cut in the sense that each of us has many. One person can be a straight white male married ruling class New England Protestant Unitedstatesean, not living with a disability, not a person living with AIDS, not a survivor (that he remembers) of childhood sexual abuse, and so on.

My example is awkward because, in contemporary global legal consciousness, the notion of identity is the descendant of the social preoccupation not with dominant but with subordinated or discriminated or persecuted identities. Identity is typically the basis of a claim against the "majority" or "dominant culture." Identity thinking alternates between essentializing what it is to have some particular trait that sets its possessors apart, in order to develop and legitimate legal claims, and trying to reconcile those claims when they conflict. Of course, straightforward nationalist claims, and claims based on class or national minority oppression are no less common today than they were in the interwar period. It is just that they are no longer paradigmatic.

Identity/rights discourse seems at first glance to be a public law and family law phenomenon. But it is in fact a true lingua franca, just as applicable to the law of the market. On the side of the typical beneficiaries of identity discourse, namely what the social jurists call "weak parties" (women, discriminated minorities, now even "the poor" understood as an identity rather than a class) formal market law no longer ignores identity. Some public and private market actors, but not others, are forbidden to discriminate against some identities, but not others, which means that they may be compelled to deal, against their will, at some economic cost, or forced to deal on more favorable terms than the identity incumbents could obtain in a "free" market. Histories of discriminatory treatment of an identity give rise to complex economic claims against private market actors or private property owners in the present.

On the side of "strong parties," employers, creditors, sellers of tangible and intangible commodities, there has been a sustained effort, emblematic of contemporary legal consciousness, to reconfigure property and contract rights as parallel to minoritarian identity/rights. Eastern European dissident rights theorists, for whom The Social was implicated if not in communism itself at least in its toleration through the years up to 1989, included private property in their catalog of what was denied under communism. The ultimate realization of this trend is Amartya Sen's inclusion of the "right to engage in entrepreneurial activity" in his catalog of human potentiality protection, probably best understood as part of the third world reaction against the social as manifested in the failed ISI regimes of the sixties and seventies.

The international business community gradually adapted to the rise of identity rights rhetoric by transforming property ownership into a minoritarian identity and government regulation into the analog of discrimination by legislative majorities. Through the WTO, for example, multinationals demand protection for intellectual property rights against the practices of third world countries that refuse to recognize patents and trademarks or to prevent "piracy" (nicely paralleling the demand of international capital that imperialist states suppress tangible piracy in the early nineteenth-century Mediterranean by colonizing North Africa).

The hope of The Social, that an institutional mechanism based on the recognition of organized groups (as in corporatism) can correctly achieve accommodation, has disappeared. Just as the people/nation complex of CLT was riven by the focus on social classes and national minorities, so the order based on classes and national minorities fragmented when the identity concept became cross cutting. The end result is that the concept of an identity, and the set of legal concepts and techniques based on the idea of a right, through which identities enter law (e.g., discrimination, accommodation, etc.), are general. But they provide only a *langue*, used to produce an infinite variety of particular arguments and particular regimes of positive law, as *parole*.[142]

Each national legal system makes its own choices about which identities to recognize and which to stigmatize. But the arguments for and against recognition are close to identical across time and space. When an identity is recognized, it will be through a typically contemporary mix of highly formal norms, of equality and nondiscrimination, with a highly negotiated, ad hoc set of norms, about tolerance or accommodation for identity defining practices like "sodomy" and the veil, and about affirmative action or reparations. In other words, public law neoformalism combined with conflicting considerations (balancing, proportionality). There will be as many "solutions" as there are law-making authorities.

Each of the traits of the third globalization has a recognizable Unitedstatesean genealogy, in the sense that, starting from our present and moving back in time, we soon come upon Unitedstatesean developments that seem at least to presage those in the global context. Public law neoformalism strongly resembles the practices of late nineteenth-century U.S. courts, which took

[142] Martha Minow, *Interpreting Rights: An Essay for Robert Cover*, 96 YALE L.J. 1860 (1987).

the CLT construction of private law and applied it to the U.S. Constitution. After WWII, liberal civil libertarians who had strongly criticized the conservative public law neoformalism of the earlier period took up the same practice through the Warren Court. Policy analysis and balancing were post-Realist U.S. developments, and the advocates of balancing were already debating public law neoformalists in the early 1950s.

The identity/rights complex, as a template for thinking about a vast range of legal issues, seems foreshadowed in the United States by the post-WWII alliance of elite WASPs, Jews, and blacks in the construction of the category of ethnicity, linking the evils of the Holocaust to those of racism in the United States as illegal discrimination. U.S. second-wave feminism is responsible for the abstraction and generalization of the category by transforming it into "identity." And it is familiar since de Toqueville that Unitedstateseans tend toward juristocracy .

Along with this conceptual genealogy, each of the main sites for the development of contemporary legal consciousness has a strong U.S. connection. I would include among these sites, first the constitutional courts, with judicial review often of issues of the distribution of powers in federal systems as well as over rights against the state, that have come into existence all over the world since 1945. Second, the rise of transnational jurisdictions, in a host of different contexts, from the European Union (EU) to the WTO to the International War Crimes Tribunal. Third, in the world of law practice there is the development of the U.S.-style large international law firm dealing with the issues of the globalized economy, and of a nonprofit NGO sector, equally globalized, understanding itself as constituting "the international community," or "international civil society."

In each of these contexts, the influence of the United States is manifest. As in the analysis of the diffusion of CLT, we can distinguish more or less violent imposition from imposition through superior bargaining power, and both from prestige. For constitutional courts, for example, the development begins with U.S. victory over Germany, Italy, and Japan in WWII, and continues through victory in the Cold War. Then there is the process by which USAID and the international financial institutions bargain with third world regimes desperate for financial bail outs, imposing rule of law reform as part of structural adjustment. U.S. courts have steadily expanded their "long arm" jurisdiction, and the way of thinking about law that goes with it, through the implicit threat that if defendant multinationals refuse to accept U.S. jurisdiction, default judgments will make it hard or impossible for them to access the U.S. market.

The analogy is to nineteenth-century imperial bargaining with the Ottoman Empire or China or Egypt for legal "capitulations" under the two threats of military intervention and refusal of trade. The rise of U.S. style transnational law firms is obviously tied to the relative dominance of U.S.

transnational corporations in the globalized world economy. Prestige seems the more relevant category for understanding the dominance of U.S.-style policy analysis in the work of the EU Brussels Commission on competition law, or for understanding quotation of U.S. Supreme Court cases by the Egyptian Constitutional Court.

On the other hand, it is easy to exaggerate the extent to which the third globalization is "really" Americanization. First, public law neoformalism and conflicting considerations have a European as well as a Unitestatesean genealogy, including, for policy analysis, Rene Demogue and Phillip Heck before WWII, and the early proportionality cases of the German Constitutional Court. Kelsenian judicial review and German ordo-liberalism undergird public law neoformalism. And as in the earlier cases of CLT and the social, there is a process of selection, in which legal elites around the world choose to be dominated in one way rather than another. The European Court of Justice is neoformalist in its interpretation of the canonical "freedoms" of movement of goods and persons in a "single market" in part, as is widely recognized, in order to drape its legislative power in the cloak of legal necessity.

Why is it that, in a goodly number of peripheral and semiperipheral national legal systems, constitutional courts established over the whole period, from the late forties (India) into the 1970s (Portugal, Spain, Greece) and the 1990s (Central Europe, Colombia, South Africa), have come to exercise significant power, successfully invalidating legislative and executive actions? The background of U.S. military hegemony, the pressures of the international financial institutions and of world capital markets, and the prestige of U.S. institutions are all part of the story. But here, too, it seems likely that selection is important.

We might interpret developments of this kind of judicial power as a strategy of a part of the local elite, the part with access to judicial power and legal discourse, to deal by mediation with a characteristic set of conflicting pressures. In the economy, these regimes were the sites of the elaboration of the institutions of the social, from land reform to import substitution industrialization, by the left and right nationalist regimes that came to power after WWII, in the context of decolonization and third worldism more generally. Beginning some time in the late 60s, rising neoliberalism, with strong links to CLT, backed by the resurgence of right-wing power in the United States and Western Europe, has been pushing for the dismantling of social regimes, and especially of ISI regimes.

Third world constitutional courts mediate between these pressures and the resistance of the intended beneficiaries of the social, peasants, the urban poor, government employees, and business interests with access to the rents generated by regulation. Sometimes the courts strike down the social measures, as for example when the Ghanaian Constitutional Court abolishes the Nkrumah era compulsory sales cooperatives of producers of domestic gin. Sometimes they soften the impact of the neoliberal roll back, as when the

Indian court, with the hearty approval of David Beatty, delayed the eviction of squatters on public streets in Mumbai until the monsoon season was over.[143]

A similar but inverse process seems to be at work for the domains of civil liberties, sex, and the family. Here the international pressure comes from the international NGOs, pressing for protection of political dissidents and for the liberalization of sexual and family legal codes. On the other side are, often, the military and traditionalist religious and nationalist organizations. Once again, the constitutional discourses of public law neoformalism and proportionality allow the legally empowered part of the elite to mediate. Clitoridectomy is not Shari'a, so the government can ban it, according to the Egyptian court.

Mediation means that neither side gets everything it wants on social issues, any more than the courts enact either the Washington consensus or the social agenda. Public law neoformalism and the method of proportionality empower judicial institutions to stand above the conflict of CLT-style neoliberalism and the surviving elements of the left-wing social, and equally above the conflict between liberalizers and social authoritarians and traditionalists. They take the conflicts out of the domain of pure politics, with all its explosive possibilities, and relocate it in the domain of legal expertise, ostensibly under suprapolitical local control.

My view is that it will be a while before it is possible to work out, retrospectively, just what the class base was for this mediating activity.[144] As a first guess, it would seem plausible that the supporters of judicial review may have included the long-established colonial or precolonial cosmopolitan elites, not fully displaced, or even strengthened by the social regimes, and the newly enriched groups, moving toward a more cosmopolitan social stance as well as into the global market, who managed to establish themselves within the social dispensation. For these groups, the Washington Consensus advocates, the liberalizing NGOs, the local military, cultural nationalists, and religious fundamentalists are all threats to be managed, accommodated but not allowed to ruin the good times and the promising future.

The process of selection, as in all of these examples, is possible because, as with the first two, the third globalization diffuses a *langue*, and permits an infinite variety of *parole* by those who learn to speak proportionality, neoformalism, rights/identity, and judicial supremacy. As the *langue* diffused, it lost its distinctive Unitedstatesean quality. The U.S. solutions to the problems that local speakers address in their own national contexts come to seem just particular instances rather than paradigmatic utterances. This process is facilitated by the parochialism of U.S. legal culture, which after WWII lost

[143] David Beatty, The Ultimate Rule of Law (2004).

[144] I found Ran Hirschl, Towards Juristocracy: The Origins and Consequences of the New Constitutionalism (2004) helpful in this regard.

the openness to the rest of the world that had been one of its striking traits when Unitedstateseans were self-conscious dwellers in the periphery. When they want to influence the *langue*, or assert proprietorship over its use, Unitedstateseans may be ineffectual because they know it in its contemporary transnational form less well than those who have been busily developing it offshore over the last fifty years.

The centrality of the judge combines, with the problematic status of juristic method in the aftermath of critiques and with the multiplication of claimant identities, to pose a new problem. In place of the question of the extent to which law should be moral, for CLT, and the question of the relation between law and society, for the social, in contemporary legal consciousness the question is the relationship between law and politics. The judge simultaneously represents law against legislative politics domestically and sovereign politics internationally, and must answer the charge that s/he is a usurper, doing "politics by other means."

Contemporary legal consciousness harbors a plethora of normative reconstruction projects, designed to transcend the opposition of CLT and the social, and thereby restore Reason to rulership in law.[145] It also harbors a plethora of methodologies through which legal theorists attempt to achieve a distanced understanding of the relation of law to other domains. In place of, or along side, the normative projects of CLT and the social – utilitarianism, natural rights, social Darwinism, Catholic natural law, Marxism, pragmatism, Comteanism, and so on – we have Legal Process, liberal rights theory (often puzzlingly combined with analytical jurisprudence[146]), efficiency analysis, republicanism, communitarianism, legal neopragmatism, feminist legal theory, critical race theory. And that is just the Unitedstatesean array. There is no more a dominant reconstruction project today than there was a dominant philosophy of law in the late nineteenth century or between the World Wars.

Among the interpretive as opposed to reconstructive projects: analytical jurisprudence, the sociology of law, the economic analysis of law, literary theorizing of law as text, the cultural study of law, critical legal studies, postmodern legal theory. Of course, the interpretive modes are no less value saturated for having eschewed prescription. Critical legal studies, the approach of this article, includes a critique of policy analysis, for its pretension to leach out, through the notion of universalizability, the inevitable particularism of political/legal choice. And it includes a critique of public law neoformalism for suppressing the moment of "governance" in political/legal choice.[147]

[145] Pierre Schlag, The Enchantment of Reason (1997).

[146] See Lopez-Medina, *supra* note 3.

[147] David Kennedy, *When Renewal Repeats: Thinking Against the Box*, in Left Legalism, Left Critique (Janet Halley & Wendy Brown, eds., 2002); David Kennedy, *The Human Rights Movement Part of the Problem*, 15 Harv. Hum. Rts. J. 99 (2002); Duncan Kennedy, Critique of Adjudication, *supra* note 2; Duncan Kennedy, *Distributive and Paternalist Motives in Contract and*

CONCLUSION

The left and right political ideologies pursued through contemporary legal consciousness are no more internally coherent than the legal dogmatics of CLT or the organicist dogmatics of the social. This point is an important antidote to the tendency to see a discussion of the politics of law, like the one above, as reducing law to politics. As I've argued at length elsewhere, the reduction is impossible because, for example, the projects of the right oscillate between libertarianism and social conservatism; those of the left, say for the family law issues just mentioned, between a feminist identity politics of protection and a queer theoretical antiidentity politics of sexual liberation.[148]

In other words, the content of left and right projects is no more reliably "axiologically decidable" (or "determinate," as we used to say in critical legal studies) than the pure question of legal validity. When one traces the phenomenology of decision under uncertainty into the choice of an interpretation of one's own politics, it turns out that there is an "hermeneutic circle." Commitments as an actor within a legal consciousness shape politics as well as the reverse.[149]

Even in Clausewitz's famous formulation,[150] war is politics *by other means*, not "just" politics. In Carl Schmitt's flip of Clausewitz, politics is war by other means, but not reducible to war.[151] War as "means" can be an end, or a means to other ends than politics. If law is politics, it is so, again, by other means, and there is much to be said, nonreductively, about those means. By analogy with Schmitt, it seems to me also true that politics is law by other means, in the sense that politics flows as much from the unmeetable demand for ethical rationality in the world[152] as from the economic interests or pure power lust with which it is so often discursively associated.

The narrative begun in this article attempts to historicize "our" situation, in the mode of left critical theory combined with modernism/postmodernism. The three globalizations are incidents in the story of military force, economic power, and ideological hegemony within the capitalist period of world history. But I understand this period not as playing out the logic of capital, but rather as the period of universal rationalization paradoxically intertwined with the death of reason.[153] The death of reason permits (but does not require or

Tort Law with Special Reference to Compulsory Terms and Unequal Bargaining Power, 41 Md. L. Rev. 563 (1983).

148 Janet Halley, *Sexuality Harassment*, in Left Legalism, Left Critique, *supra* note 144.

149 Kennedy, Critique of Adjudication 187–191, *supra* note 3.

150 Carl von Clausewitz, On War (Michael Howard & Peter Paret, trans., 2d ed. 1989) (1832).

151 Carl Schmitt, The Concept of the Political (1976).

152 Cf. Max Weber, *Politics as a Vocation*, in From Max Weber (Gerth & Mills, eds., 1946).

153 *Id.*

in itself bring about) the taking back of alienated powers that can be used for local or national or transnational change toward equality, community, and wild risky play. But they are powers whose ethical exercise starts from accepting the existential dilemmas of undecidability that legal discourse has, from globalization to globalization, staunchly denied.

3 THE "RULE OF LAW" IN DEVELOPMENT ASSISTANCE: PAST, PRESENT, AND FUTURE

David M. Trubek

The issue of the relationship between legal institutions and "development," whether development is defined narrowly in economic terms, or more broadly, was originally mooted by Max Weber 100 years ago and has continued to fascinate scholars.[1] In recent years, it also has come to interest policymakers as development institutions have placed increasing emphasis on the "rule of law" as a necessary ingredient in any development strategy. The result has been a proliferation of law reform projects and programs supported by development assistance institutions.[2]

In the 1990s, there was a massive surge in development assistance for law reform projects in developing and transition countries. These projects involve investments of many billions of dollars. The World Bank alone reports it has supported 330 "rule of law" projects and spent $2.9 billion dollars on this sector since 1990. At the beginning of this new surge of interest in law within the development community, there appeared to be a broad consensus on the reasons to create the "rule of law" in these transitional and developing economies, on what the "rule of law" meant, and on the best strategies to implement those objectives. But as more was learned about the challenges, and a burgeoning literature emerged, it has become apparent that the initial enthusiasm for the rule of law masked different, and potentially contradictory, visions and approaches. This chapter seeks to trace the origins of the current wave of interest in the rule of law, identify the contradictions that have emerged, and specify issues now on the agenda.

THE LAW AND DEVELOPMENT MOVEMENT OF THE 1960s

To understand the present fully, it is useful to go back to the first wave of interest in law in the international development assistance community. This

[1] David M. Trubek, *Max Weber on Law and the Rise of Capitalism*, 1972 WIS. L. REV. 720–753 (1972).

[2] For an overview, see David M. Trubek, *Law and Development*, INTERNATIONAL ENCYCLOPEDIA OF THE SOCIAL & BEHAVIORAL SCIENCES (N.J. Smelser and Paul B. Bates, eds., 2001).

was the law and development (L&D) movement that started in the 1960s and continued into the 1970s. This movement was led by a small band of liberal lawyers working in development agencies, foundations, and universities in the United States and Europe. They sought to interest development agencies in the importance of legal reform. Although the L&D movement was relatively small and short lived, and had little impact on the development policies of its time, it did put the issue of how law related to "development" on the intellectual agenda.

The L&D movement was built around the dominant Western development paradigm of the time that gave priority to the role of the state in the economy and the development of internal markets. This was the era of import-substitution industrialization, in which developing countries sought to build their own industrial capacity by limiting manufactured imports from advanced economies and providing subsidies for national firms. The basic economic model was one of a regulated market economy in which the state played an active role, not just through various forms of planning and industrial policy but also through state ownership of major industries and utilities.

Although the rhetoric of development stressed that the ultimate goals were freedom and democracy, not just growth, the projects focused on growth. Development policy stressed economic matters not because planners were uninterested in political democracy or social development, but because those who cared about such matters thought they would follow from economic growth. This meant that within this vision it was possible to accept – if not favor – various forms of bureaucratic authoritarian rule while professing allegiance to ideas of democracy and promotion of individual freedom. Authoritarianism could be portrayed as a temporary stage that would foster growth but automatically wither away once growth was achieved.

In this context, it is no surprise that the small band of liberal lawyers who focused on law reform as a development strategy placed great emphasis on the economic role of law and highlighted the importance of law as an instrument through which state actors could shape the economy. This meant more effective operation of state-owned economic enterprises and "modern" approaches to regulation of the private sector. The L&D movement cherished a vision of lawyers as pragmatic, instrumental problemsolvers who would facilitate state-led economic development. Depending on their role, such "modern" lawyers would help policymakers shape and enforce effective regulations, advise the managers of state enterprises how best to realize their goals, and counsel private clients in ways that would allow them to grow and profit while acting consistently with the policy objectives of the planners and law givers.[3]

[3] David M. Trubek and Marc Galanter, *Scholars in Self-Estrangement: Reflections on the Crisis of Law and Development Studies in the United States*, 1974 Wis. L. Rev. 1062–1101 (1974).

According to the L&D planners, legal systems in Latin America and other developing nations were not producing the kind of modern law and lawyers that were needed. The planners saw many obstacles to legal modernity. Foremost among them was that the legal cultures of these nations were highly "formalist." By this, the L&D planners meant rules were developed, interpreted, and applied without careful attention to policy goals. They alleged that *formalist law teachers* taught that law was an abstract system to be applied by rigid internal rules without concern for policy relevance and impact; *formalist legislatures* copied foreign models or followed abstract principles instead of studying social context and shaping rules for instrumental ends; *formalist judges* applied rules in a rigid and mechanical fashion rather than first accepting the inevitable discretion adjudication entails and then looking to the policy goals behind the rules to guide them in the application of this discretion; and *formalist practitioners* stood aloof from both the goals of the law and the objectives of their clients, issuing interpretations based on some abstract logical system or rote application of formulae thus impeding rather than fostering progress.

Formalism, in this sense, engendered other weaknesses. These included weak enforcement, inappropriate rules, and low legitimacy. Enforcement was ineffective in part because the rules adopted were inappropriate to specific national contexts and thus were easily ignored, and in part because of administrative deficiencies and corruption. The rules passed were inapposite: this was because they either had been copied from more advanced systems without real concern for national need and attention to specific national context, or because they were elaborated by some system of abstract logic equally insensitive to real policy concerns. The legitimacy of the legal system was low because the rules had little to do with the needs of the country and for that reason (among others) laws were frequently ignored.

This diagnosis led to the L&D programs that evolved in the 1960s. The primary goal of these programs was to transform legal culture and institutions through educational reform and selected transplant of "modern" institutions. If formalism was the source of bad laws, weak enforcement, and ineffective or counterproductive lawyering, then the most important thing to do was to create a new, more instrumental *legal culture.* This culturalist approach led to a heavy emphasis on reform of legal education. Legal education was seen as the source of the evils of formalism, and change of legal education as the way to transform a formalist culture into an instrumental one. Instrumentally oriented law schools would not only turn out lawyers who would approach their tasks in a pragmatic, can-do fashion, they would also be venues from which a critique of formalism in law making and application could be mounted, as well as think tanks that could produce the modern law that was so badly needed.

This culturalist approach meant that the L&D movement found itself working to a significant degree with law schools and with the legal elites that exercised substantial influence over major law schools in the developing world. Less attention was paid to the legislature, judiciary, or practicing bar. This was not because they were thought to be less important, but because it was assumed that change in the education system was the most effective way to bring about change in all other legal institutions.

Looking back, it is not wholly clear why the idea took hold that legal education was the fulcrum on which all forms of change would occur. It seems as if the planners assumed – paradoxically – that legal education was both highly autonomous and yet very influential. That is, they assumed that it would be relatively easy to bring about change in the law schools because they were freer from the forces of "formalism" than the bench or bar while at the same time they thought that once change occurred in the schools it would immediately influence modes of adjudication and methods of lawyering. The focus on legal education also may have been influenced by the importance of law schools from advanced countries in the development effort. The pioneers of the law and development movement were drawn from elite law schools in the United States and Europe and, early on, called on the schools to assist in the effort. And in the United States at least the law schools were actively involved in development assistance projects while the organized bar, bench, or attorneys general usually were not.

Legal education reform may have been an area of prime concern but it was not the sole focus of reform energies. It was also recognized that there was a need to create modern rules and legal institutions. This meant to some degree transplanting legal institutions from more advanced countries. But in accordance with the culturalist critique, this had to be done with careful attention to local needs and conditions to avoid the mimicry that seemed to have played such a major role in legal borrowing in the past.

Both in the reform of legal education and the development of modern law, the emphasis was on economic law and the training of business lawyers not just in the private sector but also in the public sector, which played such a major role in many third world economies. This emphasis on economic law was not because all L&D planners were indifferent to issues of democracy, social justice, and human rights; rather, it was because many thought that such values were best served by first getting growth going. Moreover, they believed that a more effective legal system would – by its very nature – insure protection of individual rights. Just as the development thinkers hoped (or pretended to hope) for spillover from economic growth to democracy, so the L&D movement believed there would be spillover from an effective and instrumental orientation in economic law to "democracy values" like access to justice and protection for civil rights.

What was the theory that lay behind the law and development movement of the 1960s? In a sense, there was none. Academics played a role, along with lawyers and others in development agencies, in creating the movement. But they really had no well-developed theories to explain their choice of programs and projects. Beyond a general belief in the importance of law, the relevance of western models, and the importance of a modern legal culture, it was all ad hoc and pragmatic. This was a time everyone thought it urgent to get on with the job, not theorize. Theory could – and did – come later.

The L&D movement had a brief and intense life. Of course, by today's standards it was never a major enterprise. It was focused on a few countries in Latin America and Africa. Projects were small and short lived, and funds were limited. The bulk of the funding came from foundations, not bilateral or multilateral aid agencies. USAID did support some projects, but neither the World Bank nor regional banks like the Inter-American Bank for Development directly supported the reform of legal institutions. For a brief period there was a surge of energy and activity, engaging a small but dedicated group of reformers. However, by the middle of the 1970s there was disillusion in the academy, foundation interest declined, and the official aid agencies showed no interest in moving into legal reform. So, for the moment, the L&D movement seemed to have run out of steam.[4]

CRUMBLING PILLARS: THE COLLAPSE OF THE L&D PARADIGM

The movement rested on four pillars; a cultural reform and transplantation strategy; an ad hoc approach to reform based on simplistic theoretical assumptions; faith in spillovers from the economy to democracy and human rights; and a development strategy that stressed state-led import substitution. In the course of the 1970s all four of these pillars crumbled.

As L&D actors gained more experience with Western-inspired reform projects, they began to see serious flaws in the approach initially taken. Questions arose about both the culturalist approach and its educational strategy, and the general effort to transplant Western legal institutions. The educational reform program failed to yield the results hoped for. The law schools proved more resistant to change than the reformers had imagined. And even if small gains were made in the educational sphere, and instrumental ideas were accepted by some third world lawyers and legal scholars, the projects failed to have the systemwide impact hoped for. It seemed as if the structures of law making, law applying, and practice were quite capable of resisting foreign-inspired cultural change. At the same time, many efforts at legal transplantation proved similarly disappointing. In some cases, the transplants did not "take" at all: some of the new laws promoted by the

[4] *Id.*

reformers remained on the books but were ignored in action. In others laws were captured by local elites and put to uses different from those the reformers intended.

Finally, even when change did come about in the economic sphere, leading to more instrumental thinking, effective law making, purposive approaches to adjudication and pragmatic lawyering, the hoped-for spillover to democracy and protection of individual rights did not occur. This was a real shock to Western liberal legalists who had assumed that the legal system was a seamless whole and that reform in one sphere would necessarily lead to progressive change in other areas. These chastened reformers found themselves facing the frightening possibility that legalism, instrumentalism, and authoritarianism might form a stable amalgam so that their efforts to improve economic law and lawyering could strengthen authoritarian rule.[5]

If these lessons from experience started to undermine several of the pillars on which the L&D movement rested, the edifice was further weakened by the effort to develop a theory of law and development. While the early L&D projects were put together in an ad hoc fashion and without any effort to develop a systematic theory, both the academics in the movement and some of the funding agencies sensed the need for such theory. As a result, substantial intellectual energy went into the search for a theory of law and development. Such a theory, it was hoped, would both explain and justify the earlier programmatic efforts and chart the way for future reform efforts. However, the project had effects opposite to those desired. Rather than providing a justification for what had been done, and a map for further reform, the theory-building project revealed serious flaws in the original approach without offering a robust alternative that could orient action and guide project development.

It is important to understand the context in which the theory-building effort was undertaken. The L&D movement was conceived and launched in the early days of the 1960s when liberal internationalism flourished and liberal legalism was a confident creed. The L&D projects were largely conceived by people from Western universities and aid agencies. By the end of the decade, when the project of theory building really got underway, the context had changed dramatically. The failures of the initial reform projects were beginning to become apparent. The anti-Vietnam protests, the events of 1968 in Europe, and other developments had changed the political context and radicalized students in many of the universities in which the theory project was housed. At the same time, the initial reform efforts had brought scholars and activists from the developing world into the effort and they offered perspectives very different than those of the initial U.S. and European reform

5 *See* David M. Trubek, *Back to the Future: The Short and Happy Life of the Law and Society Movement*, 18 Florida State U. L. Rev. 1–55 (1990).

groups. As chastened reformers met with sophisticated thinkers from the developing world and radicalized students, very different ideas about both law and development began to emerge.[6]

In this new context, it is not surprising that the theory project brought to light some of the simplistic assumptions on which L&D reform projects had been based. Although no explicit and well-developed theories had been put forward in the original surge of L&D interest, further analysis suggested that behind ad hoc decision making lay a set of assumptions that constituted a theory of sorts. It became clear that many project designers had employed a linear model of development. In such a model, it was assumed that all nations went through similar stages to reach a common end, represented in this kind of thought by the legal, economic, and social structures of the United States and Western Europe. This naive and ethnocentric neoevolutionist thinking made it easy for L&D planners to believe that something called modern law, not surprisingly found in their own national legal institutions, was the end toward which all legal systems were moving. Because they could imagine that legal development followed evolutionary stages linked to stages of economic growth, and that "Western law" was the higher evolutionary stage toward which all systems were moving, it was easy to believe that the process of transplanting Western legal culture and institutions would be relatively simple and straightforward. After all, weren't the reform projects, modeled as they were on the legal institutions of more "advanced" societies, just modest efforts to accelerate the forces of history? With the winds of history at their back, how could the reformers fail?

Needless to say, the moment these simplistic ideas were held up to critical scrutiny, they collapsed. These ideas probably would have fallen of their own weight under any circumstance, but it helped that the critique emerged in a period in which, amid growing concerns about neoimperialism, their was a great distrust of all forms of Western intervention in the developing world. Thus, as the 1970s rolled on, the L&D movement had to face the fact that the culturalist strategy was not working as they had hoped; transplantation often went awry; spillover was not happening, and critique had demolished the only theory they had. Things looked bad.

But if that were not enough, at the same time development policy was shifting, thus undermining the fourth pillar. While the L&D movement was going thorough this period of reflection, changes were afoot in the larger world of development policy. People began to question the effectiveness of ISI and of state-led growth. Attention focused on the inefficiencies of protectionism and the distortions of bureaucratic management of the economy. It was clear that a paradigm shift in development thought was on the way.

[6] For examples of alternate visions, see Yash Ghai, Robin Luckham, and Francis Snyder, THE POLITICAL ECONOMY OF LAW: A THIRD WORLD READER (1987).

The L&D movement, as such, never recovered from these blows. Of course, some academics continued to work on these issues and development aid for law reform did not dry up completely. But the pace slackened. Foundations lost interest in the area and the bilateral aid agencies and international financial institutions did not take up the slack. Some academics became disillusioned. The networks of academics and policymakers that were created in the 1960s started to unravel, and the study of law and development in the academy declined. Some declared that the L&D movement was dead.

THE "RULE OF LAW" REPLACES LAW AND DEVELOPMENT

The rumors of its death were greatly exaggerated. Today, the enterprise of law reform in developing and transition countries is big business, far eclipsing even the wildest dreams of the L&D pioneers. Aid agencies like the World Bank, which once focused primarily on building roads and dams and getting macroeconomic variables right, now proclaim the importance of the "rule of law" (ROL) and spend billions to reform the legal systems of countries as different as Albania and Argentina, Bangladesh and Bolivia. How did we get from L&D to "ROL"? What forces impelled the move of law from the periphery of the development agenda to its very core? And what is the difference – other than sheer scale – between the projects of today and those of the L&D era?

To answer those questions, it is useful to divide the ROL era into two periods: an initial phase in which the new paradigm took shape and massive investments in law reform began, and a more recent period in which subtle changes can be glimpsed.

The global context is transformed

Although the L&D movement took institutional form in the 1960s, it could be seen as a continuation of processes that dated to the end of WWII. The ROL era, in contrast, emerged during the latest wave of globalization and the post-Cold War era. This radical change of context helps account for the great differences between ROL and L&D.

The L&D movement emerged in a period in which international economic policy was supportive of state-led initiatives in partially closed economies. In the advanced countries of Europe and the United States, this was the era of "embedded liberalism." This regime, guaranteed by the Bretton Woods system, maintained a balance between openness, democracy, and economic fairness. Embedded liberalism was an *international regime* that operated to facilitate *domestic* politics and shield *domestic* systems of economic regulation and social protection in advanced capitalist countries from global shocks. It allowed individual nations leeway to regulate the economy, promote employment, insure against economic risks, and redistribute income. It supported democratic politics at the national level, ensuring that when governments exercised the powers safeguarded to them by the international regime they would act in the best interests of their citizens. This system combined efficiency with legitimacy: its great virtue was that once the international machinery was set in motion, the nation states had effective authority over their economies, major political choices could be made at the national level, and national governments could be held accountable through democratic processes.

Although the developing world was only marginally affected by embedded liberalism, one can see strong affinities between the broad intellectual framework the regime rested on and development policy of the 1950s and 1960s. Embedded liberalism was a compromise between those who wanted a completely open world economy and those who felt that it was important to limit the impact of exogenous economic forces and thus allow the state to play a major role in national economies. For people who accepted such a compromise for the developed world, it was easy to accept the idea of import substitution industrialization and state-led growth for the "Third World."

If the thinking behind embedded liberalism affected the overall architecture of the post-WWII era, the emphasis on state-led growth and relatively closed markets was also a way for the managers of the world economy – or at least of that part of the world economy under Western hegemony – to cope with the pressures of nationalism and demands for decolonialization. National movements seized control of states in former colonies and sought to break ties with their respective metropoles that had been built up under colonialism: this meant placing more emphasis on national development strategies and endogenous growth, a change international development policymakers accepted and supported.

Finally, there was the Cold War, and the ideological struggle with the Soviet Bloc. This required that the West promise to deliver economic growth, but do so while also claiming to promote liberal democracy. Law and development was part of the West's answer to communism, part of the promise, often not fulfilled, that a Western-led economic system could deliver economic growth with freedom.

The contemporary "Rule of Law" enterprise took shape in a very different *conjuncture*. By the 1990s when ROL really became big business, major changes had occurred in the world economy and world politics. International trade had grown substantially. The spread of industry into the "third world" and the success of export-led growth in Asia, plus the globalization strategies of major transnational corporations and rapid deregulation of capital markets, significantly increased the degree of world economic integration. The collapse of the Soviet Union helped legitimate the kinds of neoliberal economic policies that gained credence in the West under the aegis of the Reagan and Thatcher administrations. The vision of a world of partially closed national economies and state-controlled national markets gave way to a vision of a fully open global economy with minimal state involvement and free flows of goods and capital across national boundaries. This vision affected thinking about development in very profound ways, creating a new development paradigm with important implications for the law reform agenda. It implied a triple shift, from state to market, from internal to export-led growth, and from official capital flows to private foreign investment.

These shifts create multiple pressures for the internationalization of legal fields. They provide opportunities for the more cosmopolitan sectors of the legal profession, valorizing knowledge on foreign legal systems and contacts with foreign firms. They put pressure on governments to make legal changes calculated to attract foreign investors. They created the need to strengthen the legal foundations of market institutions.[7]

One of the more dramatic developments is the emergence of new actors into the legal scene. These include the growth of more internationally oriented corporate law firms in developing countries and the emergence of major multinational law firms as global players. Local law firms with cosmopolitan connections were able to expand in size and influence. And truly global institutions were constructed. Through merger, acquisition, and opening of branch offices, major law firms, led by the U.S. corporate bar and British solicitors, and joined by law subsidiaries of the Big 5 (now 4) accounting firms, created global legal practices with hundreds if not thousands of lawyers operating in many countries. While the global practice of law was not a new phenomenon, the scale of such firms and the geographic range of their activities grew geometrically in the 1980s and 1990s. The global firms often came to occupy important positions in national legal orders, thus deepening the contact between national legal systems and transnational legal ideas and actors and facilitating the spread of a new orthodoxy about law and economic development.[8]

These forces intertwined with the growing interest of the official development agencies in legal reform so that the reform projects both found responsive supporters and helped create additional support elements. Although the remainder of the chapter focuses on the development agencies and their discourse concerning law, it is important to bear in mind that they act in a broader context that is influenced by multiple actors and forces.

[7] *See* Yves Dezalay and Bryant G. Garth, The Internationalization of Palace Wars: Lawyers, Economists, and the Contest to Transform Latin American States (2002).

[8] Ruth Buchanan, John R. Davis, Yves Dezalay, and David M. Trubek, *Global Restructuring and the Law: The Internationalization of Legal Fields and the Creation of Transnational Arenas*, 44 Case Western Reserve L. Rev. 407–498 (1994).

Discovering the "rule of law": Human rights, the Washington consensus, and the emergence of law as a development assistance priority

This was the context for the rediscovery of law in the development community. One could see the ROL movement as arising from the confluence of two forces at work in this new era. These forces had different roots, were supported by different actors, and defined "development" in different ways. But they coalesced, at least at the more general level, on the importance of something called "the rule of law."

The project of democracy and the need for domestic human rights protections. The first of these could be called "the project of democracy," and came out of the human rights movement of the 1970s and 1980s. Remember that the L&D movement thought that growth and cultural transformation would lead to democracy and protection of human rights. It soon became apparent that this "spillover" would not occur automatically: human rights had to be pursued as an independent goal. As a result, "human rights" went from an idea to an organized movement and institutionalized force. The international community made great progress in specifying human rights norms, creating machinery for international action to enforce them, and ensuring that internationally recognized human rights became a part of the discourse of domestic politics in many countries.

For our story, the most important move was the recognition that purely international approaches to human rights protection were insufficient without strong counterparts in domestic law. Events such as the Helsinki process drew attention to the lack of protection for human rights in domestic institutions. The human rights movement began to look at domestic institutions, championing the creation of constitutional guarantees, judicial review, greater judicial independence, and "access to justice." This path naturally led to ideas about the construction of "the rule of law." It was understood that that project would require substantial effort both to dismantle older systems that had buttressed authoritarian rule and to create the new culture and institutions needed to protect democratic freedoms.

The project of markets and the discovery of institutions. The second, and for the understanding of development assistance the more powerful, force might be called "the project of markets." Following the decline of the 1960s statist-ISI paradigm, a new set of development policy prescriptions emerged from the Washington-based international financial institutions. This approach stressed export-led growth, free markets, privatization, and foreign investment as the keys to growth. To pursue these goals, it was necessary to create all the institutions of a market economy in former command economies and remove restrictions on markets in *dirigiste* economies such as those in many Latin American countries.

For many who promoted the project of markets, growth would be best achieved if the state stayed out of the economy except to the extent that – through law – it provided the institutions needed for the functioning of the market. These include guarantees for property rights, enforcement of contract, and protection against arbitrary use of government power and excessive regulation. All this was packaged as "good governance" and deemed important both to stimulate domestic growth and attract foreign investment.

In the very beginning, promoters of markets may have assumed that the main thing that needed to be done was to get the state out of the way, and somehow everything else would take care of itself. But it soon became apparent that markets do not create the conditions for their own operation, so that the move to markets would involve major institutional reform. As a recent World Bank Report notes:

> Subsequent practical experience suggested that reform efforts could not stop with policies designed to shrink the state and liberalize and privatize the economies.... It turned out that a lack of attention to institutions generally, especially legal ones, placed substantial limits on the reforms as a means to promote economic development and poverty reduction. [9]

The rule of law as a common goal. Once the economic development agencies realized that the neoliberal turn involved positive intervention to create the institutional conditions for markets, development agencies were committed to investing in legal reform. They found their concerns overlapped with those of the proponents of human rights and democracy. For both, the rule of law was a common goal.

While the project of democracy and the project of markets seem very different, they both identified "the rule of law" as an essential step toward their objectives. Both thought it important to have constitutional guarantees for certain rights, even if they differed on the rights to be given primacy. Both thought that an independent judiciary, preferably armed with powers of judicial review, was desirable, even though they had different ideas about what the judges were to be independent of and what was the purpose of such independence. And they agreed that efficiently functioning courts providing cost-effective access to justice were needed, although they probably had different ideas about who should get such access and for what ends they would use it.

Ironically, both the market builders and the democracy promoters showed a faith in formalism, albeit a modernized neoformalism, which was seen as an inherent part of a "rule of law." For some of the promoters of democracy and freedom, it seemed self-evident that independent judges would possess a method of adjudication that would resolve all questions without resort to

[9] World Bank, Legal and Judicial Reform: Observations, Experiences and Approach of the Legal Vice Presidency 17–18 (2002).

ideology, politics, or even policy-oriented balancing. However, at the same time that ROL proponents were championing formalism, they also were arguing that it was necessary to make legal systems more effective and efficient, and promoting instrumental thought and greater sensitivity to policy concerns.

The reform agenda that came from this curious amalgam of markets and democracy was wide-ranging, covering all aspects of the legal system from education and drafting of new rules to organization of the bar. This was especially true for programs in former command economies where, it was thought, the whole institutional structure of market society had to be built from scratch. Thus, unlike the L&D movement, which focused on education, ROL projects sought to bring about change in all aspects of the legal system. This meant that there were projects to strengthen the bar and bench as well as the academy, and to reform legal rules in almost all areas. Practicing lawyers, prosecutors, judges, and court administrators from Western countries joined legal academics in this new phase of law reform and transplantation. However, special emphasis was placed on the administration of justice. This includes the efficient management of cases, increased access to justice through the construction of alternative dispute resolution mechanisms, enhanced means of enforcing judicial decisions, and the promotion of judicial independence. While there are many reasons why the administration of justice loomed so large in the ROL programs, it is worth noting that because of their shared faith in the role of judges, this is an area in which the project of markets and the project of democracy overlap.

Several distinctive features marked the first phase of the ROL era. In addition to neoformalism and a focus on the administration of justice, there was great emphasis on contract and property, seen as core ingredients of a market economy, a strong belief in the possibility of legal transplantation, a willingness to conduct reforms at once in all parts and levels of the legal order, and a view that there was one model of "the rule of law" that made sense for all countries. Further, there was a faith that the needed reforms could be imposed from the top, and would be quickly and easily accepted.

Looking at some of the ideas and projects of this period, L&D veterans could only sigh as they saw many of the errors of the past being repeated. For them, the emphasis on top-down, one size fits all reform, suggested that little had been learned from prior experiences. What about all the experience with the limits of transplants, the need for adaptation to local contexts, the possibility of multiple paths to growth, the risk that reforms would be captured by elites for their own ends, and the gap between law on the books and law in action? And what could they make of the apparent return to formalism? After a personal encounter with the managers of the new ROL program in USAID in the early 1990s, I felt about that agency as Tallyrand felt about the Bourbons after the Restoration: they had forgotten nothing and learned nothing!

Critiques of the first phase

The first phase of the ROL enterprise had a narrow concept of the rule of law and a simplistic notion of how to bring the rule of law into existence. There were three things that could be said in criticism. The first dealt with the implementation of ideas. The others dealt with the institutional ideas themselves.

Questioning implementation methods. The first criticism has already been suggested. It focused on the method to implant the rule of law. For those who thought that there was a single model good for the whole world, attention had to be drawn to the fact that working legal institutions must be embedded in diverse contexts. Those who relied heavily on legal transplants had to be reminded of the complex and disappointing history of legal transplantation. And those who thought that reform ended with the passage of new laws needed to be lectured on the historic gap between the law on the books and the law in action.

Challenging the model itself. But doubts about the enterprise went beyond questions of timing and strategies for transplantation. There were real questions about the kind of "rule of law" that would result. Critics expressed concern about the results that would come from successful implantation of the initial rule of law model.

These more fundamental criticisms might be divided into two broad types. The first were those who agreed with the basic ideas behind the ROL enterprise, focused on the economy, but accepted a somewhat broader role for law and legal institutions than the strict, neoliberal market vision that took center stage in the first phase. Early ROL ideas rested on a particular view of the role for the state in the economy. They presupposed severe restrictions on economic regulation. Private law was presented as a neutral framework with no distributional effect. The model did include protection for human rights, but these included rights to property as well as political and civil rights, and property was emphasized. The role of the judiciary was to police the boundaries between state and market, and it was thought they would do this through a mechanistic formalism.

Critics could note that such a model was at odds with the actual existing arrangements in all advanced capitalist states. They could point out that these countries used law to intervene in markets in myriad ways to correct market failures and allocate risk. They could also note that actually existing legal systems in established market economies vary in many dimensions, and that there was no single model or set of best practices that could be copied, even if, despite the prior experience with transplants, copying could be done effectively.

While this second criticism fell well within the mainstream of liberal thought about law and development, a more radical strand may also be discerned. The more radical position would embrace the first two critiques, but go beyond them. For those who took this view, the "rule of law" should promote solidarity as well as efficiency. And they saw the law and its "rule" more as an arena in which the struggles for various values and interests could go on than as a fixed entity rigidly cabined by formal rules and processes or a technocratic machine limited exclusively to correcting market failures.

Revealing contradictions in the amalgam. If we look at the body of thought that arose in the first stage (ROL-1), we can see that it represented an uneasy amalgam of potentially contradictory strands. Emerging from an unstable alliance of the project of markets and the project of democracy, the latent within the amalgam were serious tensions. Initially, these were masked by the vagueness of the idea of the rule of law, a term sufficiently general so that different meanings might be and were read into it by partisans of differing visions.

Of course, there were areas of real overlap between the visions of the two projects: thus both believed in the idea of an independent judiciary that would serve as a shield against arbitrary state action. And it may be that both sides felt a need to play down differences in the interest of interesting policy makers in the part of the vision that they really shared. But as time has gone on, and critics have poured cynical acid on some of the initial ideas of the initial ROL effort, the contradictions always latent in ROL-1 and the neoliberal development model have become clearer. These include contradictions between:

FORMALISM AND PRAGMATISM. ROL-1 stressed the importance of a neutral framework for growth, judicial autonomy, and adherence to the rule of law while simultaneously championing the need for an instrumental approach to law, pragmatic problem solving, and policy science. Thus, it contained an unstable amalgam of legal formalism and a postrealist legal culture that not only rejected formalism, but *denied that formalism is a realizable goal.* According to the legal realist tenets embedded in postrealist pragmatist thinking about law, legal orders, private as well as public, are inherently indeterminate. As a result, any effort to revive formalism and pretend otherwise was mystification. As a result, pragmatists not only rejected the formalist option but claimed it was a myth behind which rules were being manipulated. As time goes on, the contradictions between these two inherently inconsistent strands of legal culture have become clearer.[10]

ECONOMIC CONSTITUTIONALISM AND DEMOCRATIC EMPOWERMENT. The ROL-1 amalgam favored strong constitutional or quasi-constitutional protections for basic economic freedoms including property rights, freedom of

[10] *See* Frank Upham, *Myth-Making in the Rule of Law Orthodoxy*, Working Paper No. 30, Carnegie Endowment for International Peace Rule of Law Series (2002).

contract, and protection against excessive and arbitrary regulation. At the same time, stress was placed on expanding access to justice, popular empowerment, and more democratic forms of governance. At some point, these two approaches were bound to clash if democratically elected governments chose to regulate their economies and intervene in market processes.

MARKET-ORIENTED GROWTH AND DIRECT POVERTY ALLEVIATION. The ROL-1 amalgam arose at a time when the faith in markets to spur growth and lift all boats was at its apogee. ROL accepted poverty alleviation as a goal, but in the robust version of this faith, there was no need for direct action for poverty alleviation as this would result from growth itself – yet another "spillover" idea in a field plagued by such notions. Needless to say, as time went on and the promised growth did not always materialize, or materialized but did not automatically lift all boats, this contradiction also has become more apparent.

EFFICIENCY AND DISTRIBUTION. In the ROL-1 amalgam, stress was placed on law's role in making the economy more efficient, but little was said about distribution. There were two different reasons why distributional issues were down-played. First, according to formalist thinking, the rule of law simply creates a framework for efficient allocation of resources and does not itself have distributional consequences. Second, in robust neoliberal economic thought, distributional issues are generally downplayed. But, as some in the ROL enterprise have brought to light, the inevitable distributional effects of all legal rules and institutions, and also seen the desirability of direct forms of intervention for distributional purposes, issues of distribution have reappeared in the debate.

GLOBALIZATION AND ENDOGENOUS GROWTH. Two cardinal aspects of robust neoliberalism are that everyone will benefit from greater global economic integration, and foreign investment and export-led growth are the best development strategies. In this vision, a primary goal for the rule of law is to make national economies more attractive to foreign investors. To that end, property and other economic rights should be protected and government intervention limited. At the same time, this vision stresses the importance of measures of legal harmonization and elimination of any discrimination against foreigners so that national economies can be more easily linked to larger global or regional economic entities. But as evidence came in to show that liberalization can hurt some sectors of the population, and that some economies had grown successfully while placing limits on foreign investment and stress on internal market development, the tension between globalization and economic fairness has surfaced.

ROL stage II: Cracks in the monolithic view of development and law

As one looks at policy developments and at the burgeoning law and development literature, it looks as if we are entering a new stage in the ROL era. To be sure, many of the elements of the first stage are still with us. But in recent years, critics have brought to light problems with the neoliberal Washington Consensus approach to growth and raised doubts about some aspects the program of law reform initially associated with that approach. These changes and doubts, when coupled with other developments, show that the project is more complex – and more problematic – than initially thought. As the L&D veterans feared, the project of institution building has proven more difficult than imagined. The idea that market development would by itself spur institutional reform has proven an illusion: it is one more "spillover" idea refuted by experience: we have learned that, markets do not create the conditions for their own success. All the problems of transplantation discovered decades ago have belatedly been recognized. Finally, there is a growing recognition that the original compromise between the projects of markets and the project of democracy papered over contradictions now becoming more apparent.

Changes in development policy. The first big change has come about in the broader sphere of development policy. Doubt has arisen concerning the ease of implementing policies and institutional changes dictated by the Washington Consensus. This has led to much greater attention to issues of reform sequencing, and to a recognition that active planning and implementation are needed to implement even the most neoliberal, free market order. But this questioning has gone beyond issues of timing and implementation: some more or less within the mainstream have also questioned some of the policies themselves. They have criticized the exclusive emphasis on export led growth; the strong bias against regulatory intervention; the idea that there is one and only one road to development that works for all economies; the idea that full and immediate capital market liberalization is highly desirable; the lack of concern for strong social safety nets.

As a result, a chastened neoliberalism may be emerging. In this vision the "big bang" is to be discouraged and privatization and markets phased in gradually; export led growth policies will be tempered with concern for domestic markets; limits allowed on foreign investment; state intervention permitted but only when necessary to correct market failure; and targeted poverty reduction and limited safety nets allowed.

Official ideas about the "rule of law" become complexified. The second change has occurred in official thinking about law. One can see signs that development institutions have begun to question some of the ideas that were taken as holy writ in the first stage of ROL. Mainstream voices are heard questioning formalism; raising doubts about rigid constitutional constraints on state action; recognizing failures of transplants and top-down reform; stressing need for context-specific project development; accepting need for long time horizons; recognizing the need to add labor rights, women's rights, and environmental protection to contract, property, bankruptcy, and economic regulation; acknowledging need for special efforts to ensure access to justice; and questioning the adequacy of the field's knowledge base.

Thus, the World Bank has recently expressed doubts about the earlier commitment to formalism:

> A new conventional wisdom about the rule of law and development seems to have taken root in development circles. It is asserted that formalist rule of law, which stresses institutionalized legal mechanisms and absolute autonomy from politics, is a necessity for economic development. But attempts to transplant formalist rule of law to developing and/or democratizing countries could actually be counterproductive for economic, institutional, and political development, especially when informal mechanisms would be more effective and efficient.[11]

Similarly, in a recent note posted on the Bank's legal institutions website, we see an emerging recognition of the complexity of the relationship between formalism, judicial autonomy, and development:

> The economic impact of a particular set of institutions often depends on context. For example, certain institutions make it difficult for the government to institute policy changes. In some contexts, this is beneficial for economic development, since it makes government commitments more credible.... On the other hand, in times of economic crisis or rapid change, these same institutions can hinder a government's ability to respond effectively. An independent constitutional court may encourage foreign investment by ensuring the executive does not arbitrarily seize property, but if it were to prevent the rapid adoption of policies needed to counteract a financial crisis, it might also discourage investment.[12]

These cracks in the monolithic views of the first stage of ROL parallel changes in thinking about development policy in general. Even those who think that it is possible to create perfect markets now see that such a program involves time-consuming and arduous efforts at institutional reform. But as it becomes apparent that there will always be market failures of various forms, justifying some degree of regulatory intervention, emphasis is shifting toward various forms of regulatory and administrative law. These were far from central to the vision of the first stage of ROL. Finally, the recognition that there are different legitimate paths to growth casts doubt both on the "one size fits all" idea and the sure faith in legal transplants.

Expansion of the reform agenda and refinement of methods. The changes in official views have led to changes in the reform agenda and the nature of projects now being undertaken. A quick survey of recent developments at

[11] World Bank, Legal Institutions of a Global Economy Homepage, http://www1.worldbank.org/publicsector/legal/index.htm.

[12] *Id.*

the World Bank indicates that at least some in this institution have started to rethink the paradigm. There, one can find:

- explicit recognition of the failures of transplants and of top-down methods;
- rejection of a one-size-fits-all approach and stress on the need for context-specific project development based on consultation of all "stakeholders";
- awareness that legal reform requires a long time horizon and cannot be carried out quickly;
- recognition of the importance of the rule of law for poorer segments of the population;
- support for rule of law projects that deal with labor rights, women's rights, and environmental protection; and
- acceptance of the need to make access to justice an explicit dimension of judicial reform projects.

However, as Santos points out, the Bank is not a monolith and it is premature to say that these remarks presage real change.[13]

Questioning the knowledge base. A final aspect of the current scene is that questions have begun to arise about the knowledge base on which the whole enterprise has been built. While the World Bank has acknowledged that it made mistakes in the past, its current publications stress that there is now a strong knowledge base and effective methodology to guide rule of law projects. However, even sympathetic outside observers have questioned this assurance. In a recent paper, Thomas Carothers, head of the Democracy and Rule of Law Project at the Carnegie Endowment for International Peace, challenged official thinking on a range of issues.[14] Where the World Bank is quite confident about its ROL credos, to the point of producing tables that quantify the amount of rule of law and show that the more ROL, the higher national per capital income,[15] Carothers struck a more skeptical note. He questioned the validity of key aspects of conventional ROL wisdom such as whether:

- the rule of law is necessary to attract foreign investment;
- technical improvements in the administration of justice are necessary for democracy; and
- the court system is the core of "the rule of law."

Carothers made clear that, despite the expansion of the reform agenda and the refinement of methods, ROL projects remained tied to a Western model – one might add an *idealized* Western model – in which the core of the rule of

[13] *See* Alvaro Santos' chapter in this volume.

[14] Thomas Carothers, *Promoting the Rule of Law Abroad: The Problem of Knowledge*, Working Paper No. 34, Carnegie Endowment for Int'l Peace Rule of Law Series (2003).

[15] World Bank, *supra* note 9.

law is thought be the an independent judiciary applying neutral rules in an objective manner and to the belief that the creation of such an institution will directly and unproblematically accomplish a wide range of goals from market development to poverty alleviation. Carothers suggested that despite rhetoric to the contrary, the development agencies have learned very little from their experiences and there are substantial obstacles to any systematic learning process in this field.

BEYOND CRITIQUE: WHAT FUTURE FOR THE RULE OF LAW?

Shifts in views about development and the cracks that have emerged in the original rule of law orthodoxy suggest that things are more open and fluid than they once seemed. Critics of the Washington Consensus and the legal orthodoxy it engendered have succeeded in opening up the discourse. The moment seems more open, the discourse more fluid.

But doubts remain. Are we dealing with a situation in which small concessions have been made to other ways of thinking about both law and development, but a hard orthodox core remains? Or is this a time when new ideas and new strategies might have a chance to be taken seriously? The World Bank has expanded its reform agenda and rejected the most blatant errors of implementation. It has added some "social concerns" to the economic rights core of its vision. But the Bank's view of "ROL" is still grounded on strong assumptions about the nature of law, the relationship between law and development, and the relevance of Western models, however contextualized. So the question is: in this period of rethinking and partial doubt, is there a real chance for the recognition of alternative development strategies and of very different legal paths that can be followed on the road to economic growth and political freedom? Is it possible, for example, that acceptance of pragmatism could replace faith in formalism, however "neo" the formalism may be; democratic empowerment take precedence over economic constitutionalism; poverty alleviation be a goal in itself rather than a result of "trickle down" policies or token project additions; distributive concerns be highlighted in policy making and the construction of legal rules and institutions; and a better balance struck between economic integration and endogenous growth?

My view is that there is an opening for the introduction of new ideas. I see the present as a turning point, a moment in which it is possible to go beyond critique of orthodoxy to reconstruction. Thus I think that progressive intellectuals should engage constructively with the ROL enterprise. I support such values as human dignity, equality, and fairness that are embedded in the idea of the rule of law. I recognize that actually existing legal systems do not necessarily embody these values, and to some degree can deny them while professing to uphold them. But we also know that these actually existing legal institutions are arenas in which the struggle for such values can go on in relatively bloodless ways.

That suggests that the struggle for progressive goals can be compatible with efforts to create something called "the rule of law." And it raises the possibility that ROL development projects could be shaped to serve the whole population, not just the economic elite. There are groups in the developing world who seek to do just that. Intellectuals in the north have an opportunity – and an obligation – to work with them to identify the perils and open up the possibilities of this present.

4 THE "RULE OF LAW," POLITICAL CHOICES, AND DEVELOPMENT COMMON SENSE

*David Kennedy**

Although we easily intuit that development policy making is saturated with political significance, political choices are often presented in vocabularies of economic and legal expertise that obscure the political stakes of development policy making. This chapter retells the postwar history of economic and legal expertise in the development field to highlight the possibility – and also the difficulty – of reclaiming its political significance.

I use the term political in two senses. Experts act politically when they *distribute resources among groups and individuals* – we can decode the politics of this work by associating expert choices with the interests of groups that contest one another's claims on resources in the arenas we think of as political: men and women, rich and poor, rural and urban, North and South, agricultural and industrial. Experts also act politically when they *affect the distribution of power among ideological positions* that we associate with political contestation: left, center, and right.

I tell the history of development common sense in four phases: a postwar modest interventionist consensus (1945–1970); followed by a period of crisis and retrenchment (1970–1980); a new consensus on transition from socialism, first in the third world, and then in the second (1980–1995); followed by a period of doubt, reexamination, and eclecticism (1995-the present) during which the neoliberal "Washington Consensus" has been chastened in numerous ways.

Although my goal is to decode the politics of expertise in each phase, like my coauthors, I say very little about how thinking in these phases was linked to

* My understanding of the evolving legal and economic expertise of development professionals has been enormously influenced by work and ideas shared by Duncan Kennedy and David Trubek, by my teachers Robert Meagher and Robert West, and by numerous friends and students who have been generous with their time and insights. Particular thanks to: Yishai Blanc, Alvaro Santos, Jorge Esquirol, Robert Wai, Amr Shalakany, Hani Sayed, Helena Alviar, Liliana Obregon, Arnulf Becker, James Gathii, Tony Anghie, Kerry Rittich, Leo Specht, Carlos Gouvea, and John Ohnesorge.

broader social and political events. We all suggest that the postwar consensus had something to do with broader ideas about the welfare state, embedded liberalism, the larger postwar international legal, institutional and economic order, and the possibilities opened by the Cold War. We link thinking in the 1970s intuitively to 1968, to the oil crisis, to the debt crisis, or to Vietnam. We treat it as part of a broader loss of faith in government, in the first world as in the third, and to interpretations (often wrong) about why so many countries had not developed while others – the Asian tigers in particular – had. The Washington Consensus of the 1980s and early 1990s seems inexplicable without mention of Thatcher and Reagan, and the broad discrediting of left and center-left welfare state policies in the first world. Its hold on the field seems linked to the new personnel and new terrain opened up for law and development by the shift from third world development to transition policies in ex-socialist states after 1989. The current moment of chastening seems to arise from perceptions of the failures of early transition policies. It is conventionally associated with Blair and Clinton, and often with the Asian and Latin American currency crises of the early nineties, or the new visibility for political resistance to globalization across the third world. It is often linked to criticism in intellectual circles, particularly among leading economists, of the neoliberal *idea* as a strategy for development or for transition. But these are loose suggestions, reminders of the context within which, or in relation to which, development expertise unfolded.

Nevertheless, these associations are helpful reminders that the difference between historical periods can seem to be replete with political significance. Indeed, it is now common to think of the postwar period of import substitution industrialization as "left," the crisis period of the seventies as a failed experiment in more "radical left" thinking, the neoliberalism of the 1980s as a "right" reaction, and the current period of retrenchment as one of "centrist" balance and eclecticism. There is certainly something to this.

It is also true that development professionals in every period drew from only part of the available political spectrum. It would not be overgeneralizing to say that development experts in the postwar period were political centrists – anticommunist, social democrats of one or another variety. Few were part of any political vanguard. With very few exceptions, the same could be said of the seventies, as the range of political positions in the larger global intelligentsia became broader and more volatile. Although some leading development thinkers of the neoliberal period were in the vanguard of a new, energetic – even revolutionary – right, for the most part, development policy experts were modest reformers and status quo defenders of the remnants of postwar policy making. In the current period, the spectrum among development experts runs from center left to center right, with but a few outliers on either end.

In all periods, development professionals sometimes experienced themselves, at least indirectly, to be engaged in a "political" project. If we think of politics as "distribution," there is no question that postwar development policy experts thought themselves to be engaged directly in the distribution of resources – they saw their own role in political terms. Ideologically, they understood themselves to be promoting social democracy, opposing communism. Developmentalists in the 1970s were also conscious of their political role – whether as first world defenders of a market democracy attuned to "basic needs" or as exponents of broad third-worldist and nonalignment ideologies associated with the heritage of Bandung. Some neoliberal reformers of the 1980s – and many in the post-1989 period – experienced their development policy making as part of a political vanguard, reversing what they saw as a global trend to socialism begun after the First World War, and associated as much with the name Keynes as that of Marx or Stalin. Many contemporary developmentalists understand themselves to be correcting for the excesses of the neoliberal "right" in the name of a softer, more humane and center or center-left political line.

At the same time, development professionals have also thought of their work in each period in nonpolitical terms – as the work of experts. They advised politicians, on the basis of "knowledge" about how to develop. In the postwar period, expertise advised distributional rearrangements of a society's resources – taking from agriculture and giving to industry, say. But these recommendations were less political choices or exercises of discretion than imperatives of their expertise. In the neoliberal period, the distinction was drawn more sharply still – the point was to maximize growth by enabling private allocation of resources to their most productive use – after growth was achieved, the politicians could "redistribute" the gains as they thought fit. Development was a matter of efficiency, not distribution or allocation. In the contemporary period, the vocabulary of needs and rights has brought distributional issues back to the fore, cast not as political choices but as the interpretation of preexisting entitlements and human needs. Both the neoliberals of the 1980s and their contemporary successors see it as a virtue to avoid making distributive choices, leaving them to the "market," while confining their work to correcting for "market failures," implementing consensus "human rights," eliminating "corruption," or reinforcing purely "formal" legal norms. In the same way, development professionals tend not to interpret their expert work in ideological terms – far more, they are the purveyors of something more like science, understood to pose more nuanced choices and more neutral and objective criteria for making them than "left," or "right," or "center."

This doubled self-conception makes it difficult to interpret the "politics" of development expertise with confidence. The problem is made still more difficult by the fact that in each period, right, left, and center regimes have shared the dominant mode of development thinking. At the same time, regimes in each period sharing a broadly similar approach to development were self-consciously distributed along a left-center-right axis. There were right wing import substitution regimes and left wing neoliberal regimes. We should be wary, of course, in taking the ideological labels leaders use to describe their own regimes at face value. The same is true for development experts. When they argue with one another, they often make assertions about the political implications of one or another position for the distribution of resources among groups or for the ideological authority of left, center, or right. But experts are notorious for overstating – and misunderstanding – the significance of differences between and within projects enunciated in their common expertise. In this chapter, I track the changing relationship between economic and legal ideas in development expertise to make a first stab at unraveling the mystery of their possible political associations.

PHASE ONE: POSTWAR CONSENSUS 1945–1970

The priority of economic ideas

Postwar common sense development economics emerged from dominant strands of economic thinking more broadly. At the time, mainstream economics was neoclassical in orientation. The marginal revolution had been won, the first wave of institutionalist economics (Commons) had been largely discarded, the second wave (Arrow, North, Williamson) remained in the future. The Coaseian revolution was only just beginning. Keynes remained a lodestar for thinking about macroeconomic policy, and macroeconomics continued to dominate microeconomics in thinking about what government and law should be about.

As a result, economists came to "development" sharing ideas about what an economy is – and about what economic development is. They assumed that economies were *national*, and that preindustrial economies differed fundamentally from industrialized economies. Since Adam Smith, they had seen specialization and the division of labor as the keys to increases in productivity. They saw an economy as an enormous cycle of inputs and outputs in which labor is deployed with a given technology and capital stock to produce income. When income is saved and made available for investment, the capital stock increases, permitting higher productivity in successive cycles.

They interpreted the productivity increases of the industrial revolution as a model of and definition for development. Development meant "modernization" – repeating the transformations that had occurred in the North during the industrial revolution. Only through industrialization did it seem possible to reproduce the North's productivity gains. Modernization required a sudden acceleration of the input-output cycle – the goal for economic theory was to figure out how this happens and how it could be made to happen in premodern societies.

Ricardo had taught them to focus on capital accumulation – savings and investment. Social organization and technology matter, but like the labor supply, they thought, are relatively fixed. Other things being equal, they were convinced that a given savings rate would correspond to a specific and generally stable equilibrium level of national income. The key to the rapid growth associated with industrialization was an increase in savings. Societies remained underdeveloped because their savings rate trapped them in a low-level equilibrium – they had insufficient capital to break out, to industrialize, and to begin an upward cycle of productivity gains. The key, therefore, was to identify a source of capital – a surplus in the economy – that could be harnessed to industrialization. At first, they focused on encouraging – or forcing – local savings, and on foreign aid. Later, they added the exploitation of natural resources, where possible, and the mobilization for industrial production of currently underemployed – "surplus" – rural labor.

They tended to downplay the export of primary products or inward foreign investment as sources of capital for development. There were capital shortages throughout the developed world, and capital mobility was restricted both by national law and by relatively primitive global banking and payment systems. In any event, it seemed unlikely that the gains from foreign investment could reliably be captured and redeployed for development without undermining the incentive to invest. They were also pessimistic about Less Developing Country (LDC) exports – the tropical product market seemed saturated, industrial exports seemed unlikely to be competitive. Less developed economies were likely, they thought, to be price takers while experiencing unstable prices for their exports.

They understood that mobilizing the surplus, and capturing gains for reinvestment, would mean taking resources from some groups, individuals, or economic sectors, and allocating them elsewhere. Getting distribution right was central. They were acutely aware that entire sectors could face diminishing returns if, say, landlords were to hoard or squander rather than reinvest rents. It was the task of policy to ensure that the surplus, once identified, was properly deployed, and that the gains were indeed captured for reinvestment.

Postwar development professionals had innumerable debates, both about the details of this broad economic model, and about its consequences for policy, both generally and in particular contexts. At the level of economic theory, they debated whether a single "big push" was necessary and sufficient to move a national economy to "take off" toward industrialization. Are there specific points in the economic cycle – bottlenecks – that when opened or closed will have exponential effects up- or downstream? When is it sensible to force disequilibrium to release these effects? Where are we likely to find useful forward or backward "linkages" in the economic cycle? Overall, is "balanced growth" more or less effective than prioritizing particular sectors? How significant are "tipping points" and how can they be identified? How precise do we need to be to generate a virtuous cycle? How sensitive is the economic cycle to overly rapid expansion or contraction – how precisely must macroeconomic policy be calibrated? Is the equilibrium a "knife edge" we might well ride up or down? How significant are positive cross-sector externalities in multiplying productivity gains at the moment of takeoff? Will industrialization follow the same stages in LDCs as it did in the North in the industrial revolution? What were those stages? Are there latecomer advantages to exploit or disadvantages to avoid?

Sometimes, these questions of economic theory translated rather directly into debates about policy. Which sectors should be subsidized, which taxed? Control of which prices offers the best chance to stimulate positive forward and backward linkages? Should we focus on forced savings, labor mobilization, or natural resource exploitation? How should scarce hard currency be allocated? Should we aim to balance industrial and agricultural growth, or divert resources from one to the other?

And of course, there were also debates about innumerable practical questions of method – how should returns be captured for reinvestment? – Through taxation? Where, and of what? How should this best be accomplished – price controls? Subsidies? Credit allocations? Licenses? Taxation? How should the traditional and agricultural sector be mobilized to subsidize the emerging industrial sector? Wage rates? Price controls? Government purchasing monopolies? How important was land reform – and how should it be structured? Land taken how, from whom, compensated how, distributed to whom, with what forms of tenure?

Although these economic ideas formed a background common sense among development policy professionals, these were not the only ideas on the table. This is a winner's map. At the time, these ideas were contested within economics. Keynesian macroeconomics was contested by Marxist economists, by neoclassical economists who focused on microeconomics, and by institutionalists. Had these alternative ideas been taken up, development policymakers might have focused more on the international economy, less on national government policy, or more on small scale and local cultural, legal, or informal arrangements.

Moreover, there were those who did not think about development in economic terms in the first place. Dissent came from the fields of political economy, sociology, and anthropology. Throughout the postwar period, noneconomic ideas about development faced an uphill struggle to be heard. Only in the 1960s and 1970s do we see them struggling to get in – in debates about "basic needs" or "social rights," or about ways to measure development, or about maintaining data on income distributions, levels of education and health alongside, or factored into, measures of development.

Today, the easy target in the postwar consensus seems the large role proposed for national state administrations – a recipe for corruption, rent seeking, and all manner of inefficient price distortions. At the time, however, the most salient targets were different. Critics focused on the presumption that the *national economy* was sufficiently autonomous to be the primary site for development policy, and that *industrialization* was necessary and desirable.

Some dissidents emphasized the significance of the larger world and what they saw as relations of structural dependency between the "core and periphery." For these "dependency" economists, the keys to the "development of underdevelopment" were declining terms of trade for third world economies and the relative price inelasticity and instability of primary product markets. For "world systems" political theorists, third world poverty was produced and maintained by bargaining power inequalities and a tacit alliance of world capital, first world governments, and multinational corporations to maintain an exploitative regime of "neocolonialism" throughout the newly decolonized third world.

For other dissidents, the problem was an insensitivity to local cultural endowments. For institutionalist economists, the mainstream was wrong to focus on savings rather than technology, on the management of prices rather than the reframing and harnessing of cultural attitudes and practices. They urged attention to the effects of cultural changes on economic processes – particularly the effect of changing differences between the traditional and modern sector. They urged study of the ways in which institutions and cultural commitments could hinder or stimulate cycles of cumulative causation necessary for development. Simultaneously, a range of local socialist or cooperativist experiments were initiated across the third world.

Similar institutionalist and localist themes were echoed by analysts from other fields – particularly sociology and anthropology – but with a less optimistic twist. Industrialization posed a threat to local culture, accentuated gender inequality, solidified apartheid-like divisions in the plural societies of the third world, and prevented the emergence of a national social will and ethic of collective responsibility and solidarity.

Unlike mainstream development economics, these alternative ideas did not translate well into policy options. There were exceptions, of course. David Trubek reports, for example, that the economic institutionalism of John Commons and others was influential in the USAID funded land reform institute established at the University of Wisconsin in the 1960s. By and large, however, these more alternative strands of thought seemed too pessimistic to be helpful. If the problem was "global," or the whole idea of "development" was a cultural disaster, it is harder to figure out what to do. These dissident ideas seemed to require policy at another level – global efforts to stabilize commodity markets, or strengthen the bargaining power of third world labor, capital, and government authorities in their relations with multinational corporations and first world governments.

TABLE 1. **Postwar Consensus 1945–1970**

Left counterpoint	Center and mainstream	Right
"Left-wing" modest interventionism	Modest interventionism	"Right-wing" modest interventionism
Plus:		
Dependency/world systems and institutionalism/ culturalism/localism	Host to its own left-right-center debate	

We might redraw the postwar common sense as shown in Table 1.

Implicit legal theory: The demand for law

We need to reverse engineer the legal theory of mainstream development professionals from their economic and political projects, and from the attitudes toward law they manifested in managing development policies within national administrations. A great deal of law was required to translate the leading economic theories of development into policy. "Import substitution" industrialization demanded the creation of numerous public law institutions, established by statute and implemented by public law bureaucracies: exchange controls, credit licensing schemes, tariffs, subsidy programs, tax incentives, price controls, national commodity monopolies, and so forth. Legislation was necessary to establish tariffs, subsidies, exchange controls, marketing boards, and all the other elements of the system. A vastly expanded administrative apparatus, with rule making, licensing, and other legal authority would need to be set up.

In most newly independent developing societies, this expanding legal regime was new, and brought with it new legal ideas – replacing colonial law, overturning customary law, and offering a largely public law framework for economic exchange. In the Latin American societies that had embarked on this path already before the war, this program had also come with a new set of legal ideas.

The implicit "legal theory" combined a number of ideas. In broad terms, law was understood to be *instrumental* and *purposive*. The purposes came from elsewhere – from the society, government, and the legislature. Law was subordinate to social purposes – implementing, fulfilling, and accomplishing the objectives of the society, rather than expressing a priori limits or historic commitments to be respected or purposes of its own to be achieved.

The purpose of the legal order itself was the consolidation of national economic and political authority – often associated with national self-determination and decolonization – rather than, say, the integration of local economic life into a global economy, or the facilitation of private exchange and private ordering through supplemental regulatory interventions. To the extent legal arrangements were understood to have a social purpose, the purpose was something like national "development" – law was to be interpreted to achieve the developmental purposes of the state. Where these were not express, they could be derived from analysis of the social and economic needs of the society, given its stage of economic development. Distribution was understood to be central to the work of law – allocating resources among social and economic groups – from agriculture to industry, from foreign to local financial institutions – to implement national economic policy objectives.

Within the legal order, public law was far more salient than private law. When people thought of "law," they thought about *legislation* and the pronouncements of the legislature or executive, rather than customary law, contract or property law and the pronouncements of judges. Postwar development professionals were quite optimistic about public law and about the capacity of complex administrative systems to translate policy objectives into action – to control borders, implement tariff schedules, suppress black markets, control prices, or collect taxes.

To use the vocabulary Duncan Kennedy introduces in his contribution to this volume, these are the legal ideas of the "second globalization" – the "antiformalist social" legal theory Kennedy claims entered legal consciousness first in Europe and then in the United States during the prewar period. This set of legal ideas characterized the consciousness of development economists influenced by New Deal style welfare states in the United States and Europe. In many parts of the developing world, they seemed a workable substitute for the classical legal thought associated with the colonial legacy of the Commonwealth. They had been adopted enthusiastically by the international institutions most associated with development in the prewar period – the International Labor Organization and the League of the Mandates Commission or the Bruce Report. In Latin America, they had entered legal consciousness from France, often through the emerging fields of both labor law and international law, and were often understood to reflect a particularly "American" or national revolutionary identity.

We might think of development policy asking two sorts of questions of law and legal theory: instrumentally, how can I translate my policy objectives into action, and what limits must I observe in doing so? In this period, the answer to the first we might call *legal pragmatism,* associated with "social" conceptions of law developed in the interwar period. This legal pragmatism stressed the importance of purposive reasoning to link legal arrangements with social needs and objectives, and focused attention on legislatures and administrative bureaucracies as the creators, consumers, and interpreters of law. A wide range of previously settled fields of law were opened to new legislation and interpretation in furtherance of "social" objectives of national "solidarity" required for economic development.

The law was understood to place few limits on development policy. Of course, all these new legal arrangements were unsettling to existing legal entitlements – think of land reform and the property rights of large landowners. The legal vocabulary of "rights" has often been used to slow the emergence of new economic policies. During this period, however, this was infrequent. The main legal idea that prevented acquired "rights" from seeming to present much of an obstacle to development policy was legislative and administrative positivism – the idea that the state could regulate as it pleased, altering private rights, without judicial review.

In the United States, New Deal social regulation had, of course, been systematically opposed, and for some time limited, through judicial review. Judges struck down administrative and legislative initiatives in the name of "rights" to freedom of contract and property that were understood in terms Kennedy associates with the "classical" period of the late nineteenth century. In the United States, elements of classical legal thought developed in the context of private law and had been imported into public law thinking, and were used to define the limits of various public authorities vis à vis one another. As a result, they were readily available to constrain public law expressions of national economic policy.

To counter this resistance, American legal realists developed a range of critical analytic tools to demonstrate in particular cases – before courts – that "rights" were neither clear nor compelling enough to require limits on regulatory initiatives by judicial deduction. Some of these analytic tools were present in the "social" ideas about law that underlay postwar import substitution policies in the developing world – regimes of private right were understood to have numerous conflicts, gaps, and ambiguities, which could be interpreted by reference to social needs and purposes. But the absence of judicial review and the presence of strong assumptions of legislative and administrative positivism made American legal realism an unnecessary import. The judicial assertion of rights against postwar development policies was by and large a nonproblem.

Although these basic "social" or "pragmatic" ideas about law were central to the policy imaginations of mainstream development professionals, the more detailed disputes among legal theorists *within* this common set of ideas were far less important. Legal theorists differed on numerous elements of this broad legal framework – precisely what does legislative supremacy entail, how should it be translated into administrative rule making, how and where should discretion be lodged? How should purposive interpretation be reconciled with more traditional methods of professional legal reasoning? Where in the legal fabric should one insert "social" concerns? How might social needs and purposes be reflected in legal rules – what exceptions would be necessary, what new legal forms and institutions would be required? What did Kelsen mean here – what should we take Pound to have meant there? But these legal theory debates were generally far removed from debates about development policy, and were rarely linked directly to them. Development policy was made by politicians and development experts, in the vocabulary of economics. Their legal ideas remained implicit, and debates within the legal academy largely passed them by.

At the same time, these were certainly not the only ideas about law in the air. But alternative legal ideas were rarely mobilized to contest mainstream development policy. Some jurists focused on judges and on private rather than public law. But they generally simply kept their distance from the expansion of administrative bureaucracy and legislation. Although their ideas – ideas from "classical legal thought" to use Kennedy's terminology – might have been mobilized for dissent from mainstream development policies, this seems to have been quite rare during the postwar period. Such jurists were more likely to confine themselves to their private law subject matter, perhaps focusing on comparative or historical research, or stressing their legal culture's ties to European and Roman law traditions. The tendency was to leave "national development policy" with its messy economic and political choices to others. Private law ideas and elements of the consciousness of classical legal thought would only later be mobilized to resist mainstream development policy.

There were also legal theorists, often associated with one or another strand of Marxism, who focused more on the political and social role of law. For them, the name Polanyi was more significant than Kelsen or Pound. In this period, however, their legal thinking did not differ from mainstream legal ideas in its support for import substitution development policies. It would only be later that Polanyi's account of law during the industrial revolution as a useful brake permitting the wrenching changes brought by industrialization to be politically metabolized, would seem promising to development professionals – often influenced by economic institutionalism – who sought to challenge mainstream development policies.

Having excavated the implicit "legal theory" of development professionals in the postwar period, we face an uncertain and complex undertaking identifying its politics. If we think in ideological terms, "antiformalist social" ideas about law now seem everywhere associated with the political left. Like the development policies associated with them, however, at the time they were common to left, center, and right regimes. This can be difficult for United Statesean legal scholars, unused to comparative analysis of legal method, to grasp. In the United States, the historic association of antiformalism with the New Deal defeat of Lockner-style restrictions on public law and economic regulation has given these ideas a leftish feel for generations. Of course, even in the U.S. context, we have seen antiformalist ideas harnessed to ideological projects across the political spectrum.

The impact of implicit legal ideas is extremely difficult to identify – let alone analyze in political terms. The implicit legal theory of postwar development professionals *may* have encouraged policymakers to overestimate

TABLE 2. Mainstream: 1945–1970

Basic ideas: economics	**Development policy set**	**Legal theory "Antiformalist social"**	
		Instrumental thinking	*Rights thinking*
Modest interventionism	Large regulatory state	Legal pragmatism law = policy	Legislative positivism
Homogeneity among LDCs Heterogeneity vis à vis developed world	Import substitution industrialization (ISI) Various export promotion strategies	Social law, social purposes, and social needs Administrative law bureaucracy	No judicial review Legislative and administration supremacy Legal realism critique of deduction from rights

the ease with which social purposes could, in fact, be realized through law – how easily public law initiatives could be implemented, how effective state bureaucracies were. These implicit legal ideas may have made it more difficult to imagine alternative development strategies – the dominance of "antiformalist social" legal ideas may well have made it more difficult to think up neoliberal economic policies that would have relied more heavily on private law and private ordering. They may have made it easy to underestimate the difficulty of ensuring that "law in action" reflected the increasingly complex regulatory and administrative regimes "on the books." Or to miss the potential for what has become known as "government failure," widespread corruption, and rent seeking. These legal blindspots and biases may well, in particular contexts, have had effects we could associate with the interests of particular groups or ideological positions. Identifying them would, however, be a difficult and context-specific undertaking, requiring a set of ideas of its own about the nature of law and its links to policy and outcome. As with development economics common sense, the search for the politics of legal expertise takes us back to professional questions of legal and economic theory.

We might relate mainstream economic ideas, development policies, and legal theories as shown in Table 2.

The politics of postwar common sense

How might we assess the "politics" of this postwar common sense? At the time, the broad collection of "import substitution" policies encouraged by mainstream postwar development economics were adopted by all manner of third world regimes. Governments everywhere strengthened the national management of their economies through tariffs, currency controls, price controls, credit rationing, and so on. It is difficult to say too much about the ideological color of ideas and policies common to regimes that were themselves understood at the time to exemplify the right, left, and center.

When development experts look back on the postwar period, they tend to associate its successes and failures with what they interpret as a broadly "left" ideology. Neoliberals invoke the disappointing development records of many postwar regimes to illustrate the grave wages of left thought. As disappointment with neoliberalism grew, others remembered the successes of the postwar era to illustrate the promises of a more progressive, social democratic developmentalism. At the time, it was more difficult to characterize the ideas. To participants, they seemed sharply distinct from state socialism – looking back, the differences are less pronounced. There was no well-developed "right" alternative to these ideas at the time – there were right wing, even national socialist, versions of them.

One way to think about the politics of large bodies of ideas like this is to focus on their form. For some development experts, postwar developmentalism was a loose collection of tools, hints, observations, and possibilities – for others it was a far more formal, even scientific recipe for social transformation. One could think of "stages of growth" as an iron law of history, or as a helpful sociological observation. One could imagine "declining terms of trade" as something to watch out for, or as an unfolding global logic, necessarily reproducing the "development of underdevelopment" at the periphery. The words "formalism" and "structuralism" capture something of this set of differences. Modest interventionism could seem a rulelike and objective science, autonomous from social context – or a set of broad generalizations that could inform an expert's discretion in particular contexts. The forces promoting and impeding development might be mixed and contradictory – or part of a more systematic world "structure" of power.

In the postwar period, it would be fair to say that the more formalist and structuralist one tended to be when interpreting the economic and legal ideas about development, the less mainstream, the more extreme, one's politics were likely to be. At the time, large ideological debates between, say, first world and third world experts, or American and European experts, often took on a "who is more left" quality. These also often contrasted a more theoretically modest and eclectic mode of reasoning with a more formal and structuralist mode – the first seemed more centrist, the latter more radical and leftist. In later periods, similar issues of theoretical form differentiated centrist eclectism from more radical right-wing formalism and necessitarianism about the developmental consequences of a "free market." In both cases, the broad vocabulary was shared across the ideological divide – but the vocabulary hardened as one moved to the edge.

It is difficult to link these formal dimensions of developmental expertise to the consequences of policy making. Often, rigid structuralists and modest pragmatists defended quite similar policies – where the policies of left and center developmentalists did differ, it is hard to associate the policy differences with these differences in reasoning style.

Of course, there were real differences in outcomes among import substitution/modest interventionist regimes. The enormous economic growth achieved in the South during the postwar period was by no means evenly distributed, either between or within national economies. Many national economies developed, some sustained growth and industrialized, others fell back. Some sectors and some groups prospered, others did not. It is extremely difficult to correlate these differences with more or less formal or structuralist conceptions of the dominant economic or legal ideas. Retrospective studies have sometimes attributed successes and failures to factors largely exogenous to import substitution policy altogether – pre-War manufacturing experience, cultural industriousness, the degree of income inequality at the outset, the nature of the colonial legacy, the details of factor endowments, or the quality of government control mechanisms and the civil service. Others have attributed the failures to policy sets common to the successes and vice versa.

It is difficult to link such different results to the broad mainstream consensus about what development is and how it might be achieved. Did modest interventionism have it in for some social groups? Was it fated to steer some national economies to growth and others to bankruptcy? It is even more difficult to link these different outcomes to more and less formal or structuralist conceptions of the dominant economic or legal theories. Certainly much depended on implementation, and on the choices made *within* the modest interventionist vocabulary. There were all sorts of import substitution regimes, after all, and something must have been at stake in the differences.

It is no less complex to sort out the politics of postwar development common sense by looking to their distributional effects. In general terms, we can say that everywhere resources flowed from the countryside to the city, and from agriculture to industry. Everywhere the ideas of mainstream development economics influenced the structure of the elites – strengthening the hands of those with national policy-making responsibility, and encouraging the emergence of a bourgeois class dependent on regulatory gaps and accustomed to public subsidies and oversight. Everywhere, foreign direct investment was less favored than domestic savings, export industries were less favored than import substitution, industrialization was favored over services and agriculture. Capital movements were restricted, credit allocated, the banking sector subject to government ownership or intervention, and foreign banking restricted.

If we try to become more concrete, however, the situation is far less clear. It remains extremely difficult to link particular policy choices with particular distributional outcomes even in one place and time, let alone across an entire period. For one thing, effects varied widely. Sometimes the allocation of resources to local investors encouraged an entrepreneurial break-out, at other times comprador dependency. Transformations in agricultural patterns and new modes of work and living, did change the distribution of resources between men and women – but in all sorts of different directions. The expectation that secular interests would be strengthened over religious interests was sometimes born out – and also sometimes confounded. The same for traditional cultural institutions and beliefs – sometimes wiped out, sometimes left intact, strengthened, or given new shape. In some places, the monied elites developed a "franchise" rather than an "entrepreneurial" sensibility – in others we find a consolidation of national oligopolies.

Differences within this mainstream vision often did mark ideological differences. The ideological right and left signaled their differences from the mainstream center by preferences among policy alternatives within the mainstream vernacular – to whom would the surplus be allocated, what fate for rural landholders, industrial wages, foreign investment, and traditional economic sectors – what prices stabilized, at what levels, whom to tax, whom to allocate credit, and so forth. Industrial labor could be supported or taxed in different ways, just as quite different industrial sectors could be favored. At a broader level, a "big push" might imply greater levels of state intervention, more concentrated foreign aid, less scrutiny of the details of local development projects, and more short-term tolerance for overvalued local currency. The debate between "balanced" and "unbalanced" growth often carried a political association – "unbalanced" growth would require more administrative fine tuning, more oversight, and promised to be able to be accomplished on the cheap, through precisely targeted foreign aid or investment.

Yet, despite a self-conscious focus on distribution among groups, and the widespread use of this development vocabulary to mark ideological differences within various national political cultures, the politics of these ideas remains frustratingly difficult to pin down. Associating these choices with ideological positions turns out to be more difficult than it would seem – much depends on the way specific political forces define themselves ideologically in a particular country. The apparent ideological significance of such a choice often results from the ideological predilections of whatever social groups are thought to benefit from it – industrial workers, urban commercial interests, large land owners, and so forth. Of course, where political struggle in the capital was primarily a battle between, say industrial workers (left) and urban commercial, industrial, and financial interests (right), the left/right character of policy choices might well simply ignore consequences for other players – perhaps agricultural interests, peasant labor, or traditional landholders. Other interests – foreign capital, say, or agricultural workers – might only be present by proxy, as one or another group participating in national political struggles *associated itself* with their supposed interests.

Undoubtedly, there were politics to what was *missing* from this postwar consensus – groups and interests unlikely to be candidates for surplus generation or deployment, strategies that relied less on government than on private initiative, on foreign capital rather than domestic savings, and so forth. In ideological terms, what would become the *right* of neoliberalism was missing – with the consequence that no one stood cleanly for the moral virtues and economic benefits of market-oriented freedom. At the same time, the marginalization of institutionalism and dependency meant that options requiring international coordination or distribution, or which aimed to affect the distribution of gains from trade, were off the table. Factors that have since come to be thought central to development success – the need for prior industrial experience, relative income equality, the development of national firms (rather than subsidiaries), the importance of administrative targeting, feedback, and technology transfer – were given short shrift. And these omissions undoubtedly favored some, at a cost to others.

PHASE TWO: CRISIS 1970–1980

The lead slips from economics to politics

The decade of global economic stagnation that followed the Vietnam War, the 1972 oil shock, and American abandonment of the gold standard shifted the attention of development professionals from economics to politics. In an era of simultaneous inflation and recession, Keynesian ideas about macroeconomic management seemed less robust. In the developing world, a generation had passed since the first postwar "development plans" – and the results were extremely mixed. Some economies had developed, but many remained poor and were slipping further behind. Most seemed caught in an unpredictable middle zone, unable to advance further. Rising oil prices, export stagnation and a global climate of shifting exchange rates dramatically complicated macroeconomic management throughout the developing world, leading to spiraling and unsustainable debt burdens. Efforts at macroeconomic management in the first world – primarily raising interest rates to curb inflation – dramatically increased the burden of third world debt incurred at flexible interest rates and denominated in dollars, discrediting third world capacity for macroeconomic management.

Despite rapidly changing economic conditions, this was not, by and large, a period of imaginative new thinking in development economics itself. At the national level, when crisis hit, development policy managers reached for their most familiar tools. Borrowing increased, currencies were allowed to appreciate, government spending increased, and budget deficits rose. Import substitution had always relied to some extent on export promotion to fund capital imports – many national regimes sought to expand exports, making the transition to "second stage" import substitution, or switching to a strategy of export-led growth. The policy tools remained familiar – credit was reallocated to the export sector, tariff schedules were realigned to facilitate import of the inputs for exports. Many governments established free-trade islands within their import substitution regime, cut off from the domestic economy. In dozens of small ways, import substitution regimes were adjusted and modified.

In the economic academy, talent left the development field. As developing economies became increasingly diverse – in their reliance on primary products, levels of industrialization, penetration of foreign investment, diversification of exports, openness to imports, and, most significantly, in economic performance – the opportunities for new general theories seemed few. Meanwhile, novel struggles in developed economies of the North with both stagnation and inflation presented opportunities to rethink macroeconomic orthodoxy, often on the basis of far more complex statistical and empirical analyses than had previously been possible. Those who remained in the field of development economics turned their attention to empirical analysis of the disappointing results of earlier prescriptions, in the hopes that policy prescriptions could be fine tuned, rather than to new theorizing. Some dissident ideas – dependency theory – found their way into the mainstream. Only later would it be apparent that during this period a new generation of development economists were laying the theoretical groundwork for what would become the "Chicago School," then "neoliberalism" and "the Washington Consensus" by criticizing postwar modest interventionism wholesale. Only when their ideas ripened into an alternative vision of the way forward would economics again come to drive global development policy.

In this atmosphere of retrenchment, policy elites no longer felt they could look confidently to economic theory for guidance. Political ideas and, to a lesser extent, legal ideas became more significant to development policy expertise than economic theories. At the same time, the routinization of economic policy choices gave national policy debates a more explicitly ideological, and less expert, flavor. The loss of optimism about "take off" and lower expectations about what development policy expertise could achieve made distributional decisions seem less temporary matters of technical alignment than political choices about how to share an unstable and potentially shrinking pie. At the same time, the emergence of entrenched interests committed to each element in the overall import substitution scheme made change difficult – and more a matter of winners and losers than technical policy management. In national political debates, elites focused less on how to generate development than on how to empower their constituents and ensure their access to existing national resources.

On the law side, a small group of development professionals from the North proposed a new approach to national policy making in the developing world based not on new economic thinking, but on legal reform. The efforts of these "law and development" scholars have been well chronicled by David Trubek, both in his contribution to this book and in his earlier work. They began with an intuition about why postwar development efforts had shown such mixed results. The problem lay not with the prevailing economic common sense – after all, sometimes there had been growth. The problem was imperfect implementation of modest interventionist programs. After 1980, the implementation problem at the level of national development regimes would be understood in the language of "corruption," "rent seeking," "self dealing," and "governmental failure." The law and development professionals of the 1960s and 1970s saw the problem rather as one of *resistance* – cultural, institutional, and habitual resistance by officials (often lawyers) throughout the national economic and political structure who were insufficiently *pragmatic and antiformalist* in their attitudes about law itself. Blind rule following and unimaginative bureaucratic habits were preventing law in the books from realizing its potential in action. The solution was to build a more pragmatic and antiformalist local legal culture, to facilitate the emergence of a national administrative apparatus attuned to the social needs and development purposes of the regime.

In the larger story of global development policy, this effort by North American legal elites was quite modest and short lived. Funding dried up, leading participants to lose confidence in the project and move on to other projects. It turned out to be difficult to transplant a new legal culture, even with good access to a nation's law schools. Even were they to succeed, it was not clear that a more flexible national administrative elite would, in fact, improve implementation of the national development plan – or that this would in turn generate development. The correlation between legal pragmatism and economic development was weak – while the possible correlation with authoritarianism and human rights abuses could not be ignored. Nevertheless, their story remains significant, for our purposes, because they directed attention from economic policy making to legal reform, and theorized explicitly about the relationship between law and economic development.

More significant than the turn to law were the more overtly political ideas. Indeed, an explicitly political vocabulary increasingly came to replace economics, changing thinking about what development is and how it should be achieved. The move from economics to politics had at least two quite different manifestations – loosely associated with thinking in the first world and the third. In the first world, discussions of development focused far less on "industrialization" or "modernization," and far more on improvement in specific quality of life indicators: health, housing, nutrition, education, literacy rates, infant mortality rates, and life expectancy. The World Bank's focus on "basic needs" during Robert MacNamara's tenure as president epitomized the trend. Progress on these indicators could be measured and compared globally. They could be the focus of direct and specific government programs, both nationally and internationally.

This shift represented both an expansion and a contraction of ambition. On the one hand, industrialization might not be sufficient, or might be but the first step – development now set a higher standard, national wealth *and* equitable distribution. On the other hand, development no longer required the transformation of an entire society, in a repetition of the industrial revolution. Indeed, industrialization might make things worse. The whole disappointing project of national development planning could be sidestepped – international development practitioners could intervene directly at the local level with programs designed to address these specific issues. At the same time, this approach gave the development project a more humane face – shifting the felt responsibility for the unpleasant costs of industrialization to other actors. These shifts altered the relationship between "development" and basic distributional choices in the society. On the one hand, development no longer required – and might even preclude – the sorts of massive reallocations required to harness the surplus for industrialization: from rural to urban, from agriculture to industry. In this sense, development policy could be *relatively indifferent* to national economic policy. On the other hand, development *did* require *re*distribution of a society's wealth to provide for the basic needs of its citizens. This brought a new range of humanitarian and antipoverty initiatives to the forefront of "development" policy making.

Second, and more significant in the third world, was a broader shift from the *national* to the *international* arena for development policy making. The popularization of world systems theory in political science and dependency theory in economics reinforced the notion that development would require fundamental changes in the world economic and political system. These changes would require political mobilization, rather than economic planning. The technical details of national economic policy might well be simply beside the point – swamped by the continuing effects of neocolonial exploitation. There is no question that for many third world elites, this shift was attractive precisely because it took the heat off local policy management.

There were, of course, global forces at work – debt burdens rose in response to the global oil shock and first world interest rate increases, for example. These were not the issues on which attention was focused, however, for these difficulties were only becoming apparent, and there was little appetite for shutting off the pipeline of new credit. Instead, development experts focused on what seemed two structural imbalances in the world trading system – the instability of primary product prices, and the unequal bargaining power of third world exporters. It is true, of course, that there is nothing in the economic theory of comparative advantage to ensure that the gains from trade will be equally shared among the nations participating in trade flows – all the gains might well flow to one or the other party, depending upon their relative bargaining power.

Dependency theory had begun as a series of economic hypotheses about the potential for price takers to face declining terms of trade in international commerce. LDC exports faced competitive and unstable markets, so the story went, while LDC imports came from markets dominated by monopolistic or oligopolistic practices, ensuring a long-term decline in LDC terms of trade. As it turned out, proving these hypotheses empirically in any general way had been very difficult. LDC economies differed a great deal – and competition from Asian manufacturing was beginning to undermine assumptions about the first world's natural oligopolies in manufacturing. A broader inquiry into bargaining power inequality might have uncovered a range of other institutional issues – but these were sufficient, if largely unproven, to support a broader political effort to revise the global division of labor.

This shifted attention sharply from national to international policy making. The intergovernmental institutions of the United Nations seemed the appropriate locus for international regulations aimed at compensating for the unequal bargaining power of the third world. In the 1950s, mainstream development practitioners had been largely indifferent to the United Nations, other than as a provider of technical advice to those responsible for national economic policy in the newly independent states. The financial institutions were significant, but far less than they would become in later decades. The regional development banks and the World Bank largely shared the policy priorities of the national governments – the era of "conditionality" and aggressive efforts to discipline national policy lay in the future. Private banks were not significant lenders in the third world until the 1970s, the IMF was largely supportive of national import substitution regimes, and was a less significant player before the debt crises and economic liberalization expanded the vulnerability of third world currencies. The GATT focused on tariff reduction for manufactured products and was primarily focused on trade among the industrialized world. Many developing nations were not members (including almost all of the state socialist world), and those that were benefited from a special regime of "preferences" that exempted them from participating in the discipline of multilateral tariff reduction negotiations.

Still, the United Nations *had* been involved in development policy making throughout the 1960s. It financed research and data collection and was often a source for comparative statistical information about economic performance. Often, the United Nations was a leading source for discretionary foreign capital and technical expertise. The various Specialized Agencies were all over the third world, promoting various specific health, education, illiteracy, sanitation, and other humanitarian initiatives. These international programs were sometimes more able to resist capture by local political interests and often stood somewhat outside national political debates. As the focus of development shifted from industrialization to 'basic needs' they seemed ever more at the center of things. U.N.-financed think tanks promoted development-related research by economists, lawyers, sociologists, and political scientists. The "dependency" school of development economics, in fact, was largely a product of U.N. funding in Latin America. The coordination of various U.N. humanitarian efforts in one country would often present questions of priority that could only be resolved with a view to the national development plan. The establishment of a single "U.N. Resident Representative" in many developing nations to coordinate U.N. activities often provided a locus for coordinating national development planning activities.

The reorientation from national to international came first to thinking about multilateral development aid. In the modest interventionist world of the 1950s, foreign aid did not seem particularly significant. The amounts of foreign aid were too modest, and too unreliable, to replace the mobilization of national savings, the employment of labor surpluses or the exploitation of natural resources as the trigger for takeoff. By the late 1960s and 1970s, however, foreign aid did seem significant. In some very poor countries, the amounts were significant as a percentage of GDP. It provided a source of government revenue at least partially exempt from national political vested interests. Multilateral aid also offered the opportunity to bring about development *directly*, eliminating the national government and the vagaries of national economic planning by "putting real food in the mouths of real people," as the saying went. In political terms, multilateral aid was also of great symbolic importance, both as a sign of "nonalignment" and as an example of pure *redistribution* from North to South. Less a source of capital for local industrialization than compensation, one might think, for generations of exploitation. The turn to the United Nations in the 1970s coincided, however, with a shift among donors from broad support for multilateral aid, to far more targeted support for particular international programs, or to bilateral aid schemes.

In the 1970s, third world politicians tasked the United Nations with a different approach to development – not supporting national development planning, or even an expansion in aid, but rather legislating the revision of the global economic and political order. As development professionals became convinced that changes in global political and institutional arrangements would be necessary, the United Nations offered the only global political arena in which developing nations were all represented. To enable the United Nations to take on this new function, third world scholars and diplomats focused on the structure of the United Nations itself – shifting authority from the Security Council to the General Assembly, strengthening the organs and offices associated with development, promoting the legislative capability of the General Assembly, and insisting on participation at all levels of the international institutional regime.

By the early 1970s, the U.N. system became the center for a series of proposals for changes in the global economic system, brought together as the call for a "New International Economic Order" or NIEO. Like any legislative program, it combined heterogenous elements. Various schemes (buffer stocks, international marketing boards) were proposed to stabilize the prices of primary commodities exported by developing nations. There were calls for increased multilateral aid, for global regulation of multinational corporations, for south-south cooperation and information sharing, and for the compulsory transfer of technology. To overcome the South's role as a price taker in world trade, some promoted producer cartels on the model of OPEC. Private international dispute resolution mechanisms of commercial arbitration were to be reformed to eliminate bias against third world government interests. International regulation of multinational enterprises operating in the third world, support for national efforts to regulate foreign direct investment, technical assistance in negotiating more favorable concession contracts for extractive industries – all were part of the broad NIEO agenda. Bargaining power differences between the first and third world were to be offset by placing commercial negotiations in multilateral and intergovernmental settings where sovereigns' participation was ensured and where south-south cooperation – as in the "Group of 77" – could be promoted. As the Law of the Sea negotiations got started, third world nations insisted on the equitable sharing of seabed resources as part of the "common heritage of mankind." Declarations were adopted reinforcing the legal entitlement of nation states to regulate foreign commerce, limit repatriation of profits, control – and nationalize – foreign investment, and in general determine their own economic future.

Despite the attention focused on the New International Economic Order initiatives, it was not successful, either politically or economically. Cartels proved difficult to organize and sustain. Proposals to regulate global corporate behavior were watered down, or translated into voluntary codes of conduct. It proved difficult to shift private economic negotiations to public forums, or to remake the global economic system within which national governments made economic policy. As a global legislative project, the NIEO drew resistance from across the developed world. Its most significant legacy may have been to strengthen the hands of national development planners, giving modest interventionism and import substitution a further lease on life.

In the end, the most significant innovation in the global economic order in the 1970s had nothing to do with the NIEO. The global economic order was being remade in quite a different way by the oil shock, the move to floating exchange rates, and the expansion of lending, primarily by first world private banks, to third world governments. The system for recycling petrodollars as private government guaranteed debt across the developing world required significant institutional imagination and innovation. As interest rates rose, indebtedness accelerated – the new international system that was actually built facilitated unprecedented and unsustainable levels of national indebtedness across the developing world. The explosion of debt – offered to subsidize imports made more costly by the oil shock and as a source of capital for development – would be the final undoing of modest interventionism. Debt swamped efforts to "mobilize" domestic savings. Flexible exchange rates, mounting interest payments, and balance of trade deficits swamped domestic macroeconomic policy. Expansion in government-guaranteed credit eliminated market and regulatory discipline on its use. The sums required to stabilize currencies dwarfed anything in the aid or project development field. The institutions providing such sums were in a position to demand all manner of changes in national macroeconomic policy, and felt no compulsion to respect national economic policy making.

Across the developing world, fiscal policy replaced development policy, and national governments progressively lost their margin of maneuver to foreign private banks, foreign financial experts and monetary authorities, and to the International Monetary Fund. Meanwhile, the intellectual groundwork was being laid for a new development vision, understood by its proponents as a refutation both of the economic ideas of the postwar period – import substitution, modest interventionism – and of the political ideas of the 1970s, with their focus on redistribution and public ordering at the national and international levels. These ideas would find their proponents precisely in the institutions first empowered by the debt crisis – the IMF, the U.S. Treasury, and the private banks of the North.

We might summarize the 1970 period as shown in Table 3.

The legal theory of 1970s development thinking

The legal consciousness of development professionals in the 1970s was largely continuous with that of their postwar predecessors. Law was the instrument of social purpose, the agent for implementing an economic – and political – development agenda through legislative and administrative action. Public law continued to predominate. At the national level, a pragmatic, antiformalist, "social" law continued to be the vehicle for modest interventionist development policy making. At the international level, the United Nations was seen as a centralized legislative vehicle for global policy making. International law was to provide the tools to support a nascent global welfare-state – top-down regulation to restructure relative bargaining powers of developing nations and the private market actors of the North, administrative arrangements to stabilize prices, implement social programs, and distribute resources to achieve development objectives. The New International Economic Order was promulgated in numerous legal resolutions,

TABLE 3. Crisis 1970–1980

Left	Center	Right
Falling counterpoint	**Mainstream**	**Rising counterpoint**
Problem:	**National:**	**Problem:**
Exploitation, neocolonialism	Problem: bad national implementation	Bad national policy
International:	Chastened modest interventionism	Criticism of Development Economics
Redistribution and reparations	Export-led growth / second stage ISI	**National**:
Technology transfer	Borrowing	Shift from macro to microeconomics
Tax and revenue sharing	**Law:**	**International**:
National:	Antiformalism and strengthen institutions for modest interventionism	Free trade
Nationalization	"Law and Development"	
Socialization	**International:**	
Self-Reliance	Problem: global unfairness	
Solidarity	Global modest interventionism	
Redistribution	**Politics:**	
	NIEO	
	Market stabilization, cartels, buffer stocks	
	Price controls	
	Strengthen national sovereignty	
	Improve LDC participation in global institutions	
	Promote aid / facilitate debt	

declarations, and doctrinal restatements: guaranteeing national sovereignty over natural resources and national economic management, demanding participation in established institutions, building new public sites for what had been commercial negotiations, establishing new schemes for commodity price stabilization, and technology sharing or sharing of the world's resources.

The generation of diplomats and international lawyers – often from the third world – who designed and promoted the NIEO looked to antiformalist and sociologically inspired legal thinkers like Wolfgang Friedmann for inspiration. Indeed, it would be hard to overstate the influence of his 1964 book "*The Changing Structure of International Law.*" Friedmann's ideas informed countless projects at the United Nations – expansion of U.N. administrative law, strengthening of the General Assembly's legislative capacity, a flexible interpretation of international institutional mandates to seize opportunities for "cooperation" in the fields of health, education, and poverty alleviation, and an expansion of international law to promote participation, ensure fairness, and provide space for equity. The most notable legal manifesto for the New International Economic Order was written by Mohamed Bedjaoui, a French-trained Algerian jurist who became a member, and then president of the International Court of Justice. Published by UNESCO, Bedjaoui's 1979 essay "Towards A New International Economic Order" denounced the "legal paganism" of an earlier, more "formal" and "positivist" era and called for an international law appropriate to the social and developmental needs of the age. Global interdependence required solidarity – and corresponding efforts both to reinforce the sovereignty and self-determination of the newly independent states and adjust the rules of the game to strengthen their bargaining power and ensure their representation in international institutional life.

For readers in the United States, it will be clear that the legal theories of international development experts differed in subtle ways from the dominant ideas about law in the American academy at the time. The antiformalism of international development experts owed more to the European sociological tradition than to American legal realism. At the same time, this antiformalism was coupled to a positivist and formal defense of sovereignty and normative validity that sounded, to American ears, like a throwback to classical legal thinking of the nineteenth century. Although Marxist conceptions of law were not influential among development experts, the international legal ideas advanced by jurists from the Soviet bloc, which emphasized sovereignty and national autonomy, were picked up by third world jurists. The result was often a rather unstable blend of social ideas about international cooperation and solidarity and a more conventional positivist emphasis on formal autonomy and national sovereignty.

We might say that the sociological tradition had not had the critical impact on positivist and formalist legal thought that American legal realism had had in the United States. As a result, the wide variety of postrealist reactions that emerged in American legal thought after the Second World War – most notably, the emphasis on legal process and procedures – was not particularly significant in the legal consciousness of international development experts. Other than in discussion of U.N. administrative law reform, it is hard to locate the influence of American legal process ideas. Similarly, the normative reconstructions that followed realism and pragmatism in American legal thought, with their emphasis on procedural stability, ethnical principle, and the interpretation of rights, were largely absent. In the United States, private law and private ordering continued to be a focal point for legal theory – but far less so in the thinking of international development experts. In the United States, the global regulatory framework had been reconceptualized as a horizontal – "transnational" – pastiche of often inconsistent national and local regulations and private ordering already in the 1950s. For development experts, national and global regulation remained distinct and hierarchical – the New

International Economic Order was to be not simply another transnational project, but a top-down global public law initiative parallel to the vertical public law through which development objectives were pursued nationally.

For all this continuity with the legal thinking of the postwar period, the legal ideas of developmental experts did begin to shift in the late 1960s and early 1970s. Two changes stand out – a new style of pragmatic legal thinking, and a new appreciation for the significance of formal rights and adjudication.

The "law and development" movement in the United States had exported styles of legal pragmatism and antiformalism more common in the postrealist thought of the American legal academy. At the same time, the international law thinking of those supporting the NIEO program was undergoing a series of subtle shifts, in part as a consequence of its encounter with American legal thought, and in part the result of efforts to bring the potentially contradictory antiformalist social and more formal and positivist elements in the NIEO legal program into harmony with one another. Friedmann had called these the laws of "cooperation" and "coexistence," and consigned them to different spheres – coexistence between the first and second worlds, cooperation in the third, coexistence for peace and security, cooperation for development and economic cooperation. But this solution was not sufficient – the NIEO program for development itself combined a commitment to national autonomy and formal sovereignty with a call for more social solidarity and resource sharing.

The challenge for international law in the period was to accommodate these conflicting tendencies in a way that remained purposive, pragmatic, and attuned to developmental needs. Duncan Kennedy attributes the rise of what he terms "conflicting considerations" analysis in the postwar period to the encounter between European social traditions and American postrealist legal thought. Something parallel seems to have gone on in international law – the formulation *within* legal thought of a continuum of competing policies pulling on each rule or doctrine, and the interpretation of each doctrine as a *compromise* between competing, and legitimate, purposes. Here is Wolfgang Friedmann's close friend and collaborator Oscar Schachter, also at Columbia, lauding what he takes as Dag Hammarskjold's exemplary attitude toward law in 1962.

> Hammarskjold made no sharp distinction between law and policy; in this he departed clearly from the prevailing positivist approach. He viewed the body of law not merely as a technical set of rules and procedures, but as the authoritative expression of principles that determine the goals and directions of collective action.... It is also of significance in evaluating Hammarskjold's flexibility that he characteristically expressed basic principles in terms of opposing tendencies (applying, one might say, the philosophic concept of polarity or dialectical opposition). He never lost sight of the fact that a principle, such as that of observance of human rights, was balanced by the concept of non-intervention, or that the notion of equality of states had to be considered in a context which included the special responsibilities of the great Powers. The fact that such precepts had

> contradictory implications meant that they could not provide automatic answers to particular problems, but rather that they served as criteria which had to be weighed and balanced in order to achieve a rational solution of the particular problem.... He did not, therefore, attempt to set law against power. He sought rather to find within the limits of power the elements of common interest on the basis of which joint action and agreed standards could be established.[1]

This is a different style of antiformalism – the law expresses competing social needs and purposes, which the jurist, no less than the administrator or political leader, must weigh and balance. For this interpretive task, he must cultivate a wise and open discretion. This international law less guides statesmen to new developmental or equitable purposes, than it enables them to craft novel solutions to social conflicts, to weigh and balance competing social interests and developmental objectives. In a more modest way, the same encounter with North American legal pragmatism occurred at the national level – at a minimum wherever the law and development movement had influence. The law and development scholars – largely from North America – sought less to install new social purposes in the legal fabric of developing societies than to encourage the emergence of a new more creative and discretionary sensibility among third world governmental elites – administrative and executive elites as much as judges. Their emphasis on legal education was designed less to change the law than to change the profession – to promote the practice of weighing and balancing, and the potential for discretionary innovation.

At the same time, and somewhat paradoxically, the legal pragmatism of the 1970s differed from its postwar predecessor in the new life it offered to *formalism*. Jurists influential at the United Nations – Wolfgang Friedmann, Oscar Schachter, Thomas Franck – all sought to strengthen the rulelike character of international law against the "policy"-oriented analytic style of the New Haven school associated with Myres McDougal and his collaborators. Only a law of rules, they felt, could restrain the foreign policy of the great powers. They interpreted the U.N. legal system as a liberal constitutional order, with the Charter as its constitution, rather than as a regime for public order, policy making, or collective politics. Each of the U.N. organs was thought to perform a juridical function – rule making, implementing, and adjudicating.

As this legal order opened to the participation of excolonial states, these jurists emphasized the sovereign *rights* of the newly independent states. Developing nations and their nationals were also said to have *rights* – to membership in international organizations, to participation in international fora, to staff positions at the United Nations, to the determination of their own economic policy, and to a share of the "common heritage of mankind." Bedjaoui had linked his denunciation of formal "legal paganism" with a

[1] Oscar Schachter, *Dag Hammarskjold and the Relation of Law to Politics*, 56 Amer. J. Int'l L. 1, 2–7 (1962).

strident assertion of the sovereign rights of the newly independent states and of the rights of all peoples to self-determination. New rights for U.N. officials would guarantee their autonomy – but also facilitate opening intergovernmental bureaucracies to participation by third world elites. At the same time, international lawyers working on restatements of the basic "rights and duties of states" articulated the sovereign rights of newly independent states, as well as the duties of solidarity for mankind's "common heritage."

The international human rights movement emerged during this period, offering a critique of the empowering instrumentalism of the law and development movement. There were *limits*, internationally agreed legal limits, to national governmental discretion. At the same time, the humanitarian focus on basic needs began to be articulated as a call for international social and economic *rights*. It was during this period, moreover, that international legal elites sought to transform development itself into a *right*, and development policy making into advocacy for the respect of human rights.

The focus on formal rights was often accompanied by a turn to the judiciary. International judiciaries were not yet the focal point they would become in the 1990s. Still, the International Court of Justice seemed a significant ally for third world international lawyers in the struggle for decolonization, for an expanded United Nations authority over development issues, and for resolution of disputes – primarily over territory – among third world nations. Bedjaoui would become its president. The International Court of Justice was repeatedly called upon to play a role in decolonization, affirming the right to self-determination – in Southwest Africa, in Western Sahara. Repeatedly – in territorial cases, in Nauru and East Timor, and elsewhere – the Court was asked to adjudicate the legal consequences of colonialism, the duties of excolonial powers and the rights of newly independent developing states vis à vis one another and the ex-colonial powers. Within the United Nations system, administrative tribunals increasingly found themselves presented with challenges to staffing and budgetary decisions that implicated rights to participation by developing nation and administrative discretion in the implementation of various development programs. The Law of the Sea negotiations provided a decade-long opportunity for third world conceptions of law and development to find expression. They did so not only in demands for codification, or for equitable sharing of seabed resources, but also in the articulation of a complex smorgasbord of dispute resolution mechanisms, simultaneously fragmenting and legalizing the resolution of competing claims.

Perhaps most significantly, international obligations were increasingly understood to be enforced not by the administrative action of states or international institutions, but by courts – including, most centrally, the "court" of world public opinion. International lawyers focusing on economic, social, and solidarity rights saw them implemented by the emergence of a global judicial *point of view* among the elites of the "international community," which would become the decentralized enforcement arm for the international regime. United Nations institutions were urged to adopt a "judicial" posture – detached, principled, and neutral, if also committed to justice and the long-run integration of the community. In the commercial field, moreover, development-oriented scholars promoted the emergence of a more judiciary-like commercial arbitration regime, able to weigh and balance appropriate "public policy" objectives alongside private rights in adjudication of contractual disputes between developing countries and multinational enterprises.

The emergence of a vital postcolonial formalist legal tradition was, if anything, more pronounced at the national level. The humanitarian objectives of development policy were asserted as rights – human rights – by local and multinational human rights advocates against administrative action across the developing world. At the same time, property rights began to be asserted in courts and arbitration proceedings – in the developed and developing world – against various elements of development policy. The formalism encountered by law and development scholars was not only a holdover of an earlier, more conservative, legal consciousness. It was also something new – empowering new interests in new forums. A generation of import substitution policy had created a range of new economic interests, which were increasingly understood as entitlements – to titles, licences, quotas, credit arrangements, long-standing administrative decisions, and existing contracts with the state. During this period, national judges in the third world remained largely passive in the face of such claims – their moment would come. The same could not be said for international arbitration and national courts in the North, which became increasingly important sites for the judicial review of policy decisions taken in the developing world.

These new elements – the balancing of conflicting interests, and neoformalist enthusiasm for rights and adjudication – track the legal consciousness that Duncan Kennedy associates with a "third globalization" in his contribution to this volume. The NIEO was articulated far more in this vocabulary of rights and policies, weighing and balancing, than in the postwar of an instrumental and purposive social law. Law would no longer be the instrumental expression of social needs, as understood through economic theory, but a vocabulary for balancing and selecting among diverse claims. Ever more questions seemed to present alternative, often contradictory solutions that could only be resolved by institutional deference or careful balancing on a case by case basis. This new pragmatism would take place within a "liberal constitutional" order, both internationally and nationally, in which the state's internal procedures and substantive policy choices would be limited by legal rights and procedures enforced by adjudication. In such a universe, legislative or administrative authority to make new development policy would need to be weighed carefully against an array of vested interests.

These were subtle shifts from the legal consciousness of the postwar era – it remains extremely difficult to speculate about their political significance.

There is no doubt that within the elites, the new consciousness reflected the influence of American legal thought. Needless to say, that does not make it the instrument of American hegemony. Still, the new more flexible approach to international legal obligation was often decried as indistinguishable from the "policy" consciousness of the New Haven school, widely understood to have been deployed in defense of American Cold War policies. In the 1970s, it was often asserted that more flexible styles of international legal thought favored the powerful, who could manipulate them, while more formal, rights-based styles and positivist defenses of sovereignty favored the weak and the newly independent. The opposite was also asserted, however with equal vigor – the formal, positivist approaches of the past enshrined the authority of the powerful, and only a more flexible, cooperative style could advance global social objectives. In the 1970s, rather than clear links between legal consciousness and political or ideological positions, we find that legal consciousness has become a site for ideological and political contestation.

The broad package of legal theory commitments – antiformalism, legal pragmatism, social law, human rights, liberal constitutionalism, rights-policies-adjudication – informed left, right, and center regimes at the national level, and underlay a range of left and left-center positions internationally. Nevertheless, many participants remember the move from antiformalism/social conceptions to the liberal constitutionalism of rights/policies/adjudication as a deradicalization, a move from left to center. There may have been some truth to this – attention to rights did seem both to limit the discretion of national development policymakers and moderate the goals of international development professionals. At the same time, to the extent structuralist or necessitarian styles of thinking can be associated with political extremes, the more modest, case by case legal analytic style typical of the 1970s development expert does seem amenable to interpretation as more "centrist." The transition from "development professional" to "human rights advocate" seemed to reduce attention to economics and distribution issues, even as advocates struggled for "recognition" of "economic and social rights." At the global level, ideas to the left of the NIEO package were largely discarded in the move to a liberal constitutionalism of rights. At the same time, many authoritarian regimes and stagnant national "development plans" had become entrenched in the name of legislative positivism and administrative pragmatism. The new vocabulary of liberal constitutionalism did sometimes offer an effective mode of resistance and innovation.

That said, it may well have been that this set of ideas about law constrained the range of plausible political positions in various ways. The focus on public law and institutions may have made it harder to think about use of private law as a distributive tool for development. At the global level, a liberal constitutional vision of international law and the United Nations may have focused attention on participation in the internal structure of international organizations, and on the fairness of bargaining between the first and third

TABLE 4. Mainstream: 1970–1980

Basic ideas: **Politics**	**Development policy set**	**Legal Theory** **Transition from "antiformalist social" to liberal constitutionalism and a merger of rights and policies focused on adjudication**	
		Instrumental thinking	*Rights thinking*
Dependency World systems Neocolonialism Global New Deal Antiformal and pragmatic law Human rights	**National:** Modest interventionism Retrenched export-led growth Law and development reform Legal education Pluralism, democracy Decentralization **International:** NIEO Sovereign rights International participation Global economic management Commodity price stabilization Generalized System of Preferences Common markets Petro-dollar recycling Debt	Public law pragmatism Law = policy Social law and "basic needs" Sovereignty, self-determination, and national autonomy U.N. legislation and bureaucracy Balancing social objectives	Human rights universalism Political rights Entrenched rights Economic and social rights World court, judicial viewpoint, and administrative law Balancing rights and interests

worlds, rather than on questions of global distribution. The growing attention to rights, including sovereign rights, may have gridlocked efforts to think more aggressively about reparations and sharing. The reigning legal theories may have made it more difficult to challenge the legitimacy of kleptocratic national development regimes, or to identify the costs of maladjusted administrative action.

We might summarize the legal theoretical developments of the 1970s as shown in Table 4.

The politics of these political ideas

Looking back, both the international proposals of the NIEO and the national modest interventionist programs it sought to support and supplement are now easily identifiable as "left." At the time, they appeared more centrist. The leading proponents of the NIEO were moderate "nonaligned" left regimes, in an implicit alliance with social democrats in the North, and the cosmopolitan civil servants in the U.N. system. Many development professionals – including those in the law and development movement – were moderates or centrists, American "liberals," rather than leftists. Their anticommunism was as salient as their progressivism. Their ideological strategy was flexible: coexistence where necessary, cooperation where possible. Global communism was to be contained – but not rolled back.

Although the 1970s was a period of overt ideological contestation on the global stage, policy differences over development issues were more modest. Although the "nonaligned" and the "Group of 77" were ideologically diverse, their development thinking tended to the same cluster of modest interventionist and international redistributive ideas. Elements of the NIEO project were supported by regimes of all political stripes, by communist and right-wing authoritarian regimes as well as the social democratic regimes of the first world. OPEC, the model for efforts to establish commodity cartels, embraced regimes across a wide ideological range.

In broad terms, the NIEO program was a compromise between moderate and radical visions – and it was interpreted in both ways by proponents and opponents alike. Dependency theory – and the rise of left wing ideologies across the globe – had drawn attention to global inequalities. Should the response emphasize *fairness* or *redistribution*? Was the problem a set of unfair bargains, an inequality of bargaining power – or a more profound structural bias? Were procedural solutions adequate – or would substantive redistribution of resources be necessary? Were calls for more aid, technology transfer, regulation of multinational investment efforts to preserve the global market by softening its effects – or assaults on the institution of private property worldwide? Should cartels or price stabilization schemes aim to reset the balance in bargaining – or to empower the third world for confiscatory redistributions? Were the NIEO proposals intended to supplement, smooth, and stabilize global markets – or transform them? Was its goal humanitarian relief for the poorest of the poor – or a fundamental redistribution of wealth? Should U.N. officials demonstrate professional neutrality – or an ideological commitment to nonalignment?

How one answered these questions depended, of course, on one's ideological preconceptions – and upon one's interests. When it is your money, a great deal more will look confiscatory. And the NIEO was interpreted very differently in different places. To the American financial and corporate establishment, it looked confiscatory – although liberal intellectuals were likely to interpret it more modestly, as a global version of policies that had become politically acceptable in the United States during the New Deal. For them, the goal was a level playing field. For many moderates, the more significant proposals stressed participation and procedural efforts to equalize bargaining power through information sharing, while more radical calls for redistribution or nationalization were moderated by insistence on "prompt, adequate and effective compensation." In the third world, the NIEO was often seen as the absolute minimum demanded by elemental standards of fairness.

Although these debates were carried on in quite overtly ideological terms, their effect on the ideological balance of power, either globally or within particular national political cultures, is far less clear. Often these debates had quite different resonances nationally. A pro-LDC position that seemed left wing and cosmopolitan in New York might translate into a nationalist and authoritarian position in the capital of a right-wing third world regime. Elements of the NIEO that seemed quite moderate in the United Nations context played as left wing in the United States. Looking back, the plasticity of national ideological associations for NIEO ideas that seemed center-left or left on the global stage is striking. Even on issues like the treatment of foreign investment, there were "right wing" regimes determined to tax, limit profit repatriation, even nationalize, and there were "left-wing" regimes that offered concessions for the exploitation of natural resources on extremely favorable terms.

If we think in distributional, rather than ideological terms, the politics of development thinking in the 1970s is even more difficult to assess. At the national level, right and left regimes continued to pursue versions of modest interventionist import substitution. "Right-wing" regimes were sometimes more, sometimes less, authoritarian than left-wing development regimes. In a given national context, they would typically bring a different constellation of social and economic interests to power – but which interests differed. There were right-wing regimes that favored the military, traditional landowners, the urban bourgeoisie, foreign investors – but there were also right-wing regimes that favored urban workers and rural interests, just as there were left-wing regimes that set up their import substitution regimes to favor the military – even foreign investment.

We can say that everywhere, national economic policies rooted in import substitution continued as debt burdens rose. Everywhere, national regimes seemed paralyzed in the face of new economic conditions. It would be difficult not to conclude that mainstream development thinking contributed to this paralysis. For all the rhetoric, the initiatives that emerged from the NIEO program were extremely modest – global sharing of seabed resources whose economic viability for recovery has not yet set in, modest buffer stock arrangements for a few primary commodities, and a series of nonbinding exhortations and legal pronouncements on aid and national sovereignty.

The global focus on humanitarian aid and basic needs took the pressure off national economic performance. The politicization of development policy everywhere disempowered technical experts to the advantage of entrenched interests. Across the developing world, national policymakers lost the initiative – on public and symbolic issues to the international arena of the NIEO or the United Nations, on private economic issues, to foreign banks and international financial institutions. This may have made it more difficult for national development policy to make the shift from first stage import substitution to a more targeted, diversified, and export-oriented second stage. With increased debt levels and shrinking public resources, private capital became more significant, and calls for nationalization or limits on the repatriation of profits diminished.

The politics of development thinking in the 1970s was also a consequence of what was missing. There were few challenges to modest interventionism, and national regimes stagnated in the face of rapidly changing international economic conditions. As a result of that stagnation, few of the more innovative and progressive ideas in the modest interventionist program were tried – land reforms were nominal or nonexistent, where national firms had not emerged in the earlier period, they were not created. Few national regimes eased the transition from import substitution to export promotion and diversification. The turn to humanitarianism accompanied an abandonment of social transformation as a goal for development policy. A focus on basic needs contributed to the deradicalization of development thinking, taking broader distribution issues off the table as legitimate objects of policymaking attention – shifting attention from distribution for economic development toward redistribution to meet minimum humanitarian objectives. Technical fine-tuning and targeted administrative action were broadly delegitimated in favor of more overtly political allocations of increasingly scarce resources.

If anything, the political imagination of development professionals seemed more limited in the 1970s. The image of what might be achieved at the international level was quite limited and the objectives for national development policy became ever narrower. Indeed, for all the changes in rhetoric at the global level, for all the disappointments and outright failures of modest interventionism, the policy vernacular remained relatively settled throughout the 1970s. It is difficult to conclude that the thinking of development professionals did not contribute to this stagnation.

PHASE THREE: WASHINGTON CONSENSUS 1980–1995

Economics strikes back

For all the diversity of initiatives promoted at the international and national level in the 1970s, it was not a period of optimism or confidence among theorists of development. Attention focused overwhelmingly on the disappointing results of a generation of efforts to "take off" to industrialization. Looking back, the drift from economics to politics seems to have been symptomatic of a loss of faith in the postwar development paradigm.

Over a short period between the mid-1970s and the mid-1980s, the postwar consensus was swept away by a new set of economic ideas about development, which came to be termed "neoliberalism" or "The Washington Consensus," because they came to prominence as the in-house development dogma of the U.S. Treasury, State Department, aid agencies, the International Monetary Fund, and the World Bank, all headquartered in Washington.

The basic outlines of neoliberal development policy are now well known. Within economics, the lead passed from macroeconomics to microeconomics. An economy was no longer imagined primarily as an input-output production cycle open to macroeconomic strategies to manage the relationship among economic aggregates such as "savings" or "investment," "consumption," "income," and "labor" or "technology." An economy was now imagined as a "market" in which individual economic actors transact with one another, responding to price signals and thereby allocating resources to their most productive use. Government is there less to manage the economy than to support the market. Moreover, there is no reason to think of economies in *national* terms. If things have more productive uses abroad, they will be bought, or traded for things more valued at home. In theory, the larger the market, the more opportunities there are for productive exchanges – trades from which both parties gain.

Developed and underdeveloped economies are not, in this view, fundamentally different from one another – there is no need for a special "development" economics. All societies seek to maximize economic performance and growth given their endowments. There is no path to development, there are no set stages, there is no "take-off," there is nothing magic about industrialization. There are simply people who own things, who transact, and who thereby move things from less to more productive uses. Even the term "development" fell from favor during this period, replaced by the more technical term "efficiency" used both in a technical sense, and as a loose synonym for maximizing economic performance.

The shift from macro- to microeconomic analysis, from emphasis on input-output analysis as a tool for promoting industrial growth to relative prices as the dominant method to align supply and demand, completely changed the focal point for policy. "Getting distribution right" – capturing and targeting savings to promote industrialization – was displaced by "getting prices right." The focus on prices arose from the work of economists Arrow and Debreu in the 1950s. They had demonstrated that in a perfectly competitive market, the equilibrium reached in the absence of regulation – where all prices are set by supply and demand, undistorted by government action – would be "efficient" in the specific sense that with given technology and resources, no one could be made better off without someone else being made worse off.

This theoretical insight was understood to have quite direct implications for policymakers. The basic idea was that economic policy should enable, rather than impede, market transactions. Governments should do what is necessary to support a market pricing mechanism and avoid doing anything that would distort market prices. The entire array of policy tools developed for import substitution industrialization were exactly wrong – subsidies, price controls, tariffs, licensing arrangements, exchange controls, preferential credit arrangements, tax incentives, or marketing boards were all price distorting rather than market supporting. They also cut the national economy off from world markets – both reducing the potential for gains from trade *and* eliminating the discipline of world prices that could serve as a proxy for undistorted market prices.

At the national level, the neoliberal policy agenda therefore began by dismantling the modest interventionist regimes that had been developed to pursue import substitution industrialization. Governments were encouraged to build down price distorting policies left over from their modest interventionist (and, in the case of ex-Soviet states, socialist) past and remove impediments to the penetration of national markets by global economic forces. Exchange controls, quotas, tariffs, import and export controls and licensing, restrictions on foreign investment were to be eliminated – they distort prices and limit participation in global markets. At the same time, governments should encourage the emergence of private actors through privatization of state-owned enterprises, promoting corporate law reform, strengthening the private banking sector, establishing more open and efficient financial markets, facilitating foreign investment, supporting new local enterprises, and strengthening local enterpreneurial skills and spirit. The goal was to eliminate discretionary public administration and management of economic assets. Market prices should replace administrative prices.

At the international level, the policy agenda was similar – eliminate the effort to regulate the global marketplace. Of course, efforts to regulate the global market had never been as robust as national modest interventionist regimes. Indeed, the horizontal global market, free of collectivist regulatory impulses, served as a loose model for neoliberal national markets. The New International Economic Order, with its call for global economic management by the United Nations illustrated precisely the danger to be avoided. Attention shifted away from the United Nations and public international law, with their programs to redress bargaining inequalities, regulate global markets or encourage sharing of the world's resources, to the IMF, GATT, and, to a lesser extent, the World Bank. The United Nations should stick to what it could do – humanitarian aid, disaster relief, and global security.

The neoliberal frame also led to a rethinking of foreign aid as either a necessary but temporary crutch to facilitate the move from modest interventionism to neoliberalism – in the case of "conditionality" arrangements with the IMF or the World Bank – *or* a humanitarian charity for addressing basic needs, rather than generating development. Although foreign aid might be useful as a short-term source of capital, it was no longer seen as capital for development planning, or as compensation for prior exploitation. Where capital could enhance productivity, we could expect it to be forthcoming from private investors.

International policymakers should focus on building institutions supportive of the global market – on private ordering, the world of international private law, commercial arbitration, and international finance, and to the global institutions supporting that world by stabilizing currency markets and promoting trade. The most important action was in the field of private finance – ensuring the free movement of capital and the smooth operation of global currency markets through cooperation among global banks, both public and private, and the improvement of a reliable international payment system. At the same time, a transnational regime of private commercial law was built to support increased global commerce.

Many national regimes in the third world implemented neoliberal reforms with enthusiasm – starting with Chile in the 1970s. As countries emerged from state socialism in the late 1980s and 1990s, the initial desire to "do everything differently" fit smoothly into the neoliberal prescription to reverse the interventionist policies of the postwar developmental states. But the adoption of neoliberal reform was also, and probably more importantly, the result of pressure and encouragement from international institutions. National development policy was increasingly set in negotiations with international financial institutions over debt restructing and aid, or in bilateral commercial, financial, and aid negotiations with developed nations.

As expanding hard currency debt, increasing interest rates, and economic contraction threw one national budget after another into crisis, governments turned to the IMF, to their private and public bank creditors and to the central banks of the developed world for rescheduling of debt and for temporary funding to avoid massive devaluation and inflation. Increasingly, strict fiscal discipline and implementation of the broader neoliberal policy set, was imposed as a condition for internationally sanctioned debt restructuring and receipt of IMF funding to stabilize currencies. As developing nations sought to participate more fully in international trade, membership in GATT seemed ever more significant. Accession negotiations often provided the opportunity for neoliberal dismantling of postwar interventionist regimes. The GATT was itself moving beyond its initial preoccupation with the reduction of industrial tariffs to negotiation over the elimination of a much broader range of administrative and regulatory practices that could be interpreted as price distorting "nontariff barriers" to trade.

At the same time, the transnational commercial order restricted the jurisdiction of national courts and private law systems in the third world – by developing rules for the enforcement of foreign judgments and choice of law provisions permitting first world commercial law to govern transactions in the third, by establishing an enforceable commercial arbitration regime to resolve disputes cut off from national and global considerations of "public policy," and by harmonizing private law rules to eliminate social exceptions that might offer opportunities for national judicial discretion.

In one sense, taken together, the national neoliberal program was simple – the private law regimes necessary to support market transactions should be strengthened, while the public law regulations and bureaucratic procedures that impeded private exchange were dismantled. But it was clear from the start that *some* public regulation was necessary to support the market – criminal law, antitrust law, financial and monetary regulations of various sorts, and more. The difficult question for neoliberal policy at the national level was to determine which government actions supported and which impeded market activity, and to prioritize and order market supporting initiatives in the most effective way. For this we need a more precise analytic.

The neoliberal policy analytic was a blend of three somewhat different vocabularies for analyzing government policy developed in the academic literatures of political science, economics, and political economy: public choice theory, rent-seeking, and second-best welfare economics. That the first two should have raised skepticism about modest interventionist government policy is clear – the story for the last is more complicated. Public choice theory rejected the image of the state as the institutional embodiment of a general social will, and proposed analyzing it as a site for a struggle among individual bureaucrats and legislators, administrative entities and legislative bodies, all pursuing their own interests. The boundary, moreover, between public and private entities was blurry – agencies were subject to capture, and individual bureaucrats as often pursued personal as social objectives. Needless to say, looking at third world states in this light made it more difficult to imagine them as wise managers of national economic life pursuing the national development objectives. Government "failure" was everywhere – the welfare states could not be trusted with the kind of discretion envisioned by modest interventionist policy makers of the preceding generation.

The "rent-seeking" idea linked these government failures to the problem of distorted prices. Those given discretion to manage economic resources that they do not own "for the public good" have a constant incentive to rip the public off, collecting rents by restricting use of the asset, rather than profits from its sale. In such a world, assets will be withheld from productive use, or offered for use only at prices reflecting the dead weight of rents due those with administrative discretion over their utilization. In modest interventionist regimes, the incentive for rent seeking is everywhere. As a result, tariffs, subsidies, licenses, and the rest will be administered not to bring about development – not to ensure the most productive use of the asset – but to generate the maximum rents for those within or near the state apparatus administering them.

In the field of development policy, as elsewhere, the rent-seeking and public choice ideas were deployed side by side to delegitimate the welfare state, and to promote more laissez-faire. They were often linked with ideas from economics well illustrated by Deepak Lal's 1983 paper "The Poverty of 'Development Economics.'" Indeed, Lal's paper became something of a bible for critics of what he termed the "dirigiste dogma" of postwar modest interventionism and import substitution. It is not clear, however, that the second-best welfare economic analytic that Lal develops leads inexorably to laissez-faire policy prescriptions. Lal acknowledges as much. It is worth looking at his argument in some detail, as it opens the door to appreciating the uncertain link between public choice or rent-seeking analysis and laissez-faire.

Lal argued that import substitution development policy had become a dogma. Its proponents repeatedly underestimated the significance of the price mechanism, microeconomics, and participation in global trade for developing economies, while overestimating the potential for macroeconomic management. These dogmatic beliefs, he argued, led them to *assume*, rather than demonstrate the gains to be expected from particular regulatory initiatives. Lal proposed the rigorous use of modern welfare economics to analyze the effects of particular proposals for new government regulation in the context of the existing array of regulation. Perhaps they would facilitate productive use of resources, perhaps they would not.

Modern welfare economics, he argued, begins with the crucial observation that all existing economies depart dramatically from the perfectly competitive environments for which Arrow and Debreu had demonstrated the efficiency of laissez-faire. Markets are not universal, competition is not perfect – there are all manner of transactions costs and market failures – information problems, collective action problems, goods for which it is difficult to create a market, and so on. As a result, it is extremely difficult to predict the results of any regulatory change taken on its own. Everything depends on the dynamic relationship between the existing array of imperfections and the proposed initiative. Adding – or eliminating – a given regulation might move the economy closer to the imaginable, but unattainable world of perfect competition, or it might not.

What is needed is analysis, not dogma. Lal proposes a careful comparative analysis of differing government policies against the *hypothetical* benchmark of economic activity under the "shadow prices" that would prevail under perfect competition – "reflecting the relative social (rather than private) costs and benefits of using and producing different goods and services."[2] In many cases, world prices can indeed be used as a proxy set of shadow prices for

[2] Deepak Lal (2002), at 78.

purposes of comparing differing baskets of regulatory interventions. But this is quite different from insisting that any given economy or sector move directly to trade at world prices. That might be a good idea and it might not.

This attack on economic dogma applied, as Lal repeatedly insisted, as much to devotees of deregulation as regulation. There is simply no reason to assume a priori that the elimination of a "distorting" price regulation will lead to a more efficient allocation of resources. Whether adding or subtracting a regulation would increase or decrease price distortion could only be determined in context. It might turn out that the optimal "second-best" arrangement requires a new regulation or the preservation of an existing price distortion.

Lal repeatedly castigates modest interventionists for failing to conduct the "subtle exercise" in welfare economics required to justify the regulations they propose. The debate between modest interventionists and neoliberals, he argues, is one between dogma and analysis. Lal criticizes Amartya Sen for opposing neoliberal arguments for an open economy by asserting that Korea was "interventionist" and nevertheless developed rapidly. Sen misunderstands the neoliberal project. Neoliberalism, Lal insists, is not about laissez-faire. It does not insist that one should never be interventionist or that markets always be open. Neoliberalism simply demands an *analysis* of particular interventionist practices to assess their welfare effects. Similarly, in discussing modest interventionist policy experience promoting heavy industry, Lal writes:

> There is no reason to doubt that, for large countries such as India with varied natural resources, some heavy-industry products, such as steel, would pass a social-cost benefit test of economic desirability. What is irrational is the *dirigiste* claim that there are *general* grounds for preferring one branch or type of industry over another which the government can readily discern by intuition.[3]

Lal speculates about why modest interventionists have not made more use of welfare economics to substantiate their claims for regulatory initiatives. He speculates that they are biased – suspicious of "any form of intervention which attempts to supplement rather than supplant the price mechanism."[4] He concludes, however, that the main block, other than *dirigiste* bias, is simply that "second-best welfare economics is a complex and delicate intellectual pursuit" beyond the "expertise" of developing country governments.

The observation that third world governments lack the capacity for careful analysis opens the door for Lal to depart from economic sublety in favor of default policy initiatives. Lal ends his 1983 paper by noting that in the absence of technocrats willing and able to do the difficult work of analyzing policy alternatives, it might be useful for economists to offer some broad rules

[3] *Id.* at 82.

[4] *Id.* at 78–79.

of thumb. They might well rely on recent ex-post empirical studies correlating economic performance with differing levels of government intervention. These studies, he reports, seem to suggest that governments pursuing laissez-faire did better than those that intervened. As a result, in the absence of careful analysis, laissez-faire might be the best idea to propose.

> In such circumstances, (of governments with limited expertise) the *laissez-faire* outcomes of an imperfect market economy may turn out to be better than the irrational governmental interventions which alone are feasible.[5]

In 1997, Lal republished the paper with a postscript strengthening his call for a default policy of laissez-faire. Historical studies correlating more open economies with growth had mounted, and distrust of third world governments had become more insistent. Rampant corruption, incompetence, self-dealing, and rent seeking by third world elites made it unthinkable that one could expect the type of subtle analysis required to justify regulations. Public choice and rent-seeking ideas supported a move from careful analytics to neoliberal dogma. As Lal put it in 1997, "the most important change in thinking on economic policy in the Third World has been the recognition that the assumptions about the nature of the state that underpinned planning are unrealistic."[6]

It has often been observed that the laissez-faire discipline recommended for exsocialist countries or imposed upon third world nations through structural adjustment programs was far stricter than anything existing in the first world, where market interventions and regulations remained commonplace. Rent-seeking and public choice analysis could certainly help identify weaknesses in first world regulatory regimes – the political pressure to "universalize" welfare benefits that should be targeted and the political ease of adopting and difficulty of eliminating government benefits should lead one to be wary. But the developing and exsocialist states had such severe "governance" shortfalls that they could not contemplate the emergence of the sophisticated welfare state arrangements common in more developed settings. As many have pointed out, there is much room for racism and cultural prejudice in assessments like this.

Lal's transition from analysis to dogma is troubling in other ways as well. The historical studies correlating "laissez-faire" policies with economic performance require that societies be differentiated by their degree of divergence from the perfect competition – requiring precisely the analytic exercise a default policy is designed to avoid having to make. More importantly, the application of public-choice thinking and rent-seeking ideas to the activities of *public* entities seems a function of a similar dogma that Lal criticizes. There

[5] *Id.* at 79.
[6] *Id.* at 148.

seems little reason to believe that the entrepreneurial class in third world societies is any less prone to rent seeking than the public administration. To distinguish "rents" from productive uses would require a development strategy – a way of identifying and assessing the uses made of surpluses generated in various sectors. The focus on government failures may be well advised, but also distracts attention from dangers of private monopoly, anticompetitive behavior, and administered pricing. Once laissez-faire dogma replaced welfare economic analytics, there was little room for analysis of the relative gains from trade under conditions of capital mobility and free trade. With intense foreign investor penetration, for example, there was little reason to expect the gains to accrue in the third world. There was, moreover, little reason to expect that one-time efficiency gains from movement to laissez-faire would lead to development, if by that one means either industrialization or providing for basic human needs.

Resolving these issues in particular contexts would require complex welfare economics analysis. Should this particular regulation be abandoned? How quickly should we move? How sharp should the shock to market be? How should we sequence our moves – should we focus on privatization before or after banking and credit reform? What public enterprises should remain – for defense, garbage collection, electricity, telecoms, airlines? How should privatization be conducted – how quickly, on what terms, through what scheme? Is an antitrust regime appropriate – what role for "industrial policy" within it? Is it more important to promote small-scale entrepreneurship or large-scale financial markets? As an economy opened, should one focus on inward capital mobility, tariff reduction, exchange rate stabilization? When can we usefully strategize about our comparative advantage or work to alter our factor endowments over time?

The most significant contribution of neoliberalism was not a set of answers to these questions, but a new vocabulary for debating them – part economics, part politics, part sociology. Second best welfare economics provided a starting point – default ideas about the relative significance of public and private rent-seeking, public and private governance failure, played a role as well. Government policy would be appropriate where it compensated for or eliminated a market failure. Where this was difficult to assess accurately – where the distinction between "supporting" and "distorting" the market turns out to be too complex to assess with confidence – default presumptions and policy options could step in. The broad policy vocabulary that resulted was a mix of economic ideas, historical observations, sociological preconceptions, and political biases.

The focus on microeconomics and prices, the new optimism about foreign investment and trade, the pessimism about government policy capacity, and the relative confidence in private decision making, made it difficult to justify robust public development strategies – for strategic thinking about long-term national comparative advantage, or for government action to strengthen the

TABLE 5. Washington Consensus 1980–1995

Left Largely absent	Center Counterpoint	Right Mainstream
Delinking	Further chastened modest interventionism	Neoliberalism Markets
Antidevelopment	Export-led growth	Microeconomics Get prices right
	Human rights Economic and social rights Right to development	Reverse state socialism and import substitution industrialization
	Microlending	Free trade / foreign investment
	Empowerment	Public choice theory Governance failure Rent-seeking
	Indigenous peoples rights	Second best welfare economics Efficiency and growth
	Sustainable development	No need for a special economics of "development"

bargaining power of national economic actors in their international commercial transactions. It was difficult to think dynamically about what happens *after* the one-time efficiency gain, should it emerge, generated by the move to market.

Those seeking to preserve the policy tools of modest interventionism for these purposes were thrown back on their feet by criticism of *dirigiste* dogma, rent seeking, and government failure. When they recovered, and began to subject what had become neoliberal dogma to the same analytic scrutiny, they continued to find it difficult to remember the potentials for macroeconomic thinking, of attention to productivity in a dynamic input-output cycle, of distribution as a tool of development policy, for targeting bottlenecks, for harnessing the surplus to new modes of economic activity – all that had been swept away, and they found themselves arguing for interventions only where they could be said to compensate for one market failure without causing another.

We might summarize the 1980–1990 period as shown in Table 5.

Demand for law explicit in neoliberal economic theory

At the national and international level, law was the instrument for neoliberal policy. Law remained a pragmatic and purposive instrument of policy. Building down import substitution regimes required legislative and administrative changes. Structural adjustment, conditionality, and the GATT are legal regimes. Completely new legal regimes were necessary, domestically and internationally, to support markets – financial regimes, intellectual property regimes, regimes of commercial law. New statutes and administrative rules were required – to structure the privatization of state-owned enterprises, establish financial institutions, and support new capital markets. Banking and payment systems, insurance schemes – all required a new legal framework. Investment laws, and corporate laws, insurance and securities laws were needed, and were promoted across the developing world through legal reform programs

In this sense, the neoliberal program was as *instrumentalist* and *positivist* about law as modest interventionism. National import substitution regimes were to be unbuilt by treaty, statute, and administrative decree. Particularly in the first phase, the statutes proposed to accomplish these goals were quite standardized – offered to one country after another as a kind of global "best practice." The foreign experts bringing new statutes for securities regulation, corporate law, insurance, banking or commercial law, and more, were every bit as dependent upon legislative positivism and as unconcerned about the relationship between law in the books and law in action as their modest interventionist predecessors in the immediate postwar years. Like these "social" predecessors, neoliberals understood their normative regimes to be compelled by the facts of global social organization – this time the requirements of markets, and the priority of individuals, rather than the requirements of interdependence, and the priority of groups. Neoliberals were adept at turning social antiformalist ideas to new ends.

At the same time, the legal theory implicit in neoliberal development policy was quite different from that implicit in the development thinking of the previous periods. The focus shifted from public to private law. Law emerged as a *limit* on the state – on the discretion of administrators and the mandate of legislators. Private rights, constitutional procedures, judicial review, and international obligations – all constrained the neoliberal state. The focus was less legislative positivism and sovereignty than private rights and a neoformalism about the limits of public law. Focus shifted from administrative rule making or legislation to private ordering, both nationally and transnationally. Horizontal law replaced vertical law, just as a law of rights limited the law of sovereignty.

Where the law and development reformers of the 1960s had focused on reforming the legal profession to improve the implementation of administrative and legislative law, neoliberals paid very little attention to the structure or thinking of the legal profession, or to the gap between law in the books and law in action. They were not aiming to improve the effective exercise of state power, but to more effective restraint of government rent seeking. They tended to assume that potential market actors were waiting for the right rules – once in place, they would be made use of. If that didn't happen, they were not the right rules. One didn't need to worry too much about the gap. The result was a kind of *literalism* about law and legal reform.

Courts grew in significance – central to the enforcement of market transactions and limitation of public discretion. By enforcing contracts and property rights courts both support market transactions and resist encroachment by the state. If administrative failure suggested deregulation, adjudicative failure called for judicial reform. Court enforcement of private law was thought necessary to enable market actors to make use of the new rule systems being put in place.

This is not an obvious idea – administrative agencies might as well have taken responsibility for enforcing commercial arrangements or implementing neoliberal reforms. Private actors might have been willing to make their own way, enforcing their reciprocal rights extralegally, through reputation or informal private sanctions – or, they might have been willing to lump their losses as they occurred rather than seek court enforcement. Nevertheless, neoliberal policymakers seem to have assumed that private market actors needed to see reliable courts to transact. Although potential foreign investors often *said* they wanted better courts during this period, it would take more study to understand whether this was accompanied by actual use of courts by these actors, either abroad or at home in the industrialized north. It would take still more to discover if this was a significant factor for other market actors, or was rather a collective prejudice of potential foreign investors of the day.

The focus on courts also accompanied a retreat from the legislative and administrative positivism of the modest interventionist period. With powers of *judicial review*, courts could enforce property rights against the executive, restraining its ability to mobilize resources for development and encouraging a retreat from interventionism. Of course, judicial review could be a double-edged sword. The modest interventionist regime had also generated a wide range of entitlements that were to be undone by neoliberal reforms. For judicial review to support the neoliberal reform process, courts would need to be able to distinguish inappropriate price distorting entitlement claims from "real" property rights.

The international legal regime soon found itself needing similar expertise. The United Nations of the NIEO had relied upon international public law – treaties, General Assembly resolutions, ICJ judgments, new administrative arrangements – to address political concerns about the global distribution of wealth and the fairness of international bargaining. Neoliberalism shifted attention from the United Nations to the General Agreement on Tariffs and Trade. The GATT would harness the politics of complex global bargaining sessions toward a different objective – the progressive elimination of national regulatory barriers to trade and the liberation of the global market.

This project required both formal tariff "bindings" and an apparatus – at the national and international level – for interpreting the GATT's central legal obligations ("national treatment" and "most-favored nation"), a range of vague exceptions (such as "national security") and for determining which national regulatory arrangements were *equivalent* to tariff barriers or subsidies. Interpreting these standards – to determine what counted as a "nontariff barrier" – required more than a formal application of treaty definition. National trade law regimes were always tempted to think any foreign impediment to their imports was an unfair barrier to trade – they would need a vocabulary of self-restraint. As the WTO's own interpretive machinery became increasingly juridical in nature, it would also require interpretive facility with the distinction between an unfair barrier to trade and a normal national background regulation.

A "free trade" regime requires more than the elimination of tariffs. As tariffs came down, industrial nations began to challenge all sorts of diverse pieces of one another's regulatory environment as "nontariff barriers to trade." In doing so, they were contesting elements of one another's background regime. It is an old legal realist insight that the reciprocal nature of a comparison between two legal rules – or legal regimes – makes it impossible to say which *causes* the harm – or which is "discriminatory." Is it the railroad's right of way that damages the farmer's wheat – or the farmer's property right that imposes cost on rail transport? In the trade context, we might ask whether Mexico's low minimum wage – or failure to implement its own minimum wage scheme – is an unfair "subsidy," or whether Mexican manufacturers who benefit from nonenforcement of local law are "dumping" when they export to American markets. But one might equally well ask whether it is a "nontariff barrier," an unfair or unreasonable extraterritorial reach of U.S. law, for the United States to demand higher labor standards for production of goods to be imported to its market.

Legal analysts might, at least in the first instance, draw the distinction in formal terms – if the foreign rule takes the form of a tariff or subsidy, it is an unfair barrier to trade, if not, not. But early on it was recognized that national regulators could use "nontariff barriers" to equally market restrictive effect. One might be tempted to preclude all *public* regulatory price distortions, while using antitrust to attack parallel private market distorting arrangements – but too many neoliberal regulatory initiatives might also fall under this ax. What is required is a mode of distinction that analyzes regulations for their actual market restricting or enabling potential. In the early stages, background ideas about what is "normal" served the purpose – if farmers *normally* grow wheat, a new railroad may appear to impose the cost, if the difference between American and Mexican wages is "normal," American efforts to raise Mexican standards will seem an abnormal nontariff barrier. As ever more national regulations were contested for their compatibility with national and global trade standards progressed, such default ideas seemed ever less plausible.

Managing the neoliberal regime in all these dimensions would require enormous skill and precision in rule making and interpretation. National trade regimes would need to identify and sanction foreign unfair or corrupt practices, by private and public entities alike, without descending into protectionism or rent seeking, or becoming captive to the interests of local exporters. Throughout the third world, government agencies responsible for industrial development would need to support commerce and trade, while avoiding price-distorting interventions and rent seeking. National and international agencies would need to offer technical assistance to explain privatization, as they had once explained marketing boards. Buffer stocks were out – but commodity futures markets were in, and programs were implemented to train farmers across India in the use of the Internet to check prices on the Chicago exchanges. Private arbitrators would need to distinguish contractually intended obligations from fraudulent, self-dealing, coercive arrangements of disguised rent seeking. Judges would need to rework private law to eliminate the effects of distortive "social" objectives, shrink opportunities for discretion that could be used by national officials to discriminate, and in general orient private law to encourage or mimic the pareto-optimal arrangements private parties would arrive at were they able to transact without costs. All this would require a new style of legal reasoning.

With the focus on courts, private law enforcement, and judicial review to protect property entitlements from interventionist rent-seeking, the pragmatic and flexible antiformalism that "law and development" professionals had sought to inculcate during the law and development movement, was replaced by a kind of formalism. But this was not the formalism of judicial passivity – the spread of judicial review placed courts in a far more central role. More importantly, to distinguish property entitlements whose enforcement supported the market from entitlements whose enforcement would extend the distorting effects of modest interventionism required a mode of reasoning that reached beyond formalism. A sharp and formal distinction between private rights and publicly created entitlements seemed a good place to start. But this would not be the end of the story. Judges would need to determine *which* property rights to enforce in cases of conflict, and how extensive to interpret exceptions. *Some* administratively created rights – concessions to foreign investors exploiting natural resources, tax incentives, exemptions from zoning or local regulation, and eminent domain powers – were also part of the neoliberal order. Judges would need to be able to distinguish rights that must be enforced for the market to succeed, and rent-seeking or corrupt entitlement claims that needed to be rejected. In making these distinctions, judges would need to align their interpretation of property rights with good policy sense – participating in the new discourse about the existence, extent, and prognosis for market failures and the justifications for regulation and intervention.

In this sense, neoliberalism's implicit theory of legal reasoning combined neoformalism with a policy analytics borrowed from neoliberal economics. It was not the subtle analytics of second-best welfare economics proposed by Lal, but the curious amalgam of welfare economics, more informal ideas about the type and extent of possible market failures, default ideas about likely governance failures, sporadic empiricism correlating national legal institutions and legal rules – or the reputations of these institutions – with economic performance to identify "best practices," informal deference to the attitudes of the foreign investor community, a literalism about law's instrumental potential, and professional conventions of interpretive restraint. The image of a perfectly competitive Kaldor-Hicks efficient end state provided a kind of loose reference point and target, against which to compare various judicial approaches. So whether the market failure is big or small, whether the new policy corresponds to and will correct for a transaction cost, is a matter of degree, on a continuum, in particular cases. Will the enforcement of this right, given our hunches, economic theories, and empirical awareness, put us on the track to Kaldor-Hicks efficiency or not? The legal discourse produced as answers were sought for such questions sometimes presented itself as a technical machine of formal deduction or economic analytics, but it was usually a puzzling blend of the two, interspersed with loose empirical or sociological hunches.

As neoliberalism advanced, moreover, two large default ideas about law became more salient – useful to guide interpretation in this new juridical policy vocabulary – *formalization* and *anticorruption.* During the neoliberal period, the conviction grew among development professionals that economic performance in the third world required a formalization of law and the elimination of corruption. As the evolving neoliberal policy vocabulary became ever more hazy and multifaceted, these two ideas provided a reassuring stability. Each has a long history in literature about economics and law, and each suggests a set of tactics for policy making. Each heightens the sense that the rule of law can be enhanced – and policy choices necessary for interpretation made – without making the sort of overtly political choices about distribution of resources that characterized both modest interventionism and the international proposals of the NIEO.

Although the policy vocabulary of neoliberal interpretation was extremely flexible – and became more so in the last decade – there is no question that the focus on formalization and anticorruption narrowed the range for interpretive maneuver from the more open-ended, socially oriented discourse of the preceding periods. The implicit – and sometimes explicit – legal theory of neoliberalism seemed to forget much of what had been commonplace within the domain of legal theory for more than a century about both the limits of law as an instrument of social change, and the plasticity of legal rules and standards. To observers who remained committed to the legal theories of prior periods, it could often seem that neoliberalism asked the legal order to perform feats it was unlikely to accomplish, and to remain neutral in making distinctions in ways it seemed unlikely to sustain.

One might say that neoliberals promoting formalization and anticorruption seemed to deny the necessity for interpretation, and for the difficulty of making precisely the sorts of distinctions between market ordering and market distorting made salient by their economic ideas. Indeed, the focus on formalization and anticorruption as *legal* strategies for development seemed to substitute both for the subtle exercises of welfare economic analytics initially called for by Lal, and for the more open-ended juridical policy analysis that emerged from efforts to link identification of market failures with broader empirical hunches and default assumptions.

Since at least Weber, people have asserted that "formalization" of legal entitlements, in one or another sense, is necessary for development. Necessary for transparency, for information and price signaling, to facilitate alienation of property, to reduce transaction costs, to assure security of title and economic return, or to inspire the confidence and trust needed for investment. From the start, legal formalization has meant a wide variety of things – a scheme of clear and registered titles, of contractual simplicity and reliable enforcement, a legal system of clear rules rather than vague standards, a scheme of legal doctrine whose internal structure was logical and whose interpretation could be mechanical, a system of institutions and courts whose internal hierarchy was mechanically enforced, in which the discretion of judges and administrators was reduced to a minimum, a public order of passive rule following, a priority for private over public law, and more. These ideas are all associated with the reduction of discretion and political choice in the legal system, and are defended as instantiations of the old maxim "not under the rule of man but of god and the law."

The association of legal formalization with development, however, has always seemed more problematic than this, also since at least Weber. For starters, it has also been easy to imagine, from the point of view of *other* economic actors, that formalization in each of these ways might well eliminate the chance for productive economic activity. A clear title may help me to sell or defend my claims to land – but it may impede the productive opportunities for squatters now living there or neighbors whose uses would interfere with my quiet enjoyment. A great deal will depend on what we *mean* by clear title – which of the numerous possible entitlements might go with "title to property" we choose to enforce. Clear rules about investment may make it easy for foreign investors – but by reducing the wealth now in the hands of those with local knowledge about how credit is allocated or how the government will behave. An enforceable contract will be great for the person who wants the promise enforced, but not so for the person who has to pay up. As every first year contracts student learns, it is one thing to say stable expectations need to be respected, and quite another to say whose expectations need to be respected and what those expectations should legitimately or reasonably be. To say anything about the relationship between legal formalization and *development* we would need a theory about how assets in the hands of the title holder *rather than* the squatter, the foreign *rather than* the local investor will lead to growth, and then to the sort of growth we associate with "development."

The story of development-through-formalization downplays the range of possible legal formalizations, each with its own winners and losers. Disinterest in the distributional choices one must make in designing a rule of law suitable for a policy of legal "formalization" is common in literature promoting the rule of law as a development strategy. Hernando de Soto's famous discussion of the benefits of legal formalization in his 2000 book, *The Mystery of Capital*, provides a good illustration. In discussing land reform, he is adamant that squatters be given formal title to the land on which they have settled. Doing so, he claims, will create useful capital by permitting them to eject trespassers, have the confidence to improve the land, or offer it for sale to more productive users. Of course, it will also destroy the capital of the current land owners – and, if the squatter's new rights are enforced, reduce economic opportunities for trespassers and future squatters. Formalization of title will also distribute authority *among* squatters – where families squat together, for example, formalization may well move economic discretion from women to men. The implicit assumption that squatters will make more productive use of the land than the current nominal owners may well often be correct. But de Soto provides no reason for supposing that the squatters will be more productive than the trespassers, nor for concluding that exclusive use by one or the other group is preferable to some customary arrangement of mixed use by squatters and trespassers in the shadow of an ambiguous law.

None of these observations is new. Development planners and practitioners have long struggled with precisely these problems. The puzzle is how easily one loses sight of these traditional issues of political and economic theory when the words "rule of law" come into play. There is something mesmerizing about the idea that a formal rule of law could somehow substitute for struggle over these issues and choices – or could replace contestable arguments about the consequences of different distributions with the apparent neutrality of legal best practice.

A second theme running through neoliberal ideas about the potential for using law as a development strategy focuses on eliminating corruption. Many of the advantages of eliminating corruption run parallel to those of legal formalization – eliminating corruption can seem much like eliminating judicial and administrative discretion. Indeed, sometimes "corruption" is simply a code word for public discretion – the state acts corruptly when it acts by discretion rather than mechanically, by rule. Enthusiasm for eliminating corruption as a development strategy arises from the broader idea that corruption somehow drains resources from the system as a whole – its costs are costs of transactions, not costs of the product or service purchased. Elimination of such costs lifts all boats. And such costs might as easily be quite formal and predictable as variable and discretionary. Here the desire to eliminate corruption goes beyond the desire for legal form – embracing the desire to eliminate all costs *imposed* on transactions that are not properly costs *of* the transaction. There are at least two difficulties here. First, the connection between eliminating corruption and "development" remains obscure. Even if the move from a "corrupt" legal regime to a "not corrupt" regime produces a one-time efficiency gain, there is no good economic theory predicting that this will lead to growth or development, rather than simply another stable low-level equilibrium. More troubling is the difficulty of distinguishing clearly between the "normal" or "undistorted" price of a commodity and the "costs" associated with a "corrupt" or distortive process for purchasing the commodity or service. These were precisely the sorts of distinctions first addressed by the analytics of welfare economics, then by the looser policy vocabulary of neoliberalism, for which anticorruption and formalization emerged as default substitutes.

Hernando de Soto again provides a good illustration. He repeatedly asserts that the numerous bureaucratic steps now involved in formalizing legal entitlements are mud in the gears of capital formation and commerce, retarding development. He has been a central voice urging simplification of bureaucratic procedures as a development strategy – every minute and every dollar spent going to the state to pay a fee or get a stamp is a resource lost to development. This seems intuitively plausible. But there is a difficulty – when is the state supporting a transaction by formalizing it and when is the state burdening the transaction by adding unnecessary steps or costs? The aspiration seems to be an economic life without friction, each economic act mechanically supported without costs. But legal forms, like acts of discretion, are not simply friction – they are choices, defenses of some entitlements against others. Each bureaucratic step necessary to enforce a formal title is a subsidy for the economic activity of informal users. Indeed, everything that seems friction to one economic actor will seem like an entitlement, an advantage, an opportunity to another. The point is to develop a theory for choosing among them.

In fact, it is probably more sensible to think of both the formalism and the anticorruption campaigns as political, rather than as economic projects. They were oriented far more explicitly to the perception of governance failure than to economic performance per se. They responded to the widely shared sense among development professionals that third world governments simply could not be trusted with policy making, regardless of the approach taken. If neoliberalism's energy had come, in part, from its enthusiasm for a *small* state, campaigns for formalism and against corruption were also driven by the desire for a *strong* state, capable of enforcing public order and private rights – without messing in the economy. If we think in distributional terms, there is no question that neoliberal legal theory accepted ideas about law more common in the foreign investor community than in most developing nations themselves. Many ideas about the law needed for development turned out to be about the law foreign investors wanted to see. In exsocialist countries, as elsewhere, there is no doubt that some local players were better situated to play in this new legal world and to deploy this new legal vocabulary than others.

In ideological terms, these ideas about law are quite difficult to characterize politically. Instrumentalism, positivism, and literalism about the economic consequences of legal initiatives have characterized all manner of ideological projects. Although a commitment to "formalism" was long associated in the United States with laissez-faire recollections of the nineteenth-century period of classical legal thought, it has certainly also served other masters. So also, of course, for judicial review. Projects to formalize small-scale rights to "empower" those in the informal sector to participate in the formal economy were extremely popular across the ideological spectrum, at least in the North. Formalization and anticorruption campaigns likewise. Moreover, the mode of legal reasoning about policy that developed – welfare economics, empirical observations, sociological hunches – to determine which state rules were market supporting and which were not, was used during this period by left, center, and right development professionals.

It did seem, however, that at least broadly speaking, the more market failures you thought there were, the more often you thought government initiatives might well correct them, the less certain you were about defaulting to laissez-faire, the more faith you had in third world government initiatives, the less significant a problem you felt corruption was, the slower you felt the transition to market should proceed, the more skeptical you were about the large-scale benefits of small-scale formalization, the more likely you were to be a center left of left-wing analyst. What was fascinating, however, was the relatively swift loss of a voice for "social" legal ideas as a vocabulary for the left – as well, of course, for the center and right.

The legal vocabulary of neoliberalism, however capacious ideologically, had its blind spots as well. As a policy analytic, it had little room for distributional concerns, particularly efforts to see first-order distribution as a tool for development planning. It pushed issues of redistribution, of fairness in allocation and in bargaining, off the table, and focused attention on the nature of the local public and private legal order, rather than on the international legal, political, or economic system. It does seem that the formalization and anticorruption campaigns had the effect of pushing even neoliberal policy

TABLE 6. Mainstream: 1980–1995

Basic ideas **Economics**	**Development policy set**	**Legal theory** *Classical legal thought* *Law and economics* *Rights formalism*	
		Instrumental thinking	*Rights thinking*
Neoliberalism	Politically and economically small state	Legal pragmatism	Public and private law neoformalism
Efficiency and human rights	Get prices right	Law = policy	Property and contract rights
The “transition” from socialism to the market	Strengthen private law	Efficiency and Kaldor-Hicks for judges	Formalization of entrenched rights
From totalitarianism to democracy	Weaken public law	Eliminate rent seeking and corruption	Enforce private transactions
Hayek liberalism	Facilitate participation in global market	Public law literalism and neoformalism	Limit the state
	Open markets/world prices	WTO as world constitution	Judges
	“Best practice” property law, corporate law, tax reform		Judicial review
	International financial management		Human rights
	Structural adjustment IMF/WTO/IBRD		
	Transnational private ordering		

analytics to one side, let alone the legal policy vocabularies of the “social,” or of “modest interventionism.” Development policies rooted in distributional analysis were more difficult to imagine and propose. The legal projects necessary to create a small economic state while strengthening the public order state, reemphasized distinctions between public and private legal orders and institutions that had everywhere been eroded during the same period in the North in favor of more flexible “soft law” styles of governance or public-private partnerships. This certainly responded to the stigma associated with third world governance, but it also undoubtedly reinforced it.

We might summarize the mainstream of the 1980s as shown in Table 6.

The politics of neoliberalism: From opposition to mainstream

In ideological terms, this new vocabulary was everywhere associated, at least initially, with the right. Neoliberal ideas were developed by intellectuals associated with right-wing parties in the North, and were first tried in countries self-consciously making a transition from left to right – starting with Pinochet's Chile, and continuing through the "transition" of exsocialist societies "from plan to market" after 1989. Indeed, during this period, the left largely disappeared from development thinking – into local resistance movements, hostility to development, and various visions of self-reliance and "delinking," a slogan made famous by Egyptian development economist Samir Amin. After 1980, the steam went out of the entire framework of proposals associated with the NIEO. The liberal center in the North continued to promote versions of modest interventionism, but with ever less enthusiasm – indeed, centrist thinkers became critical of top-down instrumental programs, lost interest in development economics altogether and became enamored with small-scale local development initiatives, with empowerment initiatives to encourage participation in local government, with microlending, and with the global vocabulary of human rights and dignity. By the late 1980s, the broad framework for thinking about what would have been called "development" was provided by the policy vocabulary of neoliberalism.

These ideas drew strength from their association – largely incorrectly, as it turned out – with the relative success of the Asian tigers. The economic performance of the Asian tigers – striking in comparison to the situation in Africa, Latin America, and elsewhere in the developing world – made it easy to think that they must have been doing something *completely* different. Little was known about their internal governance – but it was clear that they exported a great deal. This export orientation was interpreted as a general *openness* to the global economy – although it was not at all clear foreign investment and ownership was any more welcome than imports that competed with national firms. Openness was then commonly associated with laissez-faire – precisely the chain of associations against which Lal had warned. Nevertheless, many of the ex post empirical work correlating policy choices with development interpreted the Asian tigers in just this way – as export oriented, open economies, disciplined by world prices with governments committed to the restraint of laissez-faire. In a further leap, their success was repeatedly cited for the proposition that introducing laissez-faire through a quick dismantling of modest interventionism – a "shock" to "market" prices – was unlikely to be a wrong step.

Looking back, the differences between development regimes in Asia and elsewhere were more fine grained. There was more success outside the Asian tigers than it had seemed in 1980. All import substitution regimes promoted exports, including, after the mid-1960s, various industrial, manufactured, and processed exports. Other differences – prewar industrial experience, land reform, relative income inequality, the rise of national firms, low levels of foreign ownership, administrative quality, and precision in policy targeting – may have been more important in their relative success, as Alice Amsden has most prominently argued. There is no question that the governments of the Asian tigers were interventionist – and local prices were not always world prices. Most importantly, they had their own histories – that nowhere included the sort of "market shock" advocated by those who would imitate their success.

These various ideas coalesced around a political commitment to the sharp separation of "public" and "private" actors, institutions, and modes of thinking. Public actors were to be mistrusted. They were prone to rent seeking and other failures identified in the public choice literature. Private actors were understood to be more rational in their responsiveness to price cues. Public ordering – government action – was understood to take place upon a preexisting, even natural, background of private ordering, itself innocent of public action. Markets were understood to emerge naturally from the private bargaining of dispersed actors – while governments were more artificial constructions that could easily fail. The government action necessary to support markets could be cleanly distinguished from price distortion, rent seeking, and corruption. These ideas entered the neoliberal policy vernacular as soft background assumptions about the nature and limits of politics.

Neoliberals seemed to share a background memory of nineteenth-century liberalism as a golden age – hence the term "neoliberal." In their memory, politics and economics were cleanly separated in the liberal nineteenth-century world – a separation buttressed by a universal practice of governmental self-restraint. Combined with open borders and a stable global currency, this ideological consensus had functioned, in the words of Wilhelm Roepke, as an "as if" world government.[7] This historical memory suggested a goal for policy – to build down the legacy of collectivism, nationally and internationally, by reducing tariffs and other national price distortions through a slowly emerging transnational policy consensus.

These various intellectual influences were associated in the period with the right, and it is not surprising that neoliberalism would have been understood – is still understood – as a series of right-wing policy initiatives and theoretical preoccupations. The interesting thing, however, is that as soon as neoliberalism became a policy vocabulary combining technical criticisms and vague historical, political, and sociological observations, it became the host for debates about specific policy directions that were easy to associate with broader left-center-right ideological debates. The slower one proposed to move to market, the more regulations one defended, the more participation by the state in the economy one felt justified, the more one focused on the national economy and the less enthusiastic one was about trade liberalization or foreign investment, the more "market failures" one found, and the more willing one was to associate regulation with their amelioration, the further to the "left" one must be. Eventually, moreover, right, center, and left

[7] Wilhelm Roepke, *Economic Order and International Law*, 86 Recueil des Cours 209 (1954).

regimes adopted broadly neoliberal approaches to development – exactly as they had modest interventionist policies in the postwar period. Experts in all regimes defended their policies in a market, rather than a resource mobilization, vocabulary.

There is no question, however, that the neoliberal vocabulary as a whole, like its predecessors, also had an effect on the range of policies and the modes of justification available to any party. Most significantly, neoliberalism brought with it a sharply diminished level of political or governmental aspiration. One need not worry too much about development – if we get out of the way, private actors will allocate resources automatically to their most productive uses. It became more difficult to imagine and pursue national economic policies that made choices about resource allocation different from those made by private, and generally foreign, parties. It became more difficult for governments to develop expertise in planning and targeting. Social objectives seemed newly distinct from development – to be achieved through tax and transfer later, after the pie had grown. Distributive policies of all kinds became suspect. At the global level, it became difficult for the United Nations and the public law community to imagine a role for itself in development or economic issues.

PHASE FOUR: A CHASTENED NEOLIBERALISM 1995–2005

Rethinking: Economics, politics, society, and law

During the 1990s, disappointment with the economic, as well as the political and social results of the neoliberal "market shock" transition in East/Central Europe and Russia, the Asian and Latin American currency crises of the late 1990s, growing popular opposition to "structural adjustment" policies across the South, and a widespread feeling of vulnerability, also in the North, to "globalization" – opened a space for new thinking. Clinton administration appointees to the international financial institutions took a second look at structural adjustment and "transition" policies. Social movements in the first and third worlds assailed neoliberalism in new terms. As in the 1990s, there were new technical economic arguments about the limits of the maturing model, as well as alternative policy projects animated by ideas about politics, society, and law.

Nevertheless, the neoliberal paradigm has continued to be baseline common sense among development professionals. There has been little call for a return to modest interventionism, to import substitution industrialization or to the development economics of the postwar period. The paradigm shift from macroeconomics to microeconomics, from the idea of an input-output cycle to that of a market, from getting distribution right for the mobilization of savings to getting prices right for the efficient allocation of resources, has remained decisive. However, it is still thought that first and third world economies obey the same broad laws. Welfare economics remains the dominant economic analytic for assessing regulatory initiatives, and the looser policy discourse of market failures it spawned remains the dominant vocabulary for talking about national economic regulation. The nationalist third world welfare state remains intensely stigmatized – corrupt, inefficient, stagnant, and kleptocratic. Only the military – largely the first world military – is now thought capable of large-scale political projects of nation building or development, and doubts on that score are growing. Laissez-faire remains a potent default proposal when governments are thought inept, and the shock of world market prices is still thought a useful tonic – most recently in Iraq. Formalization and anticorruption campaigns remain vigorous.

At the same time, the neoliberal paradigm supporting this baseline common sense has been chastened. It had taken a generation for the goal of a modest interventionist "take off" to seem illusory, and for development professionals to chasten, if not abandon, the postwar paradigm of modest interventionism. Disillusionment with market shock came more quickly. To give a sense for scale – in the decade after 1989, Russian GDP was cut in half, while income inequality grew significantly – doubled in Gini coefficient terms. During the same period, China's GDP nearly doubled. The difference might have numerous explanations, but one could not help asking whether the fact that Russia embraced a market shock transition from state socialism while China did not might have had something to do with it.

As economists tried to make sense of the results of neoliberal policy in the early 1990s, many concluded, in broad terms, that there turned out to have been more market failures than they had thought. Markets in developing and transitional economies were thin, information costs high, transactions costs enormous, oligopolies and monopolies were everywhere, and so on. The need for careful, situation specific, government policy was consequently greater than anticipated. Although neoliberals had recognized that market failures could call for regulatory policy, the widespread perception of governance failure had led neoliberals to recommend laissez-faire as a kind of default best policy. The idea that an all-at-once market shock transition might stimulate *new* markets, overcoming existing market failures, had encouraged policy-makers to disregard, rather than carefully assess, the potential for market failures.

Market failure takes us back to Lal's "subtle" second-best welfare economics analytic. Many, like Lal, called for more careful analysis in these terms. When it came to policy prognostication, however, they also looked for general rules of thumb, rooted in economic analysis, but supported as well by sociological hunches, empirical study of past practices and economic performance in other societies. We might call the vernacular that emerged from this blend of economics and sociology "market failure policy analysis."

This approach began with skepticism, rather than optimism, about the disestablishment of market regulation *in particular contexts*. Although the elimination of regulation might in principle lead to efficiency gains by reducing public rent-seeking and price distortions, in particular circumstances it could turn out that the elimination of a regulation, on its own, could result in a decrease in efficiency. As economists reviewed the disappointments of neoliberalism, they developed a lengthening list of exceptional conditions that might prevent the efficient operation of markets in underdeveloped or transitional economies. The particular circumstance in which deregulation might not generate automatic efficiency gains turned out to be prevalent in developing economies. The need to go slow, to analyze carefully, to address governance failures not by eliminating government but by building regulatory capacity, came to seem paramount.

This is, of course, a quite different vocabulary for justifying regulations than the modest interventionist preoccupation with distribution and surplus mobilization. The analysis remains focused on market efficiency, and regulations are justified only as responses to market failures. Moreover, policy makers needed to address the possibility for governance failure. Nevertheless, the language of 'market failure' was extremely capacious. Developing and developed economies again seemed different, rejuvenating interest in a specialized 'development' economics. A wide variety of typical market failures suggested a range of default regulatory initiatives. But 'market failure analysis' – whether a tight analytic or a set of default judgments about necessary regulation – was not the end of the story.

Joseph Stiglitz was perhaps the most prominent mainstream economic critic of the Washington Consensus. The Clinton administration had supported his appointment as Chief Economist at the World Bank, and his work from the early 1990s was devoted to analyzing the disappointments first of market shock transition in Russia, East and Central Europe, and then of neoliberal structural adjustment policies elsewhere. His keynote address at the 1999 World Bank Annual Conference on Development Economics summarized a decade of movement away from neoliberalism, and has served as a manifesto for a new approach[8] – much as Lal's short paper had done a generation before.

Stiglitz's criticism of neoliberalism was rooted in neoinstitutionalist economics. Market failure analysis – itself a marriage of second-best welfare economics and empirical studies of best practice – was a starting point. Stiglitz went further, however, in his embrace of the need for institutional, cultural,

[8] Joseph E. Stiglitz, *Whither Reform? Ten Years of Transition*, Keynote Address at Annual World Bank Conference on Development Economics (April 28, 1999), ***available at*** http://www.worldbank.org/research/abcde/washington_11/pdfs/stiglitz.pdf, summarizing his book WHITHER SOCIALISM (1994).

and political analysis of development policy. He begins by displacing the Arrow-Debreu model as the unchallenged starting point for analysis.

> ... while AD models capture one essential aspect of a market economy – the information conveyed by price signals, and the role that those price signals serve in coordinating production – the information problems addressed by the economy are far richer. Prices do not convey all the relevant information.[9]

What conveys the relevant information turns out to be institutions, culture, and "social glue." Moreover, the dynamic development of markets can only be understood, Stiglitz argued, by taking into account the social and political effects of market shifts on institutions. Economic changes generate results in a relationship to "norms, social institutions, social capital, and trust."[10]

Stiglitz chastised neoliberals for assuming that once assets were in private hands, they would eventually find their way to productive uses through price signals. Whether they did or did not would depend on the existing institutional structure, as well as cultural and political context. He worries about obstacles to the emergence of markets after privatization – lack of capital, exceptional transactions costs, information gaps of various sorts, as well as a lack of entrepreneurial experience and culture. In analyzing the dynamic interactions of regulatory change and institutional context, Stiglitz is as concerned about the impact of private behavior – private rent seeking, private efforts to use the political process to thwart the effects of virtuous deregulatory policies, failures of private decision making and entrepreneurial culture – as he is about government failure, capture, or rent seeking.

In sequencing reforms, the effects of one reform on another must be assessed. A first reform might generate a social effect – or political response – that will in turn make later reforms more difficult or impossible. He castigated neoliberals for failing to notice the "role of the institutional blitzkrieg in destroying but not replacing the old social norms – and thus in removing the last restraints against society-threatening levels of corruption."[11]

In short, for Stiglitz, the development policy maker must reckon with the extreme interrelatedness of everything with everything else in a society. Doing so will require policy makers who can stay the course – not simply a one shot importation of best practice legislation to make "the transition" to market capitalism, but an ongoing attentiveness to institutions, culture, politics and economics. Although Stiglitz shared skepticism about the capacity of governments to do this – and to avoid doing it too much, or in the wrong way – he was equally skeptical of the notion that private actors responding to price incentives would take care of the problem. Government failure was no more or less

[9] *Id.* at 4.
[10] *Id.* at 8.
[11] *Id.*

likely than a failure of private decision-making, government rent seeking no more or less likely than private rent seeking.

It is not surprising that this demand for ongoing policy attention to the interconnectedness of everything would lead to its own default assumptions and rules of thumb. Post-1995 defaults often reversed the prescriptions of the neoliberal era. Be suspicious of best practices from elsewhere. Take it slow. Be cautious about destroying existing institutions, social networks, and economic patterns. The existing import substitution supported enterprise might well be inefficient, compared to firms elsewhere, but it would nevertheless have an elaborate network of suppliers and customers, habits of management, and patterns of employment. Third world administrative bureaucracies, as well as the economic arrangements of Soviet law should be revisited – institutional cultures and industrial forms might better be preserved, or altered only slowly. One should hesitate before throwing out this cultural capital – replacements may not automatically appear.

Stiglitz's most well-known development of this idea focused on the impact of neoliberal corporate restructuring, which led to society-wide unemployment.

> An essential part of the transition to a more efficient economy is the redeployment of resources from less productive to more productive uses. Moving workers from low productive employment to unemployment does not, by itself, increase productivity. Indeed, productivity is lowered, and some productivity is better than none. The movement into unemployment is a costly and inefficient intermediate stage – one could only defend it if there were no better way of moving workers directly from a low productivity job to a higher productivity job.[12]

The problem arises when workers, once unemployed, have no productive work to which they can move – when, for example, there is no culture of entrepreneurship to generate jobs, no capital available for new enterprises, or when the existing human capital is invested in "skills in evading government regulations, in arbitraging some of the inefficiencies in government regulations for private profit, and in operating at the interstices between the legal and illegal world."[13]

Although the initial focus was softening the more extreme market shock policies – overly rapid privatization or sudden opening to world prices – it soon became clear that an extremely wide range of policies might be defended in Stiglitzian terms. Most importantly, the analysis of cultural history and path dependence, institutional experience and political impact generated policy *choices* rather than a single right answer. There might be a range of different paths open to a given society, leading to equally efficient, but different, equilibria. One size does not – or need not – fit all.

[12] *Id.* at 6.
[13] *Id.*

As a result, policymakers will be required to make choices about the strategies to pursue. Alternative paths will doubtless have different winners and losers. To the extent these choices cannot be made through a tight analytic, a chastened neoliberalism might open the way to a more overtly political analysis. Stiglitz himself does not go this far. He recognizes that the analytic framework he proposes requires such a complex assessment of social and political factors that it may well not generate clear guidelines for policy. For him, the key is procedural rather than political: development policy making should be decentralized. In part, locating decisions as close to the ground as possible reflects a hunch that those with more local knowledge will be more able to understand the cultural, institutional and political context within which development policy will need to be made – they will make "better" decisions, more attuned to local context, culture and institutions. It is clear we have come a ways from the neoliberal's intense suspicion of government failure and the rent-seeking propensity of local elites. In part, the preference for decentralization simply reflects a sense that neoliberal policy making had erred in the other direction – stigmatizing all local knowledge and privileging the foreign expert. The emphasis on decentralization also reflected a political commitment – a shared sensibility among social democrats of the 1990s favoring "stakeholder" participation in private and public decision making, even if it was difficult to identify with precision who *are* "the stakeholders."

In short, by the mid-1990s, confidence in the availability of a decisive economic analytic for designing development policy had waned. But development professionals did not see the alternative as a set of political choices. Instead, they built a loose vernacular, rooted in market failure analysis, supplemented by default policy preferences and a preference for decentralized local decision making. The choices for policymakers were recast as questions of degree on a continuum between faster and slower movement to markets, more and less complete dismantling of dirigiste regimes, greater or lesser submission to the discipline of laissez-faire and world prices, and greater or lesser national regulatory restraint.

As confidence in the precision of economic analysis declined, development professionals also reached out in other directions. They turned increasingly to empirical studies correlating economic performance with all manner of policy choices, institutional arrangements, and cultural patterns in the effort to identify "best practices." It might be possible to sidestep the need for a good theory of development – and for detailed context specific analysis of culture, institutions, and so forth. If everywhere they did X they had good economic performance, and wherever they did not do X one found worse performance, it could hardly be a mistake to do X. Of course, correlation is not causation – X might have been the result of strong economic performance, or both might have resulted from some third element. But as economic theories of development became more complex, more situation specific, and less decisive, correlative evidence seemed more attractive as a guide for policy. Empirical studies were particularly useful in bolstering sociological hunches and default policy suggestions that emerged from the welter of more complex theoretical analysis.

Empirical study was not the only source for default preferences. Stiglitz's emphasis on "stakeholder" decentralization had introduced his own political and ethical sentiments. He was not alone. A professional interest in path dependence, context, and institutional history blurs easily into an ethical or political preference for localism, social networks, and small-scale solutions – microlending, perhaps – on the theory that development "takes a village." The appeal of "slowing down," "respecting the way things are done here," paying attention to "existing human capital," comes as well from its humanist ethics and solidarist politics.

Development professionals now share an intuitive sense about the appropriate size for the state, and the appropriate balance between public and private, which it is hard not to interpret as a political, social, or ethical sentiment about the good society rather than an analytic resolution to the problems of public and private rent seeking or governance failures. In this vision, the state is no longer the neoliberal minimalist small state, keeping the peace and enforcing private rights. But it is also not the modest interventionist state mobilizing the resources of a nation for industrialization – "nation building." The new medium-sized state is to be the economy's ally, not its engine or opponent. The political horizon of this medium-sized state was modest. In addition to these market-supporting efforts, the state needs to assure the ongoing political viability of the policies necessary for growth. It should be a stable state, oriented toward maintaining a social democratic market, integrated with the world economy. Seen longer term, the state is declining – as market failures diminish, the need for the state should lessen. In the meantime, "good governance" is crucial. Programs of institutional reform, capacity building, and technical assistance – all long part of the development policy portfolio – suddenly took on a new urgency and a new direction.

Building and maintaining this public capacity was important not only to achieve development. One might say that the institutions necessary to avoid public and private rent-seeking and ensure a stable, social democratic market, were the very definition of development. To live in a country with an appropriate state is to be developed. And only such a state can develop its citizens – responsive to their needs, investing in their human capital. There is a kind of implicit virtuous cycle here – the good state is the origin, the result, and the definition of development.

As a result, the focal point for development policy was increasingly provided less by economics than from ideas about the nature of the good state themselves provided by literatures of political science, political economy, ethics, social theory, and law. In particular, "human rights" and the "rule of law" became substantive definitions of development. One should promote human rights not to *facilitate* development – but *as* development. The rule of law was not a development *tool* – it was itself a development objective. Increasingly, law – understood as a combination of human rights, courts, property rights, formalization of entitlements, prosecution of corruption, and public order – came to define development.

The most well-known and articulate proponent of this shift has been the economist Amartya Sen. His 1999 book, *Development as Freedom*, articulates the idea. Development is a matter of human freedom and human flourishing. Freedom and flourishing require good health, nourishment, housing, and longevity – as well as the ability to own property and participate freely in a market society to develop one's potential, and support one's family and oneself. Markets are an arena for the exercise of human freedom – entrepreneurial freedom, consumer freedom, and freedom to work, save, and support oneself and one's family. Freedom is also a matter of life expectancy, education, health, and security. The state should avoid limiting freedom – by violating human rights or obstructing markets – but should also aim to expand human freedom, by providing security and promoting the fulfillment of basic human needs.

By introducing the rule of law and a social democratic state, one can accomplish development *directly*. These are the institutions – not dams or factories – that separate developed and developing economies. Dams and factories may be means, but they can never be ends. Human freedom is not a precursor to a successful market economy – markets are, among other things, necessary precursors to human freedom and human flourishing. The idea that human flourishing and freedom might be promoted directly placed a new spotlight on law, as both a means to secure freedom, and as a definition of freedom. Law was not only an instrument for new policy initiatives, nor simply a necessary precursor to markets – law, and particularly human rights, was part of the *definition* of development.

This approach reduced the felt need for a decisive policy vocabulary to analyze or compare individual policy initiatives. It had seemed crucial to determine *which* rules and institutions will best harness the surplus for take-off, *which* rules would support the market and overcome market failure, and which would distort prices. When should we rely on public, when on private, initiative: we needed a careful analysis of rent-seeking potential, the availability of competitive markets, and more to decide. It now seemed that building the rule of law – the whole rule of law, all the institutions, and all the rules – would be necessary. One should simply build a rule of law – and a state and civil society to go with it – that substantively respected human rights and market freedom. More or less any social democratic state would do. This does not help prioritize when resources are scarce – should we begin with schools, highways, or courts? – but it takes the pressure off. We will need

TABLE 7. A Chastened Neoliberalism 1995–2005

Left (Absent? rising counterpoint?)	Center Mainstream	Right Falling counterpoint
Localism	Chastened neoliberalism Stiglitz to Sen	Retrenched Washington Consensus
Antiglobalism	Market failure policy analysis	Institutionalism
Revival: dependency theory, import substitution	Institutions, culture, "social glue"	Best practices empiricism
Focus on distribution	Default preferences: Local solutions Decentralized decisionmaking "Stakeholder" democracy Multiple paths	Substantive law reform
Fair trade is free trade's destiny	Rule of law Human rights Human freedom/ human flourishing	
	Technology transfer	
	Information/human capital	
	WTO as world constitution	
	Social charter for world trade	

to build a modern, social democracy. Where we start is less significant than where we are going.

Painting with a broad brush, then, we might summarize the 1995–2005 situation as shown in Table 7.

Law and postneoliberal development policy

Certainly, law has remained instrumental and purposive – the agent of development policy. It has remained a site and vehicle for complex policy analysis – for weighing and balancing and conducting nuanced market-failure analysis. Law has also remained the repository of ontological limits to state policy. Just as neoliberalism had contested dirigiste initiatives as violations of individual – often property – rights, so neoliberalism was contested from the start by assertions of rights acquired from modest interventionist administrative and legislative arrangements. Over the last decade, however, law has also become an end in itself. The shape of law has become the shape of development. The "rule of law" defines the good developed state. "International human rights" defines human freedom and human flourishing.

As a result, implementation of familiar legal institutions and constitutional forms has become central to development policy making. In the first phases of neoliberal enthusiasm, becoming a "normal" developed country meant having familiar market institutions – a stock exchange, a banking system, a corporate law regime – interoperable with global market institutions. As faith in the neoliberal transition waned, the legal institutions that functioned as marks for "normal developed country" shifted to elections, courts, judicial review, and local human rights commissions and the legal framework for a robust "civil society."

Rule of law injection projects have generally been promoted in loosely instrumental terms – as necessary for markets to operate effectively and to attract foreign investment for development. But more than that, it also has simply seemed obvious that a liberal constitutional order was a good thing to have – an aspect of what it meant to be developed – regardless of its impact on economic indicators. Those promoting the rule of law have supported criminal prosecutors, built administrative capacity to operate new corporate and financial regulatory institutions, and trained local officials to participate in global trade negotiations and institutions.

The most important and visible institutional object of attention has been the judiciary. Judges and reliable courts seem like good ideas for lots of reasons: to enforce private arrangements, support criminal prosecution, fight administrative corruption, and review government actions for their respect of human rights, including the right to property. Moreover, many development professionals became convinced that the reputation of national judges was an important element in the investment decisions of foreign investors. It is not clear that foreign investors in fact use courts at home that often – or that they expect to when investing abroad. Indeed, there is little reason a priori to imagine that courts would be any less subject to local prejudices, incompetence or rent seeking than administrators – or any easier to reform. There was some empirical evidence that a reputation for good judging correlates with investment and economic performance, but it was hardly compelling. Nevertheless, for a period at the turn of the century, having a "reformed" judiciary with powers of judicial review became a sign for national willingness to respect investors' rights and allow profit repatriation. Alvaro Santos, in his contribution to this volume, describes well the strange institutional politics of the judicial reform initiatives that resulted in the World Bank context.

Neoliberal reforms to build down modest interventionist regimes have continued, as have efforts to reform corporate law, commercial, securities, and bankruptcy law. Development planners have remained, by and large, enthusiastic about the spread of formal property rights and the formalization of the informal economy, particularly where formalization could facilitate the spread of small scale credit arrangements – so-called "microlending" schemes, often targeting local communities of women. But with increased attention to the positive functions of the state, attention has also gone into development of law enforcement, security, and military bureaucracies, and into "capacity building" for participation in global trade, investment, and currency stabilization arrangements.

Law is also seen as the primary vehicle for managing the relationship between both public and private institutions – checking against rent seeking or capture by special interests, and ensuring that administrative agencies, courts, and legislatures keep their focus on legitimate regulation supportive of market transactions and remedying market failure, rather than distorting prices and disrupting markets. The focus on institution and state building in recent development thinking has also relied on law as a vehicle for democratic transformation – law reform, elections, checks and balances, judicial review.

This enhanced policy role for law, legal institutions, and legal analysis, coupled with a more robust role for judges in weighing acquired rights against justifications for development policies, have all placed the legal system as a whole more centrally in the development story. *Constitutions* have become development vehicles. Only through democratic checks and balances, according to some public choice theory, can the tendency to capture by special interests be blunted. The ability of national regimes to legitimate the often painful adjustment to global market conditions without succumbing to rent-seeking protectionism will depend, it is often asserted, on their constitutional character. There is much disagreement, of course, about precisely *what* constitution is required – a strong state, an open state, or a limited state – but the role of law as a constitutional vocabulary of legitimacy and self-limitation for necessary economic choices is widely accepted.

At the international level, we see a similar range of legal ideas – promotion of human rights as a development strategy, democratization, and legal reform as the vehicle for strengthening national economic performance, the emergence of "soft law" methods of rule making for social legal fields in Europe and internationally, the expansion of civil society networks as discussion partners for regulatory conversation. Indeed, the international regime is itself increasingly conceptualized in liberal constitutional terms. The WTO has transformed political negotiations over the appropriate national regulatory scheme – you drop this law and I'll drop that one – into a quasi-judicial legal process of interpretation. Commentators have promoted the WTO as a "world constitution" to facilitate the adjustment of national regulatory regimes to one another. International organizations have come to address development almost exclusively in terms of legal rights – social and economic rights, democratic rights, as well as commercial and property rights.

The most significant role played by law in current development thinking, however, is as a vocabulary for policy making. Arguments that would once have been conducted in the vernacular or economics are now made in legal terms. This reflects two tendencies – the diffusion of economic analytics into broad rules of thumb, default preferences, and conflicting considerations, and the simultaneous development within law of modes of reasoning suitable for arguing about such matters. Purposive interpretation implicates legal reasoning in argument about the appropriate pathway to broad social goals like "development." How broadly or narrowly should we interpret these regulations? Sociological reasoning attunes legal thought to considerations of context, culture, and institutional form. Policy reasoning itself has become part of legal analysis – are there lots of market failures, or few? Is this one? Will this measure correct it or make it worse?

Although one might think these questions might be better answered with a tight economic analysis, or on the basis of careful empirical study, in fact neither is usually available or decisive enough to avoid the need for a policy vocabulary more open to sociological and ideological hunches and default positions. Law, rather than economics, has become the rhetorical domain for identifying market failures and transaction costs, and attending to their elimination, for weighing and balancing institutional prerogatives, for assessing the proportionality and necessity of regulatory initiatives. Development professionals have harnessed the law to the task of perfecting the market through self-limitation – a development paralleled in the United States legal academy by the "liberal law and economics" movement. The policy vocabulary that has developed within law to implement this vision well illustrates the "conflicting considerations" style described by Duncan Kennedy as indicative of the "third globalization" in his contribution to this volume.

As a vernacular for development policy analysis, law retains elements from each of the preceding periods. It puts a wide variety of different analytic frameworks at the disposal of the development professional. The education of women, for example, might be discussed in the vocabulary of antidiscrimination, perhaps to compensate for the inefficient irrationality of market actors, which would otherwise distort the price of women's labor and disrupt the efficient allocation of resources. Or it might be discussed in the vocabulary of human capital investment and capacity building, either to compensate administratively for the collective action problems and transactions costs confronting women seeking to invest in their own skills, or as a component in a national strategy of improving comparative advantage, or mobilizing an underutilized national asset. Women's education might be discussed in a humanitarian or human rights vocabulary, as an element in human freedom, or a responsibility of human solidarity. Or simply as the right thing to do. Traces of neoliberalism, modest interventionism, and postneoliberal thinking, and of right-center-left ideological preferences, have all been sedimented into the legal vocabulary for discussing development.

These are all also technical issues. Will this educational initiative in fact respond to discrimination or be a further distorting affirmative action measure? Will the human capital investment be recouped – how does it compare to other investment opportunities for the society? What do human rights commitments require in the way of women's education? How do you compare this "right thing to do" with other basic needs? What about backlash, the social and political viability of the educational reform, the costs to other development initiatives, and so on?

As a framework for debating such issues, law has increasingly replaced economics and politics. The legal vernacular is not more decisive or analytically rigorous. It seems, however, to be more capacious. Moreover, economic analysis often requires baseline determinations it is not suited to make. Law provides a vocabulary for debating them, rather than relying on default assumptions. In the trade context, for example, to determine whether a regulation is a "nontariff barrier" to trade or part of the "normal" regulatory background on which market prices are set requires a decision exogenous to the economic analysis. Is Mexico subsidizing when it lowers its minimum wage or fails to enforce its own labor legislation, or is the United States imposing a nontariff barrier when it requires Mexico to meet minimum labor standards? The WTO's policy machinery offers an institutional and rhetorical interface between different conceptions of the appropriate answer to such questions – perhaps different national ideas about the "normal" level of wage protection. The development policy vernacular has a similar effect on issues like women's education – providing a loose argumentative vocabulary that transforms absolute questions – women's education, yes or no – into shades of gray. "Maybe here, to the extent it compensates for discrimination, but not there, where markets work," and so forth.

The legal vocabulary used in discussions is not infinitely plastic, of course. It emphasizes some things and leaves others behind. The appearance of a technical and "balanced" solution to the question whether a living wage is a "normal" or "abnormal" regulatory imposition on the market, or whether we should fear "private rent seeking" or "public rent seeking" obscures the sense in which these issues present mutually exclusive political choices. There is no technical way to figure out what level of wage support – or women's education – is normal or nondistortive or market correcting – or "required by human rights commitments." In the trade context, to decide which regulations are barriers to trade and which are "normal" complements to the market, we should ask whether a regulation is part of a nation's legitimate strategic or comparative advantage – whether we might think of a regulatory arrangement, like plentiful labor, as a factor endowment, rather than a distortion of world prices. Once we go down this road, the door is open for analysis of the distributional consequences of regulation, which would take us to a more overtly political frame for debate.

Law offers the opportunity to make these decisions without confronting them as naked political alternatives, while accepting that no economic or interpretive analytic is available to determine which way to proceed. This has revitalized the law and development field. It is difficult, however, to understand the politics of this move to law. Legal determinations present themselves as operations of logic, policy analysis, procedural necessity, economic insight, or constitutional commitment. In the background, however, lie a set of choices that are difficult to identify and contest. Legal norms and institutions define every significant entity and relationship in an economy – money, security, risk, corporate form, employment, and insurance. Law defines what it means to "own" something and how one can successfully contract to buy or sell. In this sense, both "capital" and "labor" are themselves legal institutions. Each of these many institutions and relationships can be defined in different ways – empowering different people and interests. Legal rules and institutions defining what it means to "contract" for the "sale" of "property" might be built to express quite different distributional choices and ideological commitments. One might, for example, give those in possession of land more rights – or one might treat those who would use land productively more favorably.

Although some minimum level of national institutional functionality seems necessary for economic activity of any sort, this tells us very little. For development we need to strategize about the choices that go into making one "rule of law" rather than another. Attention to the role of law offers an opportunity to focus on the political choices and economic assumptions embedded in development policy making. Unfortunately, however, those most enthusiastic about the rule of law as a development strategy have treated it as a recipe or readymade rather than as a terrain for contestation and strategy. They have treated its policy vernacular of "balancing" as more analytically decisive than it is. As a result, the politics of law in the neoinstitutionalist era has largely been the politics of politics denied.

We might summarize the legal theory of mainstream development thinking today as shown in Table 8.

Politics of postneoliberal development common sense

The postneoliberal development vocabulary has primarily been the product of the broad political center, seeking alternatives to neoliberal ideas they associated with the right without returning to the postwar "dirigiste dogma" they associated with the left. Both left and right, however, have used the neoinstitutionalist vocabulary, and it is flexible enough to support and attack a wide range of policies associated with a range of ideological positions. In fact, differences within this vocabulary have come increasingly to define ideological differences. In this sense, we might say that the new policy vocabulary *has merged* with the ideological vocabulary of political life.

The postneoliberal development policy expertise offers a series of methodological tendencies, each of which can also be used for ideological differentiation: We might say, for example, that the more market failure one sees, the

TABLE 8. Mainstream: 1995–2005

Basic ideas: Economics	Development policy set	Legal theory Liberal constitutionalism "Rights and policies and adjudication"	
		Instrumental thinking	*Rights thinking*
Chastened neoliberalism	Medium state	Law as policy	Neoformalism
Stiglitz and Sen	New social policy	Law as instrument	Acquired rights and human rights as limits on national policy discretion
Market failures	Market failure analysis	Pragmatism	Social and economic rights
Path dependence	Institutionalism	Law as policy vocabulary	Judges
Transaction costs	Build local regulatory context first, focus on sequencing and feedback loops from context	Liberal law and economics	Rule of law *as* development
Efficiency and human flourishing	Civil society	Neoinstitutionalism	
Freedom as development	Courts	Rule of law *for* development	
Culture is important	Moderate market tested regulation		
	Regulation *can* be efficient		
	Local solutions		
	Social norms and expectations		
	Microcredit		
	Local empowerment		
	Rule of law injection		
	Judicial training		
	Human rights at the IMF/IBRD/WTO		

more to the left one must be. It seems "leftist" to emphasize localism, path dependence, and the need for context-appropriate solutions, to be skeptical of empiricism and to link human freedom with larger issues of distribution and social welfare. It seems rightist to focus on local conditions as a limit on efficiency, to stress the usefulness of empirical correlations suggesting "best practice" institutional arrangements from other places, to foreground economic, rather than social or political analytics. It seems right wing to focus on human market freedom, left wing to stress human flourishing and centrist to link and balance them.

These associations are slippery, of course. At times, a focus on local cultures – as something to preserve, mobilize, and respect – marks the left.

Likewise an insistence on heterogeneity, criticism of "one size fits all," or "best practice" and preference for local solutions and decentralization. But when the right asserts a sharp distinction between traditional and modern cultures, or suggests that the institutions of developed societies may not be appropriate in developing contexts, the associations can pivot. Suddenly the left is arguing for the universality of values and continuity between developed and developing. Localism – associated in the 1950s with the left, in the 1970s with the right, and in the 1980s with the center and center-left – is now present across the spectrum from left delinking through center path dependence to right microlending and individual empowerment.

At the same time, the policy ambitions of right, left, and center have become more modest. On the right, we find a resurgence of dismay about the very idea of development as a policy objective, a kind of hand washing after the disappointments of the post-1989 period. Perhaps all we can do is offer humanitarian charity in catastrophe, along with strengthened security measures to contain refugee flows and strengthen local states able to provide the order necessary at least for the most basic natural resource extraction. The right has not been alone in this feeling of disillusionment. Throughout the 1990s the feeling grew among policy elites that there was simply not much one could do – that development policy had become controversial, the experts divided, the problems at once technical and intractable. Better to stick to basics – a relatively clean government, with low ambitions for policy performance, establishment of the key institutions familiar from developing economies and hope for the best – or see the world of development policy as simply a vehicle for funding arrangements for private or bureaucratic gain. On the left, a distrust of development and development policy and a preference for the language of ethics, and for initiatives that remain resolutely local. In this sense, as well, it was a period of "chastening" for left, right, and center. Initiatives from all quarters are vulnerable to discrediting when they begin to run into difficulty – perhaps there was nothing to do, perhaps "those people" just aren't up to it, perhaps the problem is intractable.

At the same time, many voices are stepping outside the new development paradigm altogether. On the right, one finds increasingly a sense that development may not be possible or appropriate – a vocabulary of security and political realism – the "great game" for natural resources and influence – and cultural clash replacing development as a framework for discussing third world societies. Or a vocabulary of Messianic democracy, self-help and self-reliance. On the left, one finds a parallel resistance to the cultural disruptions of economic development and enthusiasm for cultural and ecological preservation. Social movements have opposed development projects in the name of preserving local cultures, local environmental resources, or locally viable agricultural and other economic arrangements. In doing so, they have often asserted the vocabulary of human rights *against* development. Left voices have focused on economic and social rights, and expanded the objective from modest social welfare to a broader – if also more general – broadside against income inequality and poverty.

Of course, neoliberals remain, who contest the new paradigm from the right. Left voices also raise questions about the limits of the Stiglitz/Sen vision in terms that recollect earlier moments. They ask what happens *after* efficiency – how a one time efficiency gain will be transformed into *development* without focusing again on distribution, targeting, the need to maximize *indirect* gains, and head for the tipping point to an upward spiral. These themes have revived talk about distribution, and the need for national policies very much in the modest interventionist mode. At the international level, voices on the left have been more skeptical of participation in global financial markets, favoring national and regional efforts to limit the vulnerability of developing economies to speculative financial flows. Left voices have revived enthusiasm for more strategic national trade policies associated with earlier programs of import substitution and export led growth. Some have called for the movement of labor to be liberated alongside capital, goods, and services. Left voices have revived interest in the bargaining power of developing nations and firms, returning to themes first sounded in the 1970s. There are signs of new south-south cooperation in agenda setting for global trade talks – targeting agricultural subsidies in the North, or supporting one another in resisting the intellectual property rules of GATT TRIPS for pharmaceuticals. In a revival of dependency analysis, some left voices they have tried to identify and correct bias in the broad trade rules that might affect bargaining power or skew allocation of the benefits from trade, rather than relying on the factor price equalization predicted by traditional trade theory.

Taken as a whole, the current professional vernacular is extremely broad and plastic, including a range of different – inconsistent – ideas and analytic maneuvers developed throughout the postwar period. In ideological terms, development expertise has something for everyone – ideas from across the entire postwar spectrum appear in the programs of left, right, and center. To understand the politics of this broad vocabulary requires attention to its overall blindspots and biases – the policy initiatives it does not think of, those it stigmatizes.

CONCLUSION

The field of "development" expertise has existed since the middle of the last century. In successive periods, experts working in the field have defined development differently, and presented the path forward in different terms. The relative significance of economics, politics, and law has shifted – what begins as an economic analytic often becomes mixed with default preferences imported from political science, sociology, or ethics. Interestingly, the entire profession has increasingly turned to law – to define development, as the route to development, and, most importantly, as the framework and vocabulary for debating about development policy. Ideas and ideological projects from other fields find their way into the vernacular of legal policy analysis. Theories are turned into common sense assumptions, arguments, and counterarguments.

Debates about development policy carried on in this vernacular seem both saturated with political significance, and are puzzlingly difficult to pin down in political or ideological terms. Although political and ideological debate seems to take place in these terms, these terms seem strangely drained of overt ideological or political significance. Nevertheless, in each period it has been possible to identify debates within the reigning vocabulary whose poles have marked ideological differences.

As they are developed, elements in such a general vocabulary are often associated quite firmly with political projects of the left, right, or center. These associations become more difficult to pin down, however, as these ideas become part of a more general common sense. In each period, ideas about what development is and how it can best be brought about came to dominate – but they also gave rise to endless technical and political struggle about the details, and sometimes the broad direction, of implementation. In these struggles, people across the political spectrum were often arguing in the same general vocabulary – was there a market failure, how large, would the proposed remedy make things worse? In this process, very few arguments have been completely lost – we find import substitution ideas, localist ideas, all reemerging over the last decade. More commonly, as they are borrowed by various political projects, they lose their left-center-right identification. Something of the sort seems to have happened to de Soto's ideas about formalization and corruption, for example, as they have been used by left, right, and center in debates with one another.

It may be that the politics of development expertise, across the period, lies more significantly in the things taken for granted, solutions and approaches it seems impossible to imagine. There is no question that in each period, the vernacular for development policy has focused attention on some problems and ignored others, defaulted to some solutions and found others hard to fathom. We might rather think about the politics of these ideas by focusing on issues they make it difficult to see. In each period, the broad vocabulary of disputation has made some problems and some solutions less visible. Thinking about distribution seems stigmatized and old-fashioned – the more sophisticated analyst focuses on market failures. Thinking of development in directly political terms – as a series of choices between ideological associations or the material interests of opposed groups in society seems difficult in a vocabulary that transforms development questions into matters of professional expertise.

The antiformalist social legal vocabulary of the postwar period may well have made it more difficult to see the distributional effects – and policy potentials – for private law and private ordering, just as insistence on legislative or administrative positivism may have made it more difficult to build checks on corruption into the system. The liberal constitutional sensibility of the NIEO may have made it more difficult to devise global policies focused on redistribution rather than fairness, just as neoliberal attention to the world price system may have made it more difficult to focus on local social and political conditions.

I have been particularly interested in the politics of finding it difficult to focus overtly on distributional issues – a common experience in the field at least since the 1970s. Contemporary "rule of law" ideas are particularly suited to submerging attention to distribution. In each period, policymakers allocated resources, taking from some and giving to others, to maximize the potential for the broad social and economic transformations evoked by the word "development" as they understood it. The broad development strategies – import substitution, export-led growth, and neoliberal market development – expressed quite different background ideas about how and to whom resources should be distributed to maximize development. These distributive commitments – to take from agriculture and give to industry, to transfer from public to private management, to favor foreign over domestic investors or vice versa – were then written as law. Each strategy required numerous further allocative decisions – to encourage one investment, discourage another, and subsidize one industry at a cost to another.

That distributive policies of this sort characterized development in the decades of government planning after World War II is easy to see. Import substitution and export-led growth strategies depended upon discretionary decisions taken by vast planning bureaucracies interpreting all manner of complex regulations. But the market-based development strategies more common since the emergence of neoliberalism after 1980 or 1989 also require numerous distributive choices. The price mechanism may do much of the allocating, but markets come in many varieties, and prices are negotiated against the background or quite different legal regimes. Renewed interest in law as an instrument for development could offer the opportunity to view and contest these distributive choices and alternative market arrangements.

Unfortunately, too often this has been an opportunity missed. Rather than supplementing the earlier policy vocabularies of import substitution, export-led growth or neoliberalism, the rule of law has become a development policy vernacular of its own. The idea that building "the rule of law" might *itself* be a development strategy encourages the hope that choosing law *in general* could substitute for all the perplexing political and economic choices that have been at the center of development policy making for half a century. The politics of allocation is submerged. Although a legal regime offers an arena to contest those choices, it cannot substitute for them. The campaign to promote the rule of law as a development path and as a vernacular for policy refinement through "balancing" has encouraged policymakers to forego a more straightforward pragmatic and political analysis of the choices they make in building a legal regime – or to think that the choices embedded in the particular regime they graft onto a developing society represent the only possible alternative.

The ideas about development that fuel contemporary interest in the law also encourage the hope that law could simplify development policy, toning down its engagement with political and economic controversy. I encounter these ideas first in the classroom. In the first world settings where I have recently taught law and development, the field now draws numerous students from the broad center and center-left of the political spectrum. The more technocratic specialists of the center-right who flocked to the field in the 1980s and early 1990s and saw law as a technical vehicle for neoliberal market reform seem to have retreated, or have come to express themselves in more restrained terms. But gone also are the social democratic internationalists of the 1950s and 1960s who inaugurated the field after the Second World War and who saw law as an instrument for state-led development planning through the implementation of import substitution or export-led growth policies.

Contemporary students of law and development are a genial group, well meaning and liberal in outlook. They share a broadly humanitarian, cosmopolitan, and internationalist sensibility. They also seem to share a mid-level conception of "development policy" – neither a narrow matter of technical economic detail nor a broad vocabulary for political struggle, but something in between. Fifteen years ago, students of development policy in first world institutions were split between confident, largely right-wing first worlders for whom "development" was a project of technical adjustment or economic management and equally confident, if often angrier left-wing students from developing societies for whom the term "development" brought to mind the entire field of national – and international – political struggle. For both groups in those days, "development" was a universal phenomenon. For the technocrats of the north, it meant the adjustment of developing societies to economic axioms of universal validity – growth is growth. For students from the south, development meant broad questions of political economy and social theory that must be confronted by all societies, regardless of their place in the world system – politics is politics.

The last decade has chastened both groups. Today's first worlders, in retreat from one-size-fits-all neoliberalism, share an intuition that "development" must mean something particular – to the specific market conditions of transitional or developing societies, and to the cultural setting of each national economy. They are often drawn to technical accounts of what makes underdeveloped economic settings unique – characteristic market failures in particular. Demand curves that don't slope gently off to the right, oligopolies, thin markets, peculiar information problems, transaction costs, and sometimes even disparities in bargaining power. They are also eager to replace economics with the softer – and often legal – vocabularies of ethics or human rights. Third world students meet this intuition from the other direction – in flight from political generalities, they hope for a more technocratic development science. They aspire to participate in "governance" rather than government, and are also often drawn both to human rights and to more universal ethical expressions of their political aspirations.

For both groups, the economies and political systems of developing societies again seem to differ from those of the north and west – and to differ in ways that encourage attention to particular legal arrangements rather than universal economic or political theories. In this new vernacular, development policy must be attuned to specific political, social, and cultural conditions. Institutional issues are central. As politics and economics have become local, they seem to merge with the professional world of informed, empathetic, and humble expertise. On the economic side, institutional economics, transaction cost problems, and market failures are back. On the political side, attention to human rights, cultural and social costs, policy sequencing, planning, and the institutional mechanics of policy making is in. All this places law, legal institutional building, the techniques of legal policy making and implementation – the "rule of law" broadly conceived – front and center. Unfortunately, however, this new interest in "*law and development*" is often accompanied by an ambition to leach the politics from the development process and to muddle the economic analysis. Students – like policy professionals – often turn to law in flight from economic analysis and political choice.

But development policy requires sharp economic analysis and forces political choices – for neither of which is "law" a substitute. The tools for development policy making – including the legal tools – are distributional. Whether rules of private law or acts of bureaucratic discretion, they allocate resources and authority toward some and away from others. For development to occur, these distributions must put things into the hands of those whose return on their use will cause whatever we mean by "development." If we mean a transformation of the economy through industrialization, for example, resources must be allocated to those whose use of them will have the greatest multiplier effect in that direction.

There are lots of different theories about how to do this – and they are economic theories. If development means more than a one-time growth spurt – means some sort of sustained, upward spiral, or some kind of socioeconomic transformation – then one needs an idea about how a particular set of distributional choices will generate such a change. Development policy making also requires political choices – about whose ox should be gored in the name of which development path. Where there turn out to be more than one equally efficient way to the same upward spiral, political choices among possible strategies become even more salient. There is politics, in other words, right at the start – in the distributive choices that underlie the aspiration for growth and development.

Although often quite sophisticated about the broad choices facing developing societies, contemporary students of development policy tend not to think these choices implicated in efforts to build the rule of law. Some self-consciously refuse the hard choices of economic policy making, advocating instead broad and aspirational commitments to human rights, "freedom," "social welfare," "democracy," "health," or "human flourishing." For others, the tough distributional choices seem far downstream – after development gets underway, they imagine, we will face choices about what to do with our new wealth. For these young policymakers, development means "economic growth *plus*. . . . " Growth can be assured, they suggest, by implementing a technical rule of law, following the "best practices" of efficient market economies. Any later *re*distribution for social equality, education, or health will involve a completely separate policy commitment. These secondary objectives could then form the basis for all sorts of humanitarian policy campaigns – for human rights, for labor protections, for universal primary education, and so forth. In development planning, their general invocation will suffice – for now we must focus on the less contentious matter of getting growth going. The deferral of these political choices, and of any pragmatic assessment of strategies for their attainment, makes the development policy that remains seem a matter of relative consensus.

Take proposals to increase women's educational opportunities. The vocabularies I suggested earlier arise from competing – and conflicting – political and economic visions of what development is and how it might be achieved. Should we seek to harness women's productive capacity – invest in their human capital – on the theory that doing so will be more effective in generating development than other investments? Or should we seek a more efficient market in women's skills and labor? Most students of development today are uncomfortable with both ideas. They prefer to affirm the ethical importance of women's education – women's right to education – and leave vague how this relates to development. Perhaps development simply *means* women's education rather than growth, perhaps we should *assume* women's education will spur economic growth, perhaps we should think of women's education as a redistributive necessity, even at significant cost to growth. The point is not to be forced to choose among these possibilities, and not to focus on the *costs*, to others, society, growth, even to some women, of investment in women's education rather than in something else.

Focus on the rule of law as a development strategy fits well with a resistance among today's center and center-left students to think of themselves as rulers, making contestable distributive choices with real consequences. Partly this represents a retreat from the cold realization that policy making breaks eggs, imposes costs, *intervenes* in foreign places with a view to changing them. One encounters instead the vague sentiment that getting governance right, injecting the rule of law, enforcing human rights, will somehow bring a softer gentler development graciously in its wake. Partly the resistance to rulership arises from the intuition that political and economic debates about what development is and how to make it happen have not generated a technical consensus on how to bring about development. As a result, focus on politics or economics places the ruler in the awkward position of having to *choose* in a way that will have consequences that cannot be accurately predicted or guaranteed – but will undoubtedly make some people worse off. This makes people who aspire to act from expertise uncomfortable.

The "rule of law" promises an alternative – a domain of expertise, a program for action – that obscures the need for distributional choices or for clarity about how distributing things one way rather than another will, in fact, lead to development. Unfortunately, this turns out to be a false promise. The focus on rights, constitutions, government capacity, or judicial independence may all be to the good – but without a sharp sense for how one is intending to affect the economy, it is hard to compare building the rule of law with leaving the economy to operate more informally, and hard to compare building the rule of law one way with building it another.

In this, the focus on law as a development policy shares a great deal with other efforts to replace political and economic thinking with a general appeal to technical expertise and ideas about best practice. The result, by default or design, is a narrowing of the ideological range. Political choices fade from view – as do choices among different economic ideas about how development happens or what it implies for social, political, and economic life. Where once there might have been ideological and theoretical contestation, there is a somewhat muddy consensus.

It need not be this way. One could focus on law in ways that sharpened attention to distributional choices and rendered more precise the consequences of different economic theories of development. The choices between import substitution and export-led growth, or between neoliberal market-based development and strategies of either import or export promotion, offer the opportunity for sharp debate about economic theory and political preferences. Even during periods of broad consensus – on import substitution or neoliberalism – there were numerous implementation decisions to be made that required both economic theory and political commitment. The choices within and between regimes are made and implemented in legal terms.

In short, development strategy requires a detailed examination of the distributional choices effected by various legal rules and regimes to determine, as best one can, their likely impact on growth and development. It requires that we identify the choices that might lead to different development paths and compare them in social, political, and economic terms – even if we lack a strong consensus or decisive expertise about how to make them. One makes policy to distribute – by price or administrative action – hoping to allocate resources to their most productive, most developmentally promising, use. It is unfortunate that there is no distributional recipe for development, but that is our situation. There are contending ideas, contending interests, contested theories, and complex unknowables. Not knowing, we must decide. We might even experiment.

The law should be a terrain for these inquiries and a site for this experimentation – not a substitute for them. Building a legal regime involves choices that distribute differently and contribute to development in different ways. Sometimes, no doubt, increasingly formal legal rules would be a good idea. Sometimes less governmental discretion, sometimes more vigorous criminal enforcement, broader distribution of supply relationships, less local preference in contracting, all might be very helpful. But sometimes we would also expect the opposite. The emergence of the rule of law as a development strategy has become an unfortunate substitute for engagement with the politics and economics of development policy making.

5 THE DIALECTICS OF LAW AND DEVELOPMENT

Scott Newton

The story of Law and Development (L&D), that is, the legal movement or discipline, not the conceptual relationship between law and economic development that it addresses, is by now more than thirty years old. What is to be gained from yet another retelling, from this present vantage point? For one, the original telling has long since itself become an episode of a longer and more elaborate sequence, a tale within a tale. For another, the story has ceased to be a mere parochial disciplinary genealogy, because it has been taken up by all sorts of other narrators, and come to include all sorts of other characters. The L&D story is a story of development in a double sense: it is necessarily about *economic* development as the object of theoretical and practical exertions, but it is also about *historical* development as the contingent unfolding of those exertions, development as twists and turns (or moments), and the occasions (or mediations) that precipitate the twists and turns. These are the dialectics of L&D, which parallel and respond to, but with interesting deviations from, the dialectics of development theory itself. I think an account of the dialectics of L&D is both overdue and potentially useful. My hope is that it can serve both a diagnostic and heuristic function, if we are really to unleash the critical potential of L&D, which has sometimes seemed a failed promise or missed opportunity.

Whatever L&D may have been at the outset – and it has perennially frustrated attempts to fix its disciplinary boundaries and establish its guiding paradigm(s) – it becomes something else over the course of four decades. It is born North American but gets internationalized, only to be renaturalized and reinternationalized. In the same way as its fate is bound up with American ideas (like law and society or law and economics) and ideology (like modernization or neoliberalism), so is that fate bound up with interventionism and policy making. (This is not to make hegemonic claims but to recognize something native to the discourse, whatever the geographic or spiritual provenance of its exponents.) It zigzags back and forth across hemispheres in the process, and colonizes other disciplines, or gets colonized by them (comparative law, law and economics). It zigzags as well between efficiency and equity, between formalism and deformalization, hegemony and oppositionism, regularity (or uniformity) and heterogeneity, diffusionism and comparativism, internationalism and nationalism, mainstream and alternative, interventionism and quietism, Weber and Marx, Pigou and Coase, but in keeping with its dialectical development, each successive zig or zag acquires a changed significance, and L&D becomes richer and stranger.

The outline of the story runs like this. An initial U.S. modernization/law and society moment (law as a necessary aspect of modernization, rationalization of bureaucracy (public law) plus some attention to private law regimes, focus on legal systems and legal education, and legal activism) yields to a critical moment at about the same time as classic developmentalism is challenged from the left by structuralism and dependency theory. L&D gets wet, crossing Atlantic and Pacific Oceans (and the Rio Grande), and it gets political. It receives older and younger streams of thinking from comparative law (including colonial law) to neo-Marxian, class-based jurisprudence and legal anthropology, and develops further in the direction of critical political economy, which, curiously, leads it away from economic development per se (outward toward the inequities of the world economic order or inward toward non-Western/"indigenous" legal regimes). This moment itself succeeds to a (once again U.S.-anchored) formalist "vulgar-Weberian" moment of the valorization of private law and rule of law triumphalism, in the context of the postcommunist transition and the general neoliberal turn in development economics. This is simultaneously an institutionalist/law and economics moment, when the legal design of particular market institutions becomes the focus of concern and the criterion of allocative (or adaptive) efficiency paramount. In the latest moment, L&D is pressed once again by renewed critiques (of political economy and formalism and contextual and processual critiques from culture and society), and opened up (perhaps belatedly) to a range of critiques developed elsewhere (critiques of efficiency logic, determinacy – i.e. "development, or comparative, CLS") in a double-barreled challenge to (on the plane of national development policy making) even chastened market-oriented reform and (on the plane of globalization) international economic law.[1]

[1] Another way of telling this story is through shifting disciplinary allegiances: from sociolegal studies to Marxian critique/comparative law/legal anthropology to law and economics to CLS. Depending on one's own disciplinary allegiance, one can tell this story as one or another version of blundering and recovery:

1) (rightist): Lost and found: Lost in the thickets of the politics of culture and radical political economy (Marxian theories, comparative law, legal anthropology) and found again in the open ground of economics. Thus, L&D rejoins the mainstream of law and economics (as development economics rejoins the mainstream of neo-classical economics).
2) (leftist): Surrendered and reappropriated: Surrendered to proponents of an efficiency-premised economic analysis of law (because initially concerned with law as a tool of *social* change under a modernization paradigm, and not expressly with the specifically *economic*

This very broad outline is the disciplinary chronicle or genealogy put forward in this chapter. Interestingly, the discipline itself doesn't seem to have been interested in a disciplinary chronicle, save at the early point of its premature self-announcement of demise. Its afterlife is characterized by considerably less critical self-scrutiny or even self-description. As a taught subject it is canonized in the mid-1970s and as a research discipline it has acquired a paradigm of sorts at about the same time. Its subsequent fortunes, or moments, turn back on its origins in ways that, upon examination, seem calculated to baffle both its quondam adherents and its new recruits.

The present account of these moments is meant to suggest a kind of reconstruction of the missing logic of L&D, a *dialectic* logic – that is, reflecting a succession of conceptual encounters between apparently polar ideas, which are thus revealed to require and complement one another, even as the discourse is itself transformed and enlarged by institutionalizing the tension among them. It does not purport to treat the received L&D canon as canonical, but rather to recognize and tentatively constitute a strange and heterogeneous canon, which might well be justifiably disavowed by any of the authors included. It requires selective abstraction of what people examining the significance, function, and place of law in projects of economic transformation have been occupied with, irrespective of how they saw their own disciplinary affiliation. It also requires two initial caveats.

FIRST CAVEAT: Law and Development is a peculiar and heterogeneous discipline.

If we take "development" to refer to the diverse projects of comprehensive economic transformation and the accompanying social and political processes in the nonindustrialized world, then L&D could have meant any number of particular ways of framing the relation between those projects and processes, on the one hand, and law (legal discourse, institutions, professionals, culture, etc.), on the other – or all or some of them. It could have meant a broad attempt to work out a grand unified theory of law and society on the basis of abundant comparative data; it could have meant the narrower comparative study of the reception of Western private legal regimes for their relevance to economic growth (the Weberian Question), or of the implantation of public law norms, institutions, procedure, and culture via colonial bureaucracies for their significance to development policy making;

functions of law) and then reappropriated by proponents of a critical (postrealist) economic analysis of law. L&D reasserts its developmentalist roots to insist on the "developmental difference" in an era of monolithic uniformity in economic and legal-institutional policy prescription. It becomes a powerful weapon in the identification and redress of market failures and an instrument in the general critique of globalization. L&D at last has become a kind of critical counterdiscipline to international economic law: critical and fine grained and comparative where the latter is positivist, coarse grained, and universalist; attentive to differences where the latter is disdainful or neglectful of them.

it could have meant charting the effects of colonial and postcolonial legal pluralism on development strategies, or the elaboration and analysis of the legal dimensions and implications of the critique of the political economy of development.

But L&D as defined by its pioneers has a history as a theory and praxis, and denotes something specific – which, somewhat surprisingly, turns out to be none of the above. The account of its adventitious origins supplied by Trubek and Galanter[2] almost three decades ago already confronts its indeterminate status (academic movement, full-fledged subdiscipline, scholarly field or funding artifact?) and contents. It remains singularly refractory to bounding exercises. It does not appear to possess a particular normative armature or notable thematic consistency or much of a unifying logic or set of organizing principles. The most one can say is that the disciplinary range of L&D is constituted by the aggregate of studies pursued by its self-identifying adherents. The odd thing is that it continues to command allegiance of some sort, right up to the present, although the very term seems as outmoded, as dated and period bound, as say, "stages of growth," or "modernization."

Indeed, all the phenomena that at one time or another have figured in law and development discourse, the subject matter of articles, or books, the topics or themes of conference agendas and action programs, could readily (and perhaps more logically) be distributed among or subsumed within other, ostensibly more established or at least coherent, legal subdisciplines: comparative law, legal anthropology, sociolegal studies, international economic law, and law and economics. As a result there are all sorts of things that self-identifying L&D students address that concern, in one way or another, legal systems of successor states to former European colonies (land reform in Nicaragua, social action litigation in India, legal pluralism in Uganda) but are otherwise disparate and disconnected. And there are other things that would (arguably) belong at the core of L&D studies, like corporate governance in Ukraine, but that have become the scholarly domain of those who would vehemently disavow any affiliation whatsoever, whether intellectual or spiritual or professional, with self-identifying L&D adherents.

One can nonetheless descry a kind of general course, with tacks and veers, or "moments," that a discipline called for convenience "L&D" has followed over the decades, whatever the disciplinary identifications of its imputed membership. These moments follow fairly closely, albeit with a certain important lag, the wind shifts or paradigm changes of development economics itself. L&D in a certain sense has always trimmed its sails to the prevailing winds of development economics. And yet, as I shall argue, L&D responds to these wind shifts obliquely: it tacks into the wind, it doesn't simply sail

2 Trubek, David M. and Galanter, Marc, Scholars in Self-Estrangement: Some Reflections on the Crisis in Law and Development, 1974 Wisc. L. Rev. 1062–1101 (1974).

with it. Had L&D followed development economics more directly – had it run before the wind – it might have fashioned a research agenda more particularly concerned with the economic functions of law and occupied itself more centrally, with an analysis of the legal entailments or requirements of particular industrialization strategies. That it did not gives rise to a second caveat.

SECOND CAVEAT: The disciplinary story is not the only one.

Law and Development as a field of inquiry and practice famously owes its origins to the contingencies of development assistance, rather than development. But this is only half the story. Long before the pioneers of the L&D movement began to theorize the relationship, legal staffs of endless ministries of economy, or industrialization, or planning, or development, were occupied with it. There was legal work to do when Nasser nationalized cotton marketing as a development strategy in Egypt; there was legal work to do when the Asian Tigers launched themselves on the road to conquering export markets by growing "national champions" under the stewardship of industrial policy agencies.

There seem always to have been two discourses of, or approaches to, or ideas about the relation between, Law and Development. One is largely prescriptive and elaborated and external and predicated on praxis, or intervention or policy. It exists in left, right, and mainstream versions. It foregrounds law and worries greatly about what is done with it. It is instrumentalist and posits clear causal vectors. However, it is, initially at least, of modest pretensions: it does not make grand claims about the centrality of law to statist development programs of the day – import substitution or export-led growth. It confines itself for the most part to the social flatlands, leaving the commanding heights to the economists.

The other discourse may hardly deserve the name; it seems difficult to tease out. This is the L&D of development decision-makers in developing states. They needn't be lawyers, and if they are, they are apt not to be theoretically inclined. This discourse precedes the former by a couple of decades and has continued to rumble or hum along in the engine room, whatever discussions may be taking place on the bridge. It too instrumentalizes law, but sotto voce. It takes law for granted.

The story of what law and lawyers are doing and not doing in developing states with respect to development policies is a harder story to tell, and hard to place in relation to the disciplinary chronicle offered here. It has only lately come to be investigated and analyzed in its own right. The lawyers' and economists' story is in any event a much more variegated one and requires empirical and historical work of a sort that has only intermittently been entertained, and not on anything like the required scale. Just what were the lawyers at the Egyptian National Planning Commission or the Korean Economic Planning Board doing, what did they think they were doing, what consequences did their actions have for the Egyptian or Korean economies? What one surmises they must have been doing is deploying particular legal instruments (say, an industrial subsidy or a licensing scheme) for particular policy purposes, entailing a particular distribution of resources to particular groups or individuals, based on the calculated effects on growth. This necessarily close link between law and economic development policy in the minds of national legal and planning staffs is rarely considered in the academic discourse, the L&D literature. Indeed, it is only late in the history of L&D (in what is termed below the "Revivalist Moment" of the late 1980s and early 1990s) that this "economic policy gap" is closed.

This other, parallel story figures especially prominently in the case of the Asian Tigers, whose breakthrough industrialization does not receive close disciplinary attention of L&D students until the last decade. I want from time to time to advert to this other, parallel story, as a kind of corrective to my disciplinary account. For the very nature of the dialectical moments of L&D is that they provisionally foreclose even as they ultimately call forth or provoke alternative tendencies, other possible topics and themes – tendencies and topics and themes, which might nonetheless have figured or cropped up elsewhere, in unlikely places, at untimely moments (forgotten ministerial memos).

INAUGURAL MOMENT: THE DEVELOPMENTALIST DÉMARCHE 1960–1974

The Inaugural Moment is coincident with the Development Decade. Decolonization approaches completion over its course, and the statist principles and prescriptions of first-generation development economics are routinely and ubiquitously deployed. But L&D does not arise on the basis of a direct gloss by lawyers on the theories of development economics; rather it is mediated by "modernization" theory. L&D is first and foremost a lawyer's appropriation of social theory, not economic theory. From its inception, L&D stands at some distance from economics, a distance that will be closed only in the Revivalist Moment with the embrace of an expressly economic theory of law. As suggested previously in the second caveat, it also stands at a certain remove from development policy making.

The Inaugural Moment has been definitively periodized and exhaustively analyzed, no doubt most memorably by the self-proclaimed self-estranged, so much so that it is difficult to contribute anything that does not belabor conclusions and observations elaborated long since.[3] Rather than essay one

[3] Beyond Trubek Marc Galanter. (footnote 2, supra) see, as but a small sample, Merryman, John H. Comparative Law and Social Change: On the Origins, Style, Decline & Revival of the Law and Development Movement, 25 AM. J. COMP. L. 457–83 (1977); Snyder, Francis, The Failure of Law and Development, 1982 Wis. L. Rev. 373 (1982); Tamanaha, Brian, The Lessons of Law-and-Development Studies, 89 A.J.I.L. 470 (1995).

more characterization, I want to highlight a few aspects of the discipline at origin, which are fateful for its subsequent permutations: what it takes in (and what line it takes on what it takes in), what it leaves out, and what its aspirations are.

What it takes in (and what line it takes on what it takes in)

Almost the entire spectrum of elements (all the moments, with the exception of some aspects of the Post Moment) that figure in the further unfolding of L&D are already under consideration when L&D studies announce themselves: private law reception and its relation to capitalism (the Weberian nexus), deformalized "policy" law and national development strategies, postcolonial legal pluralism, political economy, law as concomitant of modernization processes, and critique from context. Nonetheless, there is a characteristic tone and emphasis that mark the enlistment of lawyers in the great development enterprise. L&D initially is allied to a modernization agenda: rationalization of legal functions, organization of legal professionals, improvement of legal education, and raising the profile of law and legal institutions. Its interventionism is not accidental, but essential. Its interventionism is nonetheless (particularly in contrast with the interventionism of the Revivalist Moment) rather peripheral or marginal, which is perhaps to be accounted for by its respectful distance from development economics and policy making.

The Inaugural Moment includes a number of one-country detailed accounts of the course of particular legal reforms conceived to promote economic development.[4] These appear to be exceptions; for the most part, the research agenda of L&D founders, like their practical agenda, is largely one of institutional strengthening and support for law and lawyers, rather than one of specific legislative proposals: a concern with *ius* rather than *lex*. Law is conceived as a tool or agent as well as an object of modernization.

What it leaves out

The North American provenance of the Inaugural Moment is not significant only for its distinctive programmatic and intervention-driven agenda, its distinctive mix of Parsonian functionalism, Weberian formalism, and home-style pragmatism, and its distinctive political and ideological juxtaposition (1960s progressive social jurisprudence in the context of anti-Castro

[4] See, e.g., Kozolchyk, Boris, Toward a Theory on Law in Economic Development: The Costa Rican USAID-ROCAP Law Reform Project, 2 LAW AND THE SOCIAL ORDER 681 (1971); Trubek, David, Law, Planning and the Development of the Brazilian Capital Market, 71–72 N.Y.U. INSTITUTE OF FINANCE BULLETIN (1971); Steiner, Henry, Legal Education and Socio-Economic Change: Brazilian Perspectives, 19 AM. J. COMP. L. 39 (1971).

hemispheric policy priorities, reflected in the "Alliance for Progess"), but also for the exaggerated significance of the "discovery" of the relevance of law and legal institutions to development goals: some first generation L&D adherents seem to imagine newly decolonized states as a kind of legal and policy *tabula rasa.*[5]

In fact, the Inaugural Moment is only notionally inaugural. L&D is distinguished as much by what and whom it leaves out of account as by what and whom it defines itself and its program. For one, it does not incorporate the colonial lawyers and comparativists of the preceding generation (i.e., it is resolutely New World and disavows any ties to imperial administration). For another, it does not incorporate the development lawyers *avant la lettre* – the legal staffs of developing country governments. The Inaugural Moment is also the heyday of developmentalism and national development strategies, when public law is marshaled and put into the service of economic policy goals. Oddly enough, the harnessing of law to the specific economic programs and policies of the day – import substitution industrialization preeminently – does not attract a great deal of attention from academic lawyers. It just gets done (by the development lawyers), and it doesn't really get much theorized or analyzed or studied, at least at this early date.

L&D scholars and actors do not typically link their programs directly and expressly to an economic project of industrialization, capital investment, and economic transformation. While there is theorizing at the grand scale, there is not much theorizing at the intermediate scale of the relation of law and legal institutions to particular economic development strategies. Moreover, while the development lawyers themselves were busily launched on the project of deformalization of law to accommodate flexible, shifting development policies, many L&D scholars meanwhile appeared to operate with strong residual formalist notions. Thus, L&D discourse diverged from the actual practice of law in economic development.

Grand ambitions

The modernization/interventionist side of the Inaugural Moment, while it receives the lion's share of later critical attention, is only part of the story. The other part, or another part, is its aspiration to a Grand Narrative, a dynamic theory of the relationship between legal change and societal transformation of the sort comprehended by development. This Olympian ambition is woven into the discursive fabric of L&D. It seems critical not to underestimate the theoretical ambitiousness of the Inaugural Moment, when L&D sets itself a challenge greater than virtually any other legal discipline of the time has posed and "with no middle flight intends to soar/ . . . while it pursues Things

5 See Merryman, footnote 3 *supra*, at 472.

unattempted yet in prose or rhyme." Indeed it is this linking of the profane and the sacred, the mundane, inglorious if not unsavory, tinkering of USAID-funded legal technical assistance to Latin America, on the one hand, with a quest for the Holy Grail of a Comprehensive Social Theory of Law,[6] on the other, which marks the Inaugural Moment.

CRITICAL MOMENT: INTERNATIONAL POLITICAL ECONOMY 1974–1985

By the time the Development Decade had run its course, and 1970s disillusionment had set in, the developmentalist project as a whole was roundly condemned as having fallen far short of expectations, if not amounting to an outright failure. Development economics was battered by the new school of international political economy, which ferociously contested developmentalism as an ideology and an internationally promoted and funded project. Burdened by accusations of failure in the past, development economics was further challenged by the notable international economic developments of the Critical Moment: the oil shocks, international economic slowdown, collapse of international monetary regulation (floating currency exchange rates), and the advent of the Third World debt crisis. These form the backdrop of the rise of the family of antidevelopmentalist theories and their impact on L&D.[7]

L&D succumbed earlier to this attack than many another development-allied discipline, evidencing its precocious dialectical tendencies. The Galilean recantation – or Maoist public self-struggle – by Trubek and Galanter has always marked the advent of disciplinary crisis. The crisis, however, appears to have been latent throughout the Inaugural Moment, as a kind of structural contradiction between the sociologically tutored, context attuned sensibilities of the scholars and the context deafness of the modernization project and paradigm (hence the "self-estrangement"). Thus, the Inaugural Moment itself could be said to have blazed the trail of critique from context, which the Critical Moment powerfully and defiantly develops: the stubborn resistance of local differences (cultural, social, political, gender, ethnic, geographic, etc).

The most significant consequences for the further development of L&D, however, did not flow from the practice of a chastened "eclectic critique" (especially critique from context) by the recanters themselves. It was the

[6] Trubek, David, Toward a Social Theory of Law: An Essay on the Study of Law and Development, 82 Yale L.J. 1 (1972); Unger, Roberto, LAW IN MODERN SOCIETY: TOWARD A CRITICISM OF SOCIAL THEORY (1977). I would claim Unger's seminal work for the L&D canon because of its preoccupation with the L&D "$64,000 question": the nature of the relation of law to economic and social transformation across time and space (diachronically in the advent of modernity and synchronically in the contemporary world of differentially developed societies).

[7] Frank, A. G., THE DEVELOPMENT OF UNDERDEVELOPMENT MONTHLY REVIEW (1966); Hopkins, T. and Wallerstein, PATTERNS OF DEVELOPMENT OF THE MODERN WORLD SYSTEM MONTHLY REVIEW (1971); Rodney, W., HOW EUROPE UNDERDEVELOPED AFRICA (1972); Escobar, A., ENCOUNTERING DEVELOPMENT: THE MAKING AND UNMAKING OF THE THIRD WORLD (1995).

collision of L&D with the proponents of one or another of the emerging varieties of counterdevelopmentalist, Marxian critique (structuralism, world systems, dependency) that proved decisive, rather than the self-critique of the L&D pioneers. A distinct (British/Commonwealth, African, and Asian) school of the political economy of law took root in reaction to Law and Development, and, far from claiming any intellectual affiliation, seemed bent on disassociation.[8] Snyder, in a gesture characteristic of this school,[9] proposed scuttling the description L&D altogether as ideologically freighted and premised on fundamental misconstructions: the existence of a neutral legal order and the posited benefits of modernization, of which it was regarded as both instrument and constituent. The Commonwealth school followed the lead of the left political theorists and political economists (Wallerstein, Frank), in rejecting developmentalism as an ideology couching neocolonial ambitions and as a practical program designed to achieve them.

What gets done

Whatever their initial qualms regarding disciplinary continuity, the Commonwealth school found themselves assuming the L&D mantle. From the mid-1970s, they embarked on an altogether different project from the American school, as they sought to bring various modes of class analysis to a study of the relation between law and legal institutions on the one hand, and the political economy (rather than "development") of the decolonized world on the other. Donor funding for L&D work dried up (with the exception of USAID-funded assistance to Latin America, in the form of the Administration of Justice program and in keeping with the Cold War U.S. foreign policy priorities that had engendered the original L&D movement), and the leftist/Commonwealth school took a dim view of developmentalist intervention by foreign donors and national elites alike. They pursued a range of studies,[10] including:

[8] Such a school is posited on the basis of the keynote productions of this period by British academic lawyers like Francis Snyder and Anthony Carty, South Asians such as Upendra Baxi, and Africans like Yash Ghai and Abdullahi An-Naim. Critical scholarship was of course not by any means confined to the anglophone world; there were significant contributions from Latin America (e.g., Boaventura de Sousa Santos) and elsewhere. Nonetheless, L&D discourse (as distinct, say, from dependency theory itself) of the period was especially a phenomenon of the English-language literature, and its principal figures shared a Commonwealth background. It must be noted that a number of them (Santos, Snyder, Ghai) also shared a background at Yale Law School in the Yale Program on Law and Modernization: The challenge to the reigning paradigm at the L&D citadel was in some sense formulated from within, in an immediately dialectical turn.

[9] Snyder, Francis, Law and Development in the Light of Dependency Theory, 14 LAW & SOC. REV. 723 (1980).

[10] An overview of the animating themes of the Critical Moment Commonwealth School is afforded by Ghai, Yash, Luckham, Robin, and Snyder, Francis, THE POLITICAL ECONOMY OF LAW: A THIRD WORLD READER (1987); the work of many of these scholars can also be found in the successive volumes of THIRD WORLD LEGAL STUDIES.

- General critiques from leftist/Marxist scholars of the Law and Development enterprise, of both liberal and radical varieties;[11]
- Domestic (one-country), occasionally but rarely comparative, studies embodying alternative philosophy and methodology, addressed to structural aspects of historical and existing legal/regulatory regimes (labor law, land law) in postcolonial states (colonial origins, class bias, etc.);[12]
- Studies of alternative legal/normative regimes: oppositional, informal, indigenous, or customary;[13]
- Accounts of and proposals for "progressive lawyering," in the form of social action litigation;[14]
- Studies of the deteriorating position of developing states vis-à-vis the industrialized world and the IFIs: debt crisis, structural adjustment policies, foreign investment, and multinational companies;[15]
- Elaboration of the right to development, foundations of "international development law"[16]

Such studies are notable for their lack of credence and/or interest in market mechanisms in general and their avoidance of policy prescription – indeed they represent a critique of the use of law in policy making quite generally. The Marxian critique of development economics and the development project itself paid scant attention to the law, regarding it as an epiphenomenon.

[11] See, e.g., Gardner, J. LEGAL IMPERIALISM: AMERICAN LAWYERS AND FOREIGN AID IN LATIN AMERICA, Univ. of Wisconsin Press (1980) (narrative history of U.S. legal assistance programs in Brazil, Chile, and Columbia and analysis of shortcomings of instrumentalism and underappreciation of role of legal culture); Snyder, Francis, The Failure of Law and Development, 1982 (review of Gardner's LEGAL IMPERIALISM: Gardner's critique attributes L&D failure to cultural not political/economic factors and so doesn't come to grips with imperialism and capitalism) 1982 WIS. L. REV. 373 (1982).

[12] See, e.g. Fitzpatrick, P. *Law and Labour in Colonial Papua New Guinea* (native labor laws in New Guinea conceived both to preserve source of labor supply and to forestall labor mobilization and organization); Snyder, F., *Labour Power and Legal Transformation* (integration of Senegalese peasants in capitalist economic relations has transformed meaning of *gamoen*, traditional form of obligation), both in Ghai, Yash, Luckham, Robin, and Snyder, Francis, THE POLITICAL ECONOMY OF LAW: A THIRD WORLD READER (1987).

[13] See, e.g., the papers addressing alternative legal strategies for rural development in 1982 THIRD WORLD LEGAL STUDIES.

[14] See, e.g., Baxi, U., *Taking Suffering Seriously: Social Action Litigation in the Supreme Court of India* (description and generally positive evaluation of first two years of Indian S.A.L., with note of caution on basis of U.S. public interest litigation experience), THIRD WORLD LEGAL STUDIES 107 (1985).

[15] See, e.g., Adelman, S. and Espiritu, C., *The Debt Crisis, Underdevelopment, and the Limits of Law* (law has played conservative not innovative role in debt crisis, protecting interests of wealthy creditors and IFIs), in Adelman, S. and Paliwala, A. 1993, Law and Crisis in the Third World, 1993.

[16] See, e.g., the papers addressing human rights and development in 1984 THIRD WORLD LEGAL STUDIES; Chowdhury, S. R., Denters, E.M.G., de Waart, P.J.I.M., eds., THE RIGHT TO DEVELOPMENT IN INTERNATIONAL LAW, 1992; articles reprinted in "Part II The debate about the right to development as a human right or state law versus people's law and the development process" in Carty, A., ed., LAW AND DEVELOPMENT (1993).

The L&D critics of the Critical Moment might have remedied the dependency theorists' lack of feel for legal-institutional design, or the distinctiveness/autonomy of legal systems, discourse, institutions, roles, and logic. They were more concerned, however, either (in their theoretical posture) to elucidate the role of colonial and postcolonial legal systems in justifying and facilitating (national and international) inequality or (in their practical posture) to engage in progressive lawyering and social jurisprudence at the margins (another, oft-forgotten, point of dialectical continuity with the Inaugural Moment).

Grand theory, Marxian variant

The Critical Moment, although it is in large measure reactive and dedicated to combating both the deleterious consequences of interventionism and the legitimation effects of modernization theory (i.e., it is strategically oppositional and theoretically delegimitating with respect to the Inaugural Moment), also has conceptual ambitions. It too conceives (albeit somewhat abortively) the ambition to develop a Grand Social Theory of Law, along more or less Marxian lines. Scholars of the Critical Moment are concerned to demonstrate the external determination of law by material conditions, or relations of production, or another designated set of "objective" factors. They are preoccupied with the putative continuity of colonial and postcolonial ("neocolonial") legal orders as evidence of their function in entrenching or legitimating or maintaining existing hierarchical relations, both in developing societies, and between them and industrialized societies. Such a theory, at least in application to the developing world, does not undergo comprehensive elaboration during the Critical Moment; the emphasis on the fixed, systemic qualities of legal-institutional orders, at the expense of their contingent, indeterminate, processual qualities, constrains the field of enquiry and the scope of the theory similarly.

Internationalization of L&D

L&D is internationalized with the Critical Moment, not only in terms of the provenance of its scholars and their perspectives (the Commonwealth L&D school apply distinctly non-American, European/Third World politicized modes of analysis), but insofar as the international economy, or the world system, becomes a necessary object of analysis. The contention, common to left critics of developmentalism, that the unit of accounting for development purposes cannot be the national economy, but must be the international economy, is dialectically incorporated in L&D. As a result, L&D must henceforth address the structural features of the international economy: international division of labor, core and periphery, declining terms of trade.

The relegation of national economic development policy making to subordinate or marginal significance by Critical Moment students is reinforced through the advent of the debt crisis and the increasing power of the International Monetary Fund over developing country debtors, as their lender of last resort. It is at this juncture that some Critical Moment scholars align themselves with the call for a New International Economic Order, and conceive the corresponding legal priority as the elaboration of a right to development and with it the foundation of an international law of development.[17] The elaboration of international development law as a novel field of international regulation, and its object in redressing international inequality as a consequence of colonialism, can be argued to have become the primary collective project of critical scholars of this period. If the praxis of the lawyers of the Inaugural Moment was in the mode of (U.S.-funded) furtherance of the modernization project on so many national stages in the newly decolonized world, the praxis of the lawyers of the Critical Moment was in the mode of (U.S.-resisted) standard setting on the international stage. The Critical Moment activist–scholars in part sought legal remedies (in the form of international obligations on the part of developed states before developing states to promote a new and more equitable international economic order) to the structural deficiencies identified by the dependency theorists in their critique of the political economy of development. Their vision of law was if anything more ambitious than that of the activist-scholars of the previous decade: not *national* law as instrument of development policy, but *international* law as Archimedean point for reconstructing international economic relations and releasing Third World economic prospects from the dead hand of the colonialist legacy.[18]

Oddly enough, given the Marxian, materialist pretensions of Critical Moment theorists, the right to development all but reverses the law/economy polarity, subordinating economic logic and the relations of production to legal logic, and rights logic at that. From the perspective of the further dialectics of L&D, the preoccupation of the Critical Moment with the right to development is significant chiefly for discursively institutionalizing the equity criterion by privileging international inequality as the subject of L&D studies.

[17] Numbers of champions of the Critical Moment played a significant role in the elaboration of the right to development and in the drafting of the Declaration on the Right to Development of 1986, as well as in the framing of the attending debate about the nature of the right. They assisted in the establishment of a new field of international law, development law, which marked the definitive moment of internationalisation.

[18] The turn to international law in L&D here raises a profound set of issues regarding the basis and bias of the international legal order in the wake of colonialism. What happens to L&D lawyers when they profess international law? See James Gathii, J., *International Law and Eurocentricity*, 9 E.J.I.L. 184–211 (1998) http://www.ejil.org/journal/Vol9/No1/br1-01.html#P52˙30481, for a discussion of the distinction between strong and weak versions of anticolonial legal scholarship.

The relentless insistence of the Critical Moment on redistribution and concomitant disregard of growth marks the high tide of the equity criterion in L&D discourse, which will rapidly ebb with the ensuing Revivalist Moment. The introduction of rights language and concepts to the relation between law and economic development, however, leaves L&D transformed – and survives the discursive institutionalization of the efficiency criterion in the Revivalist Moment (which of course also in its turn leaves L&D transformed).

What gets missed. With some notable exceptions, the Commonwealth School of the Critical Moment did not especially concern themselves with the legal dimensions of statist economic development policy.[19] Their general allergy to market dynamics, coupled with their suspicion of the developing state as an agent of international capital, inhibits them from paying much attention to the legal basis for national development strategies. Like their predecessors of the Inaugural Moment, albeit for ideological rather than disciplinary reasons, they preserve their distance from both development economics and development policy making. But the Critical Moment is also ironically the moment of the ascendancy of the Asian Tigers. Nonetheless, no one appears to have been subjecting the experience of what Alice Amsden calls the Rest to law-and-development analysis.[20] Thus, the only truly successful instances of industrialization in the developmentalist era escape contemporaneous L&D analysis.

REVIVALIST MOMENT: THE RULE OF LAW, *IUS MILITANS ET TRIUMPHANS* 1985–1995

If the challenge from the left to development economics was the defining Event of the Critical Moment, the challenge from the right was the defining Event of the Revivalist Moment.[21] There is a revolution in development economics, a fundamental shift in reigning ideas about the way to do development. So-called Development Model II (markets/private ordering, privatization, deregulation, open economies) starkly contrasts with Model I (state planning/public ordering, public enterprises, regulation, closed economies); "development" is not usefully distinguishable from "growth"

[19] Yash Ghai's and colleagues' work on public enterprises is one such exception. See Ghai, "Law and Public Enterprise" in Ghai, Yash, Luckham, Robin, and Snyder, Francis, footnote 10, supra; Ghai, Yash, ed., Law in the Political Economy of Public Enterprise: African Perspectives (1977).

[20] Amsden, Alice H., The Rise of "The Rest" Challenges to the West from Late-Industrializing Economies (2001).

[21] "Revivalist" is meant here chiefly to evoke the reanimation of L&D as an interventionist discourse and practice, a matter of projects and donor funding, and at the same time for its missionizing connotation.

in the era of market-predicated growth strategies, and the term "emerging markets" is preferred to "developing countries."[22]

L&D not only tracks this change in development economics, but is reanimated by it. Indeed, fatefully for L&D, this is the moment when an expressly economic theory of law (Chicago law and economics, supplemented by new institutional economics) is adopted as paradigm, and the economic policy gap is closed. Over the course of the 1980s, as this new development orthodoxy is promulgated as the "Washington Consensus," and neoliberalism appears everywhere ascendant with allocative efficiency its god, as the Socialist Bloc collapses, and a "crisis in governance" befalls the Third World,[23] there is a renewed interest in the legal-institutional conditions of market economic relations, and a concomitant upsurge in legal technical assistance programs. A new literature arises, which, like its ideologically polar antecedent (law and dependency theory), also disdains the association with "L&D," preferring Rule of Law (ROL).[24] (Subsequently, it willy-nilly gets reincorporated by the discipline as the "New L&D.") Its central focus is the zone of transition (Central and Eastern Europe and former Soviet Union), rather than "classical" development (Asia, Africa, Latin America) – indeed it seems as though "transition" is the new development.[25] Once again the center of discursive gravity shifts back across the waters to the United States. This time, though, it is legal practitioners and academics with expertise in relevant disciplines of economic law, rather than sociolegal specialists or comparative lawyers, who assume the lead role.

REINVENTING INTERVENTION

Like the Inaugural Moment, the Revivalist Moment appears intervention driven. If anything, it is even more of a donor phenomenon, resting on an even stronger ideological commitment. Whatever the interest among U.S. policymakers and government and private funders that law and modernization theory once upon a time generated, it never enjoyed anything approaching the prestige among donors and recipients that its successor paradigm – law and economics-cum-new institutional economics – appears to have done as reigning orthodoxy over the posttransition decade. The interventionism this

22 Salacuse, Jeswald, *From Developing Countries to Emerging Markets*, 2(3) Int'l & Comp. L. J. 277 (2000).

23 World Bank, Subsaharan Africa: From Crisis to Sustainable Growth, (1989).

24 Carothers, Thomas, *The Rule of Law Revival*, 77 Foreign Affairs 95 (1998).

25 "Transition," invoked to characterize the transformation of once-socialist economies to a market form, implies a process, which, unlike "development," is ortholinear, with fixed start- and endpoints and one conceivable trajectory between them. See Newton, Scott, "Transplantation and Transition: Legality and Legitimacy in the Kazakhstani Legislative Process," in Galligan, Denis J. and Kurkchityan, Marina, eds., Law and Informal Practices: The Post–Communist Experience (2003).

time round is also unapologetic and insistent.[26] The degree of scholarly output also appears to dwarf that of the modernization moment. The field has been vastly more crowded and prestigious (not to mention lucrative). It has also become more doctrinally narrow and less tolerant of divergent points of view. The gray L&D literature, funded through donors of one sort or another (especially the Development Banks), is by now far more voluminous than the formal refereed L&D literature. Indeed, even edited volumes have a tendency to remind the reader of how-to manuals.[27]

Principal themes of the Revivalist Moment literature, of both the commissioned and the independent sort, focus on:

- Legislative "best practice": the development of model laws for adoption by the beneficiary jurisdiction, or (more commonly) the recommendation of particular statutes, statutory provisions, or general statutory approach from a source jurisdiction (typically the home jurisdiction of the author/adviser/expert);[28]
- Analyses of proposed or existing commercial legislation, or regulatory approaches, from an economic efficiency or institutionalist standpoint; (less commonly) evaluations of the implementation of new legislation;[29]
- Institutional capacity building of the legal sector: analyses of existing weakness or deficiencies in law enforcement agencies, ministries of justice, prosecution offices, and courts with proposals for administrative reform and strengthening;[30]
- Dispute resolution: studies of the effectiveness, impartiality, and competence of state, formal, and informal modes of commercial dispute resolution, including arbitration and mediation;[31]

26 This is not necessarily to be deplored. Indeed the greater frankness about intervention and assertion of the consequences of policy choices in the Revivalist Moment is a dialectical advance, even if the policy choices are contestable, unimaginative, and so on.

27 See, e.g., Seidman, A., Seidman R. B., and Walde, T., eds., Making development work: Legislative reform for institutional transformation and good governance (1999).

28 See deLisle 1999 at 226–36 for a survey of the range of legislative model-peddling from the United States to Eastern Europe and CIS.

29 See, e.g., Fox, M., and Heller, M., Corporate Governance Lessons from Russian Enterprise Fiascoes, 75 N.Y.U.L. Rev. 1720; Kratzke, W. P., Russia's Intractable Economic Problems and the Next Steps in Legal Reform: Bankruptcy and the Depoliticization of Business, 21 Nw. J. INT'L L. & Bus. 38 (2000–2001) (critiques, respectively, of corporate governance and bankruptcy provisions in Russian legislation, on the basis of observed performance).

30 See, e.g., Boylan, S. P., Status of Judicial Reform in Russia, 13 AM. U. INT'L L. REV. 1327 (1997–1998) (survey and evaluation of dimensions of judicial reform in Russia, including procedural issues, such as jury trials and pretrial detention, and professional issues, such as salaries and appointment).

31 See, e.g., Hendrix, G. P., The Experience of Foreign Litigants in Russia's Commercial Courts, in Murrell, P., ed., *Assessing the Value of Law in Transition Economies* (2001) at 94 (analysis of case outcomes in Russian commercial courts does not yield evidence of consistent antiforeign bias).

- Legal education reform; education, training, accrediting, and regulation of legal professionals;[32]
- ROL: articles endorsing (more commonly extolling, occasionally querying) the virtues of the rule of law in jurisdictions that have been subject to discretionary, arbitrary, interventionist, or just plain socialist legal regimes;[33]
- Review articles and studies, generalizing and summarizing experiences of attempted reform efforts; comparative survey and analysis of the legislative foundation for one particular field of activity across jurisdictions, with a view toward distilling general principles.[34]

Notably absent from the initial literature are empirical studies testing the significance of legal regulation to particular spheres of market activity in transition or developing jurisdictions (these arrive later, with the Post Moment); rare are articles relating to the use of public law, such as the provision of social benefits or regulatory regimes outside the immediate commercial law arena (rarer still are articles grappling with the complexities of effective regulation, as opposed to articles addressing the desirability of deregulation). I want to confine myself to two general points about this literature (and the *mentalité* of the Revivalist Moment in general): its twin tendencies toward formalism and prescriptiveness.

Formalism and the Shihata doctrine

The Revivalist Moment marched under the banner of formalism, in the context of the "turn to governance" as a new policy emphasis in IFI activity over the course of the 1980s.[35] Legal formalism as ROL is understood as the corrective to the interventionist, deformalized excesses of developmentalist or socialist (or welfarist) economic policies: the L&D turn to formalism at this juncture (or the turn to formalism that gets taken up into L&D), although it

[32] See, e.g., Granik, L. A., Legal Education in Post-Soviet Russia and Ukraine, 72 Or. L. Rev. 963 (1993).

[33] USAID, Achievements In Building And Maintaining The Rule Of Law, http://www.usaid.gov/ourwork/democracy˙and˙governance/publications/pdfs/pnacr220.pdf 2002 (survey and regional/crossregional comparison of USAID rule-of-law programming in Latin America, Europe and Eurasia, Africa, Asia, and Middle East).

[34] See, e.g., European Bank for Reconstruction and Development, Secured Transactions Project materials, http://www.ebrd.com/country/sector/law/st/main.htm (comprehensive analysis of legal framework for secured transactions across multiple Central and Eastern European jurisdictions).

[35] Governance, in the definition of Julio Faundez, is essentially a matter of administrative competence and capacity: "The capacity of governments to formulate and implement policies and the processes by which authority is exercised in the management of a country's economic and social resources." Faundez, Julio, Legal technical assistance in Faundez, Julio, ed., Good government and law: legal and institutional reform in developing countries (1997).

has come to seem a sign of the (neoliberal) times, is actually rather curious, given the extent to which legal formalism had long since been subjected to a wide variety of critiques – indeed the story of twentieth-century jurisprudence is one of the theoretical and applied dismantling of formalism. The forgetting of the lessons of the Inaugural Moment as learned in the Critical Moment is one of the distinguishing features of the Revivalist Moment, and will be discussed shortly.

The justification for the turn to formalism is conveniently formulated in what I like to call the Shihata doctrine, espoused by the late general counsel of the World Bank.[36] In a neo-Diceyan table of constituent elements of ROL, Shihata specified:

- rules, known in advance
- actually in force
- mechanisms for proper application
- judicial/arbitral conflict resolution
- amendment procedures

The formulation is deliberately (and perhaps deceptively) elementary. Shihata had a sophisticated feel for the significance of institutional context, and indeed the World Bank's approach to ROL TA projects has been marked by increasing attention to institutional frameworks, reflecting the conceptual gain represented by the new institutional economics. However, even as suitably nuanced, qualified, and institutionally buttressed, the Shihata doctrine is curious, and puts one in mind of a kind of vulgar Weberianism. This is a Weber emptied of complexity and sociological insight – a dumbed-down Weber. The invocation of formalism in the Revivalist Moment often appears, well, formal. In pointed contrast to the two preceding L&D moments, the Revivalist Moment eschews Grand Theory and looks instead to Simple Explanation. Its philosophic sensibilities are Anglo-American, rather than Continental.[37]

Prescriptiveness and efficiency. A striking characteristic of the Revivalist Moment is the prescriptiveness of its reform proposals, at institutional, legislative, and administrative levels. Whereas the L&D actors of the Inaugural

[36] Shihata, Ibrahim, "Governance and the Role of Law in Economic Development" in Seidman, A., Seidman R. B., and Walde, T., eds., MAKING DEVELOPMENT WORK: LEGISLATIVE REFORM FOR INSTITUTIONAL TRANSFORMATION AND GOOD GOVERNANCE (1999).

[37] There do exist elaborate, sophisticated and developmentally attuned defenses of formalism. Hernando de Soto mounts a notable effort in *The Mystery of Capital*, which is a sustained and elaborated argument for the formalization of property rights in mobilizing as capital the otherwise economically inert (because not formalized and therefore not appropriately valued) assets of the poor. See de Soto, Hernando, THE MYSTERY OF CAPITAL: WHY CAPITALISM TRIUMPHS IN THE WEST AND FAILS EVERYWHERE ELSE (2000).

But for the most part, the Revivalist Moment does not address the larger questions of the origins, maintenance, and changes in the legal order characteristic of industrialized society.

Moment were content to talk in general terms about effective company law or capital markets regulation, the Revivalist Moment actors will talk about a (suitably but minimally modified) version of the Delaware Corporations Code, translated into Armenian. The theoretic justification for the turn to prescriptiveness is not so explicitly formulated as the turn to formalism, but seems clearly to rest in law and economics reasoning on grounds of efficiency.

Indeed the application to the legal regimes of developing and transition countries of the principles of the economic analysis of law (elaborated by the U.S. law and economics school, and as supplemented by the so-called new institutional economics) appears significantly more fateful for the dialectics of L&D than does the application of Weberian formal-legal rationality.[38]

Although it is the ROL formalism in the Revivalist Moment that gets the spotlight, from boosters and detractors and interested onlookers alike, it is the efficiency logic of law and economics that is the real novelty act here. Both the basic law and economics theory and its refinement in institutional economics are of U.S. origin. It is their infusion into L&D discourse that marks the Revivalist Moment as a moment of re-Americanization in an intellectual sense, more than just in a political or professional one.

The focus on the calibration of legal regimes to market functioning and on their structuring of market incentives through the imposition of transaction costs, has set off a host of detailed studies of everything from corporate governance provisions of company law to the law of security.[39] Although the bulk of this work has been undertaken in the service of prescriptive transplantation,

[38] Law and economics analysis commences with the Coase Theorem, which holds that in the absence of transaction costs any set of legal rules for conducting economic transactions would lead to the allocatively efficient result after bargaining among actors. Inasmuch as transactions costs are ubiquitous and endemic, any scheme of regulation (or approach to decision making, either legislative or judicial) should strive to approximate the ideal condition of costlessness, that is, it should minimize transaction costs. Legal rules are thus to be analyzed functionally, for their facilitation or constraint of market clearing. Public choice and new institutional economics complicated (this analysis by introducing the variable of institutions – complex, historically arising sets of rules and procedures, which constrain(channel) public decision making. Proponents of this methodology claim to be able to assess any legal framework for economic relations from the standpoint of its distance or proximity to yielding the allocatively efficient result in any sphere of economic activity or any individual transaction subject to regulation. See Mecuro, N. and Medema, S. Economics and the Law 1997, chaps. 2–4, for a discussion of the major features and relations *inter se* among law and economics, public choice, and new institutional economics, and their common predication on the neoclassical principle of allocative efficiency. For the belated introduction of law and economics analysis to law and development, see Trachtman, J. P., The Applicability of Law and Economics to Law and Development: the Case of Financial Law, in Seidman, A., Seidman, R. and Waelde, T. W. 1999 footnote 27 *supra* at 193; Newton, S., Law and Development, Law and Economics, and the Fate of Legal Technical Assistance, 2004/2 ALADIN.

[39] See, e.g., the studies in the volume: Murrell, Peter, ed., footnote 31, *supra*.

and the results remain open to perennial challenge from critical/comparative perspectives, the consequences of the incorporation of this mode of analysis in L&D studies appear fateful. It has become increasingly difficult to maintain simplistic antimarket arguments without meeting the institutionalist case on home grounds (or to maintain simplistic promarket arguments without making the detailed institutionalist case). The nature of the market/administration polarity in L&D discourse has itself been transformed by the application of this mode of argument and analysis. Either defending or attacking a market-oriented approach to a particular legal-regulatory problem now requires a significantly more closely-argued and comprehensive case: it's harder to do now than it was once upon a time, whatever one's ideological starting point. Furthermore, the way is now opened to systematic comparative studies of the dynamic role of particular modes of legal regulation and institutional design in economic development.[40]

Internationalization in the revivalist moment

The revivalist project is specifically directed at integration into a global economy. L&D had already been internationalized (and its analysis forced beyond the bounds of the national economy, another dialectical transformation) during the Critical Moment as a site of contestation and challenge to a purported world system that had sealed the fate of developing countries, forcing them into a structural hierarchy promising only diminishing returns. Now, in the Revivalist Moment, L&D becomes instead a site for coaching and preparation. There is only one race after all (and it is indeed now a collective race, in which development and transition cannot meaningfully be distinguished from one another or from growth, rather than an individual challenge, as it might have been conceived in the Inaugural Moment), and the task of developing countries is to train for it, and of L&D to deploy law to that end.

POST MOMENT: POSTDEVELOPMENTALIST, POSTSTRUCTURALIST, POSTFUNDAMENTALIST

The Post Moment is so-called because it appears to mark a time in the wake of paradigm exhaustion or collapse. It unfolds against the seismic event in development economics of the (relative) failure of the transition project across much of the former socialist bloc (especially its eastern and southern regions), and the Asian financial crisis of 1997. This debacle prompts

40 See Mattei, Ugo A., Efficiency in legal transplants: an essay in comparative law and economics, 14 International Review of Law and Economics 3 (1994); Mattei, Ugo A., Antoniolli Luisa, and Rossato, Andrea, "Comparative Law and Economics," in Bouckaert, Boudewijn and De Geest, Gerrit, eds., Encyclopedia of Law & Economics, http://encyclo.findlaw.com/0560book.pdf.

much soul searching among development economists and raises the profile of "Stiglitzians" – those broadly sympathetic to market-oriented strategies as opposed to developmentalist ones (i.e., proponents of Development Model II rather than Model I), but keenly aware of the frequency of market failures and the necessity for corrective intervention. At the same time the advent of comprehensive global economic governance, particularly as formalized in the growing body of international economic law, arguably severely constrains the legal scope for national economic policy.

As in prior moments, the discursive shifts of L&D roughly track these changes in development economics. A number of simultaneous critical moves, mounted by scholars with divergent aims and disciplinary/ideological allegiances, appear to characterize the Post Moment. Some of these represent established modes of critique from the Critical Moment (from legal realism, or comparative law, or political economy), but newly refined or elaborated. Others represent the importation (or exportation) of more recently developed modes of critique (of CLS provenance), such as the critique of determinacy, or of efficiency logic. (One might wonder, in view of the belated application of these critiques, why the post is so post in the Post Moment.) Nonetheless, for numbers of L&D actors, the Revivalist Moment still seems to hold sway, and many of its neoliberal and market-fundamentalist assumptions are simply not to be relinquished. While the discussion here focuses on the critical challenges in the Post Moment and the dialectical movement they represent, they do not exhaust the field of L&D scholarly inquiry at this juncture.

Critique from context

Scholars are once again in self-estrangement as they rediscover the perils of ethnocentricity, neglect of context, and the discounting of difference. These critiques are worked out in divergent ways, to divergent effects. For the most part, they seem to be "house critiques" of the reliance on private law, corresponding to the "house critiques" of market fundamentalism in development economics, such as Stiglitz's.[41] Such approaches, typically from a practitioner's/adviser's viewpoint, caution against neglecting local difference and local knowledge, emphasize process over product, and recommend eclecticism and pragmatism.[42]

[41] Stiglitz, Joseph, Whither Reform? Ten Years of Transition (World Bank Annual Conference on Development Economics: Keynote Address 28–20 April 1999) http://www.worldbank.org/research/abcde/washington11/pdfs/stiglitz.pdf.

[42] Holmes, Stephen, Can Foreign Aid Promote the Rule of Law? 8(4) East European Constitutional Review (1999); Waelde, T. and Gunderson, J. L., Legislative reform in transition economies – a short-cut to social market economy status? 43 ICLQ 347 (1994); Lawyers Committee for Human Rights and Venezuelan Program for Human Rights Education and Action, Halfway to reform: The World bank and the Venezuelan justice system (1996).

The contextual dependence of ROL has been asserted vigorously by numerous scholars, of divergent affiliation, in the Post Moment.[43] Accounts both of the role of law in contemporaneous economic development (preeminently the case of the Asian Tigers[44] and the postmortem of the transition cases) and of its role in historical episodes (the legal authoritarianism of Wilhelmine Germany and the Sozialjurisprudenz of Weimar Germany) have made newly manifest the heterogeneity of patterns, *contra* vulgar-Weberianism of ROL. The effect of such studies and analyses has been to historicize and relativize ROL.[45]

From critique of international political economy to critique of globalization

The renaissance of legal attention to the challenges of development, under the patronage (and often in the *palazzi* and villas) of bilateral, multilateral, and private donors, does not escape the notice of the Critical Moment toilers in L&D vineyards. They regard the Revivalist Moment as a reprise of the Inaugural Moment: modernization theory shorn of any social apologetics.[46] Initially, they continue to focus their attention on IFI-mediated structural adjustment regimes. Over the course of the 1990s, their ranks swell as a new generation of critically minded legal scholars take globalization as their chosen theme, both in its indirect effects on legal aspects of economic development

[43] See Taiwo, Olufemi, The Rule of Law: The New Leviathan?, 12 Can. J.L. & Juris. 151; West, Robin, Is the Rule of Law Cosmopolitan?19 Quinnipiac L. Rev. 259; Thomas, Jeffrey E., A Postmodern Depiction of the Rule of Law, 48 UCLA L. Rev. 1495.

[44] Jayasuriya, Kanishka, "Introduction: a framework for the analysis of legal institutions in East Asia," in Jayasuriya, Kanishka, ed., Law, Capitalism and Power in Asia: The Rule of Law and Legal Institutions (1999). For other Asian examples, see Peerenboom, R., China's long march toward rule of law, 2002 and Antons, C., ed., Law and development in East and Southeast Asia, 2003.

[45] The critique from context does not necessarily serve heterodox ideas or contest the presumptive applicability of ROL analyses and prescriptions; indeed, contextual critique of one sort – e.g., cultural, in an effort to account for the failure to take root of the rule of law in Russia or Kenya on the basis of an inhospitable or incongruent legal culture – may serve to block or check contextual critique of another sort – e.g., political. As a rule, in the prescriptions of ROL advocates of the proper function of law in transition and developing states, the economic crowds out the political. Just so, in their accounting for breakdowns in the new regime, the cultural as explanatory variable can crowd out the social or political. Thus, the failure to thrive of some element of the legal order for the market economy is attributed to something necessary and essential about the way actors construe the law, rather than contingent and circumstantial (i.e., the effects of class or relative bargaining power).

[46] Adelman, Sammy and Paliwalam Abdul, Law and Development in Crisis, in Adelman, Sammy and Paliwalam Abdul, eds., footnote 13, *supra*. The volume as a whole reflects the abiding concerns of the Commonwealth School from the Critical Moment, which has never really slackened in its concerns with exogenous factors constraining economic development.

(globalization of legal practice,[47] growth of arbitration, renewed prominence of *lex mercatoria* and increasing transnational reach of private law,[48] Amercanization of law, legal practice, attitudes, and culture[49]), and in its specifically legal entailments: the obligations assumed by developing states under international economic law (IFI "soft law" of national economic policy prescriptions, GATT/WTO, transnational regulation).

Unlike the L&D dependency critique of a generation before, the L&D globalization critique of today addresses the legal specifics of the maturing international legal framework for the global economy. It is significantly more sophisticated in its appreciation of the legal conditions, consequences, and complexities of global political economy – indeed the intervening "legalization" of the functioning of the global economy, as an aspect of "global governance," is one of its chief concerns. An emerging international political economy strand of L&D discourse in the Post Moment confronts abiding international inequality and grapples with the question, to what extent is the assumption by developing states of legal obligations to liberalize economic policy (as mediated via the structural adjustment programs of IFIs or as acquired directly through accession to the WTO), a hindrance or constraint on a state's freedom to chart development policy? Each of the two major statist developmental strategies – import substitution and export-led growth – become equally problematic under the contemporary international economic dispensation.[50] New studies have dramatically reanimated the right to development debate and reopened in rich and promising directions the issues of the prejudicial and hierarchical structures of international legal regimes.[51]

[47] Trubek, David M., Dezalay, Yves, Buchanan, Ruth and Davis, John R., Global Restructuring and the Law: Studies of the Internationalization of Legal Fields and the Creation of Transnational Arenas, 44 CASE W. RES. 407 (1944).

[48] See, e.g., Wiener, Jarrod, Globalization and disciplinary neo-liberal governance, 8(4) CONSTELLATIONS (2001) ("colonization" of domestic private law by transnational interests, via e.g., internationally harmonized banking self-regulation); Wai, Robert, Transnational Liftoff and Juridical Touchdown: The Regulatory Function of Private International Law in an Era of Globalization, 40 COLUM. J. TRANSNAT'L L. 209 (continuing salience of domestic private law for regulation of transnational business).

[49] DeLisle, Jacques, Lex Americana? footnote 28, *supra*.

[50] This loss of policy autonomy is in the minds of some critics but one aspect of the larger issue of the changing (and diminishing) face of sovereignty in a globalized age, as it affects developing countries both generally and differentially. The developing state is singularly ill-equipped to make the adjustment to the world of complex sovereignty, with its decoupling of law and the state. See Jayasuriya, Kanishka, Globalization, sovereignty, and the rule of law from political to economic constitutionalism? 8/4 CONSTELLATIONS 442 (2001).

[51] Thomas, Chantal, Causes of Inequality in the International Economic Order: Critical Race Theory and Postcolonial Development, Transnat'l L. & Contemp. Probs. 1, Orford Anne,

Critique of formalism

The critical turn (or return) of the Post Moment marks the application of fundamental legal realist insights, notably the inescapable distributive consequences and political implications of any particular legal order,[52] as indeed of the institutionalization or formalization of a legal order in the first place, to ROL vulgar-Weberianism. Thus, the contention that legal rules can create a level playing field has been held to conceal a series of moves: the neutralization of the political in the guise of the technical and the reduction of the instability and indeterminacy of rule application (adjudication) to a mechanical function. The allocative or distributional consequences of particular aspects of particular orders (insolvency law in jurisdiction X[53]) now come under scrutiny, making for an analysis that is a) finer grained and institutionally attuned (unlike those of the Critical Moment), and b) critically positioned (unlike those of the Revivalist Moment).[54]

Another critique of ROL formalism is mounted on the basis of a challenge to its own poor account of itself. A thin theory of the rule of law easily comports with a thin theory of democracy and a thin theory of markets, all of which abstract from existing rich variegation to offer a stripped-down, monochromatic, and lusterless model.[55] ROL is seen to involve the tendentious appropriation of a complex genealogy, the decoupling of legality and legitimacy, and a privileging of outcome over process. Its programmatic character, revealed by the recurring checklist of elements, represents a kind of

"Globalization and the Right to Development," in Alston, P., PEOPLE'S RIGHTS: STATE OF THE ART (2000); Gathii, J., International Law and Eurocentricity 9(1) E.J.I.L. 184, (1998).

52 "The legacy of legal realism is the knowledge that policy determinations are internal to the operation of private law rules, rather than merely the properties of legislation and regulation.It is precisely the denial of any distributive dimension to these reforms, along with the consignment of law to a management function, that permits the displacement of politics from development. In the intense focus on the place of law in enhancing the efficiency of private economic activity, its other effects – distributional, constitutive, ideological, or normative – are obscured." Rittich, Kerry, Who's Afraid of the Critique of Adjudication? Tracing the Discourses of Law in Development, 22 CARDOZO LAW REVIEW 929 (2001).

53 See, e.g., Newton, footnote 25, *supra* for an analysis of insolvency and pension laws in Kazakhstan.

54 See Rittich, Kerry, Transformed Pursuits: The Quest for Equality in Globalized Markets, 13 HARVARD HUMAN RIGHTS JOURNAL 231 (differential impact on women of dismantling of socialist enterprise-centered social benefits in context of gendered structure of labor markets) and RECHARACTERIZING RESTRUCTURING: LAW, DISTRIBUTION AND GENDER IN MARKET REFORM, Kluwer Law International 2002; Chua, A., The Paradox of Free Market Democracy: Rethinking Development Policy, 41 HARVARD INT'L. L.J. 287 (ethnically divisive and politically incendiary consequences of neoliberal development policies coupled with majoritarian democratization given role of market-dominant minorities in Southeast Asia).

55 Marks, Susan, Guarding the Gates with Two Faces: International Law and Political Reconstruction, 6 IND. J. GLOBAL LEG. STUD. 457; THE RIDDLE OF ALL CONSTITUTIONS: INTERNATIONAL LAW, DEMOCRACY, AND THE CRITIQUE OF IDEOLOGY (2000).

secondary simplification. It also serves an ideological function, used in particular ways to limit or constrain alternatives.

The critique of formalism also extends to the emphasis on judicialism in ROL literature and practice. The championship of adjudication as a sine qua non of developed market economies in the ROL literature misconstrues/simplifies the role and function of adjudication in industrialized economies, discounting the contingencies and indeterminacy of the process in the service of obscuring its political or policy implications.[56] It prescribes for the rest of the world a relentlessly outcome-oriented version of adjudication, under which discretion is held presumptively arbitrary or interested or as evidence of corruption (rather than as exercised justifiably in the face of the social, economic, and political complexity of issues of rule application).[57]

The critique of formalism in the L&D Post Moment has sparked renewed interest in the tensions between formalization and deformalization, which characterize the history of law over the course of the twentieth century, with the rise of the welfare state. These tensions have of course been a recurrent theme in L&D discourse from the Inaugural Moment, resurfacing again at the Revivalist Moment (vulgar-Weberianism). At the present juncture, in the Post Moment, they have received an added dimension thanks to the contemporary exhumation and reexamination of Weimar jurisprudence. In this connection, the idea of ordo-liberalism has been dusted off and brought up to date as economic constitutionalism: immunizing a market legal regime against political interference, claimed to lie behind a diversity of phenomena from SAPs to compliance with GATT obligations.[58] The depoliticization of economic relations through technical-legal regulation would ultimately mean only fixing their *politicization* in a particular way.

Awareness of the formalization/deformalization tension means that the critique of formalism cannot simply serve to rehabilitate the developmental state in its freewheeling resort to deformalized legal instruments to achieve policy goals. The Revivalist Moment critique of the excesses of state discretion and interference in the operation of the market has been dialectically "preserved" in the Post Moment. Some scholars draw on the aforementioned Weimar example in an attempt to salvage a defensible, critically reworked concept of ROL, to counter the perceived dangers of deformalization in both

[56] Rittich, K., footnote 52, *supra*.

[57] An ironic scenario is the zeal with which American lawyers seek to entrench private law in transition jurisdictions and simultaneously to promote the role of judges. The endlessly flogged civil/common law divide here operates to a paradoxical effect. The ideal combination is of common law rules for private ordering against a background of the relative automaticity of civilian adjudication. American friends of private law regimes, whether wittingly or not, are no friends of American-style, policy-informed adjudication.

[58] Jayasuriya, K., footnote 50, *supra* at 452.

any national, as well as the global, economic legal-regulatory framework.[59] Notwithstanding the drumbeat for ROL formalism at the national level in transition and developing states, many developments in global legal governance seem to be in the direction of deformalization and reliance on discretionary, ad-hoc modes of administration (*lex mercatoria*, increased resort to international commercial arbitration).

There is one major leftover piece of business, which has precisely to do with the use of deformalized legal instruments. A second Commonwealth school (in Australia, the United Kingdom, South and Southeast Asia) of the political economy of law has emerged to tackle the project of analyzing the role of law in East Asia.[60] As noted previously, this remained the great challenge to L&D throughout both the Critical Moment and the Revivalist Moment. Neither the first Commonwealth school championing dependency analysis nor the second American school championing ROL proved able or willing to confront the conundrum of the Tigers. The work of this second Commonwealth school, in particular its analysis of the legal requirements of "political capitalism," is of critical significance in the L&D dialectic, because it appropriates for the discipline something of the extradisciplinary discourse of policymakers, of national development lawyers and planners, which has tended to escape it.

Critique of efficiency

Simultaneously, the very prescriptiveness, or particularity of the proposals and recommendations for legal reform across transition and developing states invites closer critical scrutiny. This is something of a milestone in this chronicle of disciplinary dialectics, because it makes possible the application of an array of developed critical techniques and modes of analysis to specific instances of legal interventionism.

The "internal critique" of the efficiency logic of the economic analysis of law had long since been developed on home grounds, in the United States.[61] This critique contends that efficiency analysis never yields single determinate

59 Scheuerman, William E., Economic globalization and the rule of law, 6(1) CONSTELLATIONS 3 (1999); BETWEEN THE NORM AND THE EXCEPTION: THE FRANKFURT SCHOOL AND THE RULE OF LAW (1994).

60 See especially, Kanishka, J., Peerenboom, R., and Antons, C., 2003 footnote 44, *supra*. As previously for the Commonwealth School of the Critical Moment, revisionist scholarship in the Post Moment investigating the role of law in the East Asian "miracle" is by no means confined to academic lawyers from commonwealth jurisdictions, and the term is adopted here as suggestive shorthand. See, e.g., Ohnesorge, J., "The Rule of Law, Economic Development, and the Developmental States of Northeast Asia" in Antons, C., footnote 44, *supra*.

61 Kennedy, Duncan, Law-and-economics from the perspective of critical legal studies, INTERNATIONAL ENCYCLOPEDIA OF THE SOCIAL AND BEHAVIORAL SCIENCES; Mercurio, N., and Medema, S., ECONOMICS AND THE LAW: FROM POSNER TO POST-MODERNISM (1997).

solutions for the choice of particular legal rules or warrants a generalized preference for private legal ordering over regulatory intervention to promote efficiency. Bringing it to bear on the application of the economic analysis of law to "development" or "transition" is a natural extension (as well as another demonstration of the infusion of North American modes of analysis). The interest from the perspective of L&D is the way it might be changing L&D once it has been thrown into the mix, once it has established a beachhead, or settlement, on L&D territory.[62]

There is also a renewal of the "external critique" of efficiency logic, on the grounds that its claimed preeminence, neutrality, and rationality, as against other sorts of logic, is politically fallible and contestable. In a dialectically transformed recapitulation of the foregrounding of equity in the Critical Moment, a distinct strand of Post Moment critical activity attempts to link the ordering of economic relations through law (private autonomy) with the exercise of public reason as democratically conditioned and institutionalized. The renewed salience of the right to development in the context of international economic law offers another mode of contestation of the hegemony of efficiency logic from the outside.[63]

Farewell, grand theory

To the diverse critical strategists of the Post Moment, the way formalism and efficiency function in the Revivalist Moment as justificatory principles appears strikingly convergent: they each purport to use law to obscure or reduce the plurality of political choices and policy options in development, they beg the hard questions of economic development. This is a strange sort of legal instrumentalism, distinct from the instrumentalism of the Inaugural Moment: law as a tool for the economic reduction of social and political complexity.[64] The failure of formalism and efficiency theory (ROL plus market-friendly law) to account for either the success of the Asian Tigers or the failure of the Post-Soviet Bear Cubs stands as the epitaph of the Revivalist Moment and its reductive instrumentalism.

But the response of the Post Moment strategists to the question-begging of "ordinary language" L&D of the Revivalist Moment is not to propose the restoration of "contintental" L&D in the style of the Inaugural Moment (Weber) or the Critical Moment (Marx). Indeed, the shift of theory from a major to a minor key is distinctly audible in the Post Moment. Any lingering pretensions to a Comprehensive Social – or Economic – Theory of Law

[62] See Rittich, K., footnote 54, *supra*.

[63] See Orford, A., footnote 51, *supra*.

[64] Kennedy, David, Laws and Developments, in CONTEMPLATING COMPLEXITY: LAW AND DEVELOPMENT; FACING COMPLEXITY IN THE 21ST CENTURY, Perry, A. and Hatchard, J., eds., 2003).

appear to have been quietly surrendered by L&D, constituting one of its more dramatic dialectical transformations. This is a moment that is much more attuned to differences and apparent contradictions and tensions, or suspended between dialectical poles:

- legal/political order
- international/national legal and policy space
- institutionally determined functions/functionally determined institutions
- public/private legal ordering
- structural/policy constraints on development
- efficiency/equity

One of the most challenging aspects of the Post Moment, as the present stage of the four-decades long dialectics of L&D, is that it makes it very difficult to argue polar positions of any sort.

- If it is commonplace to dismiss the legal instrumentalism of modernization theory as narrow, ethnocentric, and outmoded, it still remains to explain the relevance of law and legal institutions to the cases of successful industrialization (Asian tigers).
- If a tutored awareness of the degree of calibration of legal institutions to market requirements prompts dismissal of dependency theory as overblown, overbroad, and too market hostile to study the legal architecture of market institutions seriously and closely, it remains confronted by the staggering levels of international inequality and the persistent international division of labor as conditioned by the emerging international economic legal regime.
- If critical analysis undermines the purported centrality of the rule of law for the neoliberal project of unleashing the power of markets, it still remains to explain the differential performance (efficiency) of particular types and instances of legally structured market institutions.
- If the interventionist practice and discourse (of IFIs and other donors) is dismissed as irrelevant or prejudicial to the free scholarly enquiry into the dynamics of law and economic growth, the activities and writings of interveners nonetheless afford extraordinary opportunities for comparative analysis and present a host of issues eminently deserving of study.
- If the neoliberal program for growth and competitiveness, as conveyed by the IFIs and buttressed by the international trade regime, is regarded as requiring legal-technical fundamentals shielded from politics and policies, the ways in which those fundamentals are instituted in particular contexts are inescapably plural and pregnant with politics.

This may be the moment when L&D as the name for this peculiar, heterogeneous, dialectically produced set of scholarly themes from different disciplines (encompassing, e.g., the relation of legal formalism to capitalist development, the distributional consequences of particular institutionalizations of property and contract, the role of public and private law regimes in various episodes of industrialization, and the international legal premises for persistent international inequality) begins to cohere as a disciplinary arena for multiple new studies. David Trubek called for “eclectic critique” as a way out of the impasse of self-estrangement in 1974: thirty years on, its time appears to have come.

6 THE FUTURE OF LAW AND DEVELOPMENT: SECOND-GENERATION REFORMS AND THE INCORPORATION OF THE SOCIAL

Kerry Rittich

INTRODUCTION

One of the most significant events in the field of development in recent years has been the effort to incorporate social concerns into the mainstream agenda of market reform and economic development. Largely excluded from the first generation reform agenda, the "social" dimension has been brought back in through the introduction of a series of additions and reforms, sometimes referred to as "second-generation" reforms or the "post-Washington Consensus," to the development agenda of the international financial institutions (IFIs).

This is a marked shift in the framing of development policy and priorities. Prior to second generation reforms, social concerns were sharply distinguished from economic concerns; especially to the extent that they were in any sense political, they were seen as not only extraneous to but sometimes even in conflict with the pursuit of economic development. Thus, second generation reforms mark not only the recognition of the social side of development policy, but an effort to make the two sides coexist more easily.

This chapter probes the manner in which the IFIs are managing the incorporation of social justice and greater participation in the development agenda, and describes how the pursuit of social objectives, in turn, is affected by the governance agenda as a whole.

A convenient marker of the second generation reforms is the appearance of the World Bank's (Bank) Comprehensive Development Framework (CDF). Originally presented as a discussion draft circulated by the Bank's president,[1] the CDF identifies two sides to the development agenda. In addition to the macroeconomic and financial aspects of economic growth, the CDF pronounces that greater attention must now be paid to its "social, structural and

[1] James D. Wolfensohn, *A Proposal for a Comprehensive Development Framework*, Ronzending Instutionele Ontwikkeling (May 1999), available at http://www.euforic.org/rondzend/may99.htm.

human" dimensions. Along with greater attention to issues such as health, education, and gender equality, factors such as human rights, good governance and the rule of law are explicitly identified as central to the achievement of development. In addition, the CDF holds that the process of development must be returned to its subjects: no longer a one-size-fits-all agenda that is orchestrated and imposed from above, second generation reforms propose greater country-ownership of the reform process and a development agenda that is generated in a more inclusive and participatory way.

The CDF represents a holistic framework that, according to the Bank, is now widely accepted as the basis for both generating development policy and achieving sustainable development.[2] The principles and norms it articulates inform the Poverty Reduction Strategy Papers that now ground the formulation of development policy for specific States[3] as well as a wide range of other development initiatives and activities. Nor is the shift embodied in the CDF solely confined to the IFIs: the move toward greater attention to concrete social objectives is confirmed on the wider international stage in the broad endorsement of the Millennium Development Goals.[4]

This analysis proceeds from the assumption that one of the most productive and revealing ways to analyze the transformative potential of second generation reforms is by analyzing the way that they are imagined and made operational at the level of legal rules and institutions. If a crucial question is whether, and to what extent, second generation reforms represent a transformative moment in development and market reform thinking and practice, there is a variety of reasons why law might provide a crucial lens on the matter.

Law is a condition of possibility of both social justice and democratic participation; even if law were not explicitly emphasized, it would remain important to assess effects of the legal and institutional environment on the realization of social goals. However, second generation reforms themselves center law in new and important ways. The instrumental value of law to development is now well established: whether under the rubric of the rule of law, good governance, or best practices, the legal and institutional environment of economic growth has become a site of intense interest and activity in the world of development.[5] Indeed, legal and institutional reforms are increasingly identified as the key to successful development. But not only is law

[2] World Bank, *What is CDF: Ten Things You Should Know About CDF*, available at http://www.worldbank.org/cdf/.

[3] For a description see *The World Bank Group PovertyNet Home*, at http://www.worldbank.org/poverty/strategies/.

[4] United Nations Millennium Development Goals, available at http://www.un.org/millenniumgoals.

[5] References to good governance are now ubiquitous; for a classic effort to articulate their place in market reforms as a whole, see the collection of essays in IBRAHIM F. I. SHIHATA, COMPLEMENTARY REFORM: ESSAYS ON LEGAL, JUDICIAL AND OTHER INSTITUTIONAL REFORMS SUPPORTED BY THE WORLD BANK (1997).

instrumentally important to development; with second generation reforms it is also definitional to development. While the simultaneous installation of law and the social as ends of development may be purely serendipitous, myriad policy documents from the IFIs themselves point to the importance of the rule of law and good governance in securing the social dimension of development. For these reasons, if no other, we might expect a widened conception of development to be reflected in the prescriptions about the legal and policy environment for economic growth and greater participation and democratization to inform the processes through which it is to be generated.

Following this intuition, this chapter considers the nature and place of legal rules and institutions in the reformed development agenda; the uses to which they are put; the values and interests they seem to advance; the justifications that underlie them; and their impact on the social objectives to which the IFIs have now committed. It also considers the way that social concerns are articulated in this agenda and how their relationship to economic growth is represented and justified. Thus, the paper explores two interrelated questions: To what extent is the regulatory and institutional frame of development altered by the inclusion of social and democratic objectives? What is the impact of the legal and institutional frame on these social and democratic objectives, and what does the current trajectory toward social justice look like as a consequence?

At this point, it seems possible to advance a number of tentative conclusions. First, second generation reforms confirm and consolidate the growing importance of law to development: in important ways, development simply is now a legal/institutional reform project. What is new in second generation reforms is that the importance of legal reform is no longer limited to its role in fostering economic growth; instead those same reforms are now also represented as critical to the achievement of social objectives. Moreover, law itself has become a constitutive element of development: respect for the rule of law; the implementation of particular institutions; and the recognition of certain legal rights have become definitional to the achievement of development itself. Second, despite the expansion of the development agenda and with the important exception of the reforms associated with access to justice initiatives, neither the basic institutional architecture nor the substantive content of the core legal reform agenda has appreciably changed. Third, despite the importance ascribed to law for certain purposes, there is also a new consciousness of the limits of law and a new interest in nonregulatory and mixed modes of governance, especially in respect of social issues. This is reflected in the emphasis on soft forms of regulation and nonlegal norms as well as the expanded role given to nonstate actors in functions ranging from norm generation to monitoring and compliance. Fourth, the effort to take greater account of social concerns appears to work both with and against the effort to preserve or expand the zone of democratic and sovereign control over development policies and priorities. It registers as a point of tension in second generation reforms, for the following reason. Conceptions of social justice are not merely being incorporated into development, they are being transformed in their encounter with and accommodation to other imperatives within the development agenda. The suggestion here is that the encounter of the economic and the social in second generation reforms has led not only to what is most apparent, an enlarged development and market reform agenda; it has led to a struggle around the nature of the social objectives and the strategies by which they should be pursued.

Second generation reforms are the result of diverse catalysts for change both internal and external to the IFIs. Among the critiques of first generation, neoliberal reforms were that they had more to do with the interests of international actors in debt recovery, market access, and the protection of investments than with economic growth of States to which they were applied.[6] In addition, reforms entailed practices that seemed obviously problematic from the standpoint of sovereignty.[7] In the view of some, they furthered a conception of development that had long been disclosed as narrow, if not pathological, in its focus.[8] In addition, they appeared to impose disproportionate risks, costs, and burdens on particular groups such as women and workers.[9] First generation reforms were also subject to a range of internal critiques, the most telling of which were that they failed in their efforts to generate economic growth and to alleviate poverty by ignoring and arguably damaging the aggregate welfare of the societies in which they operated.[10]

Second generation reforms attempt to respond to these arguments in two ways, by expanding the ambit of development reforms to encompass a greater range of concerns and objectives and by instituting or endorsing a range of procedural changes that place an enhanced emphasis on popular participation and access to services, including courts. It would be a mistake, however, to understand the transformed agenda solely as a response to these now well-publicized critiques, and it would be inadequate to explain the path

[6] See JOSEPH E. STIGLITZ, GLOBALIZATION AND ITS DISCONTENTS (2002); Balakrishnan Rajagopal, *International Law and the Development Encounter: Violence and Resistance at the Margins*, 93d American Society of International Law Proceedings 16 (1999).

[7] James T. Gathii, *Good Governance as a Counter-Insurgency Agenda to Oppositional and Transformative Social Projects in International Law*, 5 BUFF. HUM. RTS L. REV. 107 (1999).

[8] Among the best-known alternative indices is the Human Development Index found in the United Nations Development Program; see generally U.N. Development Programme, Human Development Report (New York: Oxford, various years).

[9] See GITA SEN & CAREN GROWN, DEVELOPMENT, CRISES, AND ALTERNATIVE VISIONS: THIRD WORLD WOMEN'S PERSPECTIVE (1987); for an analysis of the distributive valence of reforms in the context of transition, see Kerry Rittich, RECHARACTERIZING RESTRUCTURING: LAW, DISTRIBUTION AND GENDER IN MARKET REFORM (2002).

[10] Giovanni A. Cornia et al., Adjustment with a Human Face (1987); Stiglitz, *supra* note 6.

that second generation reforms have taken in any event. Instead, a series of other events seem to have prompted a transformation of the agenda at roughly the same time. Among them was the appearance of Amartya Sen's influential *Development as Freedom*. Following its appearance in 1999, the Bank among many others began to articulate development as a project to promote not simply economic growth but a broader set of human freedoms along with the capacities to realize them.[11] Imagining development as freedom seemed to both authorize the approach to development policy and market reform on which the IFIs had already embarked as well as signal a shift in the direction of a more humane, responsive, and mature concept of development. Imagining development as freedom also helped to explain the elevation of human rights and the rule of law to the status of development ends or objectives. In addition, the IFIs themselves had come to the conclusion that greater attention to some social issues, such as gender equality,[12] might generate better economic outcomes because they appeared to be promising routes by which to enhance levels of investment in human capital. The cultivation of human capital, in turn, had by then been identified as crucial to economic success in the emerging knowledge-based economy.[13] To put it another way, attention to some social issues that once lay outside the purview of the IFIs and beyond the gaze of market reformers became justified in the name of economic development itself. Finally systemic crises of various sorts, from the stalled or failed transition in many countries in Eastern Europe and the CIS[14] to the East-Asian financial crisis, provoked calls for a new institutional architecture. In the aggregate, these events converged to produce a development agenda that substantially enlarged the list of best practices and governance strategies that were promoted by the IFIs in the first half of the 1990s.

While restatements of the development agenda have become routine rather than exceptional in recent years, the shift toward the social seems unlikely to be transitory. The development and market reform projects of the IFIs, the Bank in particular, no longer revolve solely around the promotion of economic growth; at least at the rhetorical level, social issues have now been accepted both as ends of development in and of themselves and as important

[11] See AMARTYA SEN, DEVELOPMENT AS FREEDOM (1999). Endorsements of this idea have been widespread among the international economic institutions. See, for example, World Bank, World Development Report 2000/2001: Attacking Poverty (2001); U.N. Development Programme, Human Development Report 2000 (2000).

[12] World Bank, World Bank Policy Research Report: Engendering Development – Through Gender Equality in Rights, Resources and Voice (2001).

[13] World Bank, World Development Report 1999–2000: Knowledge for Development (1999). See also Thomas Courchene, *Human Capital in an Information Era*, 28 Can. Pub. Pol'y 73 (2002).

[14] Joseph E. Stiglitz, Whither Reform? Ten Years of Transition, Keynote Address at Annual World Bank Conference on Development Economics (April 28, 1999), available at http://www.worldbank.org/research/abcde/washington_11/pdfs/stiglitz.pdf.

factors to the achievement of general economic growth. As a result, issues ranging from human rights to gender equality no longer stand outside the development agenda, nor is their importance *to* economic development still seriously debated. Even the issue of equality is now incorporated into the agenda.[15] While some still take the position that social concerns are outside the development agenda, a distraction from the main task of generating economic growth, this perspective is now in the minority and the inclusion of the social has now been substantially normalized within the frame of development.

This evolution has shifted the center of gravity in debates around development and social justice in significant ways. Radical critiques of the development agenda remain.[16] In addition, new historical scholarship indicates that some of the social deficits now at issue may be traceable to institutional structures and practices that linger on from earlier moments in the international order.[17] Within the mainstream community, however, debates now largely focus upon the way to conceive the merged economic/social agenda, the relationship between the social and the macroeconomic or financial dimensions of globalization, and the means by which social concerns are to be furthered.

It is difficult, if not impossible, to say much about what a commitment to the importance of the social, structural, and human means in the abstract; the same might be said about claims that the reform process should now become more participatory, transparent, and democratic. Assessing the varied effects of reforms on the ground is notoriously difficult in any event; the extent to which it is safe or even possible to attribute development outcomes, whether positive or negative, to particular interventions and changes is itself one of the most deeply contested issues in contemporary development debates. Hence, the questions. Beyond the reformulated commitment at the rhetorical level, in what ways and to what extent *do* second generation reforms represent a new and different development strategy, a rupture from the past, versus a continuation or elaboration of the project that has been underway for the last decade and a half? To what extent is there either overlap or conflict between the old (and enduring) imperative of promoting economic growth and the

[15] For example, the World Bank's 2006 Word Development Report will be devoted to the theme of equity and development.

[16] For a representative selection, see generally The Post-Development Reader (Majid Rahnema and Victoria Bawtree eds., 1997).

[17] See Antony Anghie, *Time Present and Time Past: Globalization, International Financial Institutions, and the Third World*, 32 N.Y.U. J. Int'l L. & Pol. 243 (2000); Antony Anghie, *Colonialism and the Birth of International Institutions: Sovereignty, Economy, and the Mandate System of the League of Nations*, 34 N.Y.U. J. Int'l L. & Pol. 513 (2002); Balakrishnan Rajagopal, International Law from Below: Development, Social Movements and Third World Resistance (2003).

new focus on social issues? At the institutional level, what continues and what has changed?

DEFINING SECOND GENERATION REFORMS

The rise of good governance or best practice in law and institutions

The social critiques of development and market reform are directly connected to a fundamental shift in the activities of the IFIs: the move from project- to policy-based development lending, and the promotion by the IFIs of increasingly comprehensive notions of good governance in a globally integrated economy. While there were also trenchant critiques of traditional project-based lending,[18] most have been directed at the attempt to promote economic integration through policy and regulatory transformation, convergence, and harmonization in the neoliberal style. Given the mixed genesis of second generation reforms, however, it is useful to rehearse the evolution of the governance and legal project as a whole.

As has long passed into general knowledge, since the 1980s the IFIs have been among the most forceful proponents of market fundamentalism.[19] Actively promoting the market as the engine of growth and social welfare, they have sought to both reduce and redirect the role of the State in economic activity and to reconfigure the structure of entitlements governing market transactions with the aim of providing an environment conducive to private sector investment. This is a project that began with a limited focus on macroeconomic issues, expanded during the early to mid-1990s to include legal and institutional concerns, and is expanding still further in the context of second generation reforms and the inclusion of the social.

As the IFIs shifted their efforts from project- to policy-based lending, they began to attach conditions to the release of funds. Over time, they developed and deployed a variety of other soft mechanisms to promote the reforms that they regarded as optimal as well. These ranged from technical advice, including legal advice, to States; thematic reports and policy prescriptions on an increasingly wide range of development topics; and empirical research on the determinants of growth, much of which was conducted within the framework of neoclassical and institutional economic assumptions.[20] Policy interventions were originally based upon commitments to liberalization, privatization, deregulation, and the promotion of macroeconomic stability

[18] For example, objections to the Bank's engagement in the Narmada Dam project provoked the creation of an internal adjudicatory body authorized to hear a limited range of complaints about its activities. For a description, see Ibrahim F. I. Shihata, The World Bank Inspection Panel (1994).

[19] STIGLITZ, *supra* note 6.

[20] Shihata, *supra* note 5.

through inflation control, tax reform and fiscal austerity, all as prescriptions that literally came to define the Washington Consensus.[21] These factors, however, were supplemented over time by an explicit focus on the legal and regulatory framework in which economic transactions take place. This was a consequence of something that became starkly apparent in the transition economies which is that, contrary to earlier assumptions that markets would simply spring up once regulatory impediments were removed,[22] markets do not generate the conditions of their own success. The recognition that "institutions matter"[23] as well as the increasing focus on both the substantive and procedural legal reforms that have been a feature of the development of agenda since the mid-1990s, also gained force from another direction: this was the conclusion that corruption, a lack of respect for the rule of law, and various other governance failures lay at the root of the ongoing dilemmas of development, particularly in Sub-Saharan Africa.[24]

Both a consequence and a cause of the turn to institutions is that development has been reconceived largely as a question of good governance. Legal and judicial reform now regularly appear at the top of the list of fundamental structural reforms[25] and the policy documents of the IFIs are pervaded with statements to the effect that that economic development requires respect for the rule of law, protection of property and other investors' rights, and now often human rights as well.[26]

So far, deficiencies in the realm of governance are mostly attributed to national rather than international rules, norms, and institutions. There are well-recognized economic pressures on the nation-state in an era of globalization and consequent limits on its capacity to engage in institutional and policy reform independently of those constraints, especially in the absence of coordination or cooperation with other states; tax policy stands as one example. Moreover, other actors such as developed states or multinational corporations may be complicit with the corrupt practices that are typically attributed to developing states.[27] Whether or not this is the case, firm practices are certainly central to the achievement of a range of social objectives such as better environmental and workplace practices. In addition, developing states face formidable barriers to participating on an equal footing with

[21] John Williamson, *Democracy and the Washington Consensus*, 21 World Dev. 1329 (1993).

[22] On this position, see Jeffrey Sachs, Poland's Leap to the Market Economy (1993).

[23] This provoked a partial rehabilitation, under strictly disciplined conditions, of the state in the processes of economic development. See World Bank, World Development Report 1997: The State in a Changing World (1997).

[24] World Bank, Sub-Saharan Africa: From Crisis to Sustainable Growth (1989); Good Governance: The IMF's Role (1997).

[25] See, e.g., World Bank, *supra* note 2.

[26] For a description of the components and the rationale for the legal reform project, see Shihata, *supra* note 5.

[27] Jozef Ritzen, *A Chance for the World Bank* (London: Anthem Press, 2005).

industrialized states in negotiations about the design of the global institutional order and suffer predictable detriments as a result.[28] The voting structure of the IFIs, weighted to reflect the contributions of the most important donor nations, stands as one of the most prominent examples. The global trade regime, too, still provides selective protection for the markets of the developed world and permits barriers to some of the most saleable products of developing states, thus impeding the very processes by which such states are now supposed to achieve economic growth. In addition, there remain real questions about whether the current focus on a "level playing field" of rules-based economic relations based upon the protection of rights and formal equality among states is adequate to ensure the development of many low-income countries in a globalized economy, especially in the face of the "first-mover" advantages now accumulated by the developed world. In short, even assuming governance is an appropriate focus, there appear to be compelling economic, social, and political reasons to pay attention to its transnational and international dimensions. Despite these well-documented problems, "country-ownership" of reform, a hallmark of second-generation reforms, often translates simply into state responsibility for reform. Injunctions to respect the rule of law, combat corruption, and engage in institutional reform to attract investment remain the central planks of the reform agenda, suggesting that, in the eyes of the IFIs, if not elsewhere, any failures of governance are still located at the domestic level.

The basic thrust of the reform agenda since its inception has been to promote a market friendly legal and institutional order organized around the protection of property rights, the enforcement of contracts, and the provisions of other rules and institutions required to ensure a stable and attractive investment climate.[29] The argument for structural reforms is that the adoption of these rules, norms, and best practices are the precondition to participation in the global economic order, without which no state can now hope to achieve growth and escape from poverty. Nor are they irrelevant outside the developing world: rather, they apply equally to states that are already industrialized, on the theory that they are now necessary if states are to protect themselves and their citizens from irreversible declines in their fortunes and well-being in a globally integrated economy.[30]

The original impetus for the introduction of a legal agenda into the development project was law's instrumental value to development. The Bank

[28] See, e.g., Gerald K. Helleiner, Markets, Politics and Globalization: Can the Global Economy be Civilized? UNCTAD 10th Raul Prebisch Lecture (Dec. 11, 2000) (CIS, Working Paper No. 2000–1).

[29] For a more detailed consideration of the logic of the legal reform agenda, see Rittich, *supra* note 9, chapter 2.

[30] World Economic Outlook: Advancing Structural Reforms, ch. 3 (2004).

advanced a general argument about law's role in the success of reforms as a whole, as well as a set of more specific claims about the relationship of particular legal rules, for example property and contract rights, to economic efficiency and growth. These arguments retain their force; indeed, the Bank increasingly attempts to shore up these theoretical claims with empirical evidence about their connection to development outcomes.[31] With second generation reforms, however, law has also broken free of this connection; as part of the "social, structural, and human" dimension of development, law has now been invested with intrinsic value. With the move to development as freedom and the incorporation of human rights, law has become an independent objective in its own right.

The ideal regulatory agenda was originally envisioned as a regime that is relatively free of state "interventions" and regulatory encumbrances, on the theory that they were likely to impede efficient transactions and impair the extent and quality of investment. Since at least 1997,[32] the Bank has rejected a purely minimalist or night watchman conception of the state and recognized that a variety of distortions, market failures, and externalities may warrant intervention and regulatory action in at least some instances. For example, the Bank as well as other international financial and economic institutions became acutely aware as a result of the transition process that privatization prior to the installation of an adequate regulatory infrastructure could result in "the opaque transfer of ownership, corruption, and the dissipation of assets."[33] The arguments for regulation, however, remain securely tethered to the goals of enhancing the competitiveness and efficiency of markets.[34] Moreover, except to the extent that they have been reconsidered because of their clear contributions to productivity enhancement, claims about the nature of efficient and procompetitive interventions remain largely as they were in the first generation reforms. Conventional wisdom in the IFIs remains opposed to the use of regulation for purposes other than the correction of market failures; technocratic advice on policy retains a strong presumption about the likelihood of corruption and government failure whenever the state "intervenes" in the market. Together, these serve to limit both the purposes and the reach of legal reform; the presumption of government failure often undercuts the case for intervention by the state even where it might be otherwise warranted under the logic of efficiency enhancement. It is also important to note that, quite apart from these articulated concerns, the logic of regulation and intervention has always operated somewhat unevenly within and

[31] World Bank, Doing Business in 2004: Understanding Regulation (2003); World Bank, Doing Business in 2005: Removing Obstacles to Growth (2004).

[32] World Bank, World Development Report 1997: The State in a Changing World (1997).

[33] World Bank Legal Vice-Presidency, Legal and Judicial Reform: Strategic Directions 53 (2003), available at http://www4.worldbank.org/legal/legalr/GreyBookFinal2003.pdf.

[34] *Id.* at 52.

across different sectors in ways that are difficult to explain.[35] The result is that, notwithstanding the modifications to the very conception of development, the Bank retains an enduring attachment both to its initial position on "good law" for development and an abiding wariness of the State, still describing as axiomatic the proposition that growth is most likely to result from policies of deregulation and liberalization that encourage foreign investment.[36]

From critique to reform

The social critique of this project has taken two basic forms. One is that efforts to consolidate a global economic architecture around market-centered policies systemically neglected the social dimension of economic growth.[37] The second is that market reform and development policies have *themselves* produced undesirable social outcomes, either in the aggregate or for particular groups such as workers[38] or women.[39] These concerns are often articulated in the framework of human rights: either they are failures to attend adequately to human rights or are themselves breaches of human rights.[40] In addition, there seems to be evidence that market reforms and the upheavals associated with economic integration can provoke or exacerbate social conflict, especially in ethnically divided societies.[41] Both critiques gained traction, however, from a third concern, one rooted in a fundamental ordering principle of international law and institutions, namely sovereignty. This concern is simply that, however well motivated and to whatever economic effect, the constraints placed upon states by the conditionalities attached to loans were deeply invasive of sovereign power and democratic political priorities. Indeed, reforms raised fundamental questions about the legitimacy of the IFI's policy-based

35 For example, the Bank exhibits different concerns and deploys different regulatory arguments in the area of financial regulation than it does in respect of either environmental or labor regulation. See Rittich, *supra* note 9, chapter 2.

36 World Bank, *supra* note 12. See also the definition of structural reforms in IMF, *supra* note 30.

37 This was a major focus of the United Nations Summit for Social Development in 1995. See *Report of the World Summit on Social Development*, 14th plen. Mtg. at 4, U.N.Doc. A/CONF.166/9 (1995). It remains a live concern among some of the international institutions. See ILO, A Fair Globalization: Creating Opportunities for All (2004), available at http://www.ilo.org/public/english/wcsdg/index.htm.

38 Guy Standing, Global Labour Flexibility: Seeking Distributive Justice (1999).

39 Diane Elson and Nilufer Cagatay, *The Social Content of Macroeconomic Policies*, 28:7 World Dev. 1347 (2000).

40 See *Report of the World Summit for Social Development*, *supra* note 37; See also U.N. ESCOR, *Substantive Issues Arising in the Implementation of the International Covenant on Economic, Social and Cultural Rights: Poverty and the International Covenant on Economic, Social and Cultural Rights*, U.N. Doc. A/CONF.191/BP/7 (2001), available at http://www.unctad.org/en/docs/aconf191bp_7.en.pdf.

41 Amy Chua, World on Fire: How Exporting Free Market Democracy Breeds Ethnic Hatred and Global Instability (2003).

lending and the extent to which the institutions had mandates to intervene in the internal policy decisions of states.[42]

For the most part, the criticisms of first generation reforms did not focus on the legal framework of development or the broader governance agenda as such. Instead they were largely concerned with macroeconomic policies and their effects upon either specific groups or societies at large.[43] Despite the fact that their concerns intersected and sometimes directly overlapped with those who were alert to the questions of sovereignty and the distribution of power between the developed and developing world, many advocates of greater attention to the social side saw little to question or object to, and much to commend, in the whole idea of good governance. This is true *a fortiori* in the context of second generation reforms, now that good governance has come to encompass human rights.

Any decision to bracket the legal framework of development or simply to assume that good governance lives up to its advance billing and can be treated as coextensive with promoting the social side of the agenda may be a mistake,[44] however, or at the least a matter that now needs to be addressed. The basic reason is that social decisions are embedded in the very rules, institutions, and practices defined as good governance. Thus, legal and institutional reform is already in play in social debates; the terrain cannot be assumed to be neutral with respect to social norms and the generation of desirable social outcomes, especially to the extent that those norms and outcomes are themselves in contention as is now the case.

The significance of good governance and legal reform to development is conventionally attributed to their roles in enhancing the security of entitlements and the efficiency of economic transactions and their importance to the overall political and economic climate in which stable investment and human development occur.[45] In order to locate the role of law in social and distributive justice, however, as well as the democratization of development and market reform, legal rules and institutions need to be analyzed in a number of other modes as well. This is a complex and multifaceted topic; here I want only to signal those connections that seem to be most salient to the social agenda and the objectives of democratization.

42 This issue was raised inside the Bank in the early 1990s. For the Bank's effort to respond to the legal constraints on its engagement in governance issues, see Ibrahim F. I. Shihata, *Issues of "Governance" in Borrowing Members – The Extent of their Relevance Under the Bank's Articles of Agreement, in* The World Bank Legal Papers 245–282 (2000).

43 *See* Elson & Cagatay, *supra* note 39.

44 Social justice critics have often avoided deep engagement with questions of market design. A variety of factors is surely in play: division of labor along disciplinary lines; discomfort with the language and analytic tools of economists; and a tendency to rely on human rights and constitutional norms as the vehicles of transformative legal and political change.

45 Shihata, *supra* note 42.

The first is the discursive or ideological: claims about the rule of law and the nature and content of good governance can be used to legitimate attention to particular social objectives such as human rights or gender equality. But they can also be used to alternatively normalize or delegitimatize their legal or institutional expression or the frame in which they are pursued. Both on the ground and in the wider international context, such claims may make it alternatively easier or more difficult to secure support for particular reforms. This may be either beneficial or detrimental; it may also function to empower some groups at the expense of others, whether local, foreign, or some mixture of both.

This links to the second mode, the distributive: because legal rules and institutions constitute an important means of allocating power and resources to different social groups, the form and content of legal reforms can be crucially important to the question of who benefits and who loses in the course of reforms. The fact that they may be instituted to enhance competitiveness or address market failures does not change this. The manner in which reforms actually play out on the ground will undoubtedly vary, sometimes considerably, because of preexisting institutions and path dependence; because they will inevitably engender resistance as well as compliance from those whose behavior they are intended to regulate; because different groups will be differentially positioned to deploy the entitlements that they are allocated; because reforms are destined to intersect with a wide range of other normative orders, whether legal, social, or cultural; and because the process of adjudication sometimes alters, or even subverts, the initial valence of reforms.[46] Even if these complexities make it difficult to project the economic effects of reforms – whether aggregate or distributive – with complete accuracy, it also seems true that structural reforms are clearly relevant to a host of social concerns, many of which are either closely connected to or directly about the distribution of resources and power. Thus, tracking the trajectory of legal and institutional reforms remains important to understanding the rising and falling fortunes of different groups as well as the overall fate of social goals.

The third is the constitutive. Legal rules and institutions play a role in (re)constructing the very subjects and activities that they are often imagined merely to regulate. To put it another way, law "makes" societies as much as it "rules" societies. This is occasionally recognized in current development literature, particularly when, as in the references to "rule of law" respecting societies, this process of reconstruction is regarded as uncontroversially good. If legal rules and institutions are inside, rather than outside, social and economic practices, however, it seems important to consider that ideas about good governance and best practice in law and policy may themselves play a role in furthering competing ideas about social justice, and in the

46 Duncan Kennedy, *A Critique of Adjudication: Fin de siècle* (1997).

reformulation of social goals that seems to be emerging in tandem with second generation reforms. They are also likely to be implicated in defining the range of democratic options available to both states and communities. It is also worth observing that private law rules serve a political as well as an economic function; property, for example, has long been identified as a delegation of sovereignty.[47] Thus, quite apart from their distributive effects, the effort to normalize a particular structure of private rights and to confine regulatory interventions by the State will likely affect the scope of sovereign power and the extent of democratic control at the national and local levels.[48]

These observations about the properties of legal rules suggest that legal reforms might provoke or enable a variety of transformations beyond their explicit purposes. Moreover, reforms might work at cross-purposes, rather than in a clear or unitary direction; goals advanced at one level may be modified or subverted at another. Whether the idea is to assess the prospects for realizing social objectives or merely the economic objectives, a more nuanced idea of law seems in order.

Given the centrality of legal reforms to the overall development agenda and the multiple modes and registers – ideological, distributive, constitutive, regulatory, and normative – in which they resonate and operate, it seems unlikely that good governance and legal and institutional matters could be entirely separate from the realization of social objectives. Legal rules and institutions constitute the frame in which social objectives are pursued; they are part of the structure by which risk, reward, and responsibility are established. As such, they function as a key transfer point between the two sides of the development agenda. Regulatory and policy prescriptions fill out the content of general objectives, illuminating the contours of both the economic and social sides of the development project. They also disclose a great deal about how different objectives are intended to coexist; for example, they may represent an expression of the balance that is struck between distributive and efficiency concerns. Although much of the relationship between social objectives and the legal and institutional frame of development has been held in abeyance up to this point, it seems difficult to avoid confronting it directly once the social dimension of development is in play.

LAW AND GOVERNANCE IN SECOND GENERATION REFORMS: CHANGE AND STASIS

There are at least three ways in which the governance frame itself might be affected by the incorporation of the social dimension of development.

[47] Morris Cohen, *Property as Sovereignty*, 13 Cornell L.Q. 8 (1927).

[48] C. B. Macpherson, Property: Mainstream and Critical Positions, Introduction (1978).

The first, and most obvious, is that incorporation of social concerns raises the possibility of reliance upon the regulatory, redistributive state. The IFIs are latecomers to the discussion on human rights and social justice; there are already multiple analyses, platforms, statements, and normative agendas, including many that emanate from other international institutions, detailing how to promote various social objectives. They all diverge, many in significant ways, from the analyses and the prescriptions proffered by the IFIs, and most rely upon, or simply presuppose, the presence of a state with significant regulatory and redistributive capacity. Nor are these alternatives merely theoretical or aspirational. Existing norms, institutions, and practice in almost all industrialized states stand as powerful counterfactuals to the path charted by the IFIs, despite the efforts by the IFIs to depict many of these alternatives as unwise or simply unavailable in the current context.

The relationship between the social side of development and economic growth and competitiveness may also provide compelling reasons to rethink the current approach to the state and to the regulatory environment governing production and exchange. For example, the cultivation of human capital, now thought to be the foundation of successful participation in a knowledge economy, should make the capacity of governments to counter or manage, rather than merely reflect and accommodate, economic trends and pressures a more central issue, if only to avoid the medium to long term harm, economic as well as social, that may otherwise ensue from the demise or restructuring of sectors and industries in the course of market integration.[49] However, as described as follows, a central thrust of the governance agenda is to promote and legitimate a shift from the Keynesian or New Deal to the "enabling" or "postregulatory" state.[50]

Second, the incorporation of the social might call into question the adequacy of a legal and institutional order organized primarily around the promotion of efficiency and competition. For example, attention to gender and other forms of equality might compel a reexamination of the assumption that markets adequately value human capital and contributions to economic growth.[51] It might also indicate the limits of formal antidiscrimination norms as devices to ensure equality and inclusion, especially in the absence of wider

[49] The classic example here is transition; for one discussion of the costs, both economic and social, of the failure to attend to these possibilities, see ALICE AMSDEN, THE MARKET MEETS ITS MATCH: RESTRUCTURING THE ECONOMIES OF EASTERN EUROPE (1994).

[50] David M. Trubek and Louise G. Trubek, *Hard and Soft Law in the Construction of Social Europe*, SALTSA, OSE, UW Workshop on "Opening the Open Method of Coordination," European University Institute, Florence, Italy (July 2003), available at http://eucenter.wisc.edu/omc/summer03conf/trubekTrubek.pdf.

[51] For one discussion of the ways that markets transmit gender bias, see Diane Elson, *Labor Markets as Gendered Institutions: Equality, Efficiency and Empowerment Issues*, 27 WORLD DEV. 611 (1999).

structural changes.[52] This might then provoke attention to the wide range of other rules and institutions governing behavior and transactions in households and families, civil society, and the market, as well as to their distributive properties, many of which are now ignored or suppressed.

Third, attention to social concerns might also provoke a reconsideration of the nature of efficient markets and their institutional foundations. For example, it may turn out that a serious examination of labor and workplace equality issues casts doubt on the theoretical and empirical assumptions that underpin the current deregulatory approaches to labor market institutions.[53]

Although it seems unlikely that this is the final word, so far none of these possibilities is much in evidence. Instead, there are clear efforts to manage the institutional implications of the expanded development agenda by confining the growth and direction of formal legal entitlements and relying upon new forms of governance; by fashioning a new social role for the State; and by channeling many social concerns away from the State toward nonstate actors and institutions. The end result are social agendas that do not seriously disturb the established institutional and regulatory frame and that sometimes circumvent formal institutional solutions altogether.

In order to understand why this might be the case, it is useful to review the reasons that law has come to play a more central role and to rehearse the basic arguments advanced by the IFIs in respect of legal reform.

Due to the focus on institutions, law had already come to play an important role in the reform agenda prior to the introduction of second generation reforms. Arguments from law had been consistently deployed to support market reform since the IFIs became immersed in the institutional reconstruction occasioned by the transition to markets in Central and Eastern Europe and the CIS[54]; as a result, the discourse of best practices in law had been under active construction since the early to mid-1990s. Both ideas about the nature of law in the abstract and claims about necessary legal rules and institutions in market societies continue to play a central role in second generation reforms, as they did in the first. Whether it is the importance of the rule of law or the connection between property rights and security and political stability,[55] theories and arguments about law are woven throughout the governance project, helping to justify the choices and decisions that are made.

With second generation reforms, however, the IFIs have become interested in new modes of governance and begun to explore an expanded set of regulatory options; this turn is especially marked with respect to social

[52] For a collection of essays exploring this issue in the context of race, see K. Crenshaw et al., Critical Race Theory: Key Writings that Formed the Movement (1995).

[53] Simon Deakin and Frank Wilkinson, *Labour Law and Economic Theory: A Reappraisal*, in Legal Regulation of the Employment Relation 29 (Hugh Collins et al. eds., 2000).

[54] World Bank, World Development Report 1996: From Plan to Market (1996).

[55] See, e.g., World Bank, World Development Report 2002: Building Institutions for Markets (2001).

concerns. Although causal relation is uncertain – either interest in alternatives to traditional modes of regulation and governance may be driving the approach to social issues or the pressure to address social questions may itself be the catalyst for the interest in new modes of governance – the direction of change seems relatively clear. While the pursuit of economic goals continues to attract a deep interest in questions of legal rules and institutional structure, the embrace of the social coincides with a burgeoning interest in alternative modes of regulation and an increasingly nuanced set of distinctions among norms and the different modes and routes by which they can be pursued.

In the early discussions of law and development, the absence of formal law was typically represented as the absence of normativity and regulation *tout court*, coextensive with chaos, disorder, arbitrariness, and corruption – in short a Hobbesian state of nature. While the claim that the rule of law and formal legal institutions are the *sine qua non* to development remains, it is just as common now to encounter arguments that law is the problem: badly crafted rules and policies, even the regulatory state as a whole, may be impediments to growth or otherwise incompatible with the demands of a globally integrated economy. Hence, the task is to import not just law, but the right set of institutions.

With second generation reforms, however, the IFIs seem to have moved still further, beyond the point at which the goal is simply the creation of law-based societies in which sovereign control of territory is even and complete; there are no disjunctures between regulatory space and regulatory power; there are no serious gaps between regulatory objectives and the law in action; and the legal system operates seamlessly and without competition in the interests of progress and growth. Despite its centrality to securing the right climate for investment, the IFIs no longer necessarily assume that effective power resides in the State in a transnational world of commerce and production, nor are they confident that standard regulatory institutions will generate solutions to the problems of the postindustrial economy. Instead, a new regulatory paradigm may be needed; sometimes law may even be irrelevant. Hence, sometimes the role of formal law is refashioned and carved back, as governance projects demote both law and the State, or privilege it in defined forms such as private law and specific locales such as commercial regulation.

In the process, more space is created for private actors to devise their own normative regimes and alternative modes of securing compliance are encouraged. Arbitration, for example, may be promoted over adjudication, similarly consultation and cooperation among the affected actors may be preferred to regulation. For concerns such as human rights, labor standards, gender equality, and environmental issues, alternative modes of governance are especially popular: soft law is preferred over hard; frameworks, voluntary solutions, and market incentives promoted rather than rules and regulation; and negotiated compliance preferred over strict enforcement of rules and standards. In the alternative, these issues may simply be relegated to the domain of policy, where policy is understood as distinct from and subordinate to rules and institutions.

Thus, the legal reform agenda in second generation reforms is marked by both change and stasis. The argument here is that, because there is such a range of claims and logics informing the discussions of law, governance, and norm generation, and because they seem to be loosely associated with different issues, attention to both the change and the stasis is critical to understanding the direction of the social agenda and the prospects for transformation.

Change

In second generation reforms, change is clearly visible in the following interconnected areas: 1) legal restraints upon the powers of the State; 2) greater emphasis on judicial process and institutions; 3) expansion of the actors engaged in governance; 4) the turn toward soft law; 5) the recognition of nonlegal sources of normativity; and 6) the use of human rights. All mark a shift toward a much more fragmented and polycentric normative order, one in which the center of gravity in respect of governance and regulation is no longer always located in the State.

Legal restraints upon the power of the state. Because concepts such as good governance are full of history and content, but also contestable and unstable, an ongoing effort is required to manage the direction of legal and policy reform. One problem is that whatever hold market-friendly rules, policies, and institutions have in any jurisdiction, they remain vulnerable to challenge due to political pressure and regime change. There remains the possibility, present in both authoritarian and democratic regimes, that political authorities might make decisions that are suboptimal or disruptive from the standpoint of furthering investment and growth. Their capacity to do so is variably explained as evidence of corruption, arbitrariness in the exercise of power, the persistent vulnerability of the State to capture, or lack of credible commitment – in short, the malfunction or dysfunction of the State in some way.

One of the ways that these concerns play out is in efforts to decommission the political arms of the State in an expanding zone of policy and regulatory activities. The motivation is to bind the State into the future so that reforms agreed to at one point in time with one administration cannot be undone, at least without considerable expense and effort, at a later date. The Bank has now concluded that the answer to the problem of states credibly committing to "good" policies may be the delegation of a range of functions typically associated with the State to either independent agencies or external, international institutions. Taking a cue from the independence of central banks, the Bank proposes that tasks such as tax collection and trade policy might be taken out of the political or legislative arena as well.[56]

These proposals track the trend toward the constitutionalization of international economic reforms; efforts to obtain regulatory precommitment from states regarding investor rights are already well-described in the international literature.[57] While limits on state power are hardly new – restraints upon state power are a familiar part of all rules-based regimes and form the basis for constitutional oversight of the State – their traditional justification lies in the potential that the State might use its disproportionate power to oppress individuals and vulnerable groups. The logic of constitutional restraint has already been extended to nonnatural persons such as corporations; what is noteworthy about the evolution of the governance agenda in second generation reforms is the increasing tendency to tightly circumscribe the political choices of democratic electorates as well.

Such proposals represent an important moment in the struggle between governance norms and sovereignty and democracy, if only for the reason there is no necessary limit to the application of the principle of credible commitment; it might be argued that states should commit on a broad range of issues, social issues included. But whether they actually extend this far, restraints such as those described previously are likely to have important implications for the pursuit of social initiatives. For example, States that are vulnerable to investor suits for regulatory takings may experience regulatory chill in areas such as environmental or health and safety issues.[58] It is now evident that even purely economic commitments can affect the scope for responding to social issues, especially those that have resource implications (which is to say almost all of them). For this reason, States within the European Union have discovered that a monetary union quickly moves toward a fiscal union too, and that fiscal constraints quite directly affect the pursuit of social objectives, if not the fabric of the social state in its entirety.[59]

Judicial reforms. While the interest in this issue can be traced back before second generation reforms, there has been an astonishing proliferation of judicial reform projects in recent years; to date, the Bank has embarked on over 600 projects.[60] Judicial reforms encompass alterations to judicial

[56] World Bank, World Development Report 2003: Sustainable Development in a Dynamic World, ch. 6 (2002).

[57] David Schneiderman, *Investment Rules and the New Constitutionalism*, 25 Law & Soc. Inquiry 757 (2000); Deborah Z. Cass, *The "Constitutionalization" of International Trade Law: Judicial Norm-Generation as the Engine of Constitutional Development in International Trade Law*, 12 Eur. J. Int'l L. 39 (2001).

[58] See, e.g., Mexico v. Metalclad Corp., [2001] B.C.J No. 950 (2001).

[59] The recent rejection of the Euro on the part of Sweden, for example, is widely attributed to fears that the monetary union would jeopardize its welfare state.

[60] Robert Danino, Senior Vice President and General Counsel, World Bank; Address at the Conference on Human Rights and Development Towards Mutual Reinforcement (Mar. 1, 2004).

institutions and training, as well as an enhanced focus on process, procedure, and access to justice; they may involve supply side reforms, such as anticorruption efforts and reforms to judicial institutions, or demand side access to justice reforms.[61]

Some of the time, judicial reforms appear to be driven by efforts to improve the position of marginalized groups. So far supply-side concerns appear to have dominated the funding process, however. While recently there have been more access to justice projects that target specific groups such as women,[62] whether they might become a central rather than peripheral concern is unclear. At this point, much of the interest in judicial reform is clearly linked to the old goals of facilitating transactions and securing property and contract rights. Judicial reform has become a major part of the effort to promote the rule of law and secure a stable investment climate: the presence of institutions capable of enforcing property and contract rights and the appropriate attitude of judges to the adjudication of conflicting rights are both crucial if reforms are to realize their potential.[63]

New actors. A hallmark of second generation reforms, particularly since 2002, is the effort to take account of the way in which governance is dispersed across society rather than centered in the State.[64] Not only does the Bank recognize that regulation occurs in multiple sites; reform prescription actively seeks to displace governance to different sites and to empower a range of regulatory actors other than the State. Thus, more and more of the regulatory projects conventionally assumed by the State are being allocated to actors in the "third sector." The market and market actors, more particularly investors and capital holders, are becoming important sources of law, normativity, rule, and control.

It has been recognized at least since the mid-1990s that market actors can be an important source of demand for "good law."[65] Within the Bank, this is normally imagined as an uncomplicated relationship. There may be those who, seeking protection from the challenges of globalization, make demands that, if acceded to, would distort the market. Workers, for example, are often identified as a special interest group;[66] women too may seek protections or rules that deviate from market norms and introduce inefficiencies.[67] But such

61 See World Bank Legal Vice Presidency, *supra* note 33.

62 *Id.*

63 This is not to suggest that they actually deliver on these objectives; the link between judicial reforms and greater economic growth seems elusive and can be very difficult to establish.

64 See in particular, World Bank, *supra* note 55, and World Bank, *supra* note 56.

65 See World Bank, World Development Report 1996: From Plan to Market (1996). The historical roots of this claim date at least to Weber, see David M. Trubek, *Max Weber on Law and the Rise of Capitalism*, 1972 Wis. L. Rev. 720.

66 See World Bank, World Development Report 1995: Workers in an Integrating World (1995).

67 For a discussion, see World Bank, *supra* note 12.

exceptions aside, the demand that market actors create for law is normally treated as simply coextensive with the production of the framework conditions for growth.

There is also evidence of the "third sectorization" of law and policy, however, as there is of development and market reform as a whole. This has complicated the regulatory logic around development. No longer do policy debates revolve solely around the State and the market, although this relationship remains a central preoccupation. Moving from the margins closer to the center of the good governance debates is a host of actors that make up the third sector. The third sector comprises myriad nonstate, nonmarket, and civil society organizations such as voluntary associations, NGOs, and religious organizations who are now invited, indeed expected, to play a greater role in public life. Like the market, they too may serve not only as service providers or partners in public/private ventures or as sources of valuable social capital;[68] they are also sources of demand for institutional change. For example, they may serve as useful vehicles of resistance to the State, particularly where the State is pursuing policies that contravene conventional wisdom on good governance. They may also serve as conduits of information and democratic preferences to policymakers, a role they may play in competition with or even in lieu of political institutions. They are sometimes also recognized as independent sources of normative authority.

The third sector also functions as a repository of concerns that are properly excluded from the law and the State, however. Sometimes the intransigence of culture or society is invoked as a brake on expectations around social change and a ground for regulatory nonintervention on the part of the State. For example, if a problem such as gender inequality lies in cultural norms, legal and institutional remedies may be futile. Instead, social change beyond the realm of the State is needed.[69]

Soft law. Despite the belief that the fundamental institutional architecture of development is now well settled and due to ongoing concerns about government failure, a desire to confine the role of the State, one place where development is clearly visible is in the use area of soft norms and institutional processes. There is increasing reliance upon voluntary initiatives, incentives, and standards generated at the local level or by the parties most directly affected; this is particularly the case in respect to issues typically consigned to the social rather than the hard economic side of the ledger.[70] For example, while the IFIs remain deeply committed to the idea that the formalization

[68] World Bank, *supra* note 56; for a critique of the uses of social capital, see Ben Fine, *The Developmental State is Dead – Long Live Social Capital?*, 30 DEV. & CHANGE 1 (1999).

[69] World Bank, *supra* note 12.

[70] Indeed, there are increasingly complex blends of different "soft" strategies.

of property and contract rights is required to facilitate investment, production, and exchange,[71] they often propose soft norms and strategies to deal with any social concerns associated with these activities. For example, corporate codes of conduct to further human rights, labor standards, and environmental protection are classic alternative regulatory initiatives that currently find favor. This turn to soft law is not unpredictable; indeed, it is consistent with the established view that regulatory initiatives for distributive purposes are likely to impede efficiency and the ongoing concerns about regulatory intervention even where some form of regulation might be indicated.[72]

Nonlegal normativity: Informal norms, social networks, and culture. In a related turn, one of the most important elements of second generation reforms is the attention that is beginning to be given to nonlegal sources of normativity and the effort to take account of local practices and norms, especially those emanating from market actors and civil society groups. One effect is to expand the reach of good governance beyond formal law, into the interstices of societies and cultures. While the phenomenon of legal pluralism and its impact on and importance to the operation of formal legal institutions has long been noted in the legal literature,[73] the turn outside of formal institutions marks a significant shift in the regulatory approach of the IFIs. While the justification for formal law remains centered on its role in attracting investment and promoting growth, culture and society have now been partially rehabilitated and there is new interest in the role of informal norms in furthering efficiency as well as growth. Moreover, the discourse is around law becoming more complex, as at least some of the antiformalist critiques have been absorbed.

Rather than the antithesis of law, now informal norms may supplement or even supplant formal law in the facilitation of business transactions. Although the rhetoric of corruption remains as strong as ever,[74] the Bank has come around to the view that social networks can be an efficient way to close deals and convey information, even though they have tendencies to function as insider networks. They may be especially critical for the poor for whom formal law is often unavailable. In addition, such networks spread risk and raise the relative returns from market transactions, which they do by defining property

[71] See, e.g., World Bank, Policy Research Report: Land Policies for Growth and Poverty Reduction (2003).

[72] Shihata, *supra* note 5.

[73] See Harry W. Arthurs, *Labour Law Beyond the State?*, 46 U. Toronto L. J. 1 (1996).

[74] Page 1 of the World Development Report 2003, *supra* note 56, begins with the statement: "Development is sustainable if the rules of the game are transparent and the game is inclusive." See also the references to property rights and the rule of law as essential to the creation of "human-made" assets and efficient markets.

and contract rights and managing competition.[75] These are, of course, precisely the same arguments that are advanced for formal law, although the arguments for the formalization of law are rooted in the inherent limits of societies governed by culture and convention.[76]

What is perhaps most interesting is the view that civil society and the third sector also have a role in responding to market failure. While market failures are one of the classic bases for state intervention, the Bank is now of the view that nonstate bodies may be able to substitute, providing solutions to such problems in at least some cases. Part of their attraction lies in the fact that they represent an alternative to the State, a means of avoiding a return to old style, top-down regulation. Yet reliance on civil society also produces countervailing worries. For example, informal norms may serve multiple objectives rather than efficiency *simpliciter*; in particular, informal laws and norms may reflect distributive concerns.[77] Nonetheless, the extra legal has clearly been acknowledged to some extent as a source of regulatory authority and efficiency, at least for those who do not circulate in the realm of global capital.

Human rights. Human rights make a significant appearance throughout the second generation reform literature. There are countless references to the need for basic human rights such as freedom of expression and freedom of association, including the freedom to establish nongovernmental entities[78]; antidiscrimination norms too now make a regular appearance.

The IFIs have embraced human rights as part of the reformulated definition of development on a number of grounds: because they are now an official end of development; because they contribute directly to good economic outcomes; because they protect the interests of civil society groups and serve as a counterweight to the power of the State; and because they form part of the political climate necessary to attract investment and ensure growth. Thus, human rights serve both economic and social purposes. For example, freedom of association may be necessary to empower civil society groups vis-à-vis the State, while antidiscrimination norms serve to increase market access and participation for excluded or disadvantaged groups, something that is expected to enhance economic growth as well as social inclusion.

The recognition of human rights is highly significant, in part because human rights often structure the debate on issues ranging from gender equality and global labor standards to the protection of indigenous peoples and the

[75] World Bank, *supra* note 55.

[76] Here, an important contemporary influence is Hernando de Soto; see HERNANDO DE SOTO, THE MYSTERY OF CAPITAL: WHY CAPITALISM TRIUMPHS IN THE WEST AND FAILS EVERYWHERE ELSE (2000).

[77] World Bank, *supra* note 55, at 176.

[78] See World Bank, *Anti-corruption: Civil Society Participation*, available at http://www1.worldbank.org/publicsector/anticorrupt/civilsociety.htm.

environment. Progressive reformers, too, not only endorse human rights as ends in themselves; they also frame their arguments for change to development reforms and practices in the language of human rights, hoping that the moral heft provided by the framework of human rights will help to overcome arguments and resistance they otherwise encounter.

Sometimes human rights do seem to represent a point of intersection between the two sides, a common way to frame the wider social agenda. For example, basic education and health care at least occasionally are described by Bank officials as "rights to which people are entitled and should have the ability to assert."[79] It is important, however, to recognize that references to human rights within development and market reform policies are not necessarily references to human rights as they are understood by the international human rights institutions, human rights scholars, the activist community, or the wider civil society. Rather, they are inevitably references to only a limited domain of human rights, typically identified as "basic" human rights. While access to basic health care and education may sometimes be described as a right, in general the IFIs speak the language of human rights only in regard to civil and political rights. As described previously, there is support for freedom of expression, religion, and association; arguably some of the access to justice initiatives could be subsumed under the framework of human rights too, especially those that target women or other marginalized or excluded groups. The IFIs also endorse equality, as formal antidiscrimination norms are viewed as fundamental to societies organized around market participation.

But what is excluded, left behind in the process of importing human rights into development, is also telling. Apart from the protection of property and contract rights, the rules, institutions, policies, and practices that organize the economy, work, and production do not generally fall within the normative framework of human rights; this remains the case even when they appear to be essential to the realization of objectives that *are* recognized as human rights, such as gender equality or core labor rights. As described next, any assumption on the part of reformers that acceptance of the formal right entails agreement about its concrete institutional, financial, or other implications is unsafe.

There may be a sizable gap between the endorsement of human rights on the one hand and legal recognition and institutional entrenchment of those rights on the other in any event. While human rights may have been accepted at the normative level, it is unsafe to assume that this recognition has any necessary or determinate impact upon the design of institutions and legal rules. For example, despite the formal acknowledgement of freedom of association and core labor rights for workers as human rights, the IFIs continue to resist the implementation of labor market rules and institutions

[79] Nicholas Stern and Shantayanan Devarajan, *Power to the Poor People*, Globe & Mail, Sept. 24, 2003, at A23.

that facilitate collective bargaining in the face of employer intransigence or protect workers from reprisals from union organizing and respect for workers' freedom of association.[80] Despite the general endorsement of gender equality, there is similar resistance, both normative and instrumental, to a host of well-entrenched proposals to promote gender equality.[81] In short, there is selective engagement with both human rights norms and their institutional implications, at least as those implications are understood in other constituencies.

For related reasons, there is also resistance to the idea of endorsing a rights-based approach to development *tout court*. The campaign for rights-based development is an effort to get the IFIs, and a wide range of other actors and institutions both global and local, to recognize a number of rights to which people are entitled and which they would have the ability to assert in the context of development.[82] Those calling for rights-based development typically seek to subject the entire range of development and market reform policies to an overarching set of human rights and public and international law norms. This includes a range of market reform policies that human rights and social justice activists have identified as inimical to the advancement or protection of human rights, social rights in particular, such as: fiscal austerity drives that limit the resources for health, education, and other social services; macroeconomic and monetary policies that increase unemployment and aggravate the plight of the poor; and liberalization and deregulation policies that shift the balance of power among social actors domestic and foreign and increase inequality both within and among states. So far, the Bank and the International Monetary Fund (Fund) have decisively resisted this move, not because they object to human rights per se but on the basis that they have no mandate to endorse development policies that do not demonstrably lead to and may in their view actually impair economic growth. But they go still further, arguing that economic growth is itself necessary for human rights, thus subverting the argument that development and market reform projects should automatically be subordinated to human rights norms.

Stasis

The new approaches to governance and norm generation in connection with social objectives and the complexities that are visible in the encounter with human rights are difficult to account for on their own terms. They do seem

[80] For a discussion, see Kerry Rittich, *Core Labour Rights and Labour Market Flexibility: Two Paths Entwined?, Permanent Court of Arbitration, Peace Palace Papers*, in Labour Law Beyond Borders: ADR and the Internationalization of Labour Dispute Settlement 157 (The International Bureau of the Permanent Court of Arbitration ed., 2003).

[81] World Bank, Integrating Gender into the World Bank's Work: A Strategy for Action (2002).

[82] For one discussion, see UNDP, *Human Rights and Development: An Emerging Nexus*, available at http://www.undp.org/rbap/rights/Nexus.htm.

connected to the stasis in the larger legal and institutional reform agenda, however.

Despite the redefinition of the aims of development and market reform, the central role assigned to law in second generation reforms, efforts to increase the country ownership of reforms, and some alterations to the processes by which reforms are implemented as a result, the actual content of the legal reform agenda has changed surprisingly little. Discussion and policy prescription on the rules and institutions that are needed for development remain centered around concerns about the promotion of efficiency and competition through the protection of property and contract rights.[83] At the same time, corruption, transparency, and accountability remain the major preoccupations in respect of the State. As a result, the fact that the development agenda has been reformulated to include the social is almost completely unreflected in the core legal and institutional reform project.

Although one of the touchstones of second generation reforms is the rejection of a one-size-fits-all template for development and the importance of wider participation in the formulation of development goals, there is surprisingly little diversity in either the discourse or the prescriptions about the legal reforms needed for development. In part this may be due to how the process of participation is itself imagined. As one recent Bank publication put it, enhancing participation involves first diagnosing the problem and then designing reforms according to the relevant known best practices; at this point, it becomes important to get local buy-in as to priorities and sequencing.[84] Despite the reminders that context matters, there is no evident pluralization in the reform proposals. Whether one-size-fits-all, especially with respect to economic rules and regulations, still seems to be a matter of internal dispute within the Bank.[85] But even if it no longer still rules at the formal level, then its impact is yet to become visible in any substantial way.

The resulting disjuncture between the expanded development agenda and the legal reform project is stark. There is a wealth of empirical research exploring the connection between the existing best practice rules and growth; indeed second generation reforms are marked by an intensified focus on measuring the results of reforms and shoring up the empirical base of the reform agenda.[86] Research and policy reports also increasingly suggest congruence

[83] IMF, *supra* note 30, at 104–5.

[84] World Bank Legal Vice Presidency, *supra* note 33, at 55.

[85] See the discussion on "One Size Can Fit All – In the Manner of Business Regulation" in World Bank, *supra* note 31, at xvi.

[86] See activities of the World Bank Institute, available at http://web.worldbank.org/WBSITE/EXTERNAL/WBI/0,,contentMDK:20097853~menuPK:204763~pagePK:209023~piPK:207535~theSitePK:213799,00.html. See also World Bank, *supra* note 31; Norman V. Loayza and Raimundo Soto, *On the Measurement of Market-Oriented Reforms* (2003), available at http://econ.worldbank.org/files/37707_wps3371.pdf.

or an overlap between the institutional demands of social justice and economic growth.[87] But research on the distributive or other social effects of the legal reform agenda itself is sparing to nonexistent.

The result is a wall between the two sides of the development agenda, the effect of which is to make the established legal framework the background condition in which other objectives, including social objectives, must be pursued. It is as if the legal framework of investment, production, and exchange had no effect on the social and, aside from the changes described previously, the incorporation of social objectives into the development agenda had few necessary institutional implications. Yet whatever the promise of procedural reforms, it is not only lack of popular participation in the development and market reform process that has attracted concern. Nor has the social deficit necessarily been attributed to the absence of the rule of law, inadequate legal process or procedure, or lack of access to judicial institutions. Rather, much of the criticism concerns the values and interests that have been furthered and neglected in the process of reform and the groups that have been alternatively harmed or advantaged in the process.

Because of the varied properties and effects of legal reforms described at the outset, these concerns seem likely to be intimately related to, rather than separate from, the institutional choices that have governed the development and economic integration agendas. Apart from a nod in the direction of civil and political rights, however, the discussion of legal rules and institutions still largely proceeds in terms of their expected contribution to efficiency. A vast number of legal rules and institutions in contemporary market societies are of course expressly designed to further distributive and social goals: collective bargaining rules, consumer protection laws, landlord and tenant laws, and zoning laws all reallocate the bargaining power that would otherwise be obtained through contract and property law. They may also guarantee social minima, whether in respect of housing, health and safety, employment, or other concerns. But it is important not to overstate the normative or functional origins of legal rules and institutions. It is doubtful whether the structure and content of many laws, not only those that obviously further social objectives but those that further efficient transactions too, can be adequately explained apart from the conflicting interests and concerns of different constituencies and their relative weight at different moments.[88] However, despite the expansion of development objectives to include the social, there is no explanation for rules that deviate from efficiency *other* than that the regulatory process has been captured by special interests.

What is missing is any recognition that the legal and institutional reform projects may be implicated in some of the very social problems that they are

[87] See, e.g., World Bank, *supra* note 12.

[88] R. W. Gordon, "Critical Legal Histories", 36 Stan. L. Rev. 57 (1984).

now being conscripted to help solve because of their effect on the allocation of power and resources. Yet while their connection to social concerns seems to be absent, there *is* some degree of consciousness that distributive struggles may be played out in and around legal rules. For example, in a recent restatement on the relationship of law to development, the Bank makes reference to the fact that legal rules "determin[e] who gets what and when" and notes that "all institutional structures affect the *distribution* of assets, incomes, and costs as well as the incentives of market participants and the efficiency of market transactions."[89] This insight, however, is largely deployed to confirm the distinction between good and bad law and the wisdom of the established path of reform: "By distributing rights to the most efficient agent, institutions can enhance productivity and growth."[90] Similarly, a recent Fund report on the political economy of structural reforms analyzes the phenomenon of status quo bias,[91] described as the tendency of potential losers to hold up the process of regulatory reforms. This insight, however, does not provoke a more general reflection on the fact that winners and losers are routinely produced in the course of reforms.

In addition, it seems likely that some reassessment of the legal reform project may be needed expressly for the purposes of furthering the social side of the development agenda. Efforts to improve the position of groups such as workers, women, and indigenous peoples, or simply to alleviate the hardship of those who are generally dispossessed, do not always live comfortably with efforts to facilitate transactions and provide a market-friendly investment environment. While greater equality may be entirely compatible with growth,[92] typically there are real and perceived tradeoffs. And even if greater attention to inequality and other social objectives does also aid growth, there can still be critical disputes about the manner and extent to which they should be addressed through legal rules and institutions. This is a particularly live possibility in second generation reforms, as many of the routes by which social objectives either might be pursued or traditionally have been pursued conflict with the norms and assumptions that organize good governance. For all of these reasons, we might expect the introduction of social concerns to engender both contestation and change in the realm of governance and legal reform.

However, this has not happened. One possible explanation is that the core reforms from the first generation are regarded as entirely compatible with enhanced attention to the social side; as the president of the Bank announced

89 World Bank, *supra* note 13.

90 *Id.*

91 IMF, *supra* note 30.

92 Ravi Kanbur and Nora Lustig, *Why is Inequality Back on the Agenda?*, World Bank: Annual Bank Conference on Development Economics (Apr. 28–30, 1999), available at http://www.worldbank.org/poverty/wdrpoverty/kanbur499.pdf.

in 1999, what is required is simply more attention to the other side of the agenda.[93] Another possibility is that core reforms are thought to be not only compatible but necessary to the realization of social objectives. This too, has some resonance in current development discourse: as the Bank and the Fund have become fond of saying, not only does development now include human rights, the realization of human rights requires economic development.[94] Indeed, it has been argued that deficits, inflation, subsidies, and trade restrictions are themselves contrary to human rights.[95] Yet a third possibility is that core legal reforms themselves directly embody or promote social objectives, even if we never realized it before. This too forms part of the current development narrative: where before property rights were defended in the name of attracting investment and economic growth, now we learn that they are in fact of most benefit and importance to the poor and critical to the direct alleviation of poverty as well.[96] Whatever the explanation, attention to the social side of development proceeds largely through preexisting legal institutions or outside them altogether.

ASSESSING THE RISE OF THE SOCIAL

Transforming the social

There is a distinct approach within second generation reforms to the analysis of social objectives and to the policy mechanisms for pursuing the social side of development. In general, they stress the role of market forces and place enhanced emphasis on the use of market incentives to achieve particular objectives. These mechanisms, in turn, affect the nature of the social objectives themselves.

Recent discussions suggest that addressing social concerns require the following shifts. It entails more emphasis on human rights, an enhanced focus on process and procedure, and greater attention to popular participation in the formulation of development policy. It may also involve alterations to policy and resource reallocations to encourage investment in human capital and enable more highly skilled, highly valued market participation. It almost certainly involves greater involvement on the part of civil society, NGOs, and grassroots groups, whether in the formulation of norms or the delivery of services. This is turn may imply more volunteer work, especially in the context of fiscal constraints or the devolution of state responsibilities to the local level. But it also involves a cultural or psychological shift, namely becoming more

93 Wolfensohn, *supra* note 1.
94 World Bank, The World Bank and Human Rights (1998).
95 Sergio Pereira Leite, *Human Rights and the IMF*, 38 Fin. & Dev. 4 (2001).
96 World Bank Legal Vice Presidency, *supra* note 84.

alive to the possibilities of the market and moving beyond the expectation that the State is either the source or the guarantor of social entitlements.

An important part of furthering the social side centers around ensuring broad participation in the market, however, which the IFIs are promoting through a variety of what might be described as "market-centered" agendas for social justice.[97] These are projects that respond to issues ranging from gender equality[98] to improved corporate social responsibility[99] and better labor standards in the new economy, largely by relying upon market forces and market incentives. What both joins them together and distinguishes them from other social justice projects is that they present the pursuit of social objectives as essentially congruent and coterminous with the current direction of institutional reform, if only they are approached in the right spirit and with a proper consciousness of governance norms. While these efforts often collapse the distance and conflict between economic growth and social objectives that marked first generation reforms, they also reframe social objectives in ways that make them more compatible with market-centered growth.

At this point, many of these projects can at best be described as speculative. But whatever the prospects that they will actually realize their objectives, their impact upon the social goals themselves is significant. Among the results are that the object and scope of social goals are being reduced. For example, formal equality, especially in the form of participation rights, is being substituted for substantive equality. Social programs are being targeted to assist only the poorest rather than provide universal or broad-based protection.

These trends are evident in the Bank's policy research report on gender equality. In this report, the Bank sets out the case for incorporating gender equality into the development agenda, explaining it as "good for growth" while at the same time defending development as good for gender equality.[100] In the process, however, the report advances a particular definition of gender equality that explicitly rejects the goal of substantive economic equality between men and women, even as it promotes market processes and greater market participation as the engines of gender equality.[101] A similar process is at work with respect to global labor standards. When the Bank and the Fund are pressed to recognize certain core worker rights as human rights, they give a qualified endorsement, explicitly reserving their position on what the International Labor Organization (ILO) identifies as the linchpin

[97] This turn seems not unrelated to a trend already identified by human rights scholars. See, e.g., Upendra Baxi, *Voices of Suffering and the Future of Human Rights*, 8 Transnat'l L. & Contemp. Probs. 125 (1998).

[98] World Bank, *supra* note 12.

[99] United Nations, The Global Compact: Corporate Leadership in the World Economy (1999).

[100] World Bank, *supra* note 12, at 2. The Bank also argues the obverse, contending that growth is good for gender equality.

[101] *Id.*

of the global labor agenda, freedom of association, and the right to bargain collectively.[102] But just as important is that they are also reformulating the basic objectives of worker protection: according to the Bank and the Fund, the goal is not to secure the traditional collective interests of workers; this may amount to special interest protection.[103] Instead, what is important is that workers' individual rights and freedoms are respected. In their view, the economic security and welfare of workers lies not in job security protection or other labor and employment standards, but in greater flexibility and adaptability to the demands of the market.

The IFIs are also altering the mechanisms through which social objectives are achieved. While this was arguably implicit in first generation reforms, with the new attention to the social side of the agenda, the limits on those objectives are now becoming more explicit. In particular, the strategies of engagement with social concerns resist the use of market rules and institutions for distributive purposes on the basis that they can be expected to have a depressing effect on aggregate growth; similar arguments are advanced for restraining the use of tax and income transfers.

These developments all indicate a growing instrumentalization of social justice claims. Social objectives are embraced not only because they are human rights or are socially desirable, but because they enhance growth. Although with second generation reforms at least some social justice issues now have status as independent ends or goals of development, debates over social justice are increasingly conducted in terms of their contribution to economic growth.[104] Social goals are themselves being reranked: those that appear to most directly enhance the extent and quality of market participation, for example investments in human capital, such as education and worker training, are preferred over those that do not.

There is also a marked individualization of the social welfare calculus. Rather than common and universal entitlements in respect of pensions and health care, market reformers propose the establishment of individual accounts calibrated to levels of market participation. Furthermore, as described previously, workers are increasingly represented individuals with rights rather than constituencies with collective interests and demands.[105]

[102] World Bank, Core Labour Standards and the World Bank, Background Document for ICFTU/ITS/World Bank Meetings on Core Labour Standards (Jan. 20, 1998); World Bank, *supra* note 12.

[103] World Bank, *supra* note 65.

[104] This shift in the language of justification is not confined to the Bank, however; those pushing for reforms from outside now frequently frame their claims in the language of efficiency too. Even the ILO now routinely advances arguments for worker protection in terms of their contribution to economic growth, as well as their intrinsic importance. See, e.g., ILO, *supra* note 37.

[105] Bob Hepple, *Introduction*, in Social and Labour Rights in a Global Context (Bob Hepple ed., 2002).

To repeat, in their efforts to propose solutions to the social, the IFIs are as likely to reject as embrace the claims and evaluations of other international institutions, scholarly experts, and civil society groups. Whether they diverge from other norms or not, however, may matter less than the simple fact that since the inception of second generation reforms, they have established an authoritative presence in such debates. Whether the issue is gender equality, global labor standards or human rights, the IFIs routinely stake out positions on the content of social and political concerns and their policy and institutional implications.

The result is a "new normal," a reconstitution of norms at the level of subject or citizen, social institutions, and societies as a whole. Paradoxically, quintessential second generation ideas that there should be self-determination in the development process and greater attention to the social or human side of the development equation manage to coexist with the view that there must be continued fidelity to market principles and the institutions said to embody them. While there is a place for human rights, heightened attention to social concerns, and even some room for equality, they are envisaged within a fairly well-defined set of market-centered and market-promoting parameters.

At least part of the reason is not hard to intuit. The embrace of the social dimension of development risks rehabilitating goals and resuscitating strategies that have been systematically challenged if not discredited outright in the broader governance agenda as a whole. To the extent that responsiveness to social welfare and social justice concerns is reflexively associated with intervention, regulation, protection, or redistribution by the State, the IFIs (along with many other international and domestic actors and bodies) seek to break this connection.

Thus, one possibility is that efforts to promote the social are better explained in conjunction with the governance agenda than in terms of established ideas about human rights or the route to social justice themselves. There are two issues integral to governance norms that appear to have had an impact on the way that social concerns are imagined in the context of development. The first is the nature of sovereignty; the second is the emergence of the enabling State.

Recalibrating sovereignty

Second generation reforms aim to redress the concern that emerged from first generation reforms, which is that development priorities and market reforms appeared to be imposed from outside and to trench on territory that should be reserved to democratic choices and national decision-making processes. Yet while there are new "participatory" processes for generating reform strategies,[106] an increasingly wide number of issues are now classified as matters of good governance. This works to contract the zone of policy and regulatory decision making in which participation is seen as important and concerns about sovereignty appear to be legitimate.

Since its inception, policy-based lending has raised a fundamental set of concerns around sovereignty, legitimacy, and the limits of the mandates of the IFIs. The original aim behind policy-based lending was to identify and isolate a set of regulatory and institutional issues from the wider zone of political contestation, on the basis that this isolation from "normal" politics was necessary to stabilize the economy and promote growth. These efforts produced resistance, much of which was articulated in terms of the infringement of democratic processes and sovereign political priorities. The move to promote good governance, particularly in dysfunctional or failed states, has not solved this problem, despite the second generation idea that reforms should become more democratic and participatory.

This is partly explained by the fact that the development of governance norms has been coextensive with the continuous erosion of the prohibition on interference in the internal affairs of States. Distributive concerns such as human rights and gender equality had long been characterized as political issues; as such, they originally fell outside the realm of considerations that the IFIs were authorized to use as the basis of lending decisions.[107] As policy-based lending expanded into a fully-fledged governance agenda, one whose promotion became not simply normalized but central to the activities of the IFIs, the specter of the forbidden political loomed large. Faced squarely with the issue, however, the IFIs simply redefined the existing boundary between economic and political issues. Armed with an opinion issued by the Bank's legal counsel on its governance activities,[108] they proceeded to articulate a comprehensive economic rationale for engagement with domestic policies and regulations, effectively ratifying the path of action on which they had already embarked. If in the first phase of policy-based reforms, sovereignty stood as a reproach to market reform initiatives but was largely ignored, then over time sovereignty has simply been redefined.[109]

What should be stressed is that the governance opinion, and the expansion into new policy, the regulatory and institutional terrain that it purported to

[106] World Bank and the IMF, *Poverty Reduction Strategy Papers – Progress in Implementation*, September, 2004, available at: http://siteresources.worldbank.org/INTPRS1/Resources/prsp_progress_2004.pdf.

[107] Shihata, *supra* note 42, at 219.

[108] *Id.* at 245.

[109] To the extent that it resembles the process identified by Antony Anghie in the mandates in the interwar period, it suggests that the international institutions are continuing a remarkably long and well-established practice of intervention into sovereignty. See Anghie, *supra* note 17.

explain and authorize, is not only a significant marker in the recalibration of sovereignty. It is also critical to the socialization of the development project in two ways. First, it provided the conduit for the incorporation of such issues into the development and market reform agenda by establishing the principle that however otherwise political, such activities did not fall outside the institutional mandate laid out in the Articles of Agreement as long as they could be plausibly linked to economic development.[110] By determining the parameters in which the formerly excluded social and distributive issues could now be legitimately considered, however, it also helped determine the *place* of such concerns within the agenda and the language or frame in which they would materialize. Arguments for greater attention to social issues would be articulated in terms of their contribution to growth and they would be measured in terms of their impact upon economic growth, failing or succeeding along that metric.

Thus, if one of the criticisms of the Washington Consensus was that it invaded the sovereign domain of States and constrained the exercise of democratic choices, the paradox of second generation reforms is that in responding to the social deficit of the first, the development institutions seem to have increased their reach. Second generation reforms proceed in the name of democratizing the development process and returning it to its subjects. With the acknowledgement of the social dimension of development and the effort to elaborate what it does and does not involve, however, the IFIs have expanded the territory in which they operate and generated governance norms that are arguably even more disciplinary than their predecessors. This effectively places a still greater range of issues and decisions beyond politics, producing a qualified and reduced form of sovereignty.

Toward the enabling state

A key element of the current reform agenda is the effort to establish the appropriate role of the state in market societies. This too has implications for the way that social concerns are furthered in second generation reforms.

Good governance, legal reform, and rule of law projects might be understood as an effort to establish, in comprehensive ways, the institutional parameters of normal markets and normal market societies. What makes this a complex exercise, however, is that it is not simply a question of diffusing market norms to states that have failed to sufficiently assimilate them. Rather, what is "normal" *within* market states is also under active reconstruction, with settled elements of the established normal under assault. In other words, projects of diffusion and transformation are simultaneously underway.

[110] *Id.*

Second generation reforms consolidate a central element of the governance agenda, which is a fundamental reconfiguration of the place of the State in society and a new division of labor among the State, the market, the individual, and civil society in social life. It is difficult to overstate the paradigm shift in relation to the State that underpins the agenda as a whole. Arguably its most fundamental element, the linchpin of the exercise, is the shift from the "protective" and "regulatory" state to what might be described as the "enabling" state. With the shift to the enabling state, the role of the State is to protect a limited set of private rights and to create the framework conditions for the flourishing of markets. It is against this metric, rather than simply the respect for the rule of law or the capacity to implement democratic preferences, that the "goodness" of governance and the competence of the State are now measured.

With second generation reforms, the events and outcomes that the State is expected to enable has expanded; rather than merely facilitate economic transactions, now it must promote goals such as gender equality and greater social inclusion too. As described previously, however, market participation is itself now a primary vehicle for these ends: despite the inclusion of the social and the commitment to expanded citizen participation in the development process, the conception of the State's role has not fundamentally shifted.

The idea of the enabling state has clear implications for the democratic and participatory objectives. Part of what is at stake in the shift from "government" to "governance" is a challenge to the singular authority of the State in the generation of norms; now other actors are clearly involved in the process too. But the enabling State also already embodies objectives, objectives that may limit the zone and scope of democratic action, particularly in respect of social issues. Because the enabling State confines or rules out many traditional Keynesian or New Deal approaches to ensuring economic security and furthering objectives such as social justice and cohesion, intensified market participation becomes a much more attractive, perhaps necessary, strategy for addressing a wide range of social ills. Thus, it is not surprising that the main plank of the social agenda, whether it concerns gender equality, improving the position of workers in the global economy, or even the general problem of poverty alleviation, is the market.

SECOND GENERATION REFORMS: TRANSFORMATIVE POSSIBILITIES?

From a legal standpoint, the second generation reform agenda does not look particularly new; indeed, the legal and institutional framework of the ideal market economy seems remarkably unaltered by the inclusion of the social, structural, and human. Nor is it substantially altered by the injunction that development should be democratized and rendered more participatory; however these ideals are imagined, there is little evidence that they have penetrated to the level of institutional design. Even the discourse around core legal reforms is largely unchanged, notwithstanding the new objectives that development now encompasses.

There are new references to human rights, freedom of expression, and associational rights in particular. There is also enhanced emphasis on entitlements that secure or improve access to the market: while in first generation reforms, such concerns revolved around investors, now they extend to workers and women as well. Beyond this, however, few new legal entitlements appear to be envisioned for those left behind in first generation reforms.

The legal and institutional agenda is also not obviously responsive to the push to make market reform and development more democratic and participatory. Instead of the product of political conflict and democratic choice, in second generation reforms as in first, the legal and institutional frame of economic development stands largely outside the democratic process, setting the parameters in which other decisions are made. So even as the incorporation of social concerns seems to represent progress or improvement on one level, the range of options through which to address them is being constrained on another.

From another vantage point, however, the relative stasis and continuity in respect of legal entitlements and institutional forms and the change that is visible elsewhere in second generation reforms is completely explicable. The IFIs may well be committed to human rights and some version of social development; the argument is not that they do not "really mean it." It is important, however, to understand that the protection of investor interests and the commitment to efficient legal rules and institutions remains a major part, perhaps *the* major part, of their strategy to advance greater social well being and social justice. This is because of the longstanding argument advanced by the IFIs that the only real form of poverty alleviation lies in growth. While in many quarters, better social outcomes are fundamentally a distributive problem, for the IFIs they remain largely dependent upon drawing new participants into the market and generating greater aggregate wealth.

But the interest in market incentives and alternative modes of regulation and norm generation, through which to further social goals, seems deeply connected to their views about the proper role of the State. Similarly, their resistance to traditional, State-centered modes of pursuing social justice seems inseparable from their abiding belief that they cannot help but interfere with economic growth. However, the paradox of reforms, second generation as well as first, is that, even though the erosion of social entitlements is one of the most enduring effects of the globalization associated with first generation reforms,[111] arguments against legal intervention for protective, and

[111] Guy Standing, *Globalization: Eight Crises of Social Protection*, Global Tensions: Challenges and Opportunities in the World Economy 111–133 (Lourdes Beneria and Savitri Bisnath, eds., 2004).

redistributive purposes appear to cut most sharply against classic social objectives. While the pathologies of the State are invoked to discredit many standard, existing institutional methods of promoting greater equality and solidarity, the State remains entirely alive, indeed central, to promoting investor interests.

Three additional observations may be germane to the discussion. First, it is worth noting that there are two projects simultaneously in play: one is the generation of economic growth at the local and national levels; the other is building the architecture of the global economy. While the IFIs work tirelessly to suggest that these two projects are necessarily congruent, if not joined at the hip, in a globally integrated economy, it seems clear that they may diverge in normative or institutional terms at least occasionally.

Policy is theoretically formulated in light of the demands of growth in particular countries. However, the boiler-plate nature of reforms has long been noted: over and over again, states have been advised to implement the same, or remarkably similar, sets of policy and institutional reforms. This feature has not disappeared in second generation reforms, despite the official end of the "one size fits all" approach. States can still expect to hear as much as they ever did about the importance of strengthening property rights and the dangers of regulating too much. Similarly, the importance of liberalizing trade and investment and the gains to be realized from privatization, all of which were key parts of the first-generation agenda, remain not simply in place, but axiomatic even though they have sometimes been associated with severe social dislocations.

In all of this, the concerns of developed countries or their industries and investors, such as securing their investments, increased market access or access to State-held assets, may also be important reform objectives, even though this tends to be submerged in the official narrative about poverty alleviation and the other benefits that will accrue to the citizens and consumers of the States that implement reforms. Notwithstanding the efforts to link best practices in law to greater economic growth, the institutional preoccupations of the IFIs, as well as their resistance to alternative paths and proposals, may be better explained by their commitment to the second project, global economic integration along the preferred institutional parameters, than by their failure to apprehend the costs and limits of conventional reforms in particular contexts and locales. For example, arguably the most outstanding examples of both economic growth and, on some measures, social progress can be found in the newly industrializing countries of East Asia, many of whom followed policies such as the rationing and selective allocation of credit, infant-industry protection, and subsidies to particular sectors and industries. These policies have become either costly or simply unavailable to developing states in the post-Uruguay round trade regime. However, this is *not* because they were ineffective at generating economic growth or have become less so in the intervening time. Rather, developing countries were compelled to give these up or open themselves to countervailing action as the quid pro quo for participation in the global trade regime.[112]

Second, ascribing independent importance to law opens up the reform project to new objectives. This could clearly lead either to an expanded list of legal entitlements and/or a reassessment of conventional wisdom about the goals and functions of legal rules and institutions associated with development. This is a live possibility, especially in a context of heightened attention to democratic participation and greater emphasis on social concerns. As described as follows, it is now possible to find references to new legal rules in conjunction with social goals such as gender equality. However, no reassessment of conventional regulatory wisdom has happened, suggesting that it is also possible that the emphasis on law for itself could serve a conservative function, entrenching rather than destabilizing or subverting the institutional project associated with first generation reforms. This is a judgment, rather than an argument that such a result is in any way entailed by invocations of the importance of the rule of law. But given that considerable substantive content had already been embedded in the legal reform project, one possibility is that elevating law's place in development agenda may simultaneously strengthen the current direction of institutional reform.

Third, one of the results of the different iterations of the law and development movement is that there is now an archive of arguments about the relationship between law and economic growth and an array of competing and conflicting justifications for legal reforms, all of which carry some resonance at the discursive level.[113] Because they are used in both predictable and arbitrary ways, it is difficult to do more than suggest the directions such arguments might take. For example, as a consequence of the conclusion that governance activities can encompass anything that reasonably bears on prospects for economic growth, the IFIs now have a series of enabling arguments for focusing attention on issues of social and distributive justice. It is important, however, to recall that they retain two basic limiting arguments from an earlier era. The first is that such issues may be political; as such, they may fall outside the realm of factors that the IFIs are authorized to consider in their lending decisions.[114] Second, the IFIs maintain that they have no independent, free-floating mandate to act as human rights enforcers; they are strictly limited in their decisions to considerations that demonstrably further economic development. As a result, they are only able to advance objectives such as human

[112] Helleiner, *supra* note 29.

[113] Even in first generation reforms, there was a range of competing explanations and justifications for reforms. Rittich, *supra* note 9, chapter 2.

[114] International Bank for Reconstruction and Development, Feb. 16, 1989, Articles of Agreement, art. 10, sec. 4, available at http://web.worldbank.org/WBSITE/EXTERNAL/EXTABOUTUS/O,,,contentMDK:20049557~menuPK:6300601~pagePK:34542~piPK:36600~theSitePK:29708,00.html; see also Shihata, *supra* note 42, at 219–244.

rights or gender equality to the extent that they *also* contribute to economic growth. These two arguments structure the engagement with human rights, distributive concerns, and other social justice claims. On the one hand, the IFIs may invoke constitutional restrictions on interference in political affairs to preclude responses to social, egalitarian, or distributive concerns, however desirable such responses might otherwise be. But on the other hand, they may also argue that their mandate to further economic development requires reconsideration of standard regulatory and policy approaches to social questions.[115] It is this that accounts for the fact that issues conceived elsewhere as matters of human, women's, or workers' rights are either missing from second generation reforms altogether or have become the subject of soft nonregulatory initiatives rather than entitlements backed by the State.

Second generation reforms appear to create common ground among market reformers and their critics, as calls for the rule of law and human rights all sound in the register of greater social justice. Clear conceptual and normative differences around the social agenda are visible, however. As they are absorbed into the development agenda, a range of social objectives are being disaggregated and fragmented, reinterpreted and reorganized, repositioned both in relation to each other and to economic objectives, or simply rejected, usually on the basis that they are inappropriate in market-centered societies.

There are also clear conflicts at the level of strategy. The conclusion we are invited to draw by the IFIs is that the achievement of social objectives requires no necessary legal and institutional reforms apart from those that are necessary for market societies to thrive in general; the corollary is that the governance and legal frame also has no adverse impact upon the possibilities of achieving social objectives either. Here is an important fault line. The protection of private rights and a correlative disenchantment with the regulatory, protective, and redistributive state remain foundational to the governance agenda.

The incorporation of the social, however, immediately raises the following concern. Regulations that alter the structure of private rights and resource reallocations through the taxation and transfer mechanisms of the welfare state have been the primary institutional means for furthering social, egalitarian, and distributive goals in nonkinship based societies. What happens to such goals when these mechanisms are removed? Is what remains really enough to ensure their realization?

One possibility, the one that is implicit in second generation reforms, is that to the extent that changes are required in the realm of governance, the answer lies in nonregulatory, noninstitutional solutions. Constituencies

[115] The rationale for engagement in these questions is an extension of the logic set out in the general approach to governance. See I. Shihata, "Issues of "Governance" in Borrowing Members – The Extent of their Relevance Under the Bank's Articles of Agreement" *supra* note 43, at 245.

explicitly committed to social justice and progressive social change are also increasingly interested in alternative, non-, or postregulatory modes of norm generation. The result is an important contemporary debate over soft law and its capacity to substitute for hard law and to effect social change. Soft law initiatives may be preferred for a variety of reasons other than simply an aversion to state-based regulation. For example, the impossibility of reaching consensus on regulatory reform may push parties to explore alternatives. Similarly, the diversity of preexisting rules and institutions may make regulatory harmonization or convergence unlikely or simply unavailable. Or the solutions to problems may be so varied and context sensitive that the most that would be desired are either process norms and entitlements or general agreement about the direction of reforms.[116] Incentives and voluntary standards may be more effective in some contexts than sanctions alone. Both goals and methods for reaching them may be unstable; for this reason, some explicitly endorse rolling-rule regimes as the preferred mode of regulation in the contemporary context.[117] In short, the diversity of preexisting regulatory regimes, the complexity of issues and the variability of adequate responses may militate in favor of a range of approaches to regulation and norm generation rather than reliance upon traditional top-down modes of regulation by the State. This suggests that there is no reason to assume that progress on the social front will occur only in reliance upon the traditional regulatory instruments and practices of the State. Institutions continue to matter, however, especially for distributive purposes.

Soft law

One of the central questions is the interaction between the institutional structures that form the core of the legal reform agenda and the soft strategies that seem to be a favored method to further social goals. Soft law strategies may well be a strategy for transformative change in a progressive direction. There is no particular reason, however, to assume that they will have this effect, or that they will be the most effective means of achieving such goals, especially in the face of competing norms and incentives. Soft norms and processes,

[116] The exemplary case is the use of the "open method of coordination" in the European Union. For a basic introduction, see David M. Trubek and James S. Mosher, *New Governance, Employment Policy and the European Social Model*, in Governing Work and Welfare in a New Economy: European and American Experiments (Jonathan Zeitlin and David Trubek eds., 2003). See also Building Social Europe through the Open Method of Co-ordination (Caroline de la Porte and Philippe Pochet eds., 2002). For an analysis of these trends in the context of labor regulation in the European Union, see Diamond Ashiagbor, *"Flexibility" and "Adaptability" in the EU Employment Strategy*, in Legal Regulation of the Employment Relation (Hugh Collins et al. eds., 2000).

[117] For a review of this literature, see William H. Simon, *Solving Problems v. Claiming Rights: The Pragmatist Challenge of Legal Liberalism*, 46 Wm. & Mary L. Rev. 127 (2004).

especially those that are designed to address distributive questions in the market, operate within and against a set of background rules and institutions in any event. Thus, any evaluation of their prospects would need to take account of the effects of the broader regulatory context.

To query the power of soft norms is not to fetishize formal legal rules. The idea that legal rules operate in the mechanical and functionalist manner imagined in much development discourse is surely a fantasy; it remains equally mistaken when it comes from those on the left who are concerned about the alleged defects of the current order and hope to remedy those defects with other formal rules. There are myriad reasons, from the presence of competing social and legal norms and the vagaries of adjudication to the distribution of assets on the ground, that formal legal norms will produce varied rather than predictable outcomes. Reformers should be alert to the way in which formal and informal norms work in tandem, whether the object of regulation is economic or social.

But these observations also suggest why investing all of one's hopes in soft law may be chimerical too. What matters for present purposes is that, as a consequence of the larger legal reforms that are now afoot, that background context may itself be shifting in ways that are significant to the success, failure or simply the impact of soft approaches. It seems particularly significant to pay attention to these possibilities where hard and soft strategies are deployed at the same time in respect of the same field or issue, or where hard rights are available to advance the interests of one of the parties involved in a dispute, while the other relies on soft norms to further its case. For example, environmental disputes may engage conflicts between capital holders with new means to challenge environmental protections through investment protections on the one hand and consumers or citizens invoking human rights on the other.[118] Disputes in the workplace or struggles over global labor standards may involve employers who both recognize core labor rights but also enjoy deregulated labor markets that leave workers with diminished power, little social protection, and no alternatives to work except on whatever terms are offered.[119] Efforts to address health crises may, amongst other scenarios, pit pharmaceutical companies newly enriched by the extension of the terms of their patent protection against either individuals in need of the protected, and therefore more expensive, drugs or states attempting to either respond to health crises or provide basic health services to their populaces.[120]

[118] See, e.g., Mexico v. Metalclad Corp., [2001] B.C.S.C. 1529 (2001).

[119] ILO, *Report of the Director General: Decent Work*, 87th session (1999), available at www.ilo.org/public/english/standards/relm/ilc/ilc87/rep-i.htm.

[120] For an effort to address this problem, see WTO, *Draft Ministerial Declaration on the TRIPS Agreement and Public Health* (Nov. 12, 2001) available at http://www.wto.org/english/tratop_e/trips_e/mindecdraft_w312_e.htm.

Both previous and current experiments with decentralized and alternative modes of norm generation point to the importance of the background institutions in any event. Collective bargaining might be taken as a paradigmatic historic example. Negotiations between workers and employers have often required institutional structures of a distinctly hard character; in their absence, employers are inclined to rely upon their default entitlements under property and contract law to unilaterally impose the terms and conditions of employment. In the most important current laboratory of new governance in the social realm, the Open Method of Coordination (OMC) in Europe, soft norm generation takes place against a backdrop of norms and practices that are well-elaborated and well-entrenched in national institutions. The OMC is not intended to displace these institutionally entrenched entitlements, but rather to chart a path for their evolution in the future. It is possible that the soft processes of the OMC may work to erode rather than strengthen social norms in some states; indeed, the IMF suggests that the mechanisms of benchmarking and peer pressure to promote competitiveness and job creation may foster the "deregulatory" structural reforms that, in its view, are needed.[121] However, the prospect that the overall outcome will be socially progressive rather than regressive seems greater precisely because the idea is not simply to dismantle these institutional underpinnings and because employment security also remains an objective. But whether, and to what extent, this turns out to be true seems inseparable from the larger institutional context in which the OMC operates, as well as the character of any "hard" reforms to which the OMC itself leads.

As these examples suggest, soft and hard norms are likely to intersect in a variety of ways. Indeed, ideas of good governance, best practices, and optimal legal reforms may be directly implicated in the relative positions of the parties in conflict. For this reason, it may be quixotic to seek solutions that bracket the regime building now underway; rather, simultaneous attention to the larger governance frame seems crucial to assessing the prospects of any soft initiatives.

Human rights

A related question is the extent to which it is safe to vest hopes for transformative change in human rights and other public law norms. Whatever the hopes of reformers, the recognition of human rights has not paved the way toward a smooth incorporation of social issues into the larger economic project; nor has it bridged the distance between the IFIs and their critics and

[121] IMF, *World Economic Outlook: Advancing Structural Reforms* (Washington, D.C.: IMF, 2004), Chapter III, "Fostering Structural Reforms in Industrial Countries," 129, available at http://www.imf.org/external/pubs/ft/weo/2004/01/pdf/chapter3.pdf.

interlocutors, including those in other international institutions, on how to accommodate social and distributive issues within the architecture of the new economy. Rather, the debate has merely shifted to two issues: which human rights should be recognized and what it means to incorporate them into the development agenda.

Here, human rights have not proved to be the trump their proponents often hope for. If human rights have become a powerful, popular counterdiscourse to globalization and to the policies and activities of the international financial and economic organizations in particular,[122] then the counterreformation is already well underway. Not only have the IFIs resisted the pressure to adopt a rights-based approach to development. They also have a series of arguments about the "right to trade"[123] and have elevated transactional freedom, property rights, and the entitlement to participate in markets to the level of basic human rights.[124] This suggests that in second generation reforms, human rights are better understood not as the answer to the social deficit but as the terrain of struggle.

Part of the reason is that normative agreement on the value of human rights does not foreclose disagreement on other levels, such as the content or definition of the right in question or the various means by which it might be furthered or secured. Nor does it foreclose the emergence of hierarchies among rights, such as the distinction between "basic" or "core" rights and other human rights, or provide a means to adjudicate among competing rights claims. The Bank's policy research report on gender equality demonstrates why it is necessary to follow the complex institutional navigations that take place around human rights and social justice claims; it also indicates where the protection of rights may stop and equality objectives shade into the zone of policy, and where soft norms and nonlegal solutions may be substituted for entitlements and regulatory change.[125] In the view of the Bank, gender equality is itself a human right and does require respect for certain rights; in some contexts, this may require changes to legal rules. But while rules on family law, violence against women, property rights, and even political participation are identified as essential to gender equality, labor market rules and institutions as well as social protection schemes are not.[126] In the view of the Bank, rather than "rights" that are intrinsic to the protection of gender

122 For a discussion of the uses of human rights in the resistance to globalization, see MARGARET E. KECK AND KATHRYN SIKKINK, ACTIVISTS BEYOND BORDERS: ADVOCACY NETWORKS IN INTERNATIONAL POLITICS (1998).

123 See Ernst-Ulrich Petersmann, *Time for a United Nations "Global Compact" for Integrating Human Rights into the Law of Worldwide Organizations: Lessons from European Integration*, 132 Eur. J. INT'L L. 621 (2002).

124 Sen, *supra* note 11.

125 This section is drawn from a larger work in progress, Kerry Rittich, Engendering Development: A New International Paradigm for Gender Justice?

126 World Bank, *supra* note 12.

equality, they constitute "policy." Here, as elsewhere, the distinction between institutions and policy is crucial: institutions are defined as rules, enforcement mechanisms, and organizations, in short, hard regulatory mechanisms; policies, by contrast, are merely goals and desired outcomes rather than entitlements.[127] Policies must be congruent with the overall institutional scheme for good economic governance. In the course of generating good governance norms, however, the IFIs have already staked out a position on why many labor market rules are counterproductive and why, to the extent that a safety net is necessary, targeted programs are to be preferred over the provision of universal entitlements. This remains the case even in the face of powerful arguments that the reconstruction, rather than the elimination, of rules and institutions governing labor markets and the extension, rather than the reduction, of various forms of social protection and social insurance might be critical to gender equality – and to the resolution of demographic and labor market crises as well – in a market-centered world.[128]

It is not necessary to adjudicate these claims to observe that in this analysis, the norms and institutions that have been classically advanced by human rights and gender equality activists and scholars to enhance women's economic equality become separated from the right to gender equality itself. As this illustrates, it is entirely possible to endorse human rights and objectives such as gender equality in general terms, yet redefine their content and foreclose many of the routes by which they can be realized. This, in turn, displaces many of the conflicts and struggles that are entailed to the level of institutional design. It also suggests, on the one hand, the limits of a transformative legal strategy whose primary focus is human rights, and on the other, the significance of the larger regulatory environment.

CONCLUSION

It is clear that the criticisms that marked the first phase of neoliberal policy-based lending and market reform have been absorbed by their authors and reflected in a revamped conception of development. But the IFIs have also served notice that they hold a different view, if not of the value of the social, structural, and human side, then of what these dimensions of development entail in conceptual and practical terms.

The enduring significance of second generation reforms may lie in the fact that a wide range of social concerns are not merely being incorporated and assimilated into market reform and governance projects, they are being transformed at the same time. While the IFIs have conceded a place for social matters within the development agenda, they have also become their arbiters

[127] World Bank, *supra* note 55, at 6.
[128] See G. Esping-Anderson, Social Foundations of Post-industrial Economies (1999).

at the same time. They are now deeply engaged in identifying the social, distributive, and egalitarian objectives that count, or count most, in the current economic context. In the process, they are altering in both subtle and far-reaching ways the manner in which social objectives are framed and conceptualized, and they are contesting and prescribing the manner in which they should and should not be advanced. The end result is to not merely incorporate social concerns into the world of development. Rather, by articulating their relationship to economic growth and managing the processes by which they are incorporated, the IFIs are effectively ranking and ordering the importance of different social objectives and alternatively legitimizing and delegitimizing the means and strategies by which they can be pursued.

So far, their efforts to promote market-centered modes of social inclusion and equality are speculative at best and suspect at worst. Because the social and economic agendas are now on the table together, the debates that will now ensue between the IFIs and those that have other ideas about social justice will almost certainly revolve around such questions as the relationship between equity and efficiency. These questions are not simply a matter of having the right values; nor can they be determined at the abstract or general level. The content of the social – now certain to be a critical point of contention – and the possibility of overlap or conflict between economic and social, and cultural or political objectives can only be evaluated in more specific ways. To put it another way, the fate of the social can only be analyzed through a nuanced and detailed examination of the norms, rules, and institutions that structure the interactions of groups and individuals in particular contexts.

So far, the IFIs largely "own" the discussion on law and development: they have established an authoritative discourse on law for development and they have both formidable resources and effective mechanisms for disseminating their research findings and policy conclusions. So far social justice activists, whether skeptical or enthusiastic about these new developments, have not seriously disturbed these efforts; many have not even seriously engaged with them. However, if the larger governance and institutional agenda *is* implicated in the fate of the social, then engagement with this agenda is indispensable. In centering law in second generation reforms, the IFIs have already invited this engagement. Paradoxically, this involves taking law even more seriously and exploring more fully the effects that have occurred thus far. This in turn requires greatly pluralizing the forms of analysis and scholarship in the field and recuperating the many functions other than the correction of market failures that legal regulation necessarily serves.

What might this mean or involve? Different contexts will present different points of entry and require different modes of analysis. However, the following observations may provide some guidance about how and where to begin.

This discussion has indicated how the post-Washington consensus is already being defined, not simply as a matter of balancing the two sides of the development agenda, but as a matter of understanding the newly incorporated social aims and values in terms of their contribution to or coexistence with growth-enhancing strategies, while economic growth is itself represented as a principal mechanism for realizing social goals. At the same time, the institutional framework in which economic growth is generated has itself been largely consolidated, often in the language of "good governance" or in the name of values such as the rule of law. As the path of second generation reforms suggests so far, social objectives and values may be both endorsed and transformed or substantially redefined in the encounter with this larger governance agenda.

The disenchantment with "regulatory," protective, and redistributive states and the move to the enabling state are clearly bedrock commitments of the IFIs and they remain the foundation of their good governance agenda, the "social, structural, and human" notwithstanding. With respect to economic activity, the IFIs remains as securely fixed in their policy prescriptions on the goal of efficiency enhancement in the second generation as they were in the first. Their reform prescriptions often appear in "end-of-history" or "no alternative" narratives. But even where the language is more temperate and the claims nuanced rather than categorical, the average reader is likely to come to the conclusion that there is no serious debate about the appropriateness of these reforms at either the empirical or the normative level. This is particularly true to the extent that theses prescriptions are presented in technocratic legal terms. Thus, it is not surprising that even institutions and advocates devoted to promoting the social dimension of development increasingly choose to push for amplification of the reform agenda or adjustments at the margins rather than serious analysis of the overall direction and implications of legal and institutional change.[129]

This is unlikely to be enough. The broad task for social justice activists at the present moment is to engage the powerful social vision that is emerging in the norms and processes of legal and economic transformation and to query, and counter if necessary, the specific claims that are now being made about how it works and what is to be expected of it. This involves, among other things: bringing to the surface the specific social visions that are either driving the reform efforts or reflected in them so that they may be clearly debated, endorsed, altered, or rejected; recuperating for further consideration some of those that have been discarded or summarily discredited; scrutinizing, rather than merely accepting, the claims that social objectives are unwise or no longer available; altering them in light of new circumstances; or simply formulating new social and political visions altogether.

Much of this is a political task. However, it is doubtful if it can be successfully conducted without much more attention to the institutional underpinnings

[129] See for example, ILO, *A Fair Globalization: Creating Opportunities for All*, *supra*, note 38.

of different social objectives, the potential conflict and congruence between social and economic goals, and the synergies and ruptures between social goals themselves; all of these need more emphasis, more elucidation, and more airtime in public debate.

With second generation reforms, development is no longer supposed to be about growth alone; efficiency enhancement should therefore no longer automatically trump other regulatory objectives. If progress on social measures is now supposed to assist economic growth in any event, conventional regulatory assumptions may also be internally unsound to the extent that they fail to take in distributive and other considerations. Even imagining that the two sides of the agenda can be fundamentally separated may be illusory. In any event, determining the extent to which the links between the economic and the social objectives are real, imagined, solid, speculative, or simply contingent and assessing whether they are positive or negative from different perspectives requires a closer lens.

The ways in which myriad social and economic norms, rules, and institutions may affect the realization of different social objectives are likely to be ignored or vastly underestimated by those, including economists, who are focused on their efficiency-enhancing properties. Or the complex and cross-cutting effects of legal rules and other norms may simply be invisible to those who are unable to adequately assess the variety of outcomes that legal rules can generate in different social and institutional contexts, their interaction with other normative orders, and the conflicting ways that they can be interpreted and adjudicated over time.

In addition, the ideological or discursive frame in which the demands of "globalization" and the new economy are presented is profoundly important to the current direction of change, as well as to the horizon of possibilities for contesting such change. The simultaneous juridification and technocratization of debates around development and market reform means that understanding the varying arguments that are advanced in the name of legal values and concepts – the assumptions on which they rest, the range of options available within them, and the connection between these assumptions and options and larger social and economic debates – are crucial to understanding the terrain of political possibilities.

Disciplinary orientation is part of the story here. Legal scholars could both help fill in the missing links between social concerns and the regulatory agenda in a variety of ways, as part of the "comparative advantage" of legal scholars in governance and institutional reform debates lies in their capacity to demonstrate these varying possibilities by better explicating the operation of the institutions that can mediate between social norms and social outcomes "on the ground." Legal scholars are thus well positioned to illuminate some of the challenges to the realization of social objectives that may remain hidden amidst endorsements of the "social, structural, and human" at the abstract level but which become clear by focusing not only on efficiency, but on the full range of things rules and institutions actually do.

An important part of the task is simply to illustrate the point made at the outset, which is that legal norms and institutions operate in multiple modes: normative, distributive, constitutive, and disciplinary. Another is to observe that the rules that govern economic transactions in industrialized states have always served multiple functions – the enhancement of efficiency is but one. To reduce the focus of the reform of legal rules and institutions to concerns about efficiency and market failures, even assuming that the calculus that underpins these efforts is adequate,[130] is to miss many of their other properties and effects and to radically reduce in scope the aspirations driving legal regulation.

Using historical or genealogical, doctrinal, sociolegal, and other analyses, legal scholars can assist in demonstrating how and why the associations between some institutions and both economic growth and social justice may be unsafe, only loosely connected, largely contingent or alternatively more plausible and robust in any particular context. But above all, such analyses can disclose how they are variable and contested. This, in turn, might provoke a reconsideration of the status both of the rules and institutions that are in vogue and those that are currently discredited. In addition, a historical perspective of any substantial duration is likely to trouble the static image of law that often prevails in development debates, illustrates the dynamic, unstable, and transitory nature of legal forms, and suggests the reasons that legal rules and institutions might be viewed as a contingent settlement of interests, values, and concerns. However, legal scholars are also in a position to point out possible synergies between the two sides of the agenda that may exist via different institutional reforms. They may also observe internal conflicts in the commitment to economic agenda itself that remain invisible because of the ideological commitment to the current reform agenda. It is very unclear, for example, that better aggregate economic effects are necessarily generated by the "deregulated" labor markets the IFIs now favor; it is almost certainly true that categorical claims about their effects cannot be maintained across the board. But the argument also cuts in the other direction: such analyses might also remind those wedded to social justice through human rights or equality claims that social agendas can be furthered in a variety of ways, and that rights, even if institutionalized in particular ways, are no guarantee of progressive outcomes, particularly in the widely varying contexts in which they are now expected to operate.

[130] There are powerful analyses that suggest how and why both the standard modes of assessing efficiency within the IFIs and the association of efficiency enhancement with particular institutional forms and practices might be inadequate. See, for example, Deakin and Wikinson, *supra* note 54; Elson, *supra* note 52.

As described earlier, rules and institutions may be designed to provide basic levels of security or protection to particular classes or to society in general; labor and employment standards, such as minimum wage laws or health and safety standards are an example of the first, while consumer protection laws stand as an example of the second. Or, like collective bargaining laws, their explicit purpose may be to redress the balance of power among the contracting parties that would obtain in their absence and to alter the sources of rule-making authority in the context of work and production. Like environmental and consumer protection laws, they may be designed to shift the allocation of risk and/or compel parties to internalize costs that they could otherwise impose on others. Like zoning laws, by allocating different activities to different places, they may literally help constitute the urban geography of societies, chart the direction of future growth and simultaneously influence the fortunes of different groups.[131] While all of these rules and institutions may be efficient as well, efficiency is not necessarily their primary function or effect. Rather, they may be designed to redistribute power and authority.

Conversely, even rules that *are* designed to further efficiency typically generate myriad distributional consequences, consequences that may be both unexpected and far reaching. As these possibilities are often underestimated, one task is to relentlessly document, in both general and more specific ways, the distributive stakes of governance and legal reform projects advanced by the IFIs, whether first or second generation or both and whether advanced in the name of the rule of law, efficiency, equality, human rights, labor market justice, or any other value or end.[132] There is clearly similar work to be done on the legal reform agendas promoted by social justice constituencies too.[133] This form of analysis helps shift the focus from the projected, overall consequences of reforms in the long term to their more proximate effects on different sectors and populations. (Who or what constitutes the object of concern is a political question in and of themselves, the answer to which will vary from context to context.) It may also help explain why even the expected aggregate effects often fail to materialize. At minimum, this should help provoke reflection on the fact that tradeoffs among different objectives and different fates for different groups may be just as likely as seamlessly coterminous progress on both the macroeconomic and social fronts. By highlighting, rather than suppressing, the fact that *winners and losers are to be expected*, such analysis should also provoke debate over whether their

[131] Gerald E. Frug, City-Making: Building Communities Without Building Walls (2001).

[132] For one effort to engage in this type of analysis with respect to first generation reforms, see Rittich, *supra* note 9.

[133] For an exemplary analysis of the ways that strategies to promote gender equality might work at cross purposes with the interests of other marginalized or disadvantaged groups, see the discussion by Janet Halley in Brenda Cossman, Dan Danielsen, Janet Halley and Tracy Higgins, *Gender, Sexuality, and Power: Is Feminist Theory Enough?*, 12 Colum. J. Gender & L. 601 (2004).

emergence represents progress or its opposite, consideration of the standpoint from which this should be evaluated, as well as debate over whether, and how much, the losers should be compensated.

We should have no illusions that there is a magic solution; to reiterate, this is a political issue. A revival of antiformalist legal analysis is part of the task, but so is a much more far-reaching analysis of the instrumental logic that also prevails. However, it seems an error to presume that the reform logic will fall apart under the weight of its limits or inconsistencies. Yet, while not sufficient on its own, it seems hard to imagine that it is not part of the project. At minimum, the exercise can provide policymakers with alternative analyses of the context and the alternatives, and aid social justice activists in their efforts to unsettle the soft consensus that has consolidated around the idea that the standard approach to reform is both normal, clearly "right" and in any event, unchallengeable.

In short, legal scholars have a distinct analytic role to play. This is simply to refuse any automatic collapse of the social into the economic project, and to identify in concrete ways how specific elements of the governance project play out in practice and might work at cross-purposes with "social, structural, and human" ends, however defined. From this standpoint, it is clear that while growth might aid social justice, it does not inevitably do so. What the nature of social progress might be, how and where specific reforms designed to promote growth might either aid or undercut particular social objectives, whether their contribution to economic growth is an adequate lens from which to view social policies, and how social objectives themselves might conflict with each other are the future of the debate.

7 THE WORLD BANK'S USES OF THE "RULE OF LAW" PROMISE IN ECONOMIC DEVELOPMENT

*Alvaro Santos**

INTRODUCTION

Law is at the center of development discourse and practice today. The idea that the legal system is crucial for economic growth now forms part of the conventional wisdom in development theory. This idea's most common expression is the "rule of law" (ROL): a legal order consisting of predictable, enforceable and efficient rules required for a market economy to flourish. Enthusiasm for law reform as a development strategy boomed during the 1990s and resources for reforming legal systems soared everywhere.[1]

* Emerging Scholars Program Assistant Professor, University of Texas at Austin School of Law, and S.J.D. Candidate, Harvard Law School. I am particularly grateful to Dave Trubek, Duncan Kennedy, David Kennedy and Linn Hammergren for their sustained intellectual engagement and invaluable support. I want to thank Bill Alford, Helena Alviar, Ruth Buchanan, Dan Danielsen, Karen Engle, Jorge Esquirol, Jane Fair Bestor, Bryant Garth, Prabha Kotiswaran, Alejandro Lorite, Fernanda Nicola, Joel Ngugi, Moria Paz, Nathan Reilly, Annelise Riles, Kerry Rittich, Hani Sayed, Talha Syed, Chantal Thomas, and Raef Zreik for their helpful criticisms and suggestions. My deepest thanks to Philomila Tsoukala for making this project all the more intellectually exciting and enjoyable. This chapter benefited greatly from questions and comments by participants in conferences at Harvard, Wisconsin, Northeastern, Cornell, Toronto and Osgoode Hall Law School, the CPOGG-Summit at Tecnológico de Monterrey (ITESM), and from my presentation at the University of Texas at Austin School of Law. The summer internship at the World Bank was made possible by the generous support of the David Rockefeller Center for Latin American Studies at Harvard University and the Harvard Law School's Office of Public Interest Advising. The views presented in this chapter are my sole responsibility.

1 The World Bank estimates to have supported 330 "rule of law" projects dealing with legal and judicial reform in over 100 countries. *Legal and Judicial Reform Observations, Experiences, and Approach of the Legal Vice Presidency*, Legal Vice Presidency, The World Bank, p. 14, (2002) http://www4.worldbank.org/legal/publications/ljrobservations-final.pdf [hereinafter Observations, Experiences and Approach]. It has spent about $3.8 billion since 1993 (World Bank Annual Reports 2003 and 2004, p. 30 and 35, respectively). See Thomas Carothers, The rule of law revival, 77 *Foreign Affairs* 95–107 (1998) (noting the expansion of legal reform programs); Yves Dezalay and Bryant G. Garth (Eds.), Global Prescriptions: The Production, Exportation, and Importation Of A New Legal Orthodoxy (2002) (analyzing how international

After more than a decade of reforms of the legal systems, and particularly of the judiciaries of developing countries around the world we are in a position to analyze the theoretical premises of the programs and the strategies of implementation. By many compelling accounts, these projects have been disappointing, failing to deliver the expected results. On the one hand these critiques challenge the theory that a preordained legal institutional framework is necessary for economic growth. On the other, they review particular reforms of laws and of judicial systems carried out in a variety of countries. However, despite these critiques, the appeal to establishing the "rule of law" by the "right" combination of legal rules and institutions continues to spur hope and inspire reforms.

The critical energy comes from both veterans of the "Law and Development Movement"[2] and from contemporary scholars in the field.[3] In addition, a number of current participants in these reforms have voiced criticisms of the strategies and projects promoted by their institutions.[4] I endorse this critical practice and to some extent, this chapter forms part of and benefits from that enterprise. However, rather than insisting that these available and powerful critiques must be considered, I intend to explore the persistence of the assumptions about the relationship between law and development by looking at the conditions that have made the "rule of law" such an enduring strategy. Thus, the first question I explore is what makes projects of legal and

development institutions and other transnational actors participate in promoting a particular set of legal reforms, believed to be favorable to economic development and democracy).

2 For a classic account of this movement see David Trubek and Marc Galanter, *Scholars in Self-Estrangement: Some Reflections on the Crisis in Law and Development Studies in the United States* 4 WISCONSIN LAW REVIEW: 1062–1102 (1974). See Trubek's contribution to this volume for a comparison of the current boom in law and development projects with the earlier reform effort in which he took part.

3 See KERRY RITTICH, RECHARACTERIZING RESTRUCTURING: LAW, DISTRIBUTION AND GENDER IN THE STRUCTURE OF MARKET REFORM (2002); Antony Anghie, *Time Present and Time Past: Globalization, International Financial Institutions, and the Third World,* 32 N.Y.U. J. INT'L L. & POL. 243 (2000); John Ohnesorge, *The Rule of Law, Economic Development, and the Developmental States of Northeast Asia,* in LAW AND DEVELOPMENT IN EAST AND SOUTHEAST ASIA 91 (Christoph Antons, ed., 2003); Jorge Esquirol, CONTINUING FICTIONS OF LATIN AMERICAN LAW, 55 FLORIDA LAW REVIEW 41 (2003), BALAKRISHNAN RAJAGOPAL, INTERNATIONAL LAW FROM BELOW: DEVELOPMENT, SOCIAL MOVEMENTS, AND THIRD WORLD RESISTANCE, (2003); Joel Ngugi, *Re-examining the Role of Private Property in Market Democracies: Problematic Ideological Issues Raised by Land Registration,* 25 MICH. J. INT'L L. 467 (2004); James Ghatti, *Retelling Good Governance Narratives on Africa's Economic and Political Predicaments: Continuities and Discontinuities in Legal Outcomes Between Markets and States,* 45 VILLANOVA LAW REVIEW 5, 971(2000).

4 See Linn Hammergren, *International Assistance to Latin American Justice Programs: Toward an Agenda for Reforming the Reformers* 309, *in* BEYOND COMMON KNOWLEDGE, EMPIRICAL APPROACHES TO THE RULE OF LAW (Erik G. Jensen and Thomas C. Heller eds., 2003). See also Richard Messick, *Judicial Reform and Economic Development: A Survey of the Issues,* 14 The World Bank Research Observer 117 (February 1999), http://www1.worldbank.org/publicsector/legal/Research%20Observer%20Paper.doc; (raising concerns on the lack of knowledge about what these reforms should consist of and about its economic impact).

judicial reform so immune from these available critiques and from increasing evidence of their scant success. Thinking about what makes the continuation of these projects so appealing should help explain why the "rule of law" is so central to the way we speak about the process of development.

In exploring this question, my work benefits from and at the same time enters a discussion with other scholarly work on how the "rule of law" idea has lent more credibility to international financial institutions, in their promotion of a specific set of economic policies in developing countries. My work departs from this literature however to the extent that some of this work assumes that the Word Bank is a monolithic institution with a single agenda.

The starting point of many critiques of the World Bank's work is to assume a consensus within the Bank about the strategy and programs for development. I propose to invert this assumption and begin from the opposite end. What makes the projects of the different groups in the Bank "hang together" in an apparently coherent way? The internal dynamics in the Bank suggest the lack of a consensus – let's call it a dissensus – among various groups working on "rule of law" projects about how it is that law will advance economic development. Thus, when confronted with the resemblance of a unified vision and strategy among these groups, the question I would like to pose is this: what causes the reduction of the dissensus?

In this chapter, I seek to disaggregate the Bank and provide insight on the impact that particular groups have in dominant development strategies. By analyzing the internal dynamics among groups at the Bank, I aim to illuminate the rise and fall of ideas about development and their resistance to both empirical evidence and academic critique. These internal dynamics include institutional inertia and constraints, groups' struggle and competition over resources and prestige, and the relationship between groups at the Bank and the governments of borrowing countries.

My argument is that the conceptions of the rule of law behind these various projects need not be, and indeed are not, consistent with each other. They often conflict, but their inconsistencies or contradictions regularly go unnoticed due to a conceptually confused discussion coupled with the dynamics of a complex institution. To explore this point, this chapter undertakes both a conceptual analysis of the "rule of law" and an institutional analysis of the dynamics among the groups leading these projects in the Bank. I give an account of the ways in which the rule of law rhetoric within the Bank forecloses an analysis about the very policies these reforms introduce, their consequences among groups in society, and their ultimate relationship to economic development. Finally, I argue that the agenda for the rule of law is not exclusively about the role of law in economic development. It is also about defining and expanding the role of the World Bank groups in domestic policies around the world.

I develop my argument in three parts. In the first part, I will sketch four conceptions of the rule of law, developed in jurisprudence and in the literature of economic development, as a template with which to analyze the Bank's strategies and the position of the various groups on the subject. I consider the lack of conceptual agreement on the meaning of the rule of law and explore its multiple interpretations, as well as the overlap and tensions among these conceptions. I argue that these various conceptions of the rule of law, as channeled in the Bank, constitute a hodge-podge that enables different and often conflicting projects to be pursued under the same agenda.

In the second part, I provide an overview of the World Bank's engagement with the rule of law, describing the different conceptions of the rule of law introduced at various points in time. I analyze how, since its inception, the rule of law has been a powerful rhetoric to justify the Bank's involvement in reforming developing countries' legal and judicial systems and to portray this endeavor as an apolitical one. I describe how the rule of law rhetoric has dramatically expanded from an instrumental conception focused on economic considerations to an intrinsic conception that values legal and judicial reforms as good on their own right and considers them an inherent part of the development process.

The third part will look at the practice of rule of law projects and describe the various divisions in the World Bank currently engaged in reforming courts and laws. I will highlight which conceptions of the rule of law these units have adopted and describe how, despite internal disparities and conflicting views among them, their agendas reinforce each other in what seems a common position. I offer an analysis on this apparent consensus at two levels. First, I describe how the conceptual hodge-podge bonds under the same rubric different agendas and competing interests. Second, I analyze the dynamics among the various World Bank groups, and the relationships between these groups and the borrowing countries. I will show how this implicit consensus enables them to discount unfavorable results, support the continuation of their projects and validate a variety of different policies.

THE RULE OF LAW

In this discussion, my purpose is to shed light on the multiplicity of conceptions of the rule of law at play in the discourse of development institutions. I seek to explore the ways in which people deploy and articulate the different conceptions of the rule of law, in what I see as a sort of hodge-podge that remains difficult to disentangle. Moreover, I argue that this amalgam of undifferentiated conceptions greatly contributes to the strength and appeal of the rule of law as it is used today. Before I examine just how I think this hodge-podge works in World Bank practice, I will review some of the main interpretations of the rule of law and offer a classification. This framework will help to clarify how these conceptions coexist in development assistance projects, how they are used interchangeably by the groups in the Bank, and with what effects.

Anyone seeking to understand what the "rule of law" is will find that the term is unclear and ambiguous. Indeed, the meaning of the "rule of law" has been the subject of disagreements and heated debates among scholars. Whenever people invoke the rule of law, they advance one or several of this term's possible interpretations as if these were obvious or required. In this section, I will explore various conceptions of the idea of the "rule of law" that will serve as an analytical framework helping to probe deeper into the Bank's use of this idea in its strategy and projects.

Discussion of the rule of law ideal can be found in the writings of political theorists like Aristotle, Montesquieu and Locke, who were concerned with devising limits to the power of the government. For Aristotle, who proposed that law rather than any single one of the citizens ruled, the ideal was a society governed by reason and not by passion.[5] Montesquieu envisioned a system of institutional restraints that could limit governmental exercise of power against citizens and guarantee individuals' freedom from fear and the threat of violence. Achieving this goal required a political system where power could check power, preventing the whims of the king or the discretion of the legislature to fall upon individuals. An independent judiciary was needed in order to check the powers of the executive.[6] Locke reasoned that the preservation of individuals' property – the chief aim of men entering a political society – was guaranteed by three conditions: first, established law agreed by consent; second, an independent judge with power to decide controversies according to law; and third, a power to execute the sentence.[7]

Scholars writing about the rule of law rely on these and other sources for authority on what the concept means. There is however, little agreement on how the conceptions of these different authors and their positions relate to one another. Some scholars have noticed the ambivalence or vagueness of the term and the multiple ways in which it may be deployed by different actors for a variety of purposes.[8] Even a number of scholars and analysts more closely

[5] ARISTOTLE, THE POLITICS, Book III, Part 16 (Tr. T. A. Sinclair, 1962) ("He who asks Law to rule is asking God and Intelligence and no others to rule; while he who asks for the rule of a human being is bringing in a wild beast. . . . In law you have the intellect without passions.") p. 142–143.

[6] MONTESQUIEU, THE SPIRIT OF LAWS, Bk. VI, chs. 1–6 (1748) (ed. David Wallace 1977). See Judith Skhlar, Political Theory and the Rule of Law, *in* THE RULE OF LAW, IDEAL OR IDEOLOGY (Hutchinson and Monahan eds., 1987) (discussing Aristotle and Montesquieu as representatives of two distinct visions on the rule of law – one the reign of reason, the other institutional guarantees for the protection of individuals against state power).

[7] JOHN LOCKE, THE SECOND TREATISE OF GOVERNMENT, ed. Peter Laslett, 1988, pp. 350–353.

[8] See, for example, Thomas Carothers, *The Many Agendas of Rule of Law Reform, in Latin America*, in RULE OF LAW IN LATIN AMERICA: THE INTERNATIONAL PROMOTION OF JUDICIAL REFORM, pp. 4–15 (Pilar Domingo and Rachel Sieder eds., 2001); Frank Upham, *Mythmaking in the Rule of*

involved with the Bank have expressed caution about the use of the term and its imprecise nature.[9]

The following discussion presents, in a schematic form, four different conceptions of the rule of law. These conceptions are organized around two main criteria: the degree of autonomy of the legal order from other orders like morals and politics, and the degree of relative value against competing considerations. The first criterion of classification makes a distinction between an *institutional* and a *substantive* conception of the rule of law.[10] For those who support the *institutional* conception, judgment about the existence of the rule of law would be rendered based on whether the rules comply with certain requirements, internal to the legal order, that make law efficacious. This view does not pass judgment upon, and is indifferent about, the actual content of these rules. This conception provides no normative criteria to evaluate whether the law in question is a good or a bad law.[11] Thus, the rule of law can exist regardless of whether we consider it fair, democratic, or just.[12] In contrast, a *substantive* vision of the rule of law takes these formal characteristics for granted but requires that rules enshrine specific values. It requires the existence of specific rights that are considered to be inherent to such a system.[13] Existence of these rights becomes the yardstick to judge whether a law is a good law or a bad law.

The second criterion of classification distinguishes between an *instrumental* and an *intrinsic* conception of the rule of law. For those who support the

Law Orthodoxy, Carnegie Endowment Working Paper, Rule of Law Series, Democracy and Rule of Law Project, #30, September 2002; John Ohnesorge, *supra* note 3; Gianmaria Ajani, *The Transplant of Vague Notions* (on file with the author).

9 See, for example, Matthew Stephenson, *The Rule of Law as a Goal of Development Policy* (available under Rule of Law and Development section at http://www.worldbank.org/lji, and Mathew Stephenson, *A Trojan Horse Behind Chinese Walls?: Problems and Prospects of US-Sponsored "Rule of Law" Reform Projects in the PRC*, CID Working Paper #47, Center for International Development, Harvard University (2000) http://www.cid.harvard.edu/cidwp/047.htm.

10 I use the term *institutional* instead of the more-often used term *formal* to emphasize the role of society's specialized institutions, particularly that of the judiciary, in the application of rules. But apart from this qualification I use the term institutional as equivalent to formal. For an analysis of the differences between formal and substantive conceptions, see Paul Craig, *Formal and substantive conceptions of the Rule of Law: An analytical framework*, PUBLIC LAW 467, Autumn 1997, 467–487. See also ROBERTO M. UNGER, LAW IN MODERN SOCIETY (1976) 48–58 (analyzing the substantive, institutional, methodological and occupational aspects of an autonomous legal order associated with the rule of law ideal). For an excellent recent treatise on the rule of law, see BRIAN TAMANAHA, ON THE RULE OF LAW (2004).

11 See Craig, *supra* note 10 at 467.

12 For an endorsement of this formal conception see Joseph Raz, *The Rule of Law and its Virtue*, 93 LAW QUARTERLY REVIEW 195 (1977).

13 The most prominent contemporary legal philosopher upholding this position is Ronald Dworkin. Coined by him as the rights conception, this view does not distinguish between substantive justice and the rule of law. This conception requires that the formal rules reflect and enforce moral rights. See RONALD DWORKIN, A MATTER OF PRINCIPLE (1985) 11–12.

TABLE 1. Rule of Law Conceptions

		Degree of differentiation of legal norms (from other systems like morals-politics)	
		Institutional	**Substantive**
Degree of relative value against other competing considerations	**Instrumental**	Max Weber	Friedrich Hayek
	Intrinsic	A.V. Dicey	Amartya Sen

instrumental conception, the rule of law is an effective mechanism to achieve whatever goals a society has set for itself. It is, in other words, an important *means* for the realization of a society's ideals in the organization of government power, relations of production, and social order.[14] Moreover, the rule of law is certainly a value of a society's legal system, but it is one among many competing values to be considered. Sometimes, a society may want to override the rule of law because of other values deemed of higher importance, such as national emergency or substantive justice.[15] In contrast, those supporting an *intrinsic* conception of the rule of law consider it a goal in its own right. The rule of law enshrines the greatest values that societies can aspire to, such as justice, democracy, or freedom and it cannot be compromised without foregoing these values.

In the following discussion, I depict these conceptions as ideal-types, relating each conception with a scholar to explore their differences and overlapping elements. These ideal-types should be understood in a continuum rather than in opposition. Table 1 illustrates the conceptions of the rule of law just explained.

Institutional conception

An institutional conception of the rule of law is mainly concerned with the efficacy of a system of rules. Joseph Raz, a prominent advocate of this conception, highlights two fundamental aspects. First, government action should be authorized by law, and second, laws should be capable of guiding people's conduct for them to plan their life.[16] This conception emphasizes the formal

14 For an account of this instrumental conception, see DUNCAN KENNEDY, A CRITIQUE OF ADJUDICATION, (1997) pp. 13–14.

15 See Kennedy, *supra* note 14, at 14.

16 To effectively enable individuals to plan their lives, rules should be prospective and stable. Particular laws should be guided by open, general and clear rules. There should be an independent judiciary to which all citizens have access and the discretion of law enforcement agencies should not undermine the purposes of the relevant legal rules. Joseph Raz, *supra* note 12 at 196. See also Paul Craig, *supra* note 10 at 469.

characteristics of a legal system that ensure that the rules are available and that they are susceptible of being followed.[17] What are these characteristics? There is of course no definitive list, but among the elements generally included are: 1) generality, 2) notice or publicity, 3) prospectivity, 4) clarity, 5) noncontradictoriness, 6) conformability, 7) stability, and 8) congruence.[18] If the rules reflect these characteristics they will enable the addressees "to *know* what they are commanded to do" and "to *do* what is commanded of them."[19] The aim of these requirements is the establishment of "rule-like commands that can successfully induce desired behavior (whatever it is) in the addressees."[20] Thus, we may conclude that an *institutional* conception refers to the qualities and mechanisms of the rules in a legal system. This view is not concerned with the *content* of the rules and the values they uphold but rather on whether the legal system has the formal characteristics that make it work.

As anticipated above, the institutional conception can be divided in two further categories. Operating entirely with criteria internal to the legal order, it is possible to identify an instrumental version of the institutional conception of the rule of law and an intrinsic one. In the following sections, I discuss these categories with reference to the work of Max Weber and A.V. Dicey.

Instrumental version. A classic formulation of this conception of the rule of law is found in Max Weber's work on the relationship between "rational law" and economic development.[21] Weber argued that his ideal type of "logically formal rationality" as a system of general, universally applied rules was at the core of western industrialization. This type of law constituted the basis of legal domination and as such the nature of "modern" law and thus the "modern state."[22] The most important element of a legal system containing such characteristics was its high degree of stability and calculability. These features enabled individuals to predict the actions of other individuals and of the state and thus to engage securely in economic transactions. This system of rules created the social discipline necessary for a modern state where economic development could thrive.[23] Thus, these formal rules were the *means* through which individuals could enter into predictable economic transactions that would ultimately lead to economic growth.

17 See Margaret Jane Radin, *Reconsidering the Rule of Law*, 64 B.U.L.Rev. 781 (1989), 784.
18 See generally Lon Fuller, The Morality of Law 33–94 (Ed. 1969).
19 Radin, *supra* note 17, at 786.
20 Id.
21 See Max Weber, Economy and Society (1968).
22 David Trubek, *Max Weber on Law and the Rise of Capitalism*, WISC L. REV. 720 (1972).
23 See G. Myrdal, *The Soft State in Underdeveloped Countries*, 15 Ucla L.Rev. 1118 (1968) (discussing the relationship between a "soft" state and underdevelopment. 'Soft" development would be characterized as a general lack of social discipline signified by deficiencies in law observance and enforcement.)

It is worth noting that Weber was reluctant to define the modern state and its legal order based on the purpose of the political community or value judgments that inspired the belief in its legitimacy. In Weber's view, political communities could pursue any conceivable end without losing the character of a modern state just as charismatic leadership could be personified by a holy man or a tyrant.[24] The immediate implication of this position is that the rule of law, as Weber conceived it, can exist in any political order.[25]

Intrinsic version. The work that best exemplifies the intrinsic/institutional conception is that of A.V. Dicey, who set out to explain the meaning of the term "rule, supremacy, or predominance of law" as one of the distinguishing characteristics of the English institutions. He identified three features of the rule of law and accorded to them a distinctively English origin. The first meaning refers to the absence of arbitrary power on the part of the government. Dicey put it this way:

> [N]o man is punishable or can be lawfully made to suffer in body or goods except for a distinct breach of law established in the ordinary legal manner before the ordinary courts of the land. In this sense the rule of law contrasted with every system of government based on the exercise by persons in authority of wide, arbitrary, or discretionary powers of constraint.[26]

Dicey considered this feature a peculiarity of the English institutions or of those countries that had inherited English traditions. He believed that in the continental tradition the executive exercised far wider discretionary authority than the government in England. This discretion enabled government's arbitrariness and thus threatened the individual's legal freedom.[27]

In the second instance, the rule of law meant legal equality, or more precisely, that every person, regardless of his or her position, is subject to ordinary law administered by ordinary tribunals.

> [N]ot only that with us no man is above the law, but (what is a different thing) that here every man, whatever his rank or condition, is subject to the ordinary law of the realm and amenable to the jurisdiction of the ordinary tribunals.[28]

24 See Reinhard Bendix, Max Weber: An Intellectual Portrait (1978), pp. 417–420.

25 Joseph Raz makes precisely this point when he argues that the rule of law "is not to be confused with democracy, justice, equality (before the law or otherwise), human rights of any kind or respect for persons or for the dignity of man." In Raz's view, a non-democratic legal system may be perfectly capable of conforming to the rule of law ideal. See Raz, *supra* note 12, at 196.

26 A.V. Dicey, The Law of the Constitution (10th ed., 1959), p. 188.

27 Id. 188. Dicey's attribution of the rule of law to the English institutions in opposition to continental institutions has been challenged by several legal scholars, most notably by Sir Ivor Jennings (The Law and the Constitution, 1952); See also H.W. Arthurs, Without the Law, Administrative Justice and Legal Pluralism in Nineteenth Century England (1985).

28 Dicey, *supra* note 26, at 193.

Dicey saw this trait also as a particularity of England, where every official, from the prime minister to a constable, is as any other citizen, responsible for every act done without legal justification. Thus, officials acting in their official capacity but exceeding their lawful authority are brought to courts and made, in their personal capacity, liable to punishment or to the payment of damages.[29] Dicey contrasted this state of affairs with the continent, where he argued that officials acting in their official capacity were regularly protected from the ordinary law of the land, the jurisdiction of ordinary tribunals, and sometimes subject only to official law administered by official organs.[30]

Finally, in a third sense, under the rule of law constitutional norms are the result of ordinary law as established by ordinary courts. Dicey maintained that:

> [T]he general principles of the constitution (as for example the right to personal liberty or the right of public meeting) are with us the result of judicial decision determining the rights of private persons in particular cases brought before the courts, whereas under many foreign constitutions the security (such as it is) given to the rights of individuals results, or appears to result, from the general principles of the constitution.[31]

For Dicey, the English constitution is judge-made and the rights of individuals are mere generalizations drawn from decisions of the judges. In contrast, in continental Europe individual rights are deductions drawn from the principles of the constitution, which is the result of a legislative act. Dicey admits this distinction may be merely a formal one, but he considers that continental constitutionalists have defined rights without giving adequate consideration to providing the remedies to enforce such rights.

Nothing in any of these three prongs of the rule of law, as developed by Dicey, would conclusively indicate that in order to establish the rule of law countries should enact a specific *content* in their laws or possess specific individual rights. Dicey argued adamantly for the common law as a more effective technique to protect such rights as compared to continental legal systems, but he did not make the rule of law hinge upon the existence of a given set of individual rights.[32] In this sense, Dicey's conception of the rule of law is internal to the legal order and it can be qualified as *institutional*. The definition and content of the rights available depends on myriad judicial decisions that have been gradually accumulating to formulate a remedy against a wrongdoing in the form of a right.

At the same time, Dicey identifies the rule of law with particular traits of the legal system: due process, authority's submission to its own law, and

[29] Id., at 193.
[30] Id., at 195.
[31] Id., at 196.
[32] Craig, *supra* note 10, at 472–474.

a constitution consisting of judicially declared rights for which there are enforceable remedies. These qualities, which he so proudly found in the English system, are in Dicey's view constitutive elements of any political community governed by the rule of law. I would argue that Dicey's position is in this sense *intrinsic* because the rule of law must be pursued in its own right. Moreover, the rule of law should be viewed not as one virtue among many competing virtues of a constitutional political system, but as what having a constitutional system is all about. In Dicey's words, "the suspension of the constitution, as far as such a thing can be conceived possible, would mean with us nothing less than a revolution."[33]

Substantive conception

A substantive conception of the rule of law takes the formal characteristics of the institutional conception for granted but requires the existence of specific rights that are considered to be inherent in such a system. It is also possible to identify, within the substantive conception, an instrumental and an intrinsic version. I will explore them analyzing the work of Friedrich Hayek and Amartya Sen.

Instrumental version. A powerful example of this position is articulated by Friedrich Hayek. In the instrumentalist version, Hayek regards the rule of law as a system that articulates a free market economy. For Hayek, whereas under the rule of law there is a permanent framework of rules within which individual decisions guide the productive activity, under arbitrary government a central authority directs the economy.[34] The rules establishing this framework under the rule of law have certain characteristics:

> [This] type of rules can be made in advance, in the shape of *formal rules*, which do not aim at the wants and needs of particular people. They are intended to be merely instrumental in the pursuit of people's various individual ends. And they are, or ought to be, intended for such long periods that it is impossible to know whether they will assist particular people more than others. They could almost be described as a kind of instrument of production, helping people to predict the behaviour of those with whom they must collaborate, rather than as efforts toward satisfaction of particular needs.[35]

Because of the system of rules in place, individuals are able to foresee with certainty how the government would use its coercive power in given circumstances and thus plan their affairs accordingly. Individuals are able to

33 Dicey, *supra* note 26, at 202.
34 Friedrich Hayek, The Road to Serfdom (1944), p.80–96.
35 Id. 81.

calculate because the government is bound by rules laid down in advance, of which individuals have knowledge. According to Hayek:

> [U]nder the rule of law the government is prevented from stultifying individual efforts by *ad hoc* action. Within the known rules of the game the individual is free to pursue his personal ends and desires, certain that powers of government will not be used deliberately to frustrate his efforts.[36]

Hayek insists that the rule of law requires particular kinds of rules that would allow individuals to calculate and predict their interactions with other individuals and the state but also that would keep the government at bay from making decisions of production and exchange in the market. He draws a distinction between these formal rules and rules that depend on particular circumstances at a given moment and evaluate the interests of various persons and groups. In the second kind of rules, the government decides whose interest is more important, coercively imposing a new distinction of rank upon people. Thus, the most important criterion of formal rules, according to Hayek, is that we do not know their concrete effects, the ends they will pursue, or the people they will assist. In this sense, formal rules "do not involve a choice between particular ends or particular people" because we are ignorant of who will use them and for what purposes. For Hayek, not knowing the particular effects of the state's measures is in fact the rationale of the "great liberal principle of the Rule of Law."[37]

The unpredictability of the particular *effects* is what Hayek holds to be the distinguishing feature of formal laws of the liberal system. This criterion is the yardstick with which to measure individual freedom under state action. For Hayek, the Rule of Law is "the legal embodiment of freedom." As such, it is not concerned with whether government actions are legal in a juridical sense. These actions may be legal but inconsistent with the Rule of Law. If the law gives the government powers to act arbitrarily, or more precisely, if the government's use of its coercive power is not limited by pre-established rules then the Rule of Law does not prevail.[38] Hayek stresses that:

> [U]nder the rule of law the private citizen and his property are not an object of administration by the government, not a means to be used for its Purpose. It is only when the administration interferes with the private sphere of the citizen that the problem of discretion becomes relevant to us; and the principle of the rule of law, in effect, means that the administrative authorities should have no discretionary powers in this respect.[39]

In order to preclude this discretion, an independent court must be able to review the substance of administrative actions. In limiting the discretion of

[36] Id.
[37] Id. 83.
[38] Id. 91.
[39] Friedrich Hayek, The Constitution of Liberty 212 (1978).

the authority, the judiciary must look not only at whether the executive has acted within its powers – whether the authority was legally entitled to act – but also whether the substance of administrative action fell within the government's powers or impinged upon the citizen's private property.

Intrinsic version. Amartya Sen upholds an intrinsic vision of the rule of law, which propounds that the legal system ought to be judged according to whether it enables peoples' capability to exercise their rights. The rule of law and the enhancement of people's freedoms should not be viewed as means to achieve certain ends, but as ends in their own right.

Sen argues that conceptual integrity requires us to see legal development as a constitutive part of the development process, regardless of its effects on the economic, political, and social areas. Development as a whole is an *amalgam* of developments in the distinct economic, legal, political, and social domains. The point is not that legal development causally influences development as a whole but rather that development as a whole cannot be considered separately from legal development.[40] From this perspective, Sen effectively de-centers the economic aspect of development, asserting that:

> [E]ven if legal development were not to contribute one iota to economic development... even then legal and judicial reform would be a critical part of the development process."[41]

So far, Sen makes two distinct arguments. First, a conceptually integrated form of development makes it impossible to think of any given sphere of development in isolation. On the contrary, we must understand them "hanging together," in a relation of necessity with one another. The connection of each of the different domains – legal, economic, political, social – is *constitutive* of development. The point here is not one of a relation of causality between each domain and development but rather that development as a whole cannot be considered separately from the development in each domain. Development in an integrated form will consider legal development just as importantly as the economic, social, or political domains.

Second, assessing development in each domain requires us to go beyond its formal aspects. In this view, the rule of law is not "about what the law is and what the judicial system formally accepts and asserts" but rather it must constitutively consider "the enhancement of peoples' capability – their substantive freedom – to exercise the rights and entitlements. Seen in this light, development in each domain is related, indeed causally interrelated, to

40 Amartya Sen, *What is the role of legal and judicial reform in economic development?* p.8, (Lecture delivered at the first World Bank conference on Comprehensive Legal and Judicial Development, Washington, DC, June 5, 2000), http://www1.worldbank.org/publicsector/legal/legalandjudicail.pdf). See generally Amartya Sen, Development as Freedom (1999).

41 Sen, *What is the role of legal and judicial reform in economic development?* p. 10.

instruments and policies in the other domains that cannot be excluded from consideration.

If we accept Sen's view on the conceptual integrity of development, legal development "must be seen as important on its own as a part of the development process, and not merely as a means to an end of other kinds of development, such as economic development."[42] This point is crucial for Sen, who wants to challenge the exclusive focus on the market system that he considers so prevalent in development studies and policy-making.[43]

THE WORLD BANK'S USES OF THE RULE OF LAW

The ubiquitous invocation of the rule of law (ROL) by international development institutions like the World Bank is a relatively recent phenomenon. In this section, I analyze how the conceptions of the ROL just described above map out onto the rhetoric and policies of the World Bank. I trace back in time the usage of the ROL concept in the Bank and discuss how the introduction of the rule of law in the Bank was supposed to have a merely institutional meaning but it encompassed a substantive one as well. Indeed, throughout the 1990s, the World Bank's ROL rhetoric has further broadened to include the four conceptions previously discussed. Thus, starting out reflecting an instrumental conception of the ROL, both in its institutional (Weber) and substantive (Hayek) versions, the Bank gradually expanded its rhetoric to include an intrinsic conception, in its institutional (Dicey) and substantive (Sen) versions. I will conclude the section showing how current World Bank rhetoric consists of a hodge-podge reflecting multiple conceptions of the ROL.

By providing an account of its multiple uses, I seek to clarify how the rule of law has been a powerful conceptual and rhetorical tool to garner support for substantive legal reforms that have important political, social, and economic implications in the countries they are implemented. By appeal to the ROL, however, these reforms are often presented as merely institutional, economically efficient, and apolitical. Moreover, the shift in emphasis from an instrumental to an intrinsic version of the ROL is not necessarily correlated to a shift in projects. Whereas projects of legal and judicial reform have remained more or less stable, the rhetoric has shifted often making the same projects look better by the mere shift in language.

42 Id., at 13.

43 In an essay commemorating the 60th anniversary of Hayek's *The Road to Serfdom*, Sen recognized Hayek as a champion of the proposition that societal institutions, including the market, should be judged by the degree to which they promote freedom. However, Sen noted that Hayek's fascination with the market's enabling effects on freedoms made him downplay "the lack of freedom for some that may result from a complete reliance on the market system, with exclusions and imperfections, and the social effects of big disparities in the ownership of assets". Amartya Sen, *An insight into the purpose of prosperity*, Financial Times (September 27, 2004).

The policy models of the World Bank

The story of the Bank's activities on rule of law projects can be told by situating them within the main development models of the Bank in three different periods. The first period, that of "structural adjustment," goes from 1980 to 1990. The second period, which witnesses the emergence of "governance" runs from 1990 to 1999. The last period, from 1999 onward is one of "comprehensive development." These three periods attest to the changes in thinking about economic development. Broadly speaking, they encompass the rise and fall of neoliberal thinking, or the so-called Washington Consensus, and the subsequent move to an "enlightened" Washington Consensus, mediated by a decade of profound reforms and severe crisis. These periods provide the framework of the World Bank's engagement with the ROL, facilitating an analysis of the ROL rhetoric in conjunction with changes in development thinking and policy models.

"Structural adjustment" was a period of market shock and trade liberalization. In the midst of the debt crisis in the beginning of the 1980s the Bank started a lending practice that made disbursements conditional upon the implementation of reform programs in macroeconomic and financial management.[44] The Bank's involvement in reforming developing countries' laws and legal systems predates the introduction of the notion of the rule of law in the Bank's projects. The notion of the "rule of law" was not part of the development strategy and was thus absent from reform proposals. However, the Bank assisted borrowing countries in a wide variety of legal changes deemed necessary to implement the macroeconomic policies agreed to as part of structural adjustment loans. Legal reforms were thus a condition for loan disbursement. They were narrowly tailored to introduce fiscal reform, ending exchange-rate controls, liberalizing trade, securing property rights, ending subsidies, and privatizing state-owned enterprises.[45]

[44] Designed as an exception to its lending practice to address the balance of payment crisis of the late 1970s, these loans increased dramatically in the 1980s and extended to the adjustment of a wide range of sectors. These reforms required widespread legislative changes in a variety of areas; especially those "enabling business environment" such as property law, commercial law, anti-trust, foreign investment, tax, banking, and labor regulation. During the 1980s adjustment lending represented 18% of International Bank for Reconstruction and Development (IBRD) and 12% of International Development Association (IDA), the two main lending institutions of the Bank. It accounted for 33% of total IBRD disbursement and 12% of IDA's. Ibrahim Shihata, *The World Bank and "Governance" Issues in its Borrowing Members*, in 1 The World Bank in a Changing World, 53, 58 (1991).

[45] The strategy that these legal changes sought to articulate consisted of three main areas: 1) macroeconomic management (realistic exchange rates, positive real interest rates, trade liberalization), efficient resource allocation (replacement of price controls with competitive markets) and the creation of a supportive legal and regulatory framework (reducing cost of doing business and encouraging competition, streamlining procedures and reforming tax, labor, investment, credit and corporate laws), 2) privatization or restructuring of state-owned

The "governance" period was inaugurated by the dismemberment of the Soviet Union, the dramatic political transformation of Eastern Europe and a severe political crisis in the African continent in the late 1980s and early 1990s. Indeed, the term governance is supposed to have emerged from a World Bank report evaluating the crisis in Sub-Saharan Africa and advancing recommendations for a minimum institutional "governance" to create stable conditions in these countries and assure the effectiveness of development assistance.[46] In this context, the "rule of law" emerged as a central part of the strategy for transforming these countries into market economies. With the introduction of the rule of law as an area of legitimate Bank intervention, law reform became a priority and the Bank rapidly began to broaden its reach. During this period, the Bank favored a long-term approach for projects of judicial and legal reform and created independent loans, in the form of investment or technical assistance that were not necessarily subject to conditionality.[47]

The current "comprehensive development" phase was inaugurated by President James D. Wolfhenson's strategy of a Comprehensive Development Framework (CDF).[48] This strategy was launched as a response to the critiques of the neoliberal economic policies and sought to turn from a focus on economic growth to one of "interdependence" of all aspects of development. CDF seeks to reconceptualize development by going beyond its macroeconomic and financial aspects to focus on structural, social, and human concerns. The quest is for a stable, equitable and sustainable development. The reduction of poverty, or rather freedom from poverty, has been introduced as a central part of the strategy.

enterprises to guarantee efficient provision of infrastructure and services (reducing or eliminating public monopolies, privatization and contracting out), and 3) developing financial systems that mobilize and allocate financial resources efficiently (develop strong financial markets, strengthen institutions promoting the private sector, and assisting micro enterprises, small-scale agriculture, and the informal sector). Ibrahim Shihata, The World Bank Facing the 21st Century – Developments in the Eighties and Prospects for the Nineties, *in* 1 The World Bank in a Changing World 30 (1991). See also *Initiatives in Legal and Judicial Reform*, Legal Vice Presidency, The World Bank (2002) http://www4.worldbank.org/legal/publications/LJR-Initiatives-2003.pdf, p. 8.

46 World Bank, Sub-Saharan Africa: From Crisis to Sustainable Growth. A long term perspective Study (1989); See also Ibrahim Shihata, 1 The World Bank in a Changing World (1991) pp. 53–57.

47 Practically every lending operation includes, in one way or another, a component of legal reform. It would be possible to classify operations according to how central legal reform is to the project and to whether such legal reforms are conditioned. Thus, operations vary from: 1) loans for capacity building and institutional development, which include components related to legal reform, to 2) reforms stipulated as conditions of structural adjustment programs, to 3) "freestanding" legal and judicial reform projects. Freestanding projects have been used in many countries. The first of these independent loans was given to China (1994). The largest has been the Legal Reform Project in Russia, supported by a $58 million loan. See *Initiatives in Legal and Judicial Reform, supra* note 45, 6–10.

48 James D. Wolfensohn, *A Proposal for a Comprehensive Development Framework* (May 1999), available at http://siteresources.worldbank.org/CDF/Resources/cdf.pdf.

The World Bank rhetoric on the Rule of Law

In describing the incorporation of the "rule of law" agenda in the Bank, I will focus on the writings of Ibrahim Shihata, general counsel and senior vice president of the World Bank from 1983 to 1998. Shihata stands out as the main architect of the "rule of law" in the Bank and as a bridge between different phases and policy models pursued.[49]

Writing in 1990, Ibrahim Shihata inaugurated and set out to justify the Bank's work on governance.[50] Mindful of the prohibitions against intervening in countries' internal political affairs under the Bank's mandate, laid down in its Articles of Agreement,[51] Shihata undertook the task of defining governance and drawing its limits. Distinguishing those aspects of governance that fell within the Bank's mandate from those representing prohibited "political considerations" became crucial for considering intervention in borrowing countries without violating the Bank's mandate.[52] Revisiting Shihata's explanation reveals the difficulties he faced trying to expand the competence of the Bank in areas understood to be reserved to the domestic jurisdiction of States. Shihata aimed at carving out a new sphere of action for the Bank while advocating its nonpolitical character. To achieve this, he emphasized the distinction between political and economic considerations, the former outside the Bank's reach, the latter within the Bank's area of expertise. This is arguably why Shihata preferred to speak of governance rather than government. Government was unmistakably political whereas governance deemphasized the

49 Shihata was by no means alone. As can be seen by the extent and scope of his publications, he had a considerable team of collaborators who helped to formulate this new role for the Bank. Thus, when I refer to Shihata I have in mind a position or school of thought led by him but not of his sole creation. The position he developed can be found in the three volumes of IBRAHIM SHIHATA, THE WORLD BANK IN A CHANGING WORLD (1991,1995,2000); COMPLEMENTARY REFORM, ESSAYS ON LEGAL, JUDICIAL AND OTHER INSTITUTIONAL REFORMS SUPPORTED BY THE WORLD BANK (1997); and THE WORLD BANK LEGAL PAPERS (2000).

50 Shihata defined governance as "the manner in which a community is managed and directed, including the making and administration of policy in matters of political control, as well as in such economic issues as may be relevant to the management of the community's resources; it conveys the same meaning as government...." Ibrahim Shihata, *The World Bank and "Governance" Issues in its Borrowing Members*, in 1 THE WORLD BANK IN A CHANGING WORLD 53 (1991), 85 (hereinafter *The WB and Governance Issues*); See also Ibrahim Shihata, *Issues of "Governance" in Borrowing Members – The Extent of their Relevance under the Bank's Articles of Agreement*, in THE WORLD BANK LEGAL PAPERS 245 (2000), 268) (hereinafter *Issues of Governance*).

51 The Articles of Agreement of both IBRD (available at http://siteresources.worldbank.org/EXTABOUTUS/Resources/ibrd-articlesofagreement.pdf) and IDA (available at http://siteresources.worldbank.org/IDA/Resources/ida-articlesofagreement.pdf) contain three similar provisions intended to prevent political intervention of these institutions in member countries and to prohibit the former from taking political or non-economic considerations into account. These are Article III, Section 5(b); Article IV, Section 10; and Article V, Section 5(c) of the IBRD Articles, and Article V, Section 1(g); Article V, Section 6; and Article VI, Section 5(c) of the IDA Articles. See Shihata, *The WB and Governance Issues*, *supra* note 50, at 65–67.

52 See *id.* pp. 81–84.

political character and stressed "management" of administrative and economic resources.

The Rule of Law as an institutional framework. It is in this context that Shihata first appealed to the rule of law, defining the sphere of legitimate action within the Bank's action in the "governance" strategy. For Shihata, those aspects of governance consistent with the Bank's mandate were found in the meaning of "good order," understood as:

> [A] system, based on abstract rules which are actually applied, and on functioning institutions which ensure the appropriate applications of such rules. This system of rules and institutions is reflected in the concept of *the rule of law*, generally known in different legal systems and often expressed in the familiar phrase of a 'government of laws and not of men.'[53]

What are the characteristics of such a system of rules and institutions? Shihata laid down five elements:

> 1) [T]here is a set of rules which are known in advance, 2) such rules are actually in force, 3) mechanisms exist to ensure the proper application of the rules and to follow for departure from them as needed according to established procedures, 4) conflicts in the application of the rules can be resolved through binding decisions of an independent judicial body, and 5) there are known procedures for amending the rules when they no longer serve their purpose.[54]

There is nothing particularly innovative about this characterization of the rule of law, as Shihata himself recognized. Probably, the reader will already have situated Shihata's characterization of the rule of law in the upper left corner of Table 1 in the first section of this article,[55] as an institutionalist-instrumentalist approach. The sources to which Shihata refers in his discussion further confirm this categorization.[56]

Shihata noted that the concept was known in other legal systems as well under appellations such as the "supremacy of law," and that it was not always tied to the principle of separation of powers. Embarking on a brief history of the notion, he referred to U.S. constitutional sources but made clear that there was nothing particularly western in the concept, that it was known in other systems and it had played a very important role in the evolution of the Islamic legal system.[57] Shihata's most important point in this discussion seems to be that the rule of law is compatible with a variety of different legal systems and traditions. Moreover, he did not associate the rule of law with democracy or for that matter with any particular type of political system or

[53] See Shihata, *The WB and Governance Issues, supra* note 50, at 85 (emphasis added). Shihata, *Issues of Governance, supra* note 50, at 272–273.

[54] *Id.*

[55] See Table 1, p. 259.

[56] See Shihata, *The WB and Governance Issues, supra* note 50, p. 87, expressly referring to Weber's theory of the role of law in the economy.

[57] See *id.* at 85, footnote 96.

government. Nor did he argue that the rule of law should be embodied in any particular kind of political and legal institutions. Shihata considered this system of rules and institutions to be important prerequisites for developing market economies. For this proposition, he referred to Weber's ideal type of "logically formal rationality" and the establishment of legal domination in a modern state as conducive to economic growth.[58] The relevance of the rule of law in development, Shihata argued, was that the effectiveness of reform policies would depend on a system capable of articulating them into workable rules and ensuring its compliance.

Following Weber, Shihata insisted that a system containing the basic elements he had pointed out for the rule of law addressed "the *process* of the formulation and application of rules, rather than the substance."[59] Thus, apart perhaps from certain formal characteristics which legal rules should fulfill in order to be observed and enforced, this approach tells us nothing about what kind of rules have to be enacted. Shihata argued that in respect of their content or *substance*, rules "will of course reflect the policies of each government and should be based on its own choices and convictions."[60] Substantive legal reform required profound knowledge of the economic and social situation in the country involved. Thus, Shihata concluded, legal reform could not be imposed from the outside and could only be useful if it was done by the country itself in response to its own needs.[61]

The Rule of Law as substantive rights and regulations. This is not, however, the whole story of Shihata's articulation of the rule of law. In a subtle but somewhat striking turn of position, performed in the same memorandum interpreting the Bank's Articles of Agreement, Shihata proposed that the Bank assist countries in the design of laws related to its mandate, and declared that it was free to condition loan disbursements upon adoption of legal reforms needed to implement agreed economic policies. Moreover, he argued, this focus on the content of the rules was appropriate as long as it was "based on considerations of economy and efficiency."[62] This competence of the Bank was to be distinguished, however, from the institutional setup as a prerequisite of economic reform and stability.[63] After all, Shihata seemed to be arguing for the Bank's involvement in the recommendation of specific types of rules, which "based on considerations of economy and efficiency," the Bank's traditional sphere of action, can serve as best practices for development countries.

58 *Id.* at 87.

59 *Id.* at 86.

60 *Id.*

61 *Id.* at 89. He further noted that "as any student of law knows, legal evolution is normally based on the interaction of the real forces in a community and reflects the evolving interests, values and convictions that do exist with such a community."

62 *Id.* at 86.

63 Shihata, *Issues of Governance, supra* note 50, at 273.

At this point, we could interpret Shihata's position as shifting from a Weberian to a Hayekian conception of the rule of law, recommending specific property and contract rights and regulations, and focusing on the substance of the rules. Shihata justified the Bank's involvement in the *content* of countries' laws by the demand for legal reforms coming from countries. The claim that it was countries that demanded these reforms needs to be taken with caution. As is widely known, the Bank developed a lending practice that required particular legal reforms from developing countries as a condition of loan disbursement. In any event, Shihata contended that this demand came from governments' realization that the private sector could not develop in the absence of an *appropriate legal framework* and well functioning mechanisms and institutions that ensured enforcement of the law, protected property and contracts, and settled disputes effectively.[64] Shihata alluded to the importance of having "an appropriate legal system, properly administered and enforced, for creating an environment conducive to business development."[65] But Shihata referred to these substantive rules of private law as a *framework* or an *environment* conducive to business development, proposing them as *institutional*, whereas they were in effect *substantive*. Thus, the concept of substantive laws forming the *appropriate* legal system favorable to business was conflated with the *institutional* character of the legal system.[66]

Furthermore, the impression of the merely *institutional* and not *substantive* character of the Bank's work in reforming countries' private laws was reinforced by the limitations that Shihata laid down for the Bank's jurisdiction in projects of legal reform. In interpreting the Bank's Articles of Agreement, which define its mandate and scope of intervention, Shihata determined that the World Bank could not work in the area of human rights, and specifically of civil and political rights. That was, in his view, definitely a political area that had to be left in the hands of each country's political system.[67] Shihata also contrasted the Bank's jurisdiction with the one of the European Bank for

[64] *Id.* Shihata refers to training programs for judges in business law or the law of commercial transactions; or providing knowledge on how compliance with contracts can be ensured, or how courts can perform their work within a reasonable time to help the business community.

[65] *Id.*

[66] For a thorough discussion of the conflation of substantive and procedural conceptions of the rule of law, see Joel M. Ngugi, *Searching for the market criterion*, SJD Dissertation, Harvard Law School 2002 (on file with Harvard Law School library). Ngugi contends that a conflation between a procedural and a substantive conception of the rule of law legitimates economic reforms that may be emptied out of democratic content. This conflation enables the deployment of what Ngugi calls a "thick concept" of the rule of law, having both a descriptive and evaluative property. In Ngugi's view, the deployment of the rule of law as a thick concept "operates to justify programmatic [value-laden] reforms while maintaining a standard rhetoric of procedural necessity that is easily agreed upon politically." *Id.* at 139.

[67] See Ibrahim Shihata, The World Bank and Human Rights, in THE WORLD BANK IN A CHANGING WORLD 97 (1991), pp. 97–109.

Reconstruction and Development, which specified in its mandate the goal of establishing market democracies. In contrast, the Bank was not entitled to condition its lending to the establishment of democratic political processes.[68] Setting out these boundaries had the effect of portraying the Bank's work in private law reform as a matter of nonpolitical economic expertise.

At this point, it can be appreciated how Shihata swayed back and forth from a Weberian to a Hayekian version of the rule of law. On the one hand, he argued for an institutional approach in order to enable the Bank to get involved and even condition countries' legal reforms. On the other hand, Shihata promoted a substantive approach when he asserted the Bank's authority in designing specific private law rules, even though he declared the Bank's role to be merely establishing an appropriate legal framework. Portraying the Bank's intervention as merely institutional was further enhanced by declaring other areas typically thought of as more substantive or political, such as civil and political rights, outside its reach.

Thus, we can observe that from the very beginning, the Bank's relationship to the rule of law idea was characterized by an ambiguity between an institutional and substantive version, which allowed it a scope of action and intervention much wider than if it had clearly placed itself only in one or the other conception.

Expanding the Rule of Law to fight corruption. In 1996, the Bank announced its determination to begin projects aimed at fighting corruption and thus join other international efforts. James D. Wolfhenson, then just appointed president of the Bank, declared that "the international community simply must deal with the cancer of corruption, because it is a major barrier to sustainable and equitable development," thus inaugurating a new area for the Bank's involvement.[69]

In his role as legal advisor, Shihata helped to set up and implement the Bank's agenda for combating corruption. While advocating an active role for the Bank in this area, Shihata was careful to notice once again the Bank's prohibition to intervene in political affairs of States. He made clear that fighting corruption was an important part of the Bank's "governance" agenda and that, consistent with his previous interpretation of the Articles of Agreement, it was driven by the estimation of corruption's negative effects on the appropriate use of the Bank's resources in developing countries. The Bank had an interest in ensuring that countries use its financial aid for the specific purposes agreed upon in advance and in an efficient manner. Promoting reforms

68 See Shihata, *The WB and Governance Issues, supra* note 50, at 77, 79, 82, 93–95.

69 See Ibrahim Shihata, *Corruption-A General Review with an Emphasis on the Role of the World Bank*, in THE WORLD BANK IN A CHANGING WORLD 603 (1991), [hereinafter *General Corruption Review*].

to increase effectiveness of development aid would thus also be consistent with the Bank's objectives.[70]

Although Shihata initially recognized that there was no conclusive empirical evidence on the relationship between lack of corruption and economic growth, he pointed out an emerging consensus holding that the long-term effects of corruption in investment climate and peoples' welfare, weakened public institutions, and ultimately decreased economic growth.[71] Once the Bank decided to actively participate in combating corruption, Shihata enthusiastically noted that the Bank began to produce research showing a strong correlation between low levels of corruption and income per capita, infant mortality, and literacy rate. Moreover, the Bank encouraged countries to combat corruption by undertaking a variety of reforms and sought to create the demand for reforms by getting civil society involved. It established workshops, seminars, and training programs to disseminate knowledge and gain from countries' experience. Finally, the Bank initiated an internal restructuring in the Bank to monitor procurement and loan disbursement.[72]

Equally important in Shihata's justification is a concern with corruption's effects on a country's institutions. In this view, corruption is wrong not only because it may hinder or retard growth, but because it corrodes societies. It makes "governance" dysfunctional and ineffective, empowering particular individuals rather than institutions, and favoring discretion and arbitrary decision rather than rule following.[73] The Bank seems clearly concerned with corruption as it relates to an exercise of public power that lacks transparency, tends to be abusive, and is unaccountable. Thus, in this view, corruption not only produces bad effects for the country's economic progress, but it is also morally wrong. It favors the powerful and impinges upon the rights of the weak and the poor.

Shihata points out that legal scholarship treats corruption as "deviation (for private gains) from binding rules, the arbitrary exercise of discretionary powers and the illegitimate use of public resources."[74] Shihata concludes that corruption has a "devastating effect on the rule of law which . . . is substituted for by the rule of whoever has the influence or the ability and willingness to pay."[75] Thus, building the rule of law becomes a strategy to manage and reduce corruption.

[70] See *General Corruption Review, supra* note 69, at 626–630.

[71] Id. at 604–605.

[72] See Ibrahim Shihata, *Postscript* of chapter eighteen, in 3 The World Bank in a Changing World 641 (2000).

[73] The Bank embraced the agenda for fighting corruption to ensure an effective state, one that could reinvigorate the market reforms promoted in the neoliberal period, particularly policies of free-trade, market deregulation and privatization of state-owned enterprises and increase their likelihood of success. See World Development Report 1997 – The State in a Changing World, 8 (World Bank 1997).

[74] Corruption General Review, *supra* note 69, at 606.

[75] *Id.* at 607.

High among the policies that countries can implement to curb corruption are legal reforms in civil service, criminal law, administrative law, and judicial reform. Changes would aim at establishing a meritocracy in the bureaucracy, guaranteeing transparency in public administration, ensuring monitoring of government procurement processes, reducing red-tape, and curbing arbitrariness and discretion in administrative and judicial decisions.

Successful reforms will ensure that in Dicey's terms, "no man is above the law," emphasizing the need for government officials to act in accordance with previously established and publicized laws. The judiciary plays a key role in this strategy. By ensuring that public officials will be held individually responsible for their actions, these projects aim at creating checks to government discretion and arbitrary power.[76] Beyond what economic effects the reduction of corruption may bring about, the institutional changes will make for a better, more transparent, accountable and, in the end, more democratic type of government. Therefore, the Bank's rationale for fighting corruption upholds an institutional version of the rule of law that is not merely instrumental but also intrinsic.

Reinterpreting the Rule of Law to reduce poverty and enhance peoples' capabilities. The Comprehensive Development Framework sets out a role for each of the actors of development (government, private sector, civil society, development agencies) and proposes a framework for coordinating their efforts. The program keeps the stress on sequencing and phasing of reforms as well as on local ownership, while preserving the role of the private sector as the main engine for development. In this holistic approach to development of the CDF, the focus of legal and judicial reform projects has moved beyond economic growth, also promoting human rights to achieve sustainable and equitable development. In the struggle against poverty, these projects emphasize access to justice as well as empowerment, ownership, and security for the most vulnerable groups, with particular emphasis on the poor, women, and children. This agenda relies on a substantive and intrinsic (Sen-based) conception of the rule of law.

The reform strategy has broadened to acknowledge an important role for the state in *regulating* the market. The task becomes one of delimiting the *appropriate* regulation to promote and encourage business activity. The goal is to generate a market-friendly and enterprise-led growth while reducing poverty and helping people improve their quality of life.[77] In addition, the Bank has argued that "a well functioning legal and judicial system is critical

[76] See Ibrahim Shihata, *Role of the Judiciary in the Prevention and Control of Corruption*, 3 The World Bank in a Changing World 277 (2001).

[77] For a strategy that reflects this goal, see *Private Sector Development Strategy-Directions for the World Bank Group*, The World Bank (April 9, 2002). http://rru.worldbank.org/documents/PSDStrategy-April%209.pdf.

both *as an end in itself* [*intrinsic*] as well as a means to facilitate and leverage the achievement of other development objectives [*instrumental*]."[78]

Multiple Rule of Law conceptions at play. Throughout these three periods, the policy models of the World Bank signal a shift of emphasis on the rule of law discourse from an *instrumental* conception (in both its institutional and substantive versions) to an *intrinsic* one. All four versions of the rule of law seem to converge in a hodge-podge articulation as exemplified in current usage of the term in World Bank reports:

> The rule of law is essential to *equitable economic development* and *sustainable poverty reduction.* Weak legal and judicial systems undermine the fight against poverty on many fronts: they divert investment to markets with more *predictable rule-based* environments, *deprive* important sectors of the use of *productive assets,* and *mute the voice of citizens* in the decision-making process. *Vulnerable individuals,* including women and children, are unprotected from violence and other forms of abuse that exacerbate inequalities. Ineffectual enforcement of laws engenders *environmental degradation, corruption, money laundering,* and other problems that burden people and economies around the world.[79]

These conceptions are overlapping but there are also tensions and contradictions between them. It seems hard that they could all be advanced simultaneously. In the following section, I will argue that, despite the promising inclusion of an intrinsic rule of law conception, there seems to be a simultaneous use of all rule of law conceptions that works as a shield. By advocating several conceptions at once, it becomes easier to justify the goals of any given project. Criticism to any one of the conceptions can be deflected by alternating between the purposes of the different conceptions at play. Looking at how projects of legal and judicial reform are justified in practice will help to clarify how the rule of law conceptions are deployed and with what purposes.

A look at its official rhetoric enables one to see that the Bank has moved a long way from the initial justification to participate in the reform of legal

[78] See *Initiatives in Legal and Judicial Reform, supra* note 45, at 2. This shift finds support in the work of Amartya Sen, who explicitly responded to the question of *"What is the role of legal and judicial reform in the development process?"* in an address to the Bank. See Sen, *supra* note 40. Legal's most recent legal reform strategy explicitly recognizes a link between poverty reduction and human rights, based on the principle that freedom from poverty is an essential element of development. Moreover, it confirms the CDF's holistic approach proposing that the protection of economic, social, and cultural human rights is an essential element of sustainable and equitable development. See *Legal and Judicial Reform: Strategic Directions,* Legal Vice Presidency, The World Bank (2003) http://www4.worldbank.org/legal/leglr/GreyBookFinal2003.pdf [hereinafter Strategic Directions] at 46.

[79] World Bank Annual Report, 2002. p.77 (emphasis added).

and judicial systems around the world. Contrast Shihata's initial position and his efforts to justify the Bank's involvement in these projects with the Bank's current position. In his reinterpretation of the Bank's Articles of Agreement, Shihata tried hard to draw a distinction between economics and politics. The prohibition from intervening in countries' political affairs was interpreted then as meaning a more overt involvement with countries' type of government and the governments' decision-making processes. Today, the Bank's reports speak, evaluate, and propose reforms about the quality of government, the level of participation of citizens in the country's decision-making processes, the protection of individuals' rights against abuse of power, the monitoring and control of public officials, and an increasing list of subjects that seem to take us back full circle to the overt political interventions that the Bank's legal advisor had initially marked out as outside the Bank's mandate. This doesn't mean that the Bank's work on legal and judicial reform did not have strong political implications earlier. But the illusion of maintaining an apolitical stance, still very much part of the Bank's discourse, has become ever more difficult to sustain. The irony is that while the rule of law was supposed to provide a justification for the Bank's apolitical involvement in countries' reform, it has expanded to the point of making the apolitical pretension untenable.

THE PRACTICE OF REFORMING COURTS AND LAWS

Having these multiple conceptions of the ROL in mind I will move now from the realm of the rhetoric to the practice field. The question that I seek to answer is why projects of legal and judicial reform are still appealing and continue to be recommended and provided by groups in the Bank despite a number of important critiques and unfavorable evidence. To answer this question I explore the practice of Bank groups in introducing and justifying legal and judicial reform projects as well as in evaluating their work and responding to critiques. To engage in this analysis I make use of all the elements laid down and developed so far.

First, I bring back the idea of the rule of law as a hodge-podge, comprising not of one but four conceptions that are different and often conflicting. Second, I identify the use of these multiple conceptions in the Bank's rhetoric and look at how these conceptions coexist and are used simultaneously. In this section, I introduce an institutional analysis of the Bank, paying special attention to four groups that have been crucial in promoting and carrying out the transformation of developing countries' legal and judicial systems. Lastly, the analysis considers the relations between the Bank and developing countries, looking at the mechanisms that tend to perpetuate these projects regardless of their substantive merits.

Disaggregating the World Bank

This analysis builds upon my experience while working in the World Bank during the summer of 2003, where I strove to capture the understandings of the rule of law under which the Bank operated. I started this project by making a preliminary map of the different groups working on issues related to rule of law reform and identifying what their projects consist of.[80] Some people at the Bank reacted by saying that my map was too neat and I needed to add more chaos and definitely more subdivisions. The deeper I got into the study of the various Bank units engaged in rule of law projects and their respective understandings of what the concept entailed, the more this experience of fragmentation and inconsistency intensified.[81]

I think that the Bank's position, discourse, and reform agenda regarding the role of law in economic development can be better grasped if we understand it as the product of the interaction and even struggle between different groups within the institution. This analysis will help to clarify that groups within the World Bank have subscribed to different conceptions of the rule of law at different points in time. Before analyzing the dynamics between these groups, I explore the connection between the particular versions of the rule of law that the groups uphold and the specific projects that they work on.

The Legal Department. The *Legal and Judicial Reform* group of the Legal Vice Presidency,[82] commonly referred to as "Legal," is the Bank's most visible department in the business of reforming laws and courts. This group was created in the early 1990s and gave the Legal Vice Presidency direct participation in the operative part of these projects, joining other divisions in the Bank already working on reforming courts. To a great extent, for the outside

[80] I use the word "groups" in this chapter to refer to the various units or divisions in the World Bank working on projects of legal and judicial reform. It should not be confused with the five "World Bank Groups," consisting of IDRB, IDA, IFC, MIGA and ICSID.

[81] This analysis is by no means exhaustive. Trying to simplify the extremely complex structure of the Bank comes at the risk of leaving out groups doing relevant work in this area. However, the groups under analysis are undoubtedly important actors in the Bank and they merit discussion as driving forces within the institution. Other groups working in aspects that relate to legal and judicial reform include the International Law and Environment in the Legal Vice Presidency, and Gender and Civil Society in the Poverty Reduction and Economic Management sector.

[82] The Legal Vice-Presidency (LGVP) operates as one integrated unit, but is composed of eight thematic practice groups: 1) Co-financing and Project Finance, 2) Corporate Finance, 3) Institutional Administration, 4) Environment and International Law, 5) Private Sector, Infrastructure and Finance, 6) Legal and Judicial Reform, 7) Policy and Institutional Affairs, and 8) Procurement and Consultant Services, and five regional practice groups: 1) Africa, 2) East Asia and Pacific, 3) Europe and Central Asia, 4) Latin America and the Caribbean, and 5) Middle East, North Africa and South Asia. The Law and Justice Group, an umbrella that includes three groups: 1) Legal and Judicial Reform, 2) Environment and International Law, and 3) Private Sector, Infrastructure, and Finance, has prepared the latest publications of the Legal Vice Presidency concerning legal and judicial reform, assessing and redefining the work of the Bank in this area.

observer Legal represents the "official" position of the Bank's work in this area through its publications. The group serves two main functions. On one hand it is involved in the design and implementation of a number of projects.[83] On the other hand, it gathers and publishes information about all legal and judicial reform projects, including those carried out by other units.[84]

Public Sector Unit. The Public Sector Unit (Public Sector) is one of the constituent parts of the Poverty Reduction and Economic Management sector (PREM).[85] This group jump-started court reform projects in the early 1990s and it has designed and implemented a substantial part of the Bank's judicial reform projects.[86] Public Sector has focused on reforming countries' judiciaries to provide the institutional framework assumed necessary for economic development to thrive. Public Sector and Legal are the main contenders for management of judicial reform projects and are engaged in an ongoing battle for resources.

Private Sector Development Group. This group was established in 1988 in the context of the Bank's advocacy of reducing the role of the State in the economy.[87] At one with the prevailing free-market wisdom and an aversion to all things public of that time, the private sector was forecasted to be the most promising area of development assistance. More recently, the Private Sector Development Group (Private Sector) has been converted into a vice presidency, effectively creating a network of units working on issues of privatization and corporate finance. Private Sector is involved in some operational work designing laws for borrowing countries in the fields of corporations, finance, bankruptcy, and other related areas aiming to create a favorable "investment climate" where businesses can thrive.[88]

83 The group's webpage can be accessed at http://www4.worldbank.org/legal/leglr/. Legal and judicial indicators can be found at http://www4.worldbank.org/legal/database/Justice/default.htm. See also *Strategic Directions, supra* note 78, and *Observations, Experiences, and Approach, supra* note 1.

84 The group's publications are accessible at http://www4.worldbank.org/legal/leglr/publications.html.

85 PREM is a network Vice Presidency, which means that there is a PREM unit in each of the Bank's five regions plus an anchor unit.

86 Apart from judicial reform, the Public Sector unit undertakes projects of public expenditure analysis and management, tax policy and administration, civil service and administrative reform, decentralization, e-government, public enterprises, technical assistance and capacity building. I will focus on the work of Public Sector of the Latin American region, which has been perhaps the most active in judicial reform projects. The number of these projects is remarkable considering that the Inter-American Development Bank has made judicial reform one of its central reform projects too. See Christina Biebesheimer and J. Mark Payne, *IDB Experience in Justice Reform-Lessons Learned and Elements for Policy Formulation*, Inter-American Development Bank (2001), http://www.iadb.org/sds/doc/sgc-IDBExperiences-E.pdf.

87 See generally, Ibrahim Shihata, *The World Bank and Private Sector Development – A Legal Perspective*, in 1 The World Bank in a Changing World 203 (1991).

88 See Knowledge Services for Private Sector Development at http://rru.worldbank.org/.

Within the Private Sector and not directly involved in operations, the Rapid Response Unit ("Rapid Response") has clearly articulated a program for law reform, seeking to establish *appropriate* regulation for economic development. Dubbed the "Doing Business" report,[89] this project claims it has found out which legal rules promote growth and recommends their adoption to developing countries as best practices for business.[90] Rapid often presents itself as a sort of 911 for policymakers in distress. Among other online services and information available, experts provide "best practice public policy advice for private sector led growth" and prompt customized assistance for the "alleviation" of the private sector. "Do you need customized policy advice on investment climate? Click here."[91]

[89] This group's interactive webpage is http://www.doingbusiness.org/ where the "Doing Business" projects of 2004, 2005 and 2006 can be accessed.

[90] This group is closely connected with the "legal origins" scholarly project doing comparative studies of how certain legal systems are more conducive to efficient outcomes than others. The "legal origins" theorists consist of a group of leading economists working in the fields of behavioral finance, financial markets, corporate finance, and corporate governance. Making use of legal history and comparative law, these scholars have turned to "legal systems" for an explanation of countries' regulatory divergence and subsequent social and economic outcomes. Together, these scholars have written an already recognizable body of literature in comparative economics that informs the "Doing Business" reports. The head of the project in the World Bank is Simeon Djankov. The main academic figure is Harvard economics professor Andrei Shleifer, and the team includes Oliver Hart, Florencio Lopez-de Silanes, and Rafael La Porta, among others.

Proponents of the "legal origins" theory first advanced in the field of corporate finance (Rafael La Porta, Florencio Lopez-de-Silanes, Andrei Shleifer, and Robert Vishny, *Law and Finance*, 106 Journal of Political Economy 1113–1155, 1998) claim that legal tradition explains differences in countries' regulation. Adopting the conventional categorization which groups countries' legal systems into "legal families", proponents of this theory argue that regulation in common law countries is economically more efficient and leads to better growth results than in civil law countries (Edward Glaeser, and Andrei Shleifer, *Legal Origins*, 117 Quarterly Journal of Economics 1193–1229, 2002).

These theorists are prolific and have produced a vast literature, rapidly expanding from the field of corporate finance to other areas of regulation like administrative law (Simeon Djankov, Rafael La Porta, Florencio Lopez-de- Silanes, and Andrei Shleifer, The Regulation of Entry, 117 Quarterly Journal of Economics 1–37, 2002, and Rafael La Porta, Florencio Lopez-de-Silanes, Andrei Shleifer, and Robert W. Vishny, *The Quality of Government*, 15 Journal of Law, Economics, and Organization 222–279, 1999); bankruptcy (Simeon Djankov, Oliver Hart, Tatiana Nenova, and Andrei Shleifer, *The Efficiency of Bankruptcy*, Working Paper. Department of Economics, Harvard University, Cambridge, Mass., 2003); labor and employment (Juan Botero, Simeon Djankov, Rafael La Porta, Florencio Lopez-de-Silanes, and Andrei Shleifer, *The Regulation of Labor*, Working Paper 9756, National Bureau of Economic Research, Cambridge, Mass., 2003); and civil procedure (Simeon Djankov, Rafael La Porta, Florencio Lopez-de-Silanes, and Andrei Shleifer, *Courts*, 118 Quarterly Journal of Economics 342–387, 2003; and Simeon Djankov, Caralee McLiesh, and Andrei Shleifer, *Remedies in Credit Markets*, Working Paper. Department of Economics, Harvard University, Cambridge, Mass., 2003).

[91] http://rru.worldbank.org/ (as seen on December 2003). Since then, Rapid Response has nuanced its marketing to offer "customized policy research on business environment issues," which it now provides for free at http://rru.worldbank.org/AskQuestion/.

TABLE 2. World Bank Groups' Use of Multiple Rule of Law Conceptions

		Degree of differentiation of legal norms (from other systems like morals-politics)	
		Institutional	**Substantive**
Degree of relative value against other competing considerations	**Instrumental**	Legal Public Sector [Max Weber]	Rapid Response Unit [Friedrich Hayek]
	Intrinsic	World Bank Institute [A.V. Dicey]	Legal Public Sector Rapid Response Unit World Bank Institute [Amartya Sen]

World Bank Institute. This group constitutes the major research center of the Bank. The World Bank Institute (WBI) does not participate in the operational work of legal and judicial reform projects but its research agenda has made it an important player in the area. Since 1996, WBI has published the "Governance Indicators," which report on the "good governance" of most countries, claiming to measure the institutional framework of both a country's government and market. This group defines governance broadly as "the traditions and institutions by which authority in a country is exercised." It has unbundled governance into three parts: 1) the process by which governments are selected, monitored, and replaced, 2) the capacity of the government to formulate and implement sound policies effectively, and 3) the respect of citizens and the state for the institutions that govern economic and social interactions. Through the publication of its indicators, WBI has become the authority on measuring governance around the world.[92] In addition, WBI has invested resources in training programs, setting up regional and country courses for judges, advancing the idea that the judiciary is a fundamental actor in curbing corruption, and improving good governance.

Table 2 table situates the four groups under analysis and the conceptions of the rule of law that they more frequently invoke in their projects.

Judicial and legal reform projects

Looking at how these multiple rule of law conceptions are deployed by groups in the Bank in projects of legal and judicial reform can help us answer the

[92] See http://www.worldbank.org/wbi/governance/govdata/; For the most recent paper see Daniel Kaufmann, Aart Kraay, and Massimo Mastruzzi, *Governance Matters IV: Governance Indicators for 1996–2004,* (The World Bank, May 2005) http://www.worldbank.org/wbi/governance/pdf/GovMatters˙IV˙main.pdf The indicators are interactive and allow the user to compare indicators across countries as well as overall rates of particular countries across regions.

puzzle of why these projects remain so appealing regardless of scant results and continued critiques. In my view, the rule of law rhetoric has facilitated the problematic continuation of projects and has further decreased the demands for delivering the economic growth originally promised. The constant practice of slippage between these ROL conceptions and the way they are deployed by the units working on these projects has two effects. First, it allows policymakers to be unclear about what they mean when they invoke the ROL. Second, it allows policymakers to not take seriously the critiques of their projects or the evidence of disappointing results by engaging in a practice of "goal-post-shifting." When pressed by a critique of the premises with which they introduced their projects, they turn to a multiplicity of other objectives or aspirations that their projects are also supposed to pursue in relation to different conceptions of the ROL. I argue that this practice enables policymakers to disregard important critiques of their projects' premises and of unfavorable results. Finally, this slippage encourages a continued confusion among different groups that may have very different agendas. I will discuss what I consider to be other negative effects of this dynamic, namely lack of transparency, waste of resources, and justification for opportunistic behavior.

Judicial reform. I will begin with an example of how I think this practice works in analyzing projects of judicial reform, of which Public Sector Unit and Legal are in charge. These projects started with the premise that an independent and effective judiciary is a necessary precondition for economic development.[93] This premise became a marching tune and was included in these groups' reports and academic papers justifying their projects. It was argued that merely enacting property and contract laws would not suffice to attract investment unless independent and effective courts enforced them. Effective courts were in charge of setting in motion the private sector. The assumption was that courts would ensure calculability and predictability of economic transactions by effectively enforcing contracts and acting independently to prevent governments' impingement on property rights.

The first judicial reform project of the Bank was delivered as a "technical assistance loan" to Venezuela in 1992. Gradually, the scope of these projects expanded to include aspects related to judicial independence, judicial training, court administration and case management, control of corruption, appointment of judges, criminal justice, and government accountability.[94]

[93] This argument is clearly stated by Maria Dakolias, the director of the Legal and Judicial Reform group, in *A Strategy for Judicial Reform: The Experience in Latin America*, 36 Va.J. Int 167 (1995–1996).

[94] See *Initiatives in Legal and Judicial Reform*, *supra* note 45, at 3–5.

However, some tensions became apparent and the premises of these projects were subject to important objections. First, it was noted that a formal regime of property rights and contract enforcement, which the courts were deemed to make effective, is not necessarily high in the considerations of investors when deciding where to invest. Investors and business actors are generally driven by returns, and they often rely on informal mechanisms of enforcement where reputation and expectations of future transactions substitute for formal mechanisms to ensure compliance.[95]

Second, there is evidence that entrepreneurs are not all that concerned with the effectiveness of judiciaries in the countries they invest. Investors' primary interest is returns, not effective courts. A 1993 survey of sixty-eight business enterprises in Ecuador, conducted by Legal itself, to determine the constraints of private sector development found that an effective judicial system came sixth in the list, after political instability, inflation and price instability, lack of skilled labor, lack of infrastructure, and high level of taxation.[96]

Imagine investors considering business in China; it isn't hard to visualize that the size of the market and profit opportunities, not the structure of its legal and judicial system, will carry the day in investors' decisions. In mid-size economies like Brazil and Mexico, large domestic markets are a major draw for both national and foreign investors. In the case of Mexico, proximity to the United States and a free-trade agreement that strongly protects investors by bypassing – not making more effective – national courts, are also major factors in attracting investment. Indeed, the legal and judicial systems of these countries could probably be less effective than they currently are without affecting entrepreneurs' interest to invest.[97]

The legal system could represent a marginal advantage for very small countries having little else to offer. Creating market-friendly legal enclaves of weak consumer protection, minimum labor, and employment rights or low standards of environmental protection could represent an attraction for investors. But more attractive may be special concessions to entrepreneurs in the usual form of tax exemptions, public services, and bureaucratic ease. In neither case, however, does judicial reform come high in the list.

[95] For a classic argument of business reliance on informal mechanisms see Stewart Maculay, *Non-Contractual Relations in Business: A Preliminary Study*, 28 American Sociological Review 55 (1963). For an argument on investor's disregard for the institutional settings often deemed required for investment see John Hewko, *Foreign Direct Investment, Does the Rule of Law Matter?* (Carnegie Endowment for International Peace, April 2002). http://www.carnegieendowment.org/publications/index.cfm?fa=view&id=952&prog=zgp&proj=zdrl,zted

[96] See World Bank, No. 127777-EC, Ecuador: Judicial Sector Assessment 1 (1994), cited in Dakolias, *supra* note 93 at 169.

[97] These examples are taken from Linn Hammergren, *Notes on the Rule of Law and Economic Development* p.5, paper presented at Harvard Conference on Rule of Law and Economic Development, April 2002, (on file with the author).

Third, it was also noted that investors usually don't solve their disputes in courts. They frequently solve their disputes through arbitration or strive to reach a settlement. But even if entrepreneurs do go to courts, they generally had access to elite lawyers who knew the system well and had high chances of succeeding. Foreign investors, for instance, can generally find their way in the domestic legal system through high-profile legal assistance that is incorporated in the business cost. Furthermore, judicial reforms were supposed to create incentives for banks and other important creditors that already have an advantage in a judicial system where they are repeat players, know the judicial personnel, have an opportunity to influence the interpretation of the law over time, have the possibility to choose their best cases, negotiate others, and generally build a practice in a specific area.[98]

Finally, good legal systems do not guarantee investment. In Costa Rica, for example, constitutional protections, proworker and prolandless courts provide a clear, predictable, and fairly enforced legal framework but create problems for certain investments.[99]

Beyond the problems posed by the assumptions, there were also problems of implementation. The standard judicial reform project ranging from 2.5 (Yemen) to 58 (Russia) million dollars carried out by Legal or Public Sector, included building new courtrooms, implementing technology for court administration and case management, and training judges. There was practically no diagnosis on the particular conditions of the judicial system of the country in question and on why it was necessary to reform. What were the problems that needed solution, for what purposes, and with what strategy? There was simply no empirical study of how the system worked and what the red lights that needed change were. Consequently, little attention was paid to the impact of the projects on the effectiveness of judicial processes or their ultimate economic impact. This lack of diagnosis usually transpired to the evaluation of these programs. A successful project would report that infrastructure, technology, and training had been effectively introduced, but there were hardly other systematic criteria against which to evaluate the impact of these projects.

When reforms aimed at increasing the effectiveness of adjudication, they focused on decreasing backlogs and reducing the time of disposition and enforcement.[100] Critiques highlighted the lack of empirical research carried out to identify the causes of the problems, (backlogs, delays,

[98] For a seminal account of this phenomenon see Marc Galanter, *Why the "Haves" Come out Ahead: Speculations on the Limits of Legal Change*, 9 Law and Society Review 95 (1974).

[99] See Linn Hammergren, *supra* note 97 p.6.

[100] Maria Dakolias, *Court Performance Around the World: A Comparative Perspective*, 2 Yale H.R. & Dev. L.J. 87 (1999) and Edgardo Buscaglia and Maria Dakolias, *Comparative International Study of Court Performance Indicators*, The World Bank (1999) http://www4.worldbank.org/legal/publications/CourtIndicators-72.pdf.

nonenforcement) or to design the most effective strategy to address them. The results of these projects remained barely open to evaluation on the basis of the identification of a problem, or on the depth of a program of action and concrete and measurable expectations. Moreover, the few empirical studies sponsored by the Bank found that much of the "conventional wisdom" that had guided reforms was unwarranted.[101]

The results of judicial reform projects are of course hard to measure, especially if the projects provided no yardstick to monitor and assess performance. But there has been no clear empirical evidence of their success in spurring economic growth. Despite a variety of studies making a case for correlation, the relation of causality between effective courts and economic development, and its direction, is still highly contested. Indeed, economies in countries that reformed their judiciaries in the last two decades have not fared well and many of them are doing worse than before. Moreover, scholars have shown that countries that for decades experienced high rates of growth like Japan, Korea, Taiwan, and China, did not have a judicial system as the ideal type promoted by groups in the Bank.[102]

[101] A series of recent World Bank studies on "court uses and court users" in five Latin American countries show how much of the "conventional wisdom" about the problems of judiciaries and why reform is necessary rests on no empirical support and is often plainly wrong. This is the conventional wisdom that has guided the Bank for most of its involvement in the sector. See Linn Hammergren, *Uses of Empirical Research in Refocusing Judicial Reforms: Lessons from Five Countries*, PREM, and The World Bank 2003 (http://www1.worldbank.org/prem/PREMNotes/premnote65.pdf). In an empirical research of summary debt-collection proceedings in Mexico City, analysts found that the users and size of the claims were small to medium and while firms constituted barely more than half of the plaintiffs, most defendants were individuals. This was not a picture of disputes between major economic actors but of minor debts incurred for consumption or small investments. Furthermore, the overwhelming majority of judgments was in favor of the plaintiff (creditor), showing no pro-debtor bias either in the procedural norms or the judges' attitudes. Delays were overtly exaggerated by experts, and when delays occurred, plaintiffs' lawyers and bailiffs rather than judges and combative defendants seemed to be far more responsible. Findings showed a high rate of abandonment due to multiple factors such as successful out of court negotiations by the parties, the plaintiff's lack of interest in materializing the claim (filing to declare a tax), the impossibility of recuperating a debt (insolvent debtor, loans granted on creditors' poor judgment in lending decisions or troubles in identifying assets to seize) or disloyal agents (the bailiff or the plaintiff's attorney). Many of these problems were extra-judicial in origin and no amount of standard judicial reforms, as suggested by the 1996 reform undertaken in Mexico to accelerate proceedings, will solve them. Others were clearly judicial problems (the bailiff's power over the proceedings, procedural complications when dealing with multiple jurisdictions, and the execution phase) that needed well-targeted reforms to give judges a more active role in the proceedings and simplify coordination between different jurisdictions. See Report No. 22635-ME, The Juicio Ejecutivo Mercantil in the Federal District Courts of Mexico, The World Bank (2002).

[102] See Frank Upham, *Mythmaking in the Rule of Law Orthodoxy*, Carnegie Endowment Working Paper, Rule of Law Series, Democracy and Rule of Law Project # 30, September 2002, http://www.carnegieendowment.org/publications/index.cfm?fa=view&id=1063; John Ohnesorge, *supra* note 3; William Alford, *The More Law, the More... ? Measuring Legal Reform in*

Faced with these difficulties, judicial reformers can confidently claim that projects of reforming courts seek now also other objectives. Legal and Public Sector make reference to what seems a Senian conception of the ROL, arguing that these projects seek to empower vulnerable groups in society by giving them access to justice and legal aid. These groups also refer to a Diceyan conception of the ROL, claiming that establishing an independent and effective judiciary is an essential element in preventing and prosecuting corruption. In this view, independent courts that review the executive's actions ensure the prevention of arbitrary government.

There is no doubt that using the legal system to distribute resources in a way that empowers the most vulnerable groups in society and enhances their capabilities to pursue the life they have a reason to live is a worthwhile project. My point is not that these groups should remain within the boundaries of a growth-based approach to development. However, the confused use of a Weberian and a Senian conception cancels out a discussion of the expectations of both. On the one hand, Legal and Public Sector avoid a discussion on the growth effects by reference to Sen. And on the other, they thin out Sen's social vision of development by equating it with the formal and institutional characteristics of the legal system. From this perspective, when judicial reforms are taking place, the poor are being empowered.

When their projects are criticized because of their lack of diagnosis and strategy, Legal and Public Sector respond they *have* a strategy, which is involving all stakeholders and promoting ownership of the project. This may be desirable for increasing participation but does not substitute for having an idea of what is wrong with a judicial system, why it is desirable to spend resources there rather than elsewhere, and how these projects will achieve the goals they seek.

Legal reform. Let's take as a second example projects of legal reform such as formalization of property rights seeking to establish a regime of clear, secure, and registered title.[103] The institutional actors involved in these projects have been the private sector development and the legal and judicial reform group.

the People's Republic of China, in HOW FAR ACROSS THE RIVER? CHINESE POLICY REFORM IN THE CHINESE WORLD, (eds. N.C. Hope, D.T. Yang, and M.Y. Li, Stanford University Press, 2003).

103 The work of Douglas North, in particular, had a strong impact on the way development policymakers began to think about law and legal rules as institutional foundations for a market economy. North's historical work advanced the argument that legal institutions that securely enforced property rights were favorable for economic efficiency and growth. Divergence from this pattern could be attributed to special interest groups and transaction costs that explained the prevalence of inefficient property rights and lack of economic growth. It is not difficult to imagine the enthusiasm with which international development organizations, like the World Bank, embraced North's theory of institutional change. Changing developing countries' institutions, and primarily legal systems, could break the institutional path dependence responsible for countries' economic stagnation and pave the way to more efficient markets. See

Starting from a Hayekian conception of the ROL announcing that clear and secure property rights were the foundation of a market economy that would lead to growth, these units have recently incorporated a Senian conception that advocates the enhancement of peoples' capabilities as justification of their projects.[104]

Projects of formalization of property rights were implemented in several developing countries, seeking to unleash the dormant capital potential. The premise was that as long as assets remained in the informal sector, they constituted a "dead capital" that could not be used productively because no one had clear title to them. Potential entrepreneurs could not use their assets as collateral to obtain credit and could not predict the enforcement of the return on their productive use.[105] Hernando de Soto has been the main campaigner of titling projects aiming to bring assets into the formal sector and his work has been optimistically received by international development agencies and other development scholars.

The premises of these projects, however, raise a number of important objections.[106] In informal settings, as contextual legal analysis of customary norms has shown, people often have clear ideas about what they can or cannot do without formalized legal entitlements. Legal and economic scholarship has shed light on social cooperation and efficient markets that do not rely on formal entitlements or formal mechanisms of enforcement.[107] That these informal mechanisms have been found to be prominent in business circles

DOUGLASS C. NORTH, INSTITUTIONS, INSTITUTIONAL CHANGE AND ECONOMIC PERFORMANCE (1990).

[104] See *Doing Business in 2005, Removing Obstacles to Growth* 33–40 (The World Bank, 2004) http://www.doingbusiness.org/documents/DoingBusiness2005.PDF (arguing that weak property rights exclude the poor from doing business). See LAND POLICIES FOR GROWTH AND POVERTY REDUCTION, The World Bank, 2003 (arguing that securing land rights of the poor and reducing barriers to title transactions can trigger important social and economic benefits, including empowerment of women and other marginalized people, as well as increased private investment, and more rapid economic growth). See THE WORLD DEVELOPMENT REPORT 2006: *EQUITY AND DEVELOPMENT*, The World Bank, 2005 (arguing that inequality of opportunity weakens prospects for overall prosperity and economic growth. To reduce poverty more effectively the report recommends ensuring more equitable access by the poor to secure land rights, along with health care, education, jobs, and capital. It also appeals for greater equality of access to political freedoms and for improving access by the poor to justice systems and infrastructure.)

[105] See generally HERNANDO DE SOTO, THE MYSTERY OF CAPITAL (2000) and ID. THE OTHER PATH: THE INVISIBLE REVOLUTION IN THE THIRD WORLD (1990).

[106] My discussion in this section builds on David Kennedy's Laws and Developments, in CONTEMPLATING COMPLEXITY: LAW AND DEVELOPMENT IN THE 21ST CENTURY (Amanda Perry and John Hatchard eds., 2003).

[107] See ROBERT C. ELLICKSON, ORDER WITHOUT LAW: HOW NEIGHBORS SETTLE DISPUTES (1991); Avner Greif, *Contracting, Enforcement, and Efficiency: Economics Beyond the Law*, in Michael Bruno and Boris Pleskovic, eds., Annual World Bank Conference on Development Economics, 1996 Washington, D.C., World Bank.

should cast some doubt on the need of formalizing entitlements to stimulate investment and business transactions.[108] Moreover, the prevalence of credit markets in informal property rights settings may help asses the extent to which formalization holds the key to an increase in capital investment.

Assuming that formalization was needed to clarify property rights, their efficient use does not require a specific set of substantively private entitlements.[109] Economists have shown the striking growth results of programs combining private and public entitlements, like the "shareholding-cooperative system" (SCS) in China.[110]

But even if the choice is a regime of private property rights, legal scholars have long made us aware that property is not a unified ownership conception but rather a bundle of rights, comprised of a multiplicity of entitlements that define relationships of people with one another.[111] As legal historians have shown, regimes of property rights both in common law and civil law systems did not develop out of a simple unified ownership conception but rather out of a multiplicity of entitlements subject to easements and exceptions.[112]

There is the additional problem that a regime of private property rights would not be self-realizable. As it becomes operative, parties will become aware that the property law scheme, applicable to their relations, contains gaps, conflicts, and ambiguities that need to be filled, resolved, and clarified. To the extent that parties are unable to resolve their disputes and in the event that they resort to courts, it will become clear to them that resolution and enforcement of disputes cannot be reached simply by reference to rights.[113] The working out of these decisions will importantly affect this new property rights regime and transform parties' entitlements and their power vis-à-vis one another.[114]

[108] See Stewart Maculay, *supra* note 95; Id. *The Impact of Contract Law on the Economy: Less Than Meets the Eye?*, Paper given at a Conference on Law and Modernization, Lima, Peru, July, 1994.

[109] See Duncan Kennedy and Frank Michelman, *Are property and Contract Efficient?*, 8 Hofstra L. Rev. 711 (1980), and Joel Ngugi, *supra* note 3.

[110] See Dani Rodrik, *After Neoliberalism, What?* (June 2002) available at http://ksghome.harvard.edu/.drodrik.academic.ksg/After%20Neoliberalism.pdf (arguing that Chinese institutional innovations like the household responsibility system, the township and village enterprises, and the two-track pricing regime succeeded in providing effective property rights despite the lack of *private* property rights); Zhiyuan Cui, Wither China? The Discourse on Property Rights in the Chinese Reform Context, 16 Social Text 55 (1998).

[111] For a canonical exposition see Wesley Hohfeld, *Some Fundamental Legal Conceptions as Applied to Judicial Reasoning*, 23 Yale Law Journal 28 (1913).

[112] See Morton J. Horwitz, The Transformation of American Law 1780–1860; Thomas Grey, *The Disintegration of Property*, Nomos xxii: Property 69–86 (1980); Carol Rose, *Crystals and Mud in Property Law* 40 Stanford L. Rev. 577 (1988).

[113] See Hohfeld, *supra* note 111; Felix Cohen, Transcendental Nonsense and the Functional Approach, 35 Colum. L. Rev. 809 (1935); Duncan Kennedy, *supra*, note 14.

[114] See Lee J. Alston, Gary D. Libecap, and Bernardo Mueller, *Property Rights And Land Conflict: A Comparison Of Settlement Of The U.S. Western And Brazilian Amazon Frontiers*, in Latin America and the World Economy Since 1800, (eds. John H. Coatsworth and Alan M. Taylor,

It turns out to be impossible to determine in the abstract what combination of property rights entitlements would lead to more efficient outcomes. For instance, would it be better to maximize the freedom of possessors to do as they please at the expense of their neighbors' security? Or rather, would it be better to maximize the security of possessors from neighbors' free exercise of power? The first one would arguably reduce protection; the second would reduce flexibility in the ways parties can relate to one another. Moreover, we would need evidence that a one-time increase in efficiency as a result of a given arrangement of legal entitlements would generate growth, rather than just another equilibrium level.[115]

A scheme of formalization of land title in Peru could enable a squatter with new title to exclude the trespasser. But we need an explanation of why assets in the hand of the title holder, rather than the reverse, would yield the more efficient outcome that would lead to growth. So, it becomes clear that attention to context is crucial. But projects of formalization generally disregarded the need for this type of contextual analysis by assuming that what was needed was simply *clear and secure* property rights.

By accounts of outside critiques and analysts within the Bank, titling programs aimed at bringing assets into the formal sector have not had the impact that reformers hoped for. But the objections mentioned are rarely addressed. Departing from a Hayekian ROL perspective, programs of formalization of property rights seem to have incorporated a version of Sen's vision for empowering the poor, women, and other vulnerable groups.[116] A recent report advocated by the "Doing Business" project in the private sector predicts that titling will help the poor because weak property rights exclude the poor from doing business and prevent them from higher income levels.[117] But the study has stayed remote from a contextual analysis of the kind that is needed by relying on the incorporation of best practices of other regulatory areas that are supposed to keep titled assets from falling back in the informal sector.[118]

1998) p. 55–84 (providing a historical example of how land titling policies in the U.S. and Brazil gave rise to important disputes between different groups of claimants with a right to the land. It was not merely the formal property rights regime but its interplay with parties' asymmetrical power and the states' enforcement in favor of one or the other that ultimately determined the land distribution).

115 For an explanation of this type of dynamic efficiency see Gunnar Myrdal, An Approach to the Asian Drama, 1843, Appendix 1 (1970); See also Duncan Kennedy, *Law-and-Economics from the Perspective of Critical Legal Studies*, in 2 The New Palgrave Dictionary of Economics and the Law (P. Newman ed. 1998).

116 See Land Policies for Growth and The World Development Report 2006, *supra* note 104.

117 See Doing Business in 2005, *supra* note 104.

118 It should be noted that development policymakers at the Bank adopted North's theory only partially. What was taken from North's theory of institutional change was the proposition that formal legal institutions, notably a system of clear and secure property rights and contracts, were generally conducive to efficient markets and economic growth. However, this wisdom missed one of North's most important contributions, namely a theory of institutional change

I started this section by stating that this practice came at a high cost, namely lack of transparency, waste of resources, and justification for opportunistic behavior. This is a puzzle: I take people at the Bank to be serious about their commitment to improving life conditions in developing countries and I can attest to the professionalism with which they do their work. In my view, the explanation is twofold. On one hand, the answer lies on the conceptual confusion about the ROL. On the other hand, it rests on the internal dynamics between units in the Bank and the relationship between the Bank and its borrowing countries. These are both aspects of the ROL agenda within the Bank that we are still a long way from fully understanding. I believe, however, that this type of inquiry is urgently needed. I propose some lines of thought here that would hopefully lead to further research.

Internal dynamics within the World Bank

The dynamics among the Bank divisions reflect the structural incentives that foster continuation of these projects and help explain the success in portraying legal and judicial reform as a necessary and promising enterprise. At first sight there is, of course, the problem of institutional inertia. As one analyst in the Bank put it "a bank is a bank is a bank." The Bank's business is to lend money and it does so to fund projects where it has experience. Moreover, people working in the projects that I just described, have developed technical expertise and have an interest in the projects' continuation and future funding. These professional interests are motivated by career aspirations in the Bank as well as desire for status in the development assistance community more broadly.

There is also competition and struggle for power, resources, and prestige among the different units in the Bank. So, despite their doubts about the projects' potential, Legal and Public Sector are involved in a race for finding borrowers and taking on more projects while doing little to reflect on their results. Apart from competition between them, there is also rivalry within

that could account for the existence of inefficient property rights over time despite the existence of formal legal institutions and of competitive pressures. North defined institutions as "the rules of the game in a society" or as "the humanly devised constraints that shape human interaction". See North, *supra* note 103 at 3. This broad conception of institutions included not only formal and state-enforced rules but also informal and uncodified social norms that effectively constrained behavior. In North's view, these formal and informal rules, together with their enforcement mechanisms, provided the framework within which human beings interact. North's insistence on the importance of informal rules as building blocks of the institutional framework seemed to have been lost in the work of the Bank groups reforming laws and judiciaries aimed at providing an institutional framework conducive to growth. Similarly, his account on the role of organizations and of their interaction with institutions as the driving force of institutional change seems to have been left out. Finally, the impact of imperfect information and ideology on organizational actors' perception of their gain in altering institutions was simply neglected. See *id.*

Public Sector and Legal among potential project managers seeking to obtain funds and claim ownership.[119] Furthermore, as divisions of the World Bank, Legal and Public Sector also face external competition from other developing agencies and regional banks. This external competition lowers the common denominator for Legal and Public Sector when they perceive that being too demanding on borrowing countries may encourage countries to seek another lender with bigger and less conditioned loans. These institutional incentives and multiple conflicts undermine cooperation between and within Public and Legal at the expense of the projects and ultimately of results in borrowing countries.

Evaluating impact. The lack of coordination and sharing of knowledge prevents a practice of evaluation that could capitalize experience and avoid waste. There is no long-term involvement in the reform projects and thus analysts rarely take responsibility for failure. Moreover, the lack of evaluations makes it harder to detect problems and, even if setbacks were visible, nobody has an interest in pointing out that one has occurred.

For more than a decade now, Legal and Public Sector have been in a privileged position to test their assumptions. They have been involved in a wide variety of judicial reform projects in different countries and have had the opportunity to monitor their progress and evaluate their impact. In addition, these groups have access to an unparalleled breadth of relevant country data accessible to the Bank. Equally, they have access to the highest authorities in the borrowing countries and can avail themselves of the information relevant for assessing the need and impact of their projects. Moreover, they have the comparative experience that the implementation of judicial reform projects in so many different countries has given them. Thus, these groups have had the opportunity to test their theory and corroborate, refute, or modify their assumptions according to the results of their own endeavors. This seems largely an opportunity missed.[120]

One effort to scrutinize the projects' assumptions however, has been made by the Public Sector anchor group. Staffed with people not involved in reform projects, it has engaged with academic criticism and layered the Bank's discourse with a more sophisticated, nuanced, context-specific understanding

[119] In addition, Legal faces both an inter-divisional and intra-divisional struggle. Apart from its quarrels with Public Sector, there is conflict in the Legal Vice Presidency between Legal (the Legal and Judicial Reform Group) and the country lawyers.

[120] Thomas Carothers, *Promoting the Rule of Law Abroad: The problem of knowledge*, Carnegie Endowment Working Paper, Rule of Law Series, Democracy and the Rule of Law Project #34 (2003) http://www.carnegieendowment.org/files/wp34.pdf; Linn Hammergren, *Are We There Yet? Developing Empirically Based Strategies for Judicial Reform* (Feb. 2002) (on file with the author). Published in Spanish as *¿Hemos llegado? El desarrollo de estrategias empíricas para la Reforma Judicial*, Revista del CLAD Reforma y Democracia. No. 23. (Jun. 2002). Caracas. http://www.clad.org.ve/fulltext/0041020.pdf.

of the role of law and legal institutions in economic development.[121] This work has the effect of conveying that the Bank is reconsidering or moving away from its original assumptions. Unfortunately, this work bears practically no effect in the assembly line of judicial reform projects carried out by Legal and the operational groups in Public Sector.

In regard to evaluating court reforms' impact, the divisions of Development Economics (DEC) and Operation's Evaluation Department (OED) have done some research but their efforts aren't coordinated and their results don't seem to affect operations. Except for a handful of assessments published by Legal to support their own projects, there seems to be a lack of connection between the barely available research on impact and the content of operations.

Rankings as substitution of evaluation and strategy. At the same time Rapid Response and WBI, which do not directly participate in the reform of courts, have produced extensive macroeconomic indicators and statistics to advance their projects while remaining impermeable to the critiques of the assumptions in which they rely, to the self-hesitation of Legal and Public Sector and to the evidence of the Bank's decade-long involvement in reforming courts. The "knowledge," popularized by the WBI's Governance Indicators and Rapid's Doing Business, comes in handy to the operational groups as a substitute for evaluation. Thus, it is no surprise that all units in the Bank resort to the Governance Indicators and Doing Business benchmarking to justify their work. These indicators lend force to the credibility and the economic prospects of judicial reform projects while reinforcing its prominence in development assistance. To a great extent, reforming the judiciary, in itself, has become a goal of development policy. That court reform has positive effects on growth is the default position and skeptics have the burden of proof, rather than the reverse.

But WBI and Rapid also compete and often undercut each others' work to take the upper hand in the reputation market of development assistance. Moreover, users of these rankings seem to pay little attention to the inconsistencies between the two sets.[122] WBI provides Legal and Public Sector with the

[121] See http://www1.worldbank.org/publicsector/legal/index.cfm. Formerly called the *Legal Institutions of the Market Economy*, this thematic group has recently changed its name to *Law and Justice Institutions*, thus reflecting the shift of emphasis in the Bank from a market-based approach to social development. A good example of the theoretical engagement fostered here is Richard Messick, *Judicial Reform and Economic Development, supra* note 4.

[122] For example, as Linn Hammergren notices, Costa Rica and Uruguay do not score well in Doing Business but do with "Rule of Law" Governance Indicators. On the other hand, Paraguay and Nicaragua score high in Doing Business but not with Governance Indicators. Although both estimates are measuring judicial functioning and its probable effect on stimulating market activity, they seem to be measuring different things. While WBI focuses on corruption and quality, Doing Business is looking at speed. For an overview of the problems with current use of statistics to improve courts' performance, see Linn Hammergren, *Making justice count: a review of the*

"evidence" necessary to support their projects. Arguably, the WBI governance indicators have two components. The first one is descriptive, assessing country performance on each indicator and drawing a *correlation* with countries' income per capita. These governance reports purport to explain bad economic performance by identifying poor ratings in any given indicator. Even though the reports offer a correlation, the indexes derive strength from an assumed relation of causality between a given indicator and economic performance. Moreover, what is assumed is a unidirectional relation of causality, going from governance institutions to economic growth and not vice versa.

The second component is normative and puts forward an agenda for reform. Once "Governance Indicators" have identified which institutions are lacking or deficient, the need for reform becomes self-evident. It is important to notice that measuring governance institutions always entails a comparison. It provides an assessment of governance performance relative to the rating of other countries. And the project seems to suggest to developing countries that by adopting the institutions that a few developed countries have now, growth will ensue in some automatic fashion.

These indicators are widely used within the Bank and are often taken as hard evidence in both their descriptive and normative facets. For instance, a comparison of countries based on these benchmarks produces "institutional gaps." In a research entitled "Lessons from NAFTA for Latin American and Caribbean Countries,"[123] a team of World Bank economists identified institutional gaps to explain why NAFTA failed to deliver the results free trade had once promised. Concretely, they argued that institutional gaps constrained the reduction of the income per capita gap of Mexico as compared to the United States. One of the indicators in which Mexico fared worse and thus mattered most for the analysis was "rule of law." The research concluded that a crucial lesson for Latin American countries, then considering a free trade agreement with the United States, is that they must reduce "their" institutional gap to capture the benefits of trade and spur economic growth. But this vague conclusion seems to lead us back to the multiplicity of goals that the ROL may entail, and to the problem that building the rule of law by implementing the Bank's legal and judicial reform projects hasn't yielded growth results.

Moreover, WBI has produced a wide variety of data that correlate its "rule of law" indicator with other variables, showing the desirability of rule of law

issues and obstacles affecting the use of management statistics for improving Court performance in Latin America, Congreso Internacional del CLAD sobre la Reforma del Estado y de la Administración Pública, 10 (2005 Oct. 18–21 : Santiago) http://www.clad.org.ve/fulltext/0052444.pdf.

[123] Guillermo Perry, Daniel Lederman, William Maloney, and Luis Servén, World Bank (April 2003), accessible at http://wbln0018.worldbank.org/LAC/LACInfoClient.nsf/1daa46103229123885-256831005ce0eb/717aaa5b2cbdd9c885256cf00062fa44/$FILE/NAFTA-US%20v2Final.pdf.

beyond or even regardless of its impact on economic growth. A favorite datum among these, used by Legal in its latest reports, is the correlation between rule of law and reduction of infant mortality.[124] The implication is clear: attaining a high level of rule of law is good, even if it has no direct impact on growth. How are developing countries supposed to improve their institutional quality? What can help them improve their "rule of law" performance? The answer at this point is almost self-evident: judicial reform. At this point, the reasoning can become circular: judicial reform leads to higher levels of rule of law, which in turn is measured by judicial change.

In contrast to the self-doubt and hesitations expressed by Legal and Public Sector, the unit responsible for the "Doing Business" report, confidently offers a "Rapid Response." "Doing Business" provides a clear-cut solution and easy-to-implement changes in legislation that will allegedly improve targeted areas of business regulation and give a boost to economic growth. In support of its reform agenda, this project argues that the laws of most developing countries are not indigenous but rather shaped by their colonial heritage. It is "legal origins" that accounts for variation in regulation across countries. In this view, legal transplantation suggests systematic variations in regulation that are "not a consequence either of *domestic political choice* or of the pressures toward *regulatory efficiency*."[125] Therefore, the report suggests, developing countries have no compelling reason to preserve their current laws. Their national laws are neither these countries' own choices in response to their particular circumstances, nor the result of various competitive forces. Rather, they will do well to introduce the benchmark rules that have induced better economic performance around the world. The good news is, of course, that now Rapid has produced this benchmark.

The Doing Business project upholds many of the assumptions under which Legal and Public Sector started their work on judicial reform a decade ago. These assumptions face important challenges. The projects consider regulation in a vacuum, severed from the political and socioeconomic context that it is supposed to affect and presents a set of legal rules as ready-mades, packaged as a strategy for development. However, even if it were possible to identify and isolate a set of rules as crucial for a country's economic success, this project assumes that they can be transplanted and take root across the board notwithstanding different economic, social and political settings. Thus, Doing Business disregards historical institutional variation among countries with successful economic experiences as evidence that divergence is not only possible, but also desirable, as countries respond to their own conditions in their quest for better economic performance. In sum, by promoting that in

[124] See *Observations, Experiences and Approach, supra* note 1 at 3.

[125] *Doing Business in 2004: Understanding Regulation* xiv, The World Bank (2004) http://rru.worldbank.org/Documents/DoingBusiness/2004/DB2004-full-report.pdf.

the area of business regulation one-size fits all, Doing Business ignores that best practices have been importantly discredited in previous reform efforts to achieve development.[126]

Second, the project's methodology relies primarily on the law in books, adjusted by a few surveyed lawyers in each country. Doing Business competes here with the much less ambitious project of Public Sector, doing empirical studies of court users and court uses in five Latin American countries. This research has looked at time of disposition and enforcement, identified bottlenecks, considered profiles of plaintiffs and defendants and winners and losers, yielding different results.[127] Although considerably more limited in breadth and scope than Doing Business, research that looks at actual court files has found that much of the conventional wisdom on what is wrong and what needs change in countries' judicial systems is unwarranted by the available evidence.

The internal dynamics between units in the Bank respond at least in part to the question of why "rule of law" reform seems to be flourishing in the Bank on the face of scholarly criticism, a few practitioners' self-doubt, and no success stories. Legal and Public Sector, directly involved in reforming courts, have great stakes in the continuation of their projects. They compete intensely to obtain new missions without needing to pay attention to the enduring effects of their projects, for they have no time to lose and no accountability to worry about. The statistical work of WBI and Rapid, not involved in operations, comes as a great relief for and fuels the machinery of court reformers. On the other hand the continued supply of judicial reforms to borrowing countries confers greater relevance to the research units and their indicators. Jointly, the operational groups and the research units take part in a self-reinforcing mechanism, advocating the many virtues of legal and judicial reform whose continuation is of their own interest.

The World Bank and the borrowing countries

What happens inside the Bank is only part of the picture. The relevance of judicial reform in the "rule of law" discourse in development is further reinforced by the high demand of judicial reform projects by borrowing countries. These projects have not been included in the conditionality requirements of the structural adjustment projects. Rather, they stand alone as projects introduced via technical assistance loans. If these projects are not imposed by conditionality, what explains their widespread existence and their popularity?

[126] For a review of the critiques to best-practices in development theory, see Rittich *supra* note 3.

[127] Linn Hammergren, *Using case file analysis to improve judicial reform strategies: the World Bank experience in Latin America* (Nov. 2004) http://www.clad.org.ve/fulltext/0049625.pdf.

Why is their demand so high?[128] The second key to this puzzle lies on the relations between the Bank staff and government officials in developing countries and the built-in incentives to keep these projects running. Moreover, the multiple ROL conceptions that judicial reform projects purport to pursue make them attractive – for different reasons – to multiple constituencies in developing countries.

To answer this question I am calling for an analysis that would need to consider the relationships between the staff members in development institutions who promote these projects (the lenders) and the government officials who demand them (the borrowers).[129] Although there may be different levels of analysis, two are of interest at first glance. First, at the professional level, these people share networks and alliances built up along career paths. Many professionally successful individuals have held positions in their respective national governments and now occupy high or relatively important positions in the Bank.[130] And the opposite is also true, relatively successful World Bank staff members have been appointed with high responsibilities in their national governments.[131] The actual and potential mobility between national governments and international development institutions, through some sort of "revolving door," creates incentives among public officials and international development analysts in building relationships among them and supplying and demanding World Bank projects.

Second, at the level of ideas, staff in the World Bank groups and officials in national governments often share a common intellectual background that is informed by their educational formation and disciplinary commitments. Many have attended the same universities to undertake graduate studies and have worked with the same mentors. Among government officials and

[128] In an article titled *Don't Blame Our Failures on Reforms That Have Not Taken Place* (The Fraser Institute Forum, June 2003, available at http://www.fraserinstitute.ca/admin/books/chapterfiles/Dont%20Blame%20Our%20Failures%20on%20Reforms%20that%20have%20Not%20Taken%20Place-diaz0603.pdf#). Mexico's Treasury Secretary, Francisco Gil, calls for a radical judicial reform. He points out the functioning of the judicial system as the most important item for market economics to work, asserting that "respect of contracts, essential to the performance of a market economy, is a rarity" and regretted that "judicial processes are unpredictable, riddled with corruption, long, and expensive."

[129] I have in mind a sociological analysis of the kind undertaken by Yves Dezaley and Brian Garth, THE INTERNATIONALIZATION OF PALACE WARS – *Lawyers, Economists and the Contest to Transform Latin American States* (2002).

[130] A notable case in point is Roberto Dañino, the former World Bank's General Counsel and head of the Legal Vice Presidency. Dañino was the Peruvian prime minister in the early years of Toledo's presidency, and later the Peruvian Ambassador to the United States. Only in the Public Sector Group of Latin America for instance, are there former cabinet members from Peru and Bolivia.

[131] Mexico's Secretary of Foreign Affairs, Luis Ernesto Derbez, worked for fourteen years at the World Bank. He directed, structured, implemented and supervised Multilateral Economic Assistance and Structural Adjustment Programs in Chile, Costa Rica, Honduras and Guatemala.

development analysts there are also mentor-mentee relationships that gain importance as the younger generation of pupils begins to occupy higher echelons in the hierarchy ladder of international institutions. Their relationships help explain the intellectual commitments that these professionals genuinely share. These commitments include disciplinary biases and ideas about the scope of the state's participation in the market, the ideal type of government, the specific role of each of the government branches, and the fashion in which law and legal institutions matter in the development process, among many others. Thus, in this picture, people promote projects not primarily because of sheer personal interest but inspired by firm disciplinary creed. When their views are reflected in a variety of policies promoted by the Bank, such as judicial reform, professionals from both ends of the development assistance pipeline strongly advocate them.

A deeper exploration into the realm of ideas would benefit from Duncan Kennedy's contribution to this volume, using the three globalizations of legal thought as a template to situate the transmission of what today constitutes the most influential legal ideas. This inquiry will help to understand this process of globalization, exploring the flows of intellectual influence between sites of production and sites of reception through channels of economic, cultural, and military power. It can be said that groups in the Bank occupy an important position in this process and that the ascendancy of judicial reform projects is related to dominant ideas about modes of legal reasoning, institutional practices and the primary role of the judge in the United States, which have become a matter of normalcy and common sense for reformers and importers alike.

If we now look at the domestic level more deeply, governments in developing countries seem to have an incentive for implementing judicial reforms because the multiple purposes for which they are sold appeal to a broad range of groups in the political spectrum. However, the contradictions and tensions between these projects' objectives remain largely obscured by the vague promise of the rule of law. Local business communities support these projects because of their alleged prospect of creating a legal environment more favorable to business. Public officials and political parties endorse these projects because they promise to control and reduce the corruption that has plagued many of the governments which introduced the first wave of market-oriented reforms across the region. Many of the corruption scandals have involved judges who were bribed by the governments to advance their particular political interests. Governments offer these projects to the population assuring them that public funds will not be squandered again.

Judicial reform projects appeal to judges, who see their resources and their professional status increased. They are of interest to legal scholars, who participate as consultants using these projects to leverage their careers. Also, lawyers are eager to support reforms when they represent an opportunity to increase their clients and their expertise. Moreover, the CDF's emphasis on participation of local actors has brought incentives on building up a consensus among different actors in the country. This means organizing workshops and seminars with judges and scholars to design a strategy that all can agree to. It also means involving as many actors as possible in the strategy: the more stakeholders involved the more acceptance the reform will have.

In their promise to increase access for the poor and improve legal services, these projects also appeal to activists and NGOs. Public opinion and civil society organizations are also attracted by the promise to combat corruption. Moreover, they favor judicial reform projects because of the perception that the judicial system is defective and does not serve the population well. Ironically, judicial systems in Latin American countries may be more independent and enjoy more and better technology and human resources than ever before. But as the judicial system has become the center of attention and the economic promises that justified the initial judicial reforms have not been realized, perception of their performance may well have worsened.

A brief example can help illustrate the effect of these dynamics in the popularity of these projects. The prospect of a judicial reform in Peru caused bitter divisions between President Toledo and the Supreme Court of Justice over who was going to lead it.[132] The content of the judicial reform was not the cause of the conflict but rather who it was that was going to take credit for it. Each government branch may have a different political agenda and a project for judicial reform represents a good opportunity to advance it. In cases like this, the World Bank and other development agencies are called upon to assist in the design and implementation of the project serving at least two purposes. International development institutions validate countries' projects by providing the loans and government officials gain points for their country in international development institutions for having entered the club of countries undertaking judicial reforms.

CONCLUSIONS

The consensus about the need of reforming courts, despite a decade of judicial reform with scant economic results, can be better understood by a conceptual analysis of the different conceptions of the rule of law at play. The slippage in the conceptions of the rule of law sheds light on why these projects remain largely immune to the critique of the assumptions that upheld them and to their disappointing experience. The use of this "hodge-podge" conception of the rule of law and the internal dynamics between the groups can also help understand the self-reinforcing mechanisms within the Bank that make

[132] Following President Toledo's proposal of several emergency reform measures which prominently included judicial reform in his speech of July 28, 2003, the Supreme Court President announced the Judiciary's own strategy of a fourteen-point reform program, on August 4th.

judicial reform seem convenient or appropriate for each of the groups, even if their versions of the rule of law differ in mutually exclusive ways. The relations between these groups and the countries which demand these projects further sustain the high demand for judicial reform projects without any other specific plans for economic development, but for the contradictory promises of the rule of law.

The Bank's turn from a growth-based development model to a comprehensive development paradigm has led groups reforming countries' judiciaries – Public Sector and Legal – to add an intrinsic conception to their formerly primarily instrumental view of the rule of law. In a moment of self-doubt about their work, this turn has infused fresh air and has given them a renewed hope if only by changing the expectations rather than the content of their projects. Judicial reform is now desirable on its own right, as an end in itself and as part of the holistic view of development that the Comprehensive Development Framework promotes.

Through the practice of measuring the best institutions for governance or benchmarking the best rules for business, the WBI and Rapid Response validate judicial reforms set in motion by Legal and Public and free these groups from the difficult task of evaluating their effects. On the other hand, ongoing reforms stand as the products that give relevance to the indicators that WBI and Rapid Response produce.

Reform recommendations by WBI and Rapid take for granted that they can determine which institutions are *appropriate* and what the *quality* of regulation must be in each country. They assume they can plausibly identify and isolate what has worked in the world laboratory, which has *already* experimented with different institutions. These groups proceed as if these institutions could be transplanted in order to improve governance and enhance the environment for doing business across countries. Institutional reforms are recommended as proven recipes, not as complex choices with multiple linkages. WBI and Rapid advocate legal reform based on their indicators as if it was demonstrated that when governance and the business environment reach certain levels in their ranking, economic development *is* taking place.

All the World Bank groups under analysis emphasize that the cause for the gigantic growth differential among countries lies on institutions, and focus distinctively on reforming law and courts. These projects reinforce the belief that the cause for a country's economic stagnation is always local. There is a paradox in development experts relentlessly repeating that the cause for economic stagnation is local while frequently introducing a univocal agenda for reform designed elsewhere. These groups' reform recommendations strengthen the belief that what is needed is institutional convergence. The resulting consensus precludes a contestation of the choices and analysis of the effects produced by the projects and policies promoted by the World Bank in developing countries.

The Bank's apparent conclusion that all ROL objectives fit into one package is neither theoretically plausible nor supported by the projects' experience. The projects of legal and judicial reform that embody the World Bank's ROL agenda are carried out under conditions that prevent an engagement in regard of their theoretical premises and their effects. These conditions favor lack of transparency and make it harder to open these projects to scrutiny and evaluation. These projects involve considerable amounts of resources and the opportunity costs for developing countries, which pay for these projects, can be significant. Finally, these conditions create incentives for policymakers at the Bank to continue to fund these projects, despite uncertainty and disappointment about results.

In this chapter, I try to contribute to a clearer discussion of the multiple different ROL concepts at play, and to illustrate how, even though some of them may be mutually exclusive, the invocation of the "hodge-podge" ROL works to justify policy proposals by shifts in expectations. My analysis of the dynamics between the different groups of the World Bank aims at highlighting institutional factors that work to exacerbate this phenomenon. I hope that both lines of inquiry can lead to a better understanding of the workings of the ROL as a development strategy and open up some space for critical interventions that take into consideration the complex role of the World Bank.

INDEX

For EU product safety concerns, contact us at Calle de José Abascal, 56–1°, 28003 Madrid, Spain or eugpsr@cambridge.org.

www.ingramcontent.com/pod-product-compliance
Ingram Content Group UK Ltd.
Pitfield, Milton Keynes, MK11 3LW, UK
UKHW022012180926
475701UK00003B/321

* 9 7 8 0 5 2 1 6 7 7 5 7 8 *